T0259810

Lecture Notes in Computer Science   11588

Commenced Publication in 1973
Founding and Former Series Editors:
Gerhard Goos, Juris Hartmanis, and Jan van Leeuwen

More information about this series at http://www.springer.com/series/7409

Fiona Fui-Hoon Nah · Keng Siau (Eds.)

HCI in Business, Government and Organizations

eCommerce and Consumer Behavior

6th International Conference, HCIBGO 2019
Held as Part of the 21st HCI International Conference, HCII 2019
Orlando, FL, USA, July 26–31, 2019
Proceedings, Part I

 Springer

Editors
Fiona Fui-Hoon Nah
Missouri University of Science
and Technology
Rolla, MO, USA

Keng Siau
Missouri University of Science
and Technology
Rolla, MO, USA

ISSN 0302-9743   ISSN 1611-3349   (electronic)
Lecture Notes in Computer Science
ISBN 978-3-030-22334-2   ISBN 978-3-030-22335-9   (eBook)
https://doi.org/10.1007/978-3-030-22335-9

LNCS Sublibrary: SL3 – Information Systems and Applications, incl. Internet/Web, and HCI

This Springer imprint is published by the registered company Springer Nature Switzerland AG
The registered company address is: Gewerbestrasse 11, 6330 Cham, Switzerland

Foreword

The 21st International Conference on Human-Computer Interaction, HCI International 2019, was held in Orlando, FL, USA, during July 26–31, 2019. The event incorporated the 18 thematic areas and affiliated conferences listed on the following page.

A total of 5,029 individuals from academia, research institutes, industry, and governmental agencies from 73 countries submitted contributions, and 1,274 papers and 209 posters were included in the pre-conference proceedings. These contributions address the latest research and development efforts and highlight the human aspects of design and use of computing systems. The contributions thoroughly cover the entire field of human-computer interaction, addressing major advances in knowledge and effective use of computers in a variety of application areas. The volumes constituting the full set of the pre-conference proceedings are listed in the following pages.

This year the HCI International (HCII) conference introduced the new option of "late-breaking work." This applies both for papers and posters and the corresponding volume(s) of the proceedings will be published just after the conference. Full papers will be included in the *HCII 2019 Late-Breaking Work Papers Proceedings* volume of the proceedings to be published in the Springer LNCS series, while poster extended abstracts will be included as short papers in the HCII 2019 *Late-Breaking Work Poster Extended Abstracts* volume to be published in the Springer CCIS series.

I would like to thank the program board chairs and the members of the program boards of all thematic areas and affiliated conferences for their contribution to the highest scientific quality and the overall success of the HCI International 2019 conference.

This conference would not have been possible without the continuous and unwavering support and advice of the founder, Conference General Chair Emeritus and Conference Scientific Advisor Prof. Gavriel Salvendy. For his outstanding efforts, I would like to express my appreciation to the communications chair and editor of *HCI International News,* Dr. Abbas Moallem.

July 2019   Constantine Stephanidis

The original version of the book was revised: For detailed information see correction chapter. The correction to the book is available at https://doi.org/10.1007/978-3-030-22335-9_26

HCI International 2019 Thematic Areas
and Affiliated Conferences

Thematic areas:

- HCI 2019: Human-Computer Interaction
- HIMI 2019: Human Interface and the Management of Information

Affiliated conferences:

- EPCE 2019: 16th International Conference on Engineering Psychology and Cognitive Ergonomics
- UAHCI 2019: 13th International Conference on Universal Access in Human-Computer Interaction
- VAMR 2019: 11th International Conference on Virtual, Augmented and Mixed Reality
- CCD 2019: 11th International Conference on Cross-Cultural Design
- SCSM 2019: 11th International Conference on Social Computing and Social Media
- AC 2019: 13th International Conference on Augmented Cognition
- DHM 2019: 10th International Conference on Digital Human Modeling and Applications in Health, Safety, Ergonomics and Risk Management
- DUXU 2019: 8th International Conference on Design, User Experience, and Usability
- DAPI 2019: 7th International Conference on Distributed, Ambient and Pervasive Interactions
- HCIBGO 2019: 6th International Conference on HCI in Business, Government and Organizations
- LCT 2019: 6th International Conference on Learning and Collaboration Technologies
- ITAP 2019: 5th International Conference on Human Aspects of IT for the Aged Population
- HCI-CPT 2019: First International Conference on HCI for Cybersecurity, Privacy and Trust
- HCI-Games 2019: First International Conference on HCI in Games
- MobiTAS 2019: First International Conference on HCI in Mobility, Transport, and Automotive Systems
- AIS 2019: First International Conference on Adaptive Instructional Systems

Pre-conference Proceedings Volumes Full List

1. LNCS 11566, Human-Computer Interaction: Perspectives on Design (Part I), edited by Masaaki Kurosu
2. LNCS 11567, Human-Computer Interaction: Recognition and Interaction Technologies (Part II), edited by Masaaki Kurosu
3. LNCS 11568, Human-Computer Interaction: Design Practice in Contemporary Societies (Part III), edited by Masaaki Kurosu
4. LNCS 11569, Human Interface and the Management of Information: Visual Information and Knowledge Management (Part I), edited by Sakae Yamamoto and Hirohiko Mori
5. LNCS 11570, Human Interface and the Management of Information: Information in Intelligent Systems (Part II), edited by Sakae Yamamoto and Hirohiko Mori
6. LNAI 11571, Engineering Psychology and Cognitive Ergonomics, edited by Don Harris
7. LNCS 11572, Universal Access in Human-Computer Interaction: Theory, Methods and Tools (Part I), edited by Margherita Antona and Constantine Stephanidis
8. LNCS 11573, Universal Access in Human-Computer Interaction: Multimodality and Assistive Environments (Part II), edited by Margherita Antona and Constantine Stephanidis
9. LNCS 11574, Virtual, Augmented and Mixed Reality: Multimodal Interaction (Part I), edited by Jessie Y. C. Chen and Gino Fragomeni
10. LNCS 11575, Virtual, Augmented and Mixed Reality: Applications and Case Studies (Part II), edited by Jessie Y. C. Chen and Gino Fragomeni
11. LNCS 11576, Cross-Cultural Design: Methods, Tools and User Experience (Part I), edited by P. L. Patrick Rau
12. LNCS 11577, Cross-Cultural Design: Culture and Society (Part II), edited by P. L. Patrick Rau
13. LNCS 11578, Social Computing and Social Media: Design, Human Behavior and Analytics (Part I), edited by Gabriele Meiselwitz
14. LNCS 11579, Social Computing and Social Media: Communication and Social Communities (Part II), edited by Gabriele Meiselwitz
15. LNAI 11580, Augmented Cognition, edited by Dylan D. Schmorrow and Cali M. Fidopiastis
16. LNCS 11581, Digital Human Modeling and Applications in Health, Safety, Ergonomics and Risk Management: Human Body and Motion (Part I), edited by Vincent G. Duffy

34. CCIS 1033, HCI International 2019 - Posters (Part II), edited by Constantine Stephanidis
35. CCIS 1034, HCI International 2019 - Posters (Part III), edited by Constantine Stephanidis

http://2019.hci.international/proceedings

6th International Conference on HCI in Business, Government and Organizations (HCIBGO 2019)

Program Board Chair(s): **Fiona Fui-Hoon Nah**
and Keng Siau, *USA*

- Kaveh Abhari, USA
- Miguel Aguirre-Urreta, USA
- Andreas Auinger, Austria
- Michel Avital, Denmark
- Dinko Bacic, USA
- Denise Baker, USA
- Gaurav Bansal, USA
- Valerie Bartelt, USA
- Langtao Chen, USA
- Constantinos Coursaris, USA
- Soussan Djamasbi, USA
- Brenda Eschenbrenner, USA
- Ann Fruhling, USA
- JM Goh, Canada
- Richard H. Hall, USA
- Milena Head, Canada
- Netta Iivari, Finland
- Qiqi Jiang, Denmark
- Richard Johnson, USA
- Mala Kaul, USA
- Yi-Cheng Ku, Taiwan
- Nanda Kumar, USA
- Eleanor Loiacono, USA
- Murad Moqbel, USA
- Robbie Nakatsu, USA
- Chee Wei Phang, P.R. China
- Eran Rubin, USA
- Roozmehr Safi, USA
- Hamed Sarbazhosseini, Australia
- Norman Shaw, Canada
- Yani Shi, P.R. China
- Choon Ling Sia, Hong Kong, SAR China
- Austin Silva, USA
- Martin Stabauer, Austria
- Chee-Wee Tan, Denmark
- Deliang Wang, Singapore
- Werner Wetzlinger, Austria
- I-Chin Wu, Taiwan
- Dezhi Wu, USA
- Shuang Xu, USA
- Cheng Yi, P.R. China
- Dezhi Yin, USA
- Jie YU, P.R. China
- Dongsong Zhang, USA

The full list with the Program Board Chairs and the members of the Program Boards of all thematic areas and affiliated conferences is available online at:

http://www.hci.international/board-members-2019.php

HCI International 2020

The 22nd International Conference on Human-Computer Interaction, HCI International 2020, will be held jointly with the affiliated conferences in Copenhagen, Denmark, at the Bella Center Copenhagen, July 19–24, 2020. It will cover a broad spectrum of themes related to HCI, including theoretical issues, methods, tools, processes, and case studies in HCI design, as well as novel interaction techniques, interfaces, and applications. The proceedings will be published by Springer. More information will be available on the conference website: http://2020.hci.international/.

General Chair
Prof. Constantine Stephanidis
University of Crete and ICS-FORTH
Heraklion, Crete, Greece
E-mail: general_chair@hcii2020.org

http://2020.hci.international/

Contents – Part I

Contents – Part II

Social Media and Big Data Analytics in Business

Collaboration, Decision Making and Open Innovation

Electronic, Mobile and Ubiquitous Commerce

A Study of Models for Forecasting E-Commerce Sales During a Price War in the Medical Product Industry

Pei-Hsuan Hsieh[(✉)]

National Cheng Kung University, Tainan 701, Taiwan
peihsuan@mail.ncku.edu.tw

Abstract. When faced with a price war, the accuracy of forecasting sales in e-commerce greatly influences an enterprise's or a retailer's merchandise inventory strategies. When faced with a price war, an enterprise might obtain certain consumption patterns by analyzing previous sales data. This case study research was conducted in collaboration with a medical product company to explore which of the various forecasting models can better inform a company's inventory plan. The study used the company's data from Amazon.com regarding sales volume, number of views, company ranking, etc. between February 7 2016 and March 28 of 2018. Three potential methods of data mining were selected from the literature: the exponential smoothing method, the linear trend method, and the seasonal variation method. Of these, the most suitable was identified for price war situations to forecast the sales volume for April 2018 and to provide concrete information for the company's inventory plan. The results showed that the seasonal variation method is more suitable than the other two sales forecasting methods. To obtain a more accurate sales forecast during a price war, the seasonal variation method is recommended to be used in the following approaches: Adjust the seasonal index by using a simple moving average. Remove the seasonal index from the sales volume, and conduct a regression analysis using the data within the last month. The resulting predicted value (with the seasonal index removed) should be multiplied by each period's corresponding weighted moving average to obtain a more accurate sales forecast during a price war.

Keywords: E-commerce · Price war · Sales forecasting · Inventory plan

1 Introduction

In the e-commerce-driven market today, the preparation for inventory forecast is crucial. Without proper inventory plans, retailers would risk customer disappointment due to merchandise shortage, which causes income loss. However, excess inventory would lead to storage and removal problems, causing surplus-induced increased cost and affecting the overall profit [12]. Situations like these are especially serious for seasonal merchandise that are put through price wars if an enterprise cannot effectively use prior experience to forecast future sales.

© Springer Nature Switzerland AG 2019
F. F.-H. Nah and K. Siau (Eds.): HCII 2019, LNCS 11588, pp. 3–21, 2019.
https://doi.org/10.1007/978-3-030-22335-9_1

Using Amazon as an example, one sees that when two leading companies that sell similar products intend to dominate the market, they usually slash prices as a competitive strategy against each other. As soon as one company begins to lower the price to attract customers, the other will see changes in the incoming orders and will fall into a predicament if it does not respond immediately to the competitor's move. Under such circumstance, traditional forecast models are no longer effective, and new models are needed. To identify more accurate merchandise sales forecast models when faced with a price war, this study looked at some conventional forecast methods, namely, the exponential smoothing method, the linear trend method, and the seasonal variation method.

The exponential smoothing method discards no prior data; more weight is given to the more recent data and less weight to the data from the more distant past [11]. For most data, this is a very suitable and accurate forecast model. However, exponential smoothing is more suitable for forecasting short-term data and less so for long-term data [8]. Therefore, we use the linear trend method to observe the trend of an entire period and the direction of future periods' data, in order to forecast the sales volume of future periods. The seasonal variation method accounts for any notable seasonality of sales. It removes the seasonal factor prior to applying the regression model, then adds it back afterwards [36].

Overall, the study analyzed and forecasted sales data using these three models that are suitable for price wars and aimed to help enterprises accurately calculate the potential sales volume during a price war in order to more effectively control their inventory costs and to increase their overall profits.

2   Literature Review

2.1   E-Commerce in Taiwan and in the United States

E-commerce development is still flourishing in Taiwan. In 2018, the top four sales volumes in the market belonged to Shopee, PChome, ibon mart, and momo. Shopee provides customers shipping fee subsidy, charges no slotting fee or processing fee, and offers a better and more comprehensive user interface. Customers can also chat with the seller in real time, to obtain more information about the products. In addition, Shopee combines different modes of business operations: B2B2C (Shopee Mall), B2C (Shopee), and C2C (Shopee Auction). It is a one-stop shop where users searching for products are presented with items from all three modes to choose from. Compared with the other e-commerce companies operated in Taiwan, Shopee provides a better consumer experience that attracts more sellers and buyers. It has become the largest mobile e-commerce entity in Taiwan since 2017.

PChome has B2C (PChome24), B2B2C (PChome Store), and C2C (Ruten.com, an auction site). Although its user experience is not on par with Shopee, it has a strong shipping system that supports the speed of product delivery. Ibon mart has a network of over 5000 brick-and-mortar stores throughout Taiwan, which provides a comprehensive set of physical-virtual convenience services.

The ibon mart website integrates products from supermarkets and investment companies. According to quarterly financial reports, the overall performance of Q4 are better than the other quarters. This is possibly due to holidays or the Single's Day (November 11) that originated in Mainland China. Momo is a shopping network invested by digital media enterprises. It also has a relatively better Q4 performance.

Although e-commerce originated in the United States, the performance of the US e-commerce has been lukewarm compared to that of Taiwan. Other than the top-earning e-commerce company Amazon, American e-commerce has not had the same level of vigor as that of China. Amazon is currently one of the largest web-based retailers, and it also has a higher performing Q4 compared to the other quarters. The fourth quarter is a major shopping season in the US and is the busiest season for e-commerce. The seasonality is due to the holidays, starting with Halloween in October, Thanksgiving in November and the subsequent Black Friday and Cyber Monday, followed by Christmas in December. The customers of Amazon.com have shown a consistent level of satisfaction, which is higher than other enterprises such as eBay, Walmart, Best Buy, etc. [31]. In recent years, the US has been influenced by the Chinese e-commerce giant Alibaba and has started to promote sales in the trend of celebrating the Singles' Day (November 11) in the last quarter [5].

2.2 The Importance of E-Commerce

In the past, companies that wanted to run a promotion activity needed weeks or even months to plan, forecast, and calculate carefully the sales volume and target profit. Their methods usually involved buying ads and releasing coupons [28]. In the information age, in the global e-commerce market, it is pivotal to plan the inventory and the logistics based on accurate sales forecast [34]. In the age of e-commerce, sales forecast and inventory control are essential. E-commerce promotion projects can immediately push the newest information out to the relevant consumer groups through emails, social media, direct broadcast, etc. [9]. At any time, sales data should be collected and analyzed; a good forecast can enable a company to ensure that there never is a shortage of merchandise that disappoints customers and leads to profit loss [27]. On the other hand, overstocking not only increases the inventory cost that affects the final profit but also increases labor and processing costs. Price discounts might be needed for inventory clearance. Case in point, the demand for seasonal merchandise will rapidly disappear once the season is over.

The start of a price war implies the reduction of profit. Under the strict control of cost, the product quality may be affected. This leads to a vicious cycle that negatively impacts future sales [26]. Price wars usually start when there are more competitors. Price adjustment is a sales strategy that can be executed easily [15]. The literature shows that enterprises often applies price wars to compete for market share and increase product sales volume when dealing with seasonal merchandise around the various annual holidays [26]. This is especially evident when the target consumer group is highly sensitive to price [25]. Additionally, seasonal products have different attributes depending on whether they are based on daily, weekly, or annual cycles; each has a different level of impact on sales volume [22]. However, one should consider the necessary inventory cost prior to a particular holiday, consumer satisfaction, willingness to re-purchase, and other factors [27]; otherwise, the earnings resulted from promotions may not fully cover the hidden costs, causing an overall loss [32]. Similarly, the competitors do not wish to lose their existing market share and will begin myriad promotion activities including the use of sales representatives' experience-based predictions, but they still need to analyze effectively the distribution point's primary consumer's sale volume [14].

2.3 Methods of Analysis and Effectiveness of E-Commerce Big Data Forecast

Not all historical data are relevant to the current consumers' behaviors. Companies should adjust their current systems and use a large quantity of long-term sales forecast data. They should let the systems consider the historical data appropriately and distinguish the useful data from the obsolete ones, and be able to tell based on current purchase behaviors and models which aspects have remained stable and which have changed and become unstable [10]. The procedure involving big data includes data collection and data processing and analysis, each processing step having an impact on the quality of the big data [1]. During data collection, the data source will affect big data's quality including its veracity, completeness, consistency, accuracy, and security [18]. Big data analysis methods can be categorized as descriptive, predictive, and normative [4]. The purpose of descriptive analysis is to accurately predict what will happen in the future and to provide a rationale for why it will happen. Predictive analysis uses data and mathematical models to confirm and evaluate targets. Normative analysis uses optimization or A/B testing to offer suggestions to staff or managers [33].

Quick response forecasting (QRF) of big data is accepted as more predictive than the traditional point of sale (POS) system [20]. If the expected demand starts to exceed the "most likely scenario," QRF can help adjust the purchase volume to effectively decrease costs. Amazon collects big data such as individual users' habits, the prices of competitors during price wars, consumers' product preferences, records of orders, profit margin, etc. Amazon uses big data to adjust 2.5 million products' prices each day, thereby attracting more customers and resulted in a 25% increase in annual profit [2]. Overall, the key to sales forecast accuracy is the calculation behind the forecast system, since it ensures that individual distributors have enough inventory to meet the demand of potential orders [30] and are able to devise more accurate purchase strategies [1].

3 Methodologies

Utilizing appropriate sales forecast methods is important for enterprises in e-commerce. Based on the previously mentioned literature, a firm grasp of customer types and needs as well as business historical data trends are necessary for choosing better forecasting methods. Common e-commerce sales forecast methods include: naïve method (time series with steady changes, seasonal variations, trend patterns), average method (moving average, weighted moving average, exponential smoothing, double exponential smoothing, triple exponential smoothing), trend-adjusted exponential smoothing, and seasonal variations [3, 7, 17, 23].

This study's data source was a medical equipment seller on the Amazon e-commerce platform (called here the Case Company). The Case Company often conducts sales analysis and forecast for the products they offer. However, during the time of this study, the company suffered the plight of a price war, which led to unstable sales and caused the supply to severely outnumber the demand.

The Case Company provided the current research with sales data including the sales volume data obtained through the sales platform's backend services, the number of views, competitors' sales data obtained via text mining methods, etc. Because the price war for which real sales data could be collected had occurred recently (Fig. 1) and the duration was not very long, three suitable methods for this research was explored: exponential smoothing method, linear trend method, and seasonal variation method. Among these three, the most appropriate method for responding to a price war was identified. The exponential smoothing method was included to investigate price wars due to its ability to focus on recent observation periods while taking into consideration the characteristics of observations in the more distant past. The linear trend method was included because it considers all data and directly reflects the trend of sales. The seasonal variation method was included because there was a noticeable seasonality in the data. We therefore included this method to see if higher accuracy may be achieved by removing any seasonal factors prior to forecasting. This study analyzed the sales data (collected between 2/7/2016 and 3/28/2018) using the three methods to forecast the daily sales volume during the month following the data collection period (4/1/2018 to 4/30/2018).

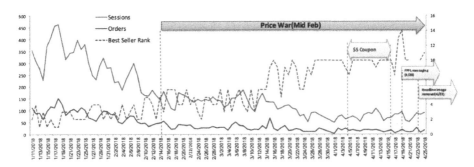

Fig. 1. The estimated period of the price war.

3.1 Exponential Smoothing Method

Smoothing value is the weighted average of forecast values and actual values. In other words, the next forecast value is the weighted average of the previous period's forecast value and its actual value. The smoothing factor (α) plays an important role. It is usually determined based on the products' characteristics and the manager's understanding of the market's sales situations along with any prior experiences with forecasted values. The closer the smoothing factor gets to 1 means that the influence of past observations decreases steeply as it was further in the past; conversely, a factor closer to 0 means that such influence decreases not as steeply. Thus, when the time series is relatively stable, one may choose a larger α, whereas a smaller α should be chosen when the time series contains more fluctuations, as to not ignore the influence of observations from earlier times. In the equation, each period's forecast value requires prior data. Therefore, the very first smoothing value must be defined. There are several ways to do that. If historical data is available from further back in time, then an overall period average from the historical data can be used as the first smoothing value. Otherwise, the first actual value may also be used as the first smoothing value as well as the second forecast value.

3.2   Linear Trend Method

This method uses time as the independent variable (x) and the function of time as the dependent variable (y) and assumes that the independent variable (time) and the forecasted function of time are linearly related. Therefore, using this method requires first a calculation of the correlation coefficient (r) between the two variables. A coefficient of 0 means no linear correlation exists and the linear trend method is not applicable. A coefficient between ± 0.2 and ± 0.3 is a weak correlation; ± 0.6 is a moderate correlation; ± 0.8 is a strong correlation. A coefficient of 1 is a perfect correlation. When the coefficient r is near 1, the linear trend method can be used to analyze the data. When r is close to 1, the linear equation in the form of $y = a + bx$ can be used to predict future changes. Based on historical data, regression can be used to find the values of a and b, thereby finding the linear equation in which the independent variable can be plugged into to produce the forecasted value of the dependent variable y.

3.3   Seasonal Variation Method

As many products' sales are cyclical or seasonal, the seasonal variation method adds to the time series forecast methods the factors that recur periodically and fluctuate regularly based on sale seasons. This enables forecasting the sales of products that are seasonal in nature. First, statistics such as the simple average method are used to compute the forecast seasonal index. Patterns of seasonal changes are also identified. These are then used to forecast the values that are sought after.

In summary, because the Case Company was faced with a price war during a short amount of time, this study used more basic methods for forecasting. Moreover, when it was uncertain whether the product had any seasonality, the linear trend method was first used to find a regression equation that predicts the sales volume; if the data's pattern was affected by the seasonality of the products, then the seasonal variation method would be added as the next step in conjunction with simple smoothing methods (simple moving average, weighted moving average, exponential smoothing) to adjust for the seasonal index.

4 Results

4.1 Application of the Exponential Smoothing Method

The most important step when using the exponential smoothing method is finding the most appropriate smoothing factor (α). We first set the α between 0.1 and 0.9, then fine-tuned the α to be between 0.01 and 0.09 to analyze the data collected between 2/7/2016 and 3/28/2018 in order to predict the sales volume for April 2018. With each month being a period, there were a total of 30 periods usable for forecasting sales volume for just one month (April 2018). Before using any equations under this method, we set the sales volume of the forecast period to be 0. The difference between the forecast value and the actual value was squared for each of the 30 periods, then the 30 squared differences were summed. The results of the equations are listed in Table 1. When $\alpha = 0.1$, the month's overall forecast error was the smallest, especially when $\alpha = 0.06$, the sum of error was the least of all. Then, comparing the April 2018's sum of actual values against the sum of forecast values, it was confirmed that when α was 0.05 and 0.06, the sum of the predicted values was 460 and 374 (only off by 39 and 47), respectively, which were very close to the actual values. On the contrary, when α was set to 0.04 and 0.07, the differences were larger than 100.

Next, each day was treated as a period and was used to forecast the next day (i.e., on April 1 we predicted the sales of April 2, and on April 2 we predicted the sales on April 3, etc.). The actual data from April 2018 was used instead of the predetermined 0. Setting the α value again between 0.1 and 0.9, it was found that $\alpha = 0.2$ yielded the least sum of error. All other α values also yielded smaller errors compared to when computations were based on monthly periods. It is evident, then, that a daily period yields higher accuracy than a monthly forecast and has more tolerance for α errors. Therefore, when facing a short-term price war, the forecast analyst can use this method to avoid severe forecast inaccuracy caused by mistakes in setting the α.

4.2 Application of the Linear Trend Method

A longer-term price war implies that the forecast period should also be elongated. In this case, the exponential smoothing method is not suitable due to the difficulty of choosing the appropriate α value; hence, a different method is needed. Here, we tested the applicability of the linear trend method. A regression analysis of the data between 2/7/2016 and 3/28/2018 yielded the linear equation $y = -0.0076x + 53.311$, meaning, the Case Company's sales were declining at a rate of -0.0076. Then, this equation was used to forecast the upcoming month's values (between 4/1/2018 and 4/30/2018). The daily differences between actual and forecast sales were squared, and the sum of the squares was 34068. The sum of the predicted values for April 2018 was 1417, which was vastly different from the month's actual sales total of 421 (Table 2). Furthermore, Fig. 2 shows that the data contained a seasonal pattern. The linear trend method was unable to respond to such seasonality, making the forecast sales volume noticeably different from the actual values.

Table 1. Applying the exponential smoothing method to find the most suitable α value.

KPI	Week	Units Ordered	0.01	0.02	0.03	0.04	0.05	0.06	0.07	0.08	0.09
		Alpha: T=	784	784	784	784	784	784	784	784	784
4/1/2018	112	3	45.81978	42.37974	37,42327	32.84675	29.26438	26.61914	24.6869	23.2548	22,16333
4/2/2018	112	25	45.36158	41.53215	36.30058	31.53288	27.80116	25.02199	22.95882	21.39441	20.16863
4/3/2018	112	17	44.90797	40.7015	35.21156	30.27157	26.4111	23.52067	21.3517	19.68286	18.35345
4/4/2018	113	24	44.45889	39.88747	34.15521	29.0607	25.09055	22.10943	19.85708	18.10823	16.70164
4/5/2018	113	14	44.0143	39.08972	33.13056	27.89828	23.83602	20.78287	18.46709	16.65957	15.1985
4/6/2018	113	18	43.57416	38.30793	32.13664	26.78234	22.64422	19.5359	17.17439	15.32681	13.83063
4/7/2018	113	14	43.13841	37.54177	31.17254	25.71105	21.51201	1S.3G374	15.97219	14.10066	12.53587
4/24/2018	115	7	36.36323	26.62919	18.57341	12.8449	8.994608	6.414085	4.651301	3.416903	2.532719
4/25/2018	116	17	35.9996	26.09561	18.01621	12.33111	8.544878	5.029239	4.32571	3.143551	2.304775
4/26/2018	116	11	35.6396	25.57468	17.47572	11.83786	8.117634	5.667485	4,02291	2.892066	2.097345
4/27/2018	116	16	35.28321	25.06318	15.95145	11.34435	7.711752	5.327435	3.741307	2.650701	1.908584
4/28/2018	116	6	34.93033	24.56192	16.44291	10.90977	7.326165	5.00779	3.479415	2.447845	1.736811
4/29/2018	116	9	34.58107	24.07068	15.94962	10.47338	5.959855	4.707322	3.235856	2.252017	1.580498
4/30/2018	116	14	34.23526	23.58927	15.47113	10.05445	6.611864	4.424883	$.009346	2.071856	1.438253
		SSD	20834.62	11158.62	5161.545	2530.183	1724.355	1704.598	1977.197	2336.242	2701.601
		Min	V								
SUM:	421		1193	963	747	580	460	374	313	267	232

Table 2. Applying the linear trend method to compute the sum of predicted sales volume (SUM) and the sum of squared differences (SSD).

Unit (x)	Date	Sales volume (v)	Forecasting model (yi = −0.0076x +53.311)
782	4/1/2018	3	47.3678
783	4/2/2018	25	47.3602
784	4/3/2018	17	47.3526
785	4/4/2018	24	47.345
786	4/5/2018	14	47.3374
787	4/6/2018	18	47.3298
788	4/7/2018	14	47.3222
789	4/8/2018	12	47.3146
790	4/9/2018	18	47.307
791	4/10/2018	18	47.2994
792	4/11/2018	16	47.2918
793	4/12/2018	19	47.2842
794	4/13/2018	14	47.2766
795	4/14/2018	9	47.269
796	4/15/2018	13	47.2614
797	4/16/2018	17	47.2538
798	4/17/2018	5	47.2462
799	4/18/2018	11	47.2386
800	4/19/2018	18	47.231
801	4/20/2018	10	47.2234
802	4/21/2018	9	47.2158
803	4/22/2018	10	47.2082
804	4/23/2018	27	47.2006
805	4/24/2018	7	47.193
806	4/25/2018	17	47.1854
807	4/26/2018	11	47.1778
808	4/27/2018	16	47.1702
809	4/28/2018	6	47.1626
810	4/29/2018	9	47.155
811	4/30/2018	14	47.1474
			SUM = 1417.728
			SSD = 34068.30735

4.3   Application of the Seasonal Variation Method

Because the data showed seasonal patterns, it was not appropriate to use the linear trend method to produce a linear equation. Therefore, the seasonal variation method was used. Additionally, different moving or smoothing methods were used to adjust for the seasonal index: simple average, simple moving average, weighted moving average, and exponential smoothing.

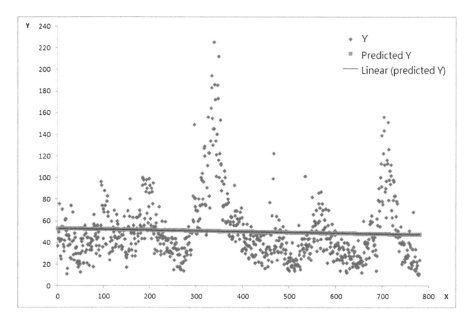

Fig. 2. The data shows a clear seasonal pattern.

Table 3. Applying the simple average method to compute the predicted sales volume.

Unit (x)	Date	Sales volume	ASI	SA (y)	Forecasting Model (yi = −0.0005x + 1.1999)	Predicted sales volume
1	2016/2/7	37	63.333	0.584210526	1.199342788	75.95837656
2	2016/2/B	44	68.333	0.643902439	1.198831652	81.92016292
3	2016/2/9	50	60.333	0.828729282	1.1983205117	72.2986712
4	2016/2/10	76	60.333	1.259668508	1.197809382	72.2678327
5	2016/2/11	44	56.333	0.781065089	1.197298246	67.44780121
6	2016/2/12	41	40.000	1.025	1.196787111	47.87148444
7	2016/2/13	28	38.000	0.736842105	1.196275976	45.45848708
8	2016/2/14	25	42.667	0.5859375	1.19576484	51.01929985
9	2016/2/15	43	49.667	0.865771812	1.195253705	59.36426735
10	2016/2/16	55	58.000	0.948275862	1.19474257	69.29506904
11	2016/2/17	71	57.667	1.231213873	1.194231434	68.86734604
12	2016/2/18	55	39.333	1.398305085	1.193720299	46.95299842
13	2016/2/19	38	35.000	1.085714286	1.193209164	41.76232072
14	2016/2/20	32	39.667	0.806722689	1.192698028	47.31035512
15	2016/2/21	36	45.000	0.8	1.192186893	53.64841018
16	2016/2/22	42	45.333	0.926470588	1.191675757	54.02263434
17	2016/2/23	61	64.333	0.948186528	1.191164622	76.63159069
18	2016/2/24	62	52.000	1.192307692	1.190653487	61.91398131

Simple Average Method. First, each date was converted to an ordinal number such that January 1 is Day 1 and January 2 is Day 2, etc. The mean of the data for the same day of every year was computed; this was the average seasonal index (ASI) for that day. For example, to compute the ASI of Day 37, compute: [(Day 37 of 2016) + (Day 37 of 2017) + (Day 37 of 2018)]/3. Then, the daily sales volume between 2/7/2016 and 3/28/2018 was divided by each day's ASI, which resulted in a set of y-value that has been adjusted for seasonality. The seasonally adjusted (SA) data was analyzed through linear regression, which resulted in the equation $y = -0.0005x + 1.1999$. The final predicted sales volume was computed by multiplying the seasonally adjusted predicted value by each period's ASI (Table 3). The sum of squared differences between the predictions and the actual sales of each day during April 2018 was large (SSD = 11221). Compared to the actual total sales of 421, the predicted sales of 914 was off by quite a bit. This was possibly due to the limited number of years for which data was available, where each period only had two or three prior data to be averaged. If one period had an outlier, the ASI would be severely skewed and unable to properly reflect the true seasonality.

Simple Moving Average Method. A simple moving average was calculated using the ASI of 10 periods, which was found to be optimal after some calculations. The goal was to smooth out the short-term fluctuations and to reflect any long-term trends or periodicities. For example, to compute the 10-period simple moving ASI for Day 88, every year's ASIs for Days 79–88 will be simply averaged. To calculate the simple 10-period moving ASI for 4/2/2018, the ten ASIs between 3/23/2018 and 4/2/2018 were averaged. Then, the daily sales volumes between 2/7/2016 and 3/28/2018 were divided by the 10-period simple moving ASIs to obtain the seasonally adjusted values. A regression analysis of these values produced the equation $y_i = -0.0005x + 1.2019$. Then, the seasonally adjusted predicted values were multiplied by their corresponding 10-period simple moving ASI to generate the final predicted sales volume (Table 4).

The resulted forecast was considerably larger than the actual sales data of April 2018. The sum of squared differences of actual daily sales values was still relatively large (SSD = 7383). The sum of the predicted values for the month was 849, which was much larger than the actual sales total of 421. It was possible that when the price war started in February 2018, the residuals in the regression model started to deviate from the regression line that was based on the data from the 2/7/2016–3/28/2018 timeframe. Using a 10-period simple moving ASI as an example, we saw that the sum of residuals was 0.557114352 in January 2018, −1.085087416 in February 2018, and −3.474345163 in March 2018.

Consequently, the next step was to analyze only the data during the price war (i.e., the data in March 2018). The seasonally adjusted values (y) were obtained when dividing each day's (row's) sales volume by its corresponding 10-period simple moving ASI. (It can be observed from Table 5 that using 10-period data for simple moving averages yielded the optimal data for this study.) Then, these seasonally adjusted values were analyzed using regression, resulting in the equation $y_i = -0.0099x + 8.2569$. The equation shows that the Case Company's sales volume decreased at a noticeably faster rate once the price war began. Multiplying the seasonally adjusted predicted values by each period's corresponding moving ASI, the final

Table 4. Applying simple moving average method to compute the predicted sales volume.

Unit (x)	Date	Sales volume	ASI {10}	SA (y)	Forecasting model (yi = −0.0005x + 1.2019)	Predicted sales volume
1	2016/2/7	37	74.13333333	0.498764323	1.197769261	88.85451635
2	2016/2/8	44	75.16666667	0.585365854	1.197251898	89.99343432
3	2016/2/9	50	73.6	0.679347826	1.196734534	88.07966174
4	2016/2/10	76	71.03333333	1.069920225	1.196217171	84.97129306
5	2016/2/11	44	67.16666667	0.655086849	1.195699808	80.31117042
6	2016/2/12	41	61.71666667	0.664326222	1.195182444	73.76267653
7	2016/2/13	28	56.36666667	0.496747487	1.194665081	67.33928841
8	2016/2/14	25	54.28333333	0.460546515	1.194147718	64.82231861
9	2016/2/15	43	54	0.796296296	1.193630354	64.45603914
10	2016/2/16	55	53.7	1.024208566	1.193112991	64.07016762
11	2016/2/17	71	53.13333333	1.336260979	1.192595628	63.36658102
12	2016/2/18	55	50.23333333	1.094890511	1.192078264	59.88206482
13	2016/2/19	38	47.7	0.796645702	1.191560901	56.83745498
14	2016/2/20	32	45.63333333	0.701241782	1.191043538	54.35128677
15	2016/2/21	36	44.5	0.808988764	1.190526174	52.97841476
16	2016/2/22	42	45.03333333	0.932642487	1.190008811	53.59006346
17	2016/2/23	61	47.66666667	1.27972028	1.189491448	56.69909235
18	2016/2/24	62	48.6	1.275720165	1.188974084	57.78414051

predicted sales volume values were generated. Lastly, when comparing the forecast against the actual sales of April 2018, the sum of squared differences was relatively small (SSD = 901). Furthermore, the total sum of predicted sales was 442, which was very close to the actual total of 421.

Table 5. Finding the optimal period length for the simple moving average method.

Period	5	7	10	13	15
Total sales volume for the month	575	501	441	384	347
SSD	1383.2	1106	900.77	931.52	1112.6

Weighted Moving Average (WMA) Method. Because ASI data may be off compared with real data, it is advisable to use a 3-period ASI to calculate weighted moving averages in order to smooth out short-term fluctuations and to reflect any long-term trends or periodicities. For example, to calculate the weighted moving ASI for 4/1/2018, the ASI was weighted at 0.2 for 3/27/2018, at 0.3 for 3/28/2018, and 0.5 for 4/1/2018 (Note: No data retrieval activity occurred on 3/29-30/2018 due to staff errors). The three ASIs were then summed. Next, the daily sales volumes between 3/1/2018 and 3/28/2018 were divided by their corresponding weighted moving ASIs to obtain the seasonally adjusted value (y). Then, these y-values were analyzed through regression and resulted in the equation $y_i = -0.0042x + 3.9115$. Each seasonally adjusted predicted value was multiplied by its corresponding weighted moving ASI to obtain the final predicted sales volume (Table 6). Lastly, comparing the predicted values against the actual daily sales volumes of April 2018, the sum of squared differences proved to be relatively small (SSD = 3035). Furthermore, the month's predicted total sales was 653, which was fairly close to the actual sales total of 421.

Table 6. Applying the weight moving average method to compute the predicted sales volume.

Unit (x)	Date	Sales volume	WMA	SA (y)	Forcasting Model ($y_i = -0.0042x + 3.9115$)	Predicted sales volume
754	3/1/2018	26	42.600	0.610328638	0.751438908	32.0112975
755	3/2/2018	29	42.300	0.685579196	0.747247873	31.60858505
756	3/3/2018	28	41.367	0.676873489	0.743056838	30.73778455
757	3/4/2018	17	39.233	0.433305013	0.738865803	28.98816835
753	3/5/2018	40	37.633	1.062887511	0.734674768	27.64826044
759	3/6/2018	51	41.500	1.228915663	0.730483733	30.31507492
760	3/7/2018	38	51.067	0.744125326	0.726292698	37.08934711
761	3/8/2018	36	50.367	0.714758438	0.722101663	36.36985376
762	3/9/2018	21	48.233	0.435383552	0.717910628	34.62722262
763	3/10/2018	16	47.167	0.339222615	0.713719593	33.66377413
764	3/11/2018	21	39.467	0.532094595	0.709528558	28.00272708
765	3/12/2018	19	32.967	0.576339737	0.705337523	23.252627
766	3/13/2018	34	33.700	1.008902077	0.701146488	23.62863663
767	3/14/2018	23	36.800	0.625	0.696955453	25.64796065
768	3/15/2018	68	45.900	1.481481481	0.692764417	31.79788676
769	3/16/2018	23	40.233	0.571665286	0.688573382	27.70360242
770	3/17/2018	15	33.767	0.444225074	0.684382347	23.10931059
771	3/18/2018	27	30.100	0.897009967	0.680191312	20.4737585

Exponential Smoothing Method. The next attempt was applying the exponential smoothing method to the seasonal index. A damping parameter of 0.7 was used to smooth out short-term fluctuations and to reflect any long-term trends or periodicities. Dividing the daily sales volumes between 3/1/2018 and 3/28/2018 by the exponential smoothing seasonal index generated the seasonally adjusted values (y). Then, these values were analyzed through regression and resulted in the equation $y_i = -0.003x + 3.0488$. Multiplying each seasonally adjusted predicted value by its corresponding weighted moving ASI, the final predicted sales volume data was obtained (Table 7). Lastly, comparing the predicted values against the actual daily sales volumes, the sum of squared difference was very large (SSD = 3608). Furthermore, the month's predicted total sales was 704, which was quite different from the actual sales total of 421. It can be concluded that using the exponential smoothing method to adjust for the seasonal index is not effective, possibly due to the size of the damping parameter

Table 7. Applying the exponential smoothing method to compute the predicted sales volume.

Unit (x)	Date	Sales Volume	DP (0.7)	SA (y)	Forcasting Model (yi = -0.003x + 3.0488)	Predicted Sales Volume
754	3/1/2018	26	40.494	0.642075003	0.754946637	30.57059137
755	3/2/2018	29	43.648	0.664404431	0.751904374	32.81920743
756	3/3/2018	28	41.561	0.673706892	0.748862111	31.1235336
757	3/4/2018	17	40.702	0.417673346	0.745819848	30.35610852
758	3/5/2018	40	38.810	1.030648947	0.742777585	28.82756877
759	3/6/2018	51	37.076	1.375534997	0.739735322	27.42678413
760	3/7/2018	38	43.323	0.877133354	0.736693059	31.91571282
761	3/8/2018	36	54.997	0.654582546	0.733650796	40.34850736
762	3/9/2018	21	48.932	0.429163513	0.730608533	35.75042781
763	3/10/2018	16	45.946	0.348231958	0.727566271	33.42904084
764	3/11/2018	21	48.084	0.436736477	0.724524008	34.83795142
765	3/12/2018	19	36.592	0.519241428	0.721481745	26.40034559
766	3/13/2018	34	30.111	1.129159742	0.718439482	21.63284916
767	3/14/2018	23	35.867	0.641265149	0.715397219	25.65886522
768	3/15/2018	68	38.527	1.765012177	0.712354956	27.44464749
769	3/16/2018	23	48.425	0.474964609	0.709312693	34.34822641
770	3/17/2018	15	37.627	0.398645687	0.70627043	26.5751187
771	3/18/2018	27	29.955	0.901355455	0.703228167	21.06511967

(DP) being too large at 0.7. Thus, excessive focus on the ASIs of the current period and the period immediately before would not produce satisfactory results in smoothing out extreme values.

5   Discussion and Conclusion

The current study chose a medical equipment company on the American e-commerce platform Amazon as the object of the research. This company had recently been impacted by a price war that caused significant overstocking and increased the company's inventory cost. Because of the impact of the price war, the existing mathematical model of the overall sales trend was not as reliable as it had been in the past when there was no price war. Thus, this study focused on exploring how a company can respond in a price war in terms of choosing sales forecast models to analyze forecast data. Three forecast methods were studied: the exponential smoothing method, the linear trend method, and the seasonal variation method. The results indicate that the seasonal variation method was the most suitable method for the data in this study because the original sales volumes data contained patterns that reflected seasonality and holiday influences. In the process of applying the seasonal variation method, it was found that the simple moving average method that used a 10-period simple moving ASI offered the best results for removing the seasonal influence from the data and was therefore identified as the most suitable forecast method for this case. The results are expected to help the medical equipment vendor accurately calculate the sales volume during a price war, reduce inventory cost, and increase overall profit.

5.1   Discussion of Results

This study found that the exponential smoothing method is constrained by the antecedent variable and must use the prior period's forecast. Thus, the forecast values in this method will trend toward 0 in long-term situations.

While the linear trend method does reflect the company's overall sales trend, the data in the study had an annual periodicity. If the goal is to forecast values for the upcoming month, this method would no longer offer accurate predictions due to its negligence of seasonality.

Among the three potential methods, the seasonal variation was the most suitable for the data in this study. We first used a simple average to calculate the seasonal index, then removed the seasonal index from all past sales volume values before doing the regression analysis, then multiplied the predicted values by their corresponding seasonal indexes. However, the results of this approach showed that because of insufficient data points (each period only had 2 or 3 values to be averaged), it was unable to approximate the true seasonal index. Any unusually high or low outliers would cause it to deviate considerably. Therefore, the seasonal index was calculated with a moving average or an exponential smoothing average to smooth out the short-term fluctuations and to reflect any long-term trends or periodicities. As a price war had started recently, using the overall historical data for regression would overlook the near-term trend of rapid sales decline. Thus, the study tested several scenarios and found that the data that yielded the most accurate regression equation for sales trend was the data from the month immediately prior to the forecast period that was also within the price war duration. After exploring the moving average, weighted moving average, and exponential smoothing methods to smooth out seasonal short-term fluctuations, it was found that the simple moving average of 10 periods was the most effective in eliminating seasonal influence from the data in this study and was the most suitable forecast method for this case. From the comparison presented in Table 8, it is clear which method is the best for companies facing a price war.

Table 8. Comparing the various methods for computing predicted sales volume and SSD.

Forecast period/Predicted Sales Volume and SSD	Linear trend method	Simple ASI	Simple moving 10-period ASI	Weighted moving ASI	Exponential smoothing seasonal index
2016/02/07–2018/03/28	1417 SSD = 34068	914 SSD = 11221	849 SSD = 7383	910 SSD = 9659	930 SSD = 9852
2018/02/01–2018/03/28	−21.3654 SSD = 8323	594 SSD = 2932	550 SSD = 1526	608 SSD = 2359	655 SSD = 2701
2018/03/01–2018/03/28	153.1 SSD = 3844	649 SSD = 3852	442 SSD = 900	652 SSD = 3035	704 SSD = 3607

Currently, the most common manufacturing method in industries is the "just in time" (JIT) model, which means that the manufacturers responsible for production would only produce items when demands arise. This is a manufacturing and purchasing strategy for minimizing or eliminating inventory that helps reduce inventory cost and increase overall profit. JIT was first proposed in 1953 by Taiichi Ohno, an executive of the Japanese company Toyota. The idea is to keep information flow and logistics parallel during production, in order to have the exact quantity of necessary materials to produce the exact quantity of necessary products at the right time [29]. This was done to shorten labor hours, reduce inventory, decrease production cost, and increase manufacturing efficiency [16].

As manufacturers adopt the JIT model, the pressure of managing inventory falls on the distributors. Generally, from the order of merchandise to product delivery takes about three months (a lead time of 90 days). This means that a distributor would need to predict at least three months' worth of merchandise sales volume when placing an order with the manufacturer. Otherwise, most manufacturers would not accept the order. For this reason, sales forecast is very important for distributors. If the three-month sales forecast is inaccurate, the distributor would be faced with inventory-related stress. If the forecast is larger than actual sales, the distributor would suffer a large inventory cost. When the distributor has originally planned for a low inventory, having overstock due to erroneous forecast would result in even more damaging consequences. In addition, consumers may not like buying products that have been sitting in the inventory for a long time, especially if the products have expiration dates [6]. For example, some products use lithium batteries, which may lose the battery power as they are kept in inventory for a prolonged period and result in lower durability than what the consumers expect. On the other hand, if the forecast is less than the actual sales, then the distributor is faced with the problem of merchandise shortage. Not only does the distributor miss out on sales opportunities, but it might also cause mistrust in its customers.

Moreover, more enterprises are using different social media to meet the customer's needs. Social media are now deeply rooted in modern life and have become a new way for companies to communicate with consumers [13]. According to prior research, including public sentiment variables in sales forecast models can increase the significance of the models. Because public sentiment variables are significantly related to certain products' sales outcomes, they are also valuable for these products' sales forecast [21, 35]. However, consumers often ignore social media ads because the ads and the consumer's preferences are mismatched [19]. Accordingly, enterprises should properly utilize social media, not only providing the target consumers with ads contents but also collecting and conducting time-series analysis on the big data around consumer's social media affective variables. Of course, social media platform administrators should also ensure the security of information and transactions, so that companies may properly use social networks to contact other companies and customers and so that customers can trust the newest information about the distributed merchandise [24].

5.2   Research Limitation and Future Research Suggestions

From the above discussion, it can be concluded that the importance of sales forecast is unquestionable. However, in the past, mathematical forecast models were not usually discussed when a company faced price wars to see how the forecast method might be adjusted. For this reason, this study provides some potential quantitative methods (exponential smoothing method, linear trend method, and seasonal variation method) that would allow companies to accurately predict sales in a price war and place orders accordingly.

The main challenge that this study encountered was that the Case Company was unwilling to make available its social media interaction data. Thus, we were unable to access data such as the level of product popularity or customer feedback. These missing data lowered the accuracy of our forecast results. If the Case Company could provide earlier historical sales data, we would be able to find the optimal ASI for the available dataset. If it could provide additional data such as number of orders placed, inventory cost, ideal quantity of inventory reserve, and delivery time, etc., we would be able to calculate the economic ordering quantity (EOQ) as a way to provide the company with the best reorder point. Future research might consider using public opinion analysis to understand the public's response to certain target products and to adjust the mathematical model accordingly in order to increase the overall accuracy of the forecast.

Acknowledgement. I would like to express my special thanks of gratitude to my four undergraduate students (Pin-Yuan Chen, Yun-Che Lin, Jun-Da Shu and Hirosato Song) who had tried so hard to manage a large dataset provided by the Case company. I would also like to thank the representative of the Case company for his clear direction in advising us to adopt certain data analysis methods. Without his help, my students and I would not be able to find a better forecasting sales model during a price war on Amazon e-commerce website for the Case company.

References

1. Avinash, B., Babu, S.: Big data technologies for e-business- Future opportunities, challenges ahead and growing trends. Int. J. Adv. Res. Comput. Sci. **9**(2), 328–332 (2018)
2. B2C, written by Volan, P., August 18, 2018, Price wars in the e-commerce industry: How big data helps businesses to gain market share. https://www.business2community.com/big-data/price-wars-in-the-e-commerce-industry-how-big-data-helps-businesses-to-gain-market-share-02109204. Accessed 22 Jan 2019
3. Brown, R.G.: Exponential smoothing for predicting demand 1956. http://legacy.library.ucsf.edu/tid/dae94e00. Accessed 21 Jan 2016
4. Brynjolfsson, E., Geva, T., Reichman, S.: Crowd-squared: amplifying the predictive power of search trend data. MIS Q. **40**(4), 941–961 (2016)
5. Business Insider, written by Green, D., November 24, 2017, These are the most popular items sold online for Black Friday so far, according to the data. http://www.businessinsider.com/black-fridays-most-popular-items-online-2017-11. Accessed 21 Jan 2019
6. Chan, T.K.H., Cheung, C.M.K., Lee, Z.W.Y.: The state of online impulse-buying research: a literature analysis. Inf. Manag. **54**(2), 204–217 (2017)

7. Chou, Y.L.: Statistical Analysis with Business and Economic Applications, 2nd edn. Continuum International Publishing Group Ltd., New York (1975)
8. Christiaanse, W.R.: Short-term load forecasting using general exponential smoothing. IEEE Trans. Power Apparatus Syst. **90**(2), 900–911 (1971)
9. Cui, R., Gallino, S., Moreno, A., Zhang, D.J.: The operational value of social media information. Prod. Oper. Manag. **27**(10), 1749–1769 (2017)
10. Currie, C.S., Rowley, I.T.: Consumer behaviour and sales forecast accuracy: what's going on and how should revenue managers respond? J. Revenue Pricing Manag. **9**(4), 374–376 (2010)
11. Everette, G.S.: Exponential smoothing: the state of the art. J. Forcasting **4**(1), 1–28 (1985)
12. Gahan, P., Pattnaik, M.: Optimization in fuzzy economic order quantity (FEOQ) model with promotional effort cost and units lost due to deterioration. LogForum **13**(1), 61–76 (2017)
13. Gallup, published by The Wall Street Journal, June 11, 2014, The myth of social media. http://online.wsj.com/public/resources/documents/sac_report_11_socialmedia_061114.pdf. Accessed 22 Jan 2019
14. Gilliland, M.: Role of the sales force in forecasting. Foresight Int. J. Appl. Forecast. **35**, 8–13 (2014)
15. Gonzalez, R., Hasker, K., Sickles, R.: An analysis of strategic behavior in eBay auctions. Singap. Econ. Rev. **54**(3), 441–472 (2009)
16. Hirano, H., Makota, F.: Just in Time is Flow: Practice and Principles of Lean Manufacturing. PCS Press, Vancouver (2006)
17. Hyndman, R.J., Athanasopoulos, G.: Forcasting: Principles and practice, 3.1 Some simple forecasting methods 2018. https://otexts.com/fpp2/. Accessed 21 Nov 2016
18. Janssen, M., van der Voort, H., Wahyudi, A.: Factors influencing big data decision-making quality. J. Bus. Res. **70**, 338–345 (2017)
19. Kietzmann, J.H., Hermkens, K., McCarthy, I.P., Silvestre, B.S.: Social media? Get serious! Understanding the functional building blocks of social media. Bus. Horiz. **54**(3), 241–251 (2011)
20. Lapide, L.: Are you capturing enough "quick-response" revenue? Supply Chain Manag. Revi. InSights **22**(2), 4–6 (2018)
21. Ma, Q., Zhang, W.: Public mood and consumption choices: evidence from sales of Sony cameras on Taobao. PLoS ONE **10**(4), e0123129 (2015)
22. McElroy, T.: Multivariate seasonal adjustment, economic identities, and seasonal taxonomy. J. Bus. Econ. Stat. **35**, 611–625 (2016)
23. Moon, S., Hicks, C., Simpson, A.: The development of a hierarchical forecasting method for predicting spare parts demand in the South Korean Navy—a case study. Int. J. Prod. Econ. **140**(2), 794–802 (2012)
24. Ramanathan, U., Subramanian, N., Parrott, G.: Role of social media in retail network operations and marketing to enhance customer satisfaction. Int. J. Oper. Prod. Manag. **37**(1), 105–123 (2017)
25. Rao, A., Bergen, M., Davis, S.: How to fight a price war. Harvard Bus. Rev. **78**(2, March/April), 107–116 (2000)
26. Reinmoeller, P.: How to win a price war. MIT Sloan Manag. Rev. **55**(3), 15–17 (2014)
27. Sagaert, Y.R., Aghezzaf, E.H., Kourentzes, N., Desmet, B.: Tactical sales forecasting using a very large set of macroeconomic indicators. Eur. J. Oper. Res. **264**(2), 558–569 (2018)
28. Seaman, B.: Considerations of a retail forecasting practitioner. Int. J. Forecast. **34**(4), 822–829 (2018)
29. Shah, R., Ward, P.T.: Lean manufacturing: context, practice bundles, and performance. J. Oper. Manag. **21**(2), 129–149 (2003)

30. Sillitoe, B.: Retailers urged to change approach to demand forecasting. Comput. Wkly., 15 June 2017. https://www.computerweekly.com/. Accessed 28 May 2019
31. Statistics on Key Figures of E-Commerce, surveyed by ACSI, February 2018, U.S. customer satisfaction with Amazon.com from 2000 to 2017 (index score). https://www.statista.com/statistics/185788/us-customer-satisfaction-with-amazon/. Accessed 21 Jan 2019
32. Vahid, M., Farokhi, M., Ibrahim, O., Nilashi, M.: A user satisfaction model for e-commerce recommender systems. J. Soft Comput. Dec. Support System **3**(3), 42–54 (2016)
33. Wang, G., Gunasekaran, A., Eric Ngai, W.T., Papadopoulos, T.: Big data analytics in logistics and supply chain management: certain investigations for research and applications. Int. J. Prod. Econ. **176**(C), 98–110 (2016)
34. Wild, T.: Best practice in inventory management, 3rd edn. Routledge, New York, NY (2018)
35. Yousef, M.I.: Social media with its role in supporting e-commerce and its challenges. J. Fundam. Appl. Sci. **10**(4S), 336–340 (2018)
36. Zhang, P.G., Qi, M.: Neural network forecasting for seasonal and trend time series. Eur. J. Oper. Res. **160**(2), 501–514 (2005)

Current State of Mixed Reality Technology for Digital Retail: A Literature Review

Shubham Jain[✉] and Dirk Werth

AWS-Institut für digitale Produkte und Prozesse, Saarbrücken, Germany
{shubham.jain,dirk.werth}@aws-institut.de

Abstract. Immersive 3D environments have been a major research area in different scientific domains such as Human-Computer Interaction, display devices, etc. Mixed Reality (MR) technologies are one of the most interesting sections of immersive environments that have a huge potential of deployment in a diverse range of industries, Retail being one of them. Retail started from traditional physical in-store setups and has been evolving ever since. Integration of technologies gave birth to Digital and Omnichannel Retail and for efficient development and deployment of MR in Omnichannel Retail, appropriate research must be made to provide proper frameworks and guidelines to developers and managers to optimize User Experiences. This paper investigates the current state of the art of MR in Retail by reviewing the present literature in the domain. It proposes important research gaps based on the analysis and understanding to provide further researches a clear picture of the different aspects associated with optimal application of MR technology in Retail sector.

Keywords: Mixed Reality · Digital Retail · User Experience

1 Introduction

Mixed Reality technology has been expanding ever since it was defined in 1994 [1]. Different industries and firms have been trying to deploy this technology in their respective sectors as it is projected as the future technology by different authors in print and picture media. Despite its existence for several decades, there are gaps and voids that need to be filled for reliable and efficient use of Mixed Reality environments. In the following paper, the current state of the art is discussed by reviewing the existing literature for Mixed Reality and immersive media; the research and development that has been going on around it and the dynamics of its deployment in Retail environments to enhance product experience. From the definition of 'digitization' of Retail mentioned in [75] and the trend of Digital Retail mentioned in [3], Digital Retail can be understood as Retail built around or using different digital technologies. It started with Online Retail stores and eventually is moving towards Omnichannel Retailing which integrates traditional physical retailing and Digital Retail in different forms. The paper focuses on analyzing three separate domains: Mixed Reality, Digital Retail and User Experience and tries to blend them to conclude the current state of the art and project future researches on the topic. The aim is to analyze the present literature in Mixed Reality technology in the context of Digital and Omnichannel Retail to identify gaps

The original version of this chapter was revised: This chapter was mistakenly published as a regular chapter instead of open access. The correction to this chapter is available at https://doi.org/10.1007/978-3-030-22335-9_26

F. F.-H. Nah and K. Siau (Eds.): HCII 2019, LNCS 11588, pp. 22–37, 2019.
https://doi.org/10.1007/978-3-030-22335-9_2

and propose a future research framework based on these gaps, which could facilitate research and development in the field.

Despite existence of several definitions of Mixed Reality by different authors e.g. [55, 63], we follow the original definition which describes Mixed Reality environment as "one in which real world and virtual world objects are presented together within a single display, that is, anywhere between the extrema of the Virtuality continuum" [1]. The author proposed a whole continuum of immersive environments known as the Virtuality continuum shown in Fig. 1 which encompasses the display devices ranging from physical reality to fully immersive computer-generated environments.

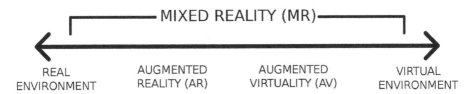

Fig. 1. Virtuality continuum by Milgram et al. [1]

As described by Microsoft [62], domains like perception and HCI (Human Computer Interaction) are a crucial part of MR as a science. Display technologies have been studied with regards to quality of experience to evaluate perception and Human-Computer Interaction (discussed in Sect. 3) which makes it important to study User Experience which is also crucial to study Omnichannel Retail because the concept of Omnichannel Retail is based on customer holistic experiences (discussed in Sect. 4).

The paper is divided into six further sections, starting with presenting the research methodology. The article then goes on by reviewing the ongoing research and applications of Mixed Reality technology and devices. Section 4 talks about the current state of Mixed Reality environments in Digital and Omnichannel Retail, and the researches and developments that are related to the scenario. The article furthers down to analysis structure in Sect. 5 and description of research gaps in Sect. 6 followed by conclusion, acknowledgement and the used references.

2   Methodology

In the presented article, the used methods for selection of search results merged a protocol-driven methodology (the search strategy is defined at the beginning of the study) with a snowballing technique (the search strategy emerges as the study unfolds) as mentioned in Greenhalgh and Peacock [72] and Ravasi and Stigliani [75]. We used the Google Scholar database and articles were selected by reading abstracts and titles and evaluating the relevance to the topic and the purpose.

The initial search was made to understand the basics of the Mixed Reality technology reaching out to the first published article using the keyword "Mixed Reality" in Google Scholar. Reaching out to the references of the paper, a total collection of 8 articles was made. Two other definitions of MR were established by reaching out to websites of Microsoft and Intel. Another article reviewing Microsoft HoloLens was added from Google Scholar with the search term "Microsoft HoloLens" and industry applications of MR was studied with websites of IKEA, Magic Leap, BMW, and Volvo. Another article was selected from Google scholar to briefly study Pokémon Go with the keyword "Pokémon Go". These articles combined to form a collection of 16.

In the next phase, search was made with keywords: "3D" + "quality" + "evaluation", and along with snowballing technique, we collected a set of another 28 articles. The phrase "Mixed Reality user acceptance" was used and snowballed to include another 4 articles. "Product experience" was searched and 15 articles were included. Another 10 articles were obtained using the keywords:" Mixed Reality" + "Retail" giving a total of 73 articles to define the scope of the paper. The research was more focused on studying proven concepts and standards to develop a state of the art and less on identifying pros and cons of individual studies.

3   Mixed Reality Technology

The authors in [1] defined Mixed Reality as a subset of Virtual Reality (VR) displays and taxonomized it into further six classes of displays. Mobile Augmented Reality (AR) which can be considered as class 4 "video see-through" MR displays, has become a major trend among all the other Mixed Reality environments as it has certain advantages such as availability and ease of use; and some trendy applications like Pokémon Go [65] and IKEA Place [66] helped in popularizing it. Class 3 MR display technology is through optical see-through head-mounted displays such as Microsoft HoloLens which was projected as "the future of Augmented Reality" by Microsoft in 2016 [2]. Some early examples of optical see-through displays are [54, 56–58]. HoloLens interactions mostly constitute of the 'HoloLens two core gestures', some voice-based interactions, gaze-controlled UI pointers and Cortana. As mentioned in [2], we agree to the fact that despite certain hardware and software limitations and shortcomings of the developer version, "future iterations of the HoloLens could profoundly change how we relate to our computers and even to our environment" because users will be able to relate to the physical environment with more digital information and possible interactions, and will be relating to the computer just in a form of daily-usable eye glasses if the designers overcome the hardware limitations. Contrary to the definition followed, Intel describes VR as an umbrella term for all the three technologies: VR, AR and MR and differentiates between AR and MR in parallel [63] which points out the presence of ambiguity of understandings in the domain.

As MR is an immersive display technology, content for the technology is produced in the form of 3D digital objects (often in the form of point clouds and meshes) blended with real environments to different degrees. Different authors have been trying to put up researches to determine the quality and general characteristics associated with 3D content. Visual quality and user perception of the 2D media has been standardized since long, along with standard objective metrics and subjective experimentation methodologies which are important to facilitate perception of the content [67–70]. The present literature suggests that the visual quality of 3D content goes beyond the concept of just pixel density or resolution like in 2D media. In [46], the authors propose a model-based perception quality assessment for meshes which makes use of both spatial and temporal features. In [43], the authors experimented with geometric and texture noises of 3D objects subjectively and concluded results such as "human viewers are far more sensitive to the distortion of texture than to that of geometry". In [44], "based on analysis of the subjective quality results, the authors proposed two new metrics for visual quality assessment of textured mesh, as optimized linear combinations of accurate geometry and texture quality measurements. These proposed perceptual metrics outperform their counterparts in terms of correlation with human opinion". In [28], authors experimented with visual quality features like data corruption in point clouds by noise, simplification, and compression; and concluded that "when the contents are subject to compression like distortions, the underlying surface and shape of the content seem to play a significant role". In [31], authors worked on contrast sensitivity and discrimination. In [33], geometric distortions introduced by compressing point clouds have been evaluated by subjective and objective methods. In [34], different configurations of the acquisition methodology have been evaluated with subjective methods for multi-view videos. [35] talks about improving techniques for surface construction in 3D models from point cloud data. [37] evaluated quality for 3D point cloud models and concluded important insights about the correlation between human visual system and factors like resolution change and color change in 3D models along with the result that shape has more impact than the color on the quality of 3D model if they are added the almost same amount noise. In [38], authors worked on quality analysis with different network characteristics for 3D videos. In [48], the authors talk about Just Noticeable Difference models for 3D meshes. [32, 40] and [50] talk about quality levels in free viewpoint videos and 3D videos; [36] talks about light field imaging which is another form of immersive 3D environment. Other mentionable works for 3D media are [39, 45, 47] and [51].

As perception of the 3D content is important in Mixed Reality technology as mentioned in [62], determining the quality and User Experience around the content and how it is perceived by the users becomes important. The study around User Experience include topics like HCI which traditionally talks about understanding and optimizing interactions through efficient computer interfaces. The concept of User Interfaces (UI) extended to become User Experience (UX) as recommended in [10], "the term User Experience to be scoped to products, systems, services, and objects that a person interacts with through a user interface". UX further created the domain of QoE (quality of experience) where researchers and developers are trying to create a holistic hedonic experience for users considering factors like visualization environments, hardware properties, and psychological human factors along with the quality of the content to be visualized [29, 45]. Quality of experience is defined as "the degree of delight or annoyance of the user of an application or service. It results from the fulfillment of his or her expectations with respect to the utility and/or enjoyment of the application or service in the light of the user's personality and current state" [29]. As per our understanding, a QoE centric system is more than just a point and click interface and aims to optimize all the factors that can affect a user's perception of the content. Factors that could affect the quality of experience are divided into three broad categories of influence factors (IFs) namely Human influence factors, System influence factors, and Context influence factors in [29]. Authors in [47] modeled QoE factors differently into six different categories while [30] describes visual quality in a 3D environment is influenced by three factors: image quality, comfort, and realism.

4 Digital Retail and Mixed Reality

Traditional physical and online retail has been evolved into Multi-channel due to the synergies between online and offline channels of Retail. Multi-channel Retail has been projected to transform into Omnichannel Retail [60] where the concept of channels will slowly diminish, and focus will be more centered on points of contact. "Omnichannel Retail refers to the integration of retail channels like stores, online, and mobile into a single, seamless customer experience" [60]. Authors in [60], which is a Delphi study for the future of Omnichannel Retail, participants agreed that omnichannel will become the new normal over the next ten years and that "the line between [channels] will blur and by the point where no distinction is made". The authors pointed out some major key trends, challenges, important technologies and main customer touch points in Omnichannel Retail in the coming decade. The authors also pointed out "omnichannel is all about customer convenience [...]. detail of the purchase will become competitive". In 2009, Bourlakis et al. [64] identified a shift from a product orientation to a consumer experience orientation in Retail.

Consumer or customer experience can be studied as a form of User Experience (UX) in the context of Retail when the primary users are the customers. Authors in [10] also tried to define User Experience in a broad domain with the help of experts from industry and academia. Work done in [22] presents a dialogue on User Experience (UX) with an experimental perspective on product quality. In Retail environments, User Experience also extends to product experience which is defined "as the awareness of the psychological effects elicited by the interaction with a product, including the degree to which all our senses are stimulated, the meanings and values we attach to the product, and the feelings and emotions that are elicited" [11]. Another work where product experience is discussed in [16], where the authors talk about product expressions and clustering of those expressions while the work in [23] presents a product experience framework dependent on aesthetic experience, emotional experience, and experience of meaning. In the scope of the paper, the definition in [11] is followed. A conceptual framework for customer experience enhancement is proposed in [20] shown in Fig. 2, that could help the retailers to identify and work on specific "offer zones" to be focused on while designing customer experience in businesses.

Customer experience is closely associated with customer satisfaction as more satisfied the customer feels with the environment, better the perception will be. The work done in [12] provides a comparison between different scales to measure customer satisfaction based on six criteria: reliability, convergent and discriminant validity, predictive validity, skewness, face validity and managerial value and argued that a 5-point disconfirmation scales would be the preferred method to measure customer satisfaction in contrast to performance and satisfaction scales. In [18], the author suggests that between 10 and 30 customers can be interviewed for one hour to understand the customer needs in a business in a typical study for customer behavior. One of the important works that talks about immersive environments in Retail is [53],

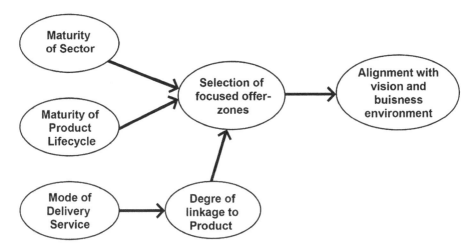

Fig. 2. Conceptual framework for customer experience enhancement [20]

which suggests that both enjoyment and engagement positively influence user satisfaction with the simulated Retail environment which influences the intention to purchase the item involved. It also suggests that engagement in the immersive environment explains perceived enjoyment better.

Customer experience is also associated with the acceptance of the technology in Digital Retail environments as it gives an insight to how does the users perceive the used technology based on different factors. Traditionally, there exists some TAM (Technology acceptance models) [15, 26] that have been used to study user acceptance and User Experience for Mixed Reality systems in Digital Retail. In [8], authors study the acceptance and potential of AR applications in Retail point of sale and concluded positively that AR-users rate the offer of information in the store better than non-users and AR-users agree to have found all the information they needed in the store more strongly. User acceptance of MR has been broadly studied in [9] using the traditional constructs like perceived usefulness (PU), perceived ease of use (PEOU), and the intention to use (ITU) [24] along with added constructs: personal innovativeness (PI), perceived enjoyment (PE). Though the work focusses mainly on Mixed Reality technology in education and the acceptance was tested with Mixed Reality regenerative concept (MRRC) for biomedical students, it gives us strong insights about the acceptance of Mixed Reality and the methodology that could be used for testing the acceptance of the technology. More User Experience, product experience and technology acceptance work can be found in [17, 19, 21, 25, 52] and [27]. The authors in [13] studies the current and future of specifically AR in Retail and argues that customer experiences are more realistic when they are embedded, embodied and extended.

MR immersive environments along with providing a more stimulated environment [53] and adding hedonic value to the Retail sector, can also add utilitarian value. Authors in [14] presented a mobile Augmented Reality application that provides customers with product information to assist them in making buying decisions. Pedro Lopes et al. [7] present a smart phone based Mixed Reality application (SPMRA) and concluded through subjective experiments in Germany and Sri Lanka that 84.1% of SPRMA users agreed to the fact that the application assisted and influenced them in making their buying decisions in stores. Automobile manufacturers such as BMW [4] and Volvo [5] has been using Microsoft HoloLens to visualize 3D holograms of automobiles, models, prototypes without the presence of the actual machinery assisting both the manufacturing and the customer showroom experience.

5 Analysis Structure

The three major concepts that were studied in the context of this paper were Mixed Reality, User Experience and Digital/Omnichannel Retail. The collected articles were given a read and the mentioned domains were tried to be synthesized. The articles that contributed to identification of basic concepts including definitions and trends are as follows:

- Mixed Reality: [1, 4–6, 54–59, 62, 63, 65, 66, 71]
- User Experience: [10, 22]
- Digital/Omnichannel Retail: [3, 60, 61, 64, 74]

The collected articles were then grouped according to the reoccurring themes and concepts found in the articles. These clusters were made by interpreting the overall themes of articles. We identified that evaluating and optimizing experience plays an important role in both Omnichannel Retail and MR developments. The reoccurring themes and concepts were as follows:

- Customer experience: [7, 11, 12, 16, 17, 19, 20, 25, 53, 73]
- Product experience: [7, 21, 23, 24]
- QoE: [29, 30, 45, 47, 49]
- Influence factors in QoE: [28, 31, 33–41, 43, 44, 46, 48]
- Pipeline/Analysis of 3D environments: [50, 51, 67–70]
- Acceptance of technologies: [9, 15, 24, 26, 27]
- Methodologies to evaluate experience: [8, 9, 12, 18]
- Use cases of MR: [7–9, 13, 14, 66]

Now the articles clustered as customer experience and product experience talk about different experience frameworks in Retail. They also talk about different components and constraints attached to the experience factors. Extending these frameworks to specifically MR Retail environments couldn't be described precisely with the literature.

Apart from these frameworks there are factors and models described in immersive environments. The articles clustered as QoE and 'Influence factors in QoE' talk about these constraints that affect the perception of a user in 3D immersive environments. When these factors are identified for MR in Retail specifically, the present knowledge is limited and, the relationship with the major customer experience frameworks couldn't be described properly.

The other four clusters 'Pipeline/Analysis of 3D environments', 'Acceptance of technologies', 'Methodologies to evaluate experience' and 'Use cases of MR' described methodologies, analysis deployments that could help in defining the relationship gaps mentioned above.

There are other articles for e.g., [52] that talk about several constraints to customer experience without proposing a holistic experience. The relationship of these factors to the QoE models and ultimately holistic customer experience models couldn't be described with the present literature in an explicit manner.

Other actors of a Retail ecosystem can also take advantage of MR environments, but the relationship among these actors in context to experience frameworks can be described with very little knowledge.

Initial research gap localization based on these knowledge gaps is shown in Fig. 3.

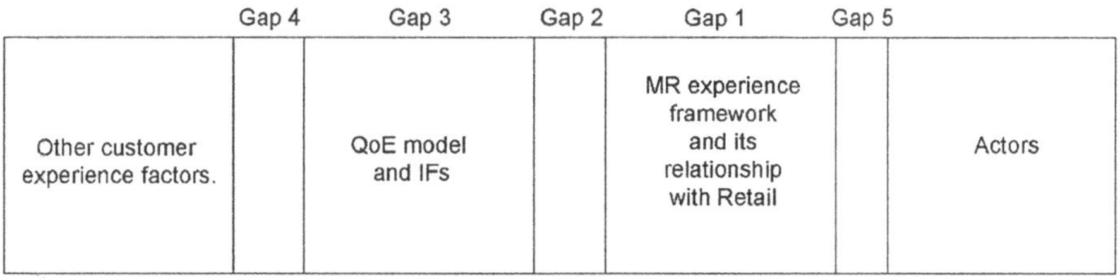

Gap 4		Gap 3		Gap 2		Gap 1		Gap 5
Other customer experience factors.		QoE model and IFs				MR experience framework and its relationship with Retail		Actors

Fig. 3. Initial localization of knowledge gaps.

The proposed framework in Fig. 4 was majorly based on customer experience, quality of experience, the QoE influence factors, and the actors in a retail ecosystem. The relationship is described in Sect. 6 clearly. During the analysis, the articles were mapped on to the model. Several experience frameworks were discussed in the article, but the one in [53] and [73] was chosen as it best describes the relationship between immersive environments and customer experience which is the center node of Omnichannel experience. Though no relevant knowledge was found extending this model to MR retail environments in precision. The QoE model was studied in relation to the influence factors. The relationship between the IFs, the antecedents of customer experience, and the customer experience model couldn't be described precisely with the present literature. Also, the relationship among the actors in the Retail ecosystem and towards the experience framework could not be defined precisely in MR retail environments towards an omnichannel approach.

6   Description of Research Gaps

The proposed research plan starts with an initial analysis of the conceptual model used in [53] and originally proposed in [73] where the important factors that are ultimately leading to increased engagement, enjoyment, satisfaction, and ultimately an increased intention to purchase are hedonic experience, utilitarian experience, and simulation experience. Though mostly, only utilitarian and hedonic values are considered as underlying dimensions of customer experience value [52]. The literature suggests that evaluating and optimizing User Experience is an important aspect of MR Omnichannel environments considering customers as the main user of the environments because the concept of Omnichannel Retail is centered around customer holistic experience. Hence, the main objective of integrating MR technologies in Retail should be enhanced customer experience and as [53] suggests, "in the immersive, 3D environment, experience is more associated with engagement and enjoyment, leading to greater purchase intention". These works talk about the relationships between the components mentioned in the model. This model has been tested on desktop virtual environments and special glasses equipped with "polarised lenses". Though the authors conceptualize different relationships in virtual and immersive environments in Retail, it lacks its validation in MR Retail environments. We propose the **first** gap as the validity of this customer experience framework and the different relationships among the components of the model in an MR Retail environment.

The factors included in defining the simulation experience: colour vividness, graphics vividness, and 3D authenticity can be categorized as Content IFs in the QoE model proposed in [29], as they are characteristics of the 3D content in an immersive environment. 'Control' as a constraint in simulation experience can be categorized under Context IFs. The proven effect of these characteristics of 3D environments on the components and considering the definition of QoE in [29], these IFs determine the degree of delight or annoyance when perceived by the users, which in the case of Omnichannel Retail are customers. Hence, we conceptualize a relationship between the model proposed in [73] and the QoE factors proposed in [29]. Other Content IFs, broadly System IFs, Context IFs along with Human IFs need to be studied for their impact on hedonic experience, utilitarian experience, engagement, etc. to define this relationship. These proposed studies on the IFs collectively is identified as the **second** major gap in the present literature. For simplification, this relationship is denoted by an arrow between the two models in the proposed research framework in Fig. 4.

As there exists many IFs that affects the quality and perception of an immersive MR environment, the present literature points out a huge gap of a specific MR customer/User Experience framework in Retail which could point out and taxonomize the MR IFs specifically in Retail, which is the **third** identified gap.

Some of these IFs are studied in the literature [28–51] for general user perception. Mostly Content IFs are studied widely in these works, but more research is needed in optimizing constraints like physical environment and the social environment of the MR customer experience as mentioned in [52]. The effect of staff characteristics [52] on the perception of MR content is also an open issue. Evaluating the impact of these "Antecedents of customer experience Value" [52] in MR Retail setups can be regarded as the **fourth** gap in the present literature. As these antecedents can be regarded as influence factors in a Retail environment, they can be categorized or described under the QoE model [29]. Hence, this relationship is represented by an arrow between the QoE model and the model that lists out the antecedents.

We also hypothesize that, as MR environment is a blend of real and digital environments, physical environment can have a huge impact on the user's perception. The impact of physical environment constraints like the physical hardware constraints to an HMD (Head Mounted Display) mentioned in [45] can be studied to find quantitative correlations that can help further development of MR environments.

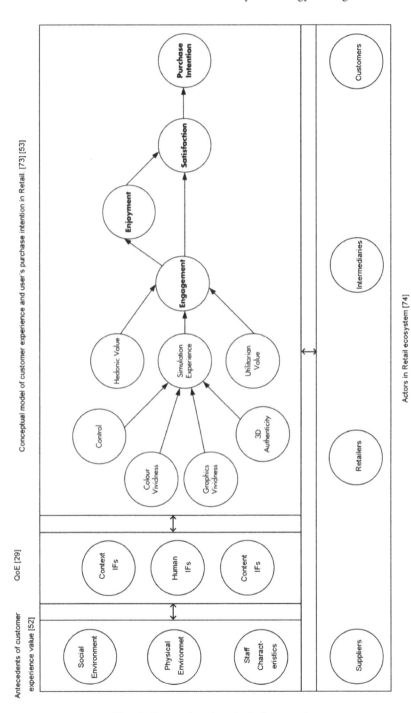

Fig. 4. Research and analysis framework

These customer experience enhancement frameworks which are based on hedonic and utilitarian value perceived by customers can be extended to other key actors in the sector mentioned in [74] like retailers, suppliers and other intermediaries. The relationship between the experience enhancement framework and different actors is represented by an arrow between the conceptual model and the model that lists out different actors of Retail. The **fifth** identified gap can be considered as the correlation of perception between different actors in the Retail eco-system which could eventually lead to a unified general perception framework for Retail or a collection of different frameworks for different actors. Retailers like Volvo have already started using it at the designing phase of the production. This gap is could be studied a bit differently as actors which are not customers, have different intentions of using the digital environments.

Use cases like these can add value to the whole Retail eco-system and give insights in different ways if deployed correctly and accepted by the user as technology acceptance is defined as the way people perceive, accept, and adopt technology use [9]. The definition suggest that acceptance of the technology is closely related to user perception of the technology which in turn is related to the experience of the user as if the user has a bad perception about the technology, the holistic experience will not be good for the user. We encourage researchers to build prototype and use cases based on the user perception framework discussed earlier and test them for user acceptance, and further use the results as proof of concept in the Retail sector.

7   Conclusion

In the presented article, three domains: Mixed Reality, User Experience and Digital Retail were studied and synthesized together to analyze the current state of the art. It was evident from the readings that the Retail sector is moving towards Omnichannel Retail model which is centered around customer holistic experience which includes hedonic and utilitarian experience of customers. To provide an efficient hedonic and utilitarian experience, immersive environments in general have proven to be of value. Mixed Reality immersive environments can add value to Omnichannel Retail by getting deployed in Retail ecosystem for different purposes. For efficient deployment of MR into Retail, the relationship between MR, the factors that affect user's experience of MR and customer experience model in Retail must be defined to facilitate different actors in the Retail ecosystem like developers, managers, customer, etc. This Omnichannel experience model can further be extended to other actors like suppliers, intermediaries, Retailers, etc. to deploy certain use cases for these actors. We identified 5 major gaps based on these relationships between the components of MR technology and Digital Retail that can be acknowledge and studied in the future and help the Retail sector to transition smoothly to customer centric model of Omnichannel approach with qualitative and quantitative studies.

Acknowledgement.

This research is a part of the European Training Network project PER-FORM that has received funding from the European Union's Horizon 2020 research and innovation programme under the Marie Skłodowska-Curie grant agreement No. 765395. This research reflects only the authors' view, the European Commission is not responsible for any use that may be made of the information it contains.

References

1. Milgram, P., Kishino, F.: A taxonomy of mixed reality visual displays. IEICE Trans. Inf. Syst. **12**(12), 1321–1329 (1994)
2. Furlan, R.: The future of augmented reality. HoloLens - Microsoft's AR headset shines despite rough edges [Resources Tools and Toys]. IEEE Spectr. **53**(6), 21 (2016)
3. Rigby, D.: The future of shopping. Harvard Bus. Rev. **89**, 65–76 (2011)
4. BMW Blog. https://www.bmwblog.com/2018/04/18/video-heres-how-bmw-is-using-mixed-reality-to-develop-cars/. Accessed 5 Dec 2018
5. Volvo webpage about collaboration with HoloLens. https://www.volvocars.com/uk/about/humanmade/projects/hololens. Accessed 5 Dec 2018
6. Lopes, P., You, S., Ion, A., Baudisch, P.: Adding force feedback to mixed reality experiences and games using electrical muscle stimulation. In: Proceedings of the 2018 CHI Conference on Human Factors in Computing Systems (CHI 2018), Paper 446, 13 pages. ACM, Montréal, Canada (2018)
7. Meegahapola, L., Perera, I.: Enhanced in-store shopping experience through smart phone based Mixed Reality application. In: Proceedings of the 2017 Seventeenth International Conference on Advances in ICT for Emerging Regions (ICTer), pp. 1–8. IEEE, Colombo (2017)
8. Spreer, P., Katrin, K.: Augmented reality in retail: assessing the acceptance and potential for multimedia product presentation at the PoS. Trans. Market. Res. **1**, 20–25 (2014)
9. Yusoff, R.C.M., Zaman, H.B., Ahmad, A.: Evaluation of user acceptance of Mixed Reality technology. Australas. J. Educ. Technol. **27**(Special issue, 8), 1369–1387 (2011)
10. Law, E.L., Roto, V., Hassenzahl, M., Vermeeren, A.P.O.S., Kort, J.: Understanding, scoping and defining user experience: a survey approach. In: Proceedings of the SIGCHI Conference on Human Factors in Computing Systems (CHI 2009), pp. 719–72. ACM, Boston (2009)
11. Hekkert, P., Schifferstein, H.N.J.: Product Experience, 1st edn. Elsevier, Oxford (2008)
12. Danaher, P.J., Haddrell, V.: A comparison of question scales used for measuring customer satisfaction. Int. J. Serv. Ind. Manag. **7**(4), 4–26 (1996)
13. Hilken, T., Heller, J., Chylinski, M., Keeling, D.I., Mahr, D., Ruyter, K.D.: Making omnichannel an augmented reality: the current and future state of the art. J. Res. Interact. Mark. **12**(4), 509–523 (2018)
14. Güven, S., Oda, O., Podlaseck, M., Stavropoulos, H., Kolluri, S., Pingali, G.: Social mobile augmented reality for retail. In: Proceedings of the 2009 IEEE International Conference on Pervasive Computing and Communications, pp. 1–3. IEEE, Galveston (2009)
15. Davis, F.D.: A Technology Acceptance Model for Empirically Testing New End-User Information Systems: Theory and Results. Doctoral dissertation, MIT Sloan School of Management. Cambridge (1986)
16. Rompay, T.V., Hekkert, P., Muller, W.: The bodily basis of product experience. Des. Stud. **26**(4), 359–377 (2005)

17. Schonowski, J.: User experience enhanced product cycle - industry spanning modular user experience paradigms. In: Proceedings of the Ninth International Conference on Enterprise Information Systems ICEIS, vol. 5, pp. 337–339. Funchal, Madeira – Portugal (2007)
18. Griffin, A., Hauser, J.: The voice of the customer. Mark. Sci. 12(1), 1–27 (1991)
19. Botha, J., Kruger, P., De Vries, M.: Enhancing customer experience through business process improvement: an introduction to the Enhanced Customer Experience Framework (ECEF). In: Proceedings of the 40th International Conference on Computers & Industrial Engineering, pp. 1–6. IEEE, Awaji (2010)
20. Kalyanaram, G., Aung, Z.Z.: Value-added ecosystem and customer experience enhancement framework. Kindai Manag. Rev. 3, 49–62 (2015)
21. Hoch, S.J.: Product experience is seductive. J. Consum. Res. 29(3), 448–454 (2002)
22. Hassenzahl, M.: User experience (UX): towards an experiential perspective on product quality. In: Proceedings of the 20th Conference on l'Interaction Homme-Machine, pp. 11–15. ACM, Metz (2008)
23. Desmet, P.M.A., Hekkert, P.: Framework of product experience. Int. J. Des. 1(1), 13–23 (2007)
24. Davis, F.D.: Perceived usefulness, perceived ease of use, and user acceptance of information technology. MIS Q. 3(3), 319–340 (1989)
25. Cetin, G., Dincer, F.I.: Influence of customer experience on loyalty and word-of-mouth in hospitality operations. Anatolia 25, 2 (2014)
26. Davis, F.D., Bagozzi, R.P., Warshaw, P.R.: User acceptance of computer technology: a comparison of two theoretical models. Manage. Sci. 35, 982–1003 (1989)
27. Pantano, E., De Pietro, L.: Understanding consumer's acceptance of technology-based innovations in retailing [S.l.]. J. Technol. Manag. Innov. 7(4), 1–19 (2012)
28. Alexiou, E., Upenik, E., Ebrahimi, T.: Towards subjective quality assessment of point cloud imaging in augmented reality. In: Proceedings of the 2017 IEEE 19th International Workshop on Multimedia Signal Processing (MMSP), pp. 1–6. IEEE, Luton, UK (2017)
29. Le Callet, P., Möller, S., Perkis, A. (eds.): Qualinet White paper on definitions of quality of experience. In: European Network on Quality of Experience in Multimedia Systems and Services (COST Action IC 1003) Version 1.1. Lausanne, Switzerland (2012)
30. Vlad, R., Ladret, P., Guérin-Dugué, A.: Three factors that influence the overall quality of the stereoscopic 3D content: image quality, comfort, and realism. In: Proceedings of the SPIE: Human Vision and Electronic Imaging XVIII 8653, pp. 865309. Burlingame, CA, USA (2013)
31. Nader, G., Wang, K., Hétroy-Wheeler, F., Dupont, F.: Visual contrast sensitivity and discrimination for 3D meshes and their applications. Comput. Graph. Forum 35(7), 497–506 (2016)
32. Collet, A., et al.: High-quality streamable free-viewpoint video. ACM Trans. Graph. (TOG) 34(4), 13 pages (2015). Article 69
33. Javaheri, A., Brites, C., Pereira, F., Ascenso, J.: Subjective and objective quality evaluation of compressed point clouds. In: Proceedings of the 2017 IEEE 19th International Workshop on Multimedia Signal Processing (MMSP), pp. 1–6. IEEE, Luton (2017)
34. Carballeira, P., Gutiérrez, J., Morán, F., Cabrera, J., García, N.: Subjective evaluation of super multiview video in consumer 3D displays. In: Proceedings of the 2015 Seventh International Workshop on Quality of Multimedia Experience (QoMEX), pp. 1–6. IEEE, Pylos-Nestoras (2015)
35. Guarda, A.F.R., Bioucas-Dias, J.M., Rodrigues, N.M.M., Pereira, F.: Improving point cloud to surface reconstruction with generalized Tikhonov regularization. In: Proceedings of the 2017 IEEE 19th International Workshop on Multimedia Signal Processing (MMSP), pp. 1–6. IEEE, Luton (2017)

36. Viola, I., Řeřábek, M., Ebrahimi, T.: Comparison and evaluation of light field image coding approaches. IEEE J. Sel. Top. Signal Process. **11**(7), 1092–1106 (2017)
37. Zhang, J., Huang, W., Zhu, X., Hwang, J.: A subjective quality evaluation for 3D point cloud models. In: Proceedings of the 2014 International Conference on Audio, Language and Image Processing, pp. 827–831. IEEE, Shanghai, China (2014)
38. Yasakethu, S.L.P., Hewage, C.T.E.R., Fernando, W.A.C., Kondoz, A.M.: Quality analysis for 3D video using 2D video quality models. IEEE Trans. Consum. Electron. **54**(4), 1969–1976 (2008)
39. Bulbul, A., Capin, T., Lavoué, G., Preda, M.: Assessing visual quality of 3-D POLYGONAL MODELS. IEEE Signal Process. Mag. **28**(6), 80–90 (2011)
40. Kilner, J., Starck, J., Guillemaut, J.Y., Hilton, A.: Objective quality assessment in free-viewpoint video production. Signal Process. Image Commun. **24**(1–2), 3–16 (2009)
41. Lavoué, G., Cheng, I., Basu, A.: Perceptual quality metrics for 3D meshes: towards an optimal multi-attribute computational model. In: Proceedings of the 2013 IEEE International Conference on Systems, Man, and Cybernetics, pp. 3271–3276. IEEE, Manchester (2013)
42. Lavoué, G., Larabi, M.C., Váša, L.: On the efficiency of image metrics for evaluating the visual quality of 3D models. IEEE Trans. Visual Comput. Graphics **22**(8), 1987–1999 (2015)
43. Pan, Y., Cheng, I., Basu, A.: Quality metric for approximating subjective evaluation of 3-D objects. IEEE Trans. Multimedia **7**(2), 269–279 (2005)
44. Guo, J., Vidal, V., Cheng, I., Basu, A., Baskurt, A., Lavoue, G.: Subjective and objective visual quality assessment of textured 3D meshes. ACM Trans. Appl. Percept. **14**(2), 20 pages (2015). Article 11
45. Video Quality Experts Group (VQEG). QoE evaluation of emerging immersive media technologies, including the current hot topics of virtual reality, omnidirectional content, point cloud and light field technologies. VQEG eLetter **3**(1), (2013)
46. Torkhani, F., Wang, K., Chassery, J.: Perceptual quality assessment of 3D dynamic meshes: Subjective and objective studies. Sig. Process. Image Commun. **31**(2), 185–204 (2015)
47. Moldovan, A., Ghergulescu, I., Weibelzahl, S., Muntean, C.H.: User-centered EEG-based multimedia quality assessment. In: Proceedings of the 2013 IEEE International Symposium on Broadband Multimedia Systems and Broadcasting (BMSB), pp. 1–8. IEEE, London (2013)
48. Nader, G., Wang, K., Hétroy-Wheeler, F., Dupont, F.: Just noticeable distortion profile for flat-shaded 3D mesh surfaces. IEEE Trans. Visual. Comput. Graph. **22**(11), 2423–2436 (2016). Institute of Electrical and Electronics Engineers
49. Moving Pictures Expert Group Technical report of the joint ad hoc group for digital representations of light/sound fields for immersive media applications. MPEG-115, Geneva, Switzerland (2015)
50. Smolic, A.: 3D video and free viewpoint video-From capture to display. Pattern Recogn. **44**(9), 1958–1968 (2011)
51. Li, Z., Bampis, C.: Recover subjective quality scores from noisy measurements. In: Proceedings of the 2017 Data Compression Conference (DCC), pp. 52–61. IEEE, Snowbird (2016)
52. Eiamkanchanalai, S.: Factors influencing customer experience management and customer experience value. Global Bus. Econ. Anthology **2**, 211–225 (2010)
53. Papagiannidis, S., Pantano, E., See-To, E.W.K., Dennis, C., Bourlakis, M.: To immerse or not? Experimenting with two virtual retail environments. Inf. Technol. People **30**(1), 163–188 (2017)

54. Bajura, M., Fuchs, H., Ohbuchi, R.: Merging virtual objects with the real world: Seeing ultrasound imagery within the patient. In: Proceedings of the 19th Annual Conference on Computer Graphics and Interactive Techniques, vol. 26, no. (2), 203–210. ACM, Chicago (1992)

55. Pan, Z., Cheok, A.D., Yang, H., Zhu, J., Shi, J.: Virtual reality and mixed reality for virtual learning environments. Comput. Graph. **30**(1), 20–28 (2006)

56. Ellis, S.R., Bucher, U.J.: Depth perception of stereoscopically presented virtual objects interacting with real background patterns. Bull. Psychon. Soc. **30**(6), 443 (1992)

57. Feiner, S., MacIntyre, B., Haupt, M., Solomon, E.: Windows on the world: 2D windows for 3D augmented reality. In: Proceedings of the 6th Annual ACM Symposium on User Interface Software and Technology (UIST 1993), pp. 145–155. ACM, Atlanta (1993)

58. Janin, A.L., Mizell, D.W., Caudell, T.P.: Calibration of head-mounted displays for augmented reality. In: Proceedings of the IEEE Virtual Reality International Symposium (VRAIS 1993), pp. 246–255. IEEE, Seattle (1993)

59. Magic Leap devices. https://www.magicleap.com/magic-leap-one. Accessed 5 Dec 2018

60. Briel, F.V.: The future of Omnichannel retail: a four stage Delphi study. Technol. Forecast. Soc. Chang. **132**, 217–229 (2018)

61. Wiener, M., Hoßbach, N., Saunders, C.: Omnichannel businesses in the publishing and retailing industries: synergies and tensions between coexisting online and offline business models. Decis. Support Syst. **109**, 15–26 (2017)

62. Microsoft webpage for mixed reality. https://www.microsoft.com/en-us/windows/windows-mixed-reality. Accessed 5 Dec 2018

63. Intel. https://www.intel.com/content/www/us/en/tech-tips-and-tricks/virtual-reality-vs-augmented-reality.html. Accessed 5 Dec 2018

64. Bourlakis, M., Papagiannidis, S., Li, F.: Retail spatial evolution: paving the way from traditional to metaverse retailing. Electron. Commer. Res. **9**(1), 135–148 (2009)

65. Althoff, T., White, R.W., Horvitz, E.: Influence of pokémon go on physical activity: study and implications. Int. J. Med. Internet Res. **18**(12), 315 (2016)

66. IKEA Place. https://www.ikea.com/au/en/apps/IKEAPlace.html. Accessed 5 Dec 2018

67. International Telecommunication Union (ITU) Radio communication Sector. Methodology for the subjective assessment of the quality of television pictures. International Telecommunication Union, ITU-R BT.500-11 (2002)

68. International Telecommunication Union (ITU) Radio communication Sector. Subjective assessment methods for 3D video quality. International Telecommunication Union, ITU-T P.915 (2016)

69. International Telecommunication Union (ITU) Radio communication Sector. Methods for the subjective assessment of video quality, audio quality and audiovisual quality of Internet video and distribution quality television in any environment. International Telecommunication Union, ITU-T P.913 (2014)

70. International Telecommunication Union (ITU) Radio communication Sector. Methodology for the subjective assessment of the quality of television pictures. International Telecommunication Union, ITU-R BT.500-13 68 (2012)

71. Caudell, T.P., Mizell, D.: Augmented reality: an application of heads-up display technology to manual manufacturing processes. In: Proceedings of the Twenty-Fifth Hawaii International Conference on System Sciences, vol. 2, pp. 659–669. IEEE, Hawaii (2004)

72. Greenhalgh, T., Peacock, R.: Effectiveness and efficiency of search methods in systematic reviews of complex evidence: audit of primary sources. BMJ **331**(7524), 1064–1065 (2005)

73. Papagiannidis, S., Pantano, E., See-To, E., Bourlakis, M.: Modelling the determinants of a simulated experience in a virtual retail store and users' product purchasing intentions. J. Mark. Manage. **29**(13–14), 1462–1492 (2013)
74. Vrechopoulos, A.P.: Mass customisation challenges in Internet retailing through information management. Int. J. Inf. Manage. **24**, 59–71 (2004)
75. Ravasi, D., Stigliani, I.: Product design: a review and re- search agenda for management studies. Int. J. Manag. Rev. **14**(4), 464–488 (2012)

Key Success Factors Analysis of Integration of O2O into 7-Eleven Convenient Store

Chung-Chi Kao[1], Che-Hung Liu[2(✉)], Yang-Ming Lu[3],
and Chia-Fen Hsieh[3]

[1] Taiwan Uni-President Company, Tainan, Taiwan
[2] Department of Business and Management,
National University of Tainan, Tainan, Taiwan
chehung@mail.nutn.edu.tw
[3] Department of Electrical Engineering,
National University of Tainan, Tainan, Taiwan

Abstract. As information technology becomes more varied, the era of the Internet has come. The connection among the retailing industry, the Internet and online/offline integration is centered surrounded the consumers. The pattern of Internet management across all channel integration called consumer behavior. The dependence of full-path retailing on the use of Wi-Fi has become heavier and heavier as days go by, with the consumers being the core and connecting the management pattern of the Internet. It integrates critical factors in a cross-channel fashion. It develops Apps for 7–11 convenience stores and can solve future online Internet and offline store integration and create the best management values. This study combine the views that the literature in Taiwan on real/virtual integration, supported by the results of the questionnaires devised by AHP experts. It can test the crucial factors involved in the success of real/virtual integration.

Twelve crucial factors responsible for the real/virtual integration of cloud stores were found and listed based on previous literature. After eighteen 7–11 middle management, the order of priority were calculated according to AHP analysis as follows:

- The weighted average of the development of APP is 26.1%, ranking first.
- The weighted average of full-path retailing pattern is 12.7%, ranking second.
- The weighted average of automatic cashier is 8.1%, ranking third.
- The weighted average of finance technology is 7.7%, ranking fourth.

It is hoped that via this study retailing 4.0 and big data online-offline integration ideas or practice; driving APP development transformation and the connection between the internal convenience store with seamless virtual market and offline equipment real store. It provides experience in full-path purchase.

Keywords: 7-Eleven · O2O · Retailing industry · Key success factors · Analytic hierarchy process analysis

© Springer Nature Switzerland AG 2019
F. F.-H. Nah and K. Siau (Eds.): HCII 2019, LNCS 11588, pp. 38–50, 2019.
https://doi.org/10.1007/978-3-030-22335-9_3

1 Introduction

Recently, Taiwan Uni-President Company, which owns 7–11 brand and has 5000 7–11 convenience stores, has moved toward an international and diversified business model. It has built a logistics support system with the advantage of access, and combined with offline entities and online virtual access networks to create consumer-wide retail convenience. In 2016, the consolidated total revenue was 215.36 billion NTD and after-tax net profit was 9.84 billion NTD. It was not only a record high, but also won the top 250 retail sales in the world for three consecutive years.

The 7–11 physical store is based on the customer's comfort and shopping space as the spatial planning concept, creating a unique design sense. The online virtual store is a combination of a dense store network, continuous upgrade of the ibon machine function and the ibon APP digital service platform to create consumer convenience, time-saving services, and strengthen the physical merchandise and e-commerce platform cooperation shop picking up, creating a virtual and integrated business model to meet the fast-growing e-commerce logistics distribution and storage needs.

However, compared with the physical channel, the unified super-business into the e-commerce business started late, such as the 7-Net business situation is not ideal. This paper hopes to explore the problem points, and to find out the opportunities of unified super-business in the development of virtual and real integration with the foreign O2O model or the new trend of retail 4.0, and formulate the future executable strategy and development [1]. The new retail model of the business, in order to respond to the current situation of entity super business operations dilemma. This paper collected several key factors, attributes, categories, and facets by collecting literature, discourse, expert opinions, or articles published on the Internet, and compile the structural map of the key factors of cloud super-business integration [2].

This study developed the structural data of key factors of virtual and real integration through the retail 4.0 model, interviewed professional managers and operational supervisors to conduct expert questionnaires, discussed the reasons and reasons for possible derivation, designed AHP expert questionnaires as a hierarchical analysis method, and the resulted of the questionnaires. The weighting data table of key factors was calculated by AHP weighting. Through the literature exploration and the professional ideas of the interviewees, the key factors of the new retail trend super-commercial integration are gathered, thereby providing a unified headquarters retail 4.0 for entity super-business. Consolidate the opportunity points and lay the next step for the e-commerce road.

2 Research Methodology

2.1 Key Success Factors

Hofer [3] analyzes the key success factors, covering the three major aspects of the main environment, the industrial environment or the corporate environment. The key factors and strategic planning procedures are used to link the three levels of the company's external environmental competitors in the industry. Competition with other companies in the industry must have the lowest level of each critical success factor. Key success factors must be in a particular industry and must be technically or asset-successful to compete with others. The key factors for success are context, variables, and characteristics; proper and appropriate support, maintenance, and management, and organizations in the industry have an advantage in moving toward success. This study is a key factor in the success of scholars' interpretation. This factor will change over time. Enterprises and organizations will be affected by the current situation and future market operations and competition. The key success factors also affect the competitive position of enterprises and organizations in the market. Advantage.

2.2   Analytic Hierarchy Process, AHP

Analytic Hierarchy Process (AHP) is one of the analysis methods of Multiple Criteria Decision Making. AHP is to disassemble a problem into a dendritic structure level, which is carried out by AHP analysis method. It is the main key success factor for the offline and virtual integration of super-commercial online and offline. AHP is designed as a systematic decision-making method when problems need to be made, complex factors are often found, and the problems are affected by tangible and intangible factors. AHP has been viewed as one methodology that can provide better decision-making schemes and reduce the number of decision-making errors. The theory of AHP is to systematically classify problems with high complexity, classify them at different levels, and find ways to implement them after quantification. Comprehensive assessment, and then provide decision makers to make the most appropriate decision-making plan.

This study used small sample semi-structured and closed interviews as the main focus, so that the content of the interview can be focused on, avoiding the scope of open interviews too large, thus obscuring the acquisition of important key messages. The interviewees of this study were based on the professional managers and operations supervisors at the headquarters. The headquarters is strategically planning the unit entities, categories, virtual and integrated information systems and medium and long-term O2O development units of the national entity, through the marketing department managers of the headquarters and the physical store is dominated by consumers and the first-line operators of the national business executives. The basis of the hierarchical analysis theory is used. The evaluation is based on the respondents' suggestions, and the key factors are ranked in order. From the assessment content, check the selection. A strategic approach to development can be implemented.

The researcher has served the unified super-business for more than 10 years, engaged in the operation of the first-line counseling management operators and the convenience needs of consumers to understand the shopping behavior, initially based on self-experience, drafting the relevant factors of super-commercial real integration as preliminary information, supplemented by half the structured interview method was interviewed by three experts, the general manager of the technology company in China with more than 25 years of experience in the development of unlimited communication systems, the manager of the business management and regional marketing strategy with more than 25 years of experience, and the 20-year experience. The above medical supervision experience regional hospital medical supervision. The interviewers initially drafted the topic on the super-commercial integration factor, interviewed three experts respectively, and gave the respondents free expressions of ideas and suggestions, with the revised data as the basis for the research data. Finally, four major facets are obtained. The contents were described as follows:

In terms of external facets, the three major directions are the full-channel retail model, segment marketing, and social media. The full-channel retail model, the transformation of retail enterprises in the future will be full coverage of virtual and real channels, consumers can buy favorite products in any channel, with the integration of online and offline development, O2O mode will be an important step towards the full channel. A full-channel shopping model that collects big data, mobile shopping, and social integration is evoking more consumer engagement. The SoLoMo community is not only a local ethnic group, but also generates consumer desires and ideas anytime, anywhere, and can purchase and consume at any time and any place [4].

1. The transformation of the retail enterprise is a virtual and full-scale coverage, integrating online and offline resources, opening up consumer shopping channels and accessing information, providing kinds of seamless retail services with no inconsistency and consistency, and opening up N contact points with consumers. Products are promoted to consumers, information is pushed to consumers, and consumers can be purchased at any time and without any means. Smart mobile device users can generate purchases and consumption behaviors anytime and anywhere. The all-channel retail model integrates online and offline channels, provides a consistent service retail model, connects to the Internet, builds a community O2O life service platform, and integrates online and offline channels to provide consumers with shopping convenience.

2. The rise of the network red economy is the best opportunity for brand influence. The socialization of the community and the current community are reunited according to the "interest" of shopping. The focus must start from understanding the customer behavior, according to the purpose of brand advertising, recruitment, maintenance, growth or Revitalize the development of a marketing strategy. The target customer group is connected to the marketing media and through the Internet information and offline information to integrate the consumer's "pre-transaction" shopping content data, record the customer's "no export" shopping demand, and effectively grasp the existing consumption. In addition to the customer base, it is also possible to develop potential consumer groups.

3. The brand image builds a self-fan group through the social media platform, provides potential consumers with pre- and post-value-added services, and releases new products and promotional information. The purpose is to achieve one-time service quality and establish a membership system to attract consumers to the second time. Buy and synchronize to create consumer surprises. Word-of-mouth communication is a spontaneous sharing and dissemination of things in the social circle. It has a strong influence on consumer shopping. It uses the interpersonal communication channel to connect with the loved ones and friends of the consumers, and provides social media platforms with high-quality services for consumers. Answering questions, interacting and accepting suggestions, social media is a new channel spreader for word-of-mouth communication that quickly delivers messages to tens of millions of people.

The internal facets are analyzed in terms of management innovation, staff quality, and information sharing. The business of super-business is people-oriented. It is organized by internal staff members and consumers. It is organized by the organization. The staff of the three classes, namely, the store staff and the operators, form the structure of the store, from a management perspective. In the pre-service, middle- and post-education training, improve the quality of personnel, and encourage, praise, reward and other leadership models, provide employees with surprises in their work, encourage employees to encourage them, and replace blame to influence the high turnover rate of organizational personnel; From information sharing, the company's upstream and downstream manufacturers can combine the Internet business philosophy, single-category access, use technology-based information technology, physical storefronts to connect with manufacturers' information devices, and data integration links to market customers from physical storefronts to confirm goods. After the order and payment, the manufacturer can deliver to the designated entity merchant or home delivery to the government within the next 4 h or less, to achieve unlimited shopping and pick-up, to satisfy the consumer shopping experience.

1. The internal management innovation of the organization, management structure and departmental establishment will change due to the marketing model. The single-channel customer source is easy to manage, and the multi-channel is moving towards virtual and real integration. The personnel must be able to plan physical activities and have network marketing capabilities. The organization should understand the mobile application technology, and must establish the concept of all-market marketing consensus, from push-to-pull marketing [5].
2. The education and training system determines online and offline sales. Whether it can be promoted continuously becomes an important factor. With the factors of the employee training system, the factors affecting the training effectiveness are difficult to control. The quality of employees and education and training are all important parts of solving consumers.
3. The physical store recruits new members and processes through software APP downloads. The specific member APP can know the identity of the member, learn the consumption record data and send coupons and points activities through the APP to drive online consumption power. APP's built-in store information and LBS Localization Based Service can guide the online customer base to the store, allowing the entity's business performance to cross physical and virtual [6].

The technology facet analyzes two aspects of developing APP and intelligent cashier. It connects online virtual stores and offline physical stores through APP software to provide customers with shopping experience, marketing strategies, use or login actions, and provide services. Coupons, discounts or bonus points activities enhance customer's repeated purchase rate; the software application level is broad, the development of software registration to provide customers, after logging in to the software to purchase goods, can quickly pick up goods at a specific time, specify physical goods or home delivery to the government, information software combination, customized to meet customer convenience needs; low manpower trends, high labor costs, hardware equipment settings to develop unmanned stores, to intelligent cashier. The way or the consumer uses a third-party payment method, which does not require human service and generates consumer shopping queues for too long, providing convenience to satisfy consumers' shopping behavior [7].

1. The specific member APP can know the identity of the member, learn the consumption record data and send coupons and points activities through the APP to drive online consumption power. APP's built-in store information and LBS Localization Based Service can guide the online customer base to the store, allowing the entity's business performance to cross physical and virtual [8].

2. The consumer selects product to join the mobile shopping cart, and the new product barcode is outputted in the shopping cart. After completing the purchase selection, the barcode is automatically scanned on the product, the queue is checked out, the payment is completed through the mobile payment, the self-service is completed, and the person can be designated. Or no one's cashier's point of payment is paid in the traditional way or in a contactless e-wallet. Consumers get the store bar code on the Internet, use the mobile phone to check the Internet before the store scans the payment or shop, and check the store to see if there is a discount [9].

The government has three levels of analysis to analyze the "government regulations", "financial supervision" and "third-party payment outlook". Under the continuous changes of regulations, personnel costs have increased, and human resources distribution, designated entity business distribution and home delivery are fast to the cost of goods flow. The increase is reflected in the sales price of commodities; the financial supervisor provides the stored value service for the cooperation between the open bank and the third-party payment service industry, and the third-party payment provider entrusts the financial industry to provide identity authentication and stored value services. The stored value is limited to financial Industry supervision, in the absence of management costs and risks, if e-commerce provides stored value services, it can charge consumers the amount, when the operating conditions cause problems, there will be consumer insecurity and money laundering problems. The volume of e-commerce transactions is increasing day by day. Virtual store merchants and physical merchants complete the business transaction behavior by means of third-party payment. The network platform will become the basic shopping demand of the whole market, and the consumer demand and the shopping platform will be combined with the dividend distribution and distribution mechanism. If the designated time is delivered to the government, the designated merchants are delivered, or the value-added services such as theft of the customer must be prevented, the retail enterprise provides full-channel payment service, and the full payment credit card machine will perform functions such as credit card, scan code and inductive payment. The machine provides a variety of payment function convenience, reducing the cost of the business, shortening the checkout process and quickly paying for service functions. The entity merchant payment card machine service, through the financial institution cooperation system equipment credit card machine payment service, create a new retail super business transformation full channel digital payment service.

1. In the scope of the Labor Standards Law, the warehousing tally, the online logistics staff, the increase in personnel costs and the logistics cost of goods delivered by freight drivers, consumers expect goods to arrive quickly, and the price of goods is also affected by the rapid arrival of goods. The price of the item.
2. The government open bank cooperates with third-party payment service providers to provide stored value services. Third-party payment providers can provide financial institutions with identity certification and stored value services. Banks are highly financially supervised and have no management costs and risks. If the open e-commerce provider provides stored value services, the industry can pre-charge a large amount of money to consumers. If there is a mis-management, it may derive consumer rights (no deposit insurance protection) and implement money laundering prevention and other issues.
3. China's mobile payment market is limited by the lack of motivation for consumers, and the cooperation model between telecom, financial institutions and retailers with mobile payment systems has not yet formed, and data security issues may arise; various action payment emerging technologies and industry standards are born. Under the traditional financial institutions, retail entities and e-commerce cooperation is more diversified [10].

3   Result

The number of sample design questionnaires in this study was 20, and the respondents were mainly heads of professional managers and operations directors. The interviewees took the experience of management, marketing, system integration and head office strategic planning as a priority. The 20 professional managers and operations supervisors conducted face-to-face interviews by the author in a one-to-one manner to complete the questionnaire. The average interview time was about 30 min. In order to make the results of the questionnaire closer to the idea of super-commercial medium- and long-term planning, and to balance the background of professional professionals, retain the head office category management experts and first-line operation supervisors; improve the screening qualifications of category managers and business executives, leaving only the seniority >=5 years of questionnaire data, expecting to reflect the consumer shopping demand and the entity merchants super-business in response to consumer behavior through the results of senior and professional questionnaires, infinitely extending the feasibility of satisfying the consumer demand and the development strategy of super-commercial integration.

The importance of respondents' analysis of the matrices of external facets, internal facets, technological facets, and government facets is shown in the following Table. Among them, the "technical facets" have the highest weight, with an average of 0.342. For the "external facet", the average is 0.266; the other is "government facet" with an average of 0.224; the last is "internal facet" with an average of 0.168. The results of the competition show that professional managers and operational supervisors attach more importance to the technical and external structure than the government's facet and internal facets. In the test of C.I. and C.R. consistency, the C.I. value is 0.011 < 0.1, and the C.R. value is 0.012 < 0.1; indicating that the respondents have consistency in the importance of the criteria.

	External	Internal	Tech.	Gov.	Average	Weight	C.I.
External	0.257	0.335	0.243	0.231	0.266	1.077	4.043
Internal	0.125	0.164	0.179	0.203	0.168	0.675	4.021
Technology	0.366	0.317	0.346	0.339	0.342	1.379	4.036
Government	0.252	0.184	0.232	0.227	0.224	0.904	4.035

The interviewed experts ranked the importance of the four major facets in order. 1. The technical facet is 34.2% > 2. The external facet is 26.6% > 3. The government facet is 22.4% > 4. The internal facet is 16.8%. Respondents had a view on facet evaluation, with the highest data being 34.2% of the technical facets and the lowest being 16.8% internal facets. The results of this layer's facet evaluation, the data are falling below the median value of 20%, the gap value is not large, showing that the respondent's important appraisal of the facet does not have a very significant attention or preference.

AHP project factor "third level" importance analysis results, ranked by experts in the important ranking of the eight major projects through the calculation of weights followed by 1. Development APP 26.1% > 2. Full-channel retail mode 12.7% > 3. Intelligence Cashier 8.1% > 4. Financial supervision 7.7% > 5. Third-party payment outlook 7.4% 6. Focus marketing 7.3% > 7. Government regulations 7.3% > 8. Social media 6.7% > 9. Management innovation 6.4% > 10. Information Sharing 5.8% > 11. Employee Quality 4.6%.

Ranked first is the development of APP strategy factors for technology facets, with a weight of 26.1%. Compared with the smart facet factor of the same facet, the development of APP is the best strategic factor; 76.4% is in favor of the need to develop APP strategy. Very high, from the significant data, it is known that the interviewed experts attaches great importance to the development of the APP, and it is obvious that the first place is important.

Also ranked second is the external channel's full-channel retail model with a weight of 12.7%. Compared with the same facet of segmented marketing and social media, the full-channel retail model covers consumer purchases in unlimited network coverage. Under the circumstance, smart mobile devices will be popularized, and products can be purchased on the information platform or purchased from physical stores anytime and anywhere to form a seamless retail; this is an external facet project, which can be known to have a great impact on virtual and real integration.

In particular, the financial supervision of the internal facet and the third-party payment outlook are the two items. After passing the AHP questionnaire, the importance of the project in the fourth and fifth places is known to the retail industry. Supervision, third-party payment outlook pays attention to the degree. The government's facet was ranked third in the first appraisal, but when it entered the second-tier appraisal, the ranking was upgraded to the fourth and fifth place, showing the respondents and experts, although the government policy There is no special preference, but it is very important for financial supervision and third-party payment - especially the fourth financial supervisor has a weight of 7.7% (34.5%), and the fifth third-party payment weight is 7.4% (32.9%). There are two project system factors in the government's facet, ranking fourth and fifth. This ratio of high proportions has led to an upward increase in the government's facet rankings. It also allows the author to know that the super-commercial integration is successful, and that the super-business executives and category managers need to have confidence in government policies.

The results of the analysis of the key factors of the third level, the results of the comprehensive ranking, the respondents integrated 12 key factors, the ranking by weight processing is 1. Development APP 26.1% > 2. Full-channel retail mode 12.7% > 3. Smart Cashier 8.1% > 4. Financial Supervision 7.7% > 5. Third Party Payment Outlook 7.4% 6. Focus Marketing 7.3% > 7. Government Regulations 7.3% > 8. Social Media 6.7% > 9. Management Innovation 6.4% > 10 Information Sharing 5.8% > 11. Employee Quality 4.6%.

This level is ranked by the four major facets, the eleven major projects and the AHP analysis weight value data. The first place to be ranked is the development app of the technology facet. Through the literature, we can know that this part is to let the industrial staff, the large users of large LBS operators (LBS in the localization push function), to achieve lower visitor realization. Shopping behavior, retail enterprises analyze and manage customer data, construct a channel bonus mechanism and platform, and integrate big data with online and offline virtual businesses.

The super-business category managers and supervisors highlight the evaluation of this factor, agree with the importance of APP development in the cloud super-commercial integration, and present uniqueness; APP development is a precise marketing mobile device newsletter, sending valuable information to provide Consumers who need it can download coupons or purchase merchandise accumulating dividends points and other incentives in smart mobile devices, and use mobile wallet to pay for the purchases and frequency of the purchases. Group push coupons. Therefore, this factor in the AHP questionnaire is a unique high proportion and has become the most important key factor.

The full-channel retail model is the second place. The transformation of the retail enterprise in the future is a virtual and full-channel coverage. It can purchase favorite products in any channel, and with the integration of online and offline development, the O2O model will move toward the full channel [11]. Collecting all-channel shopping models of big data, mobile shopping and social integration, evoking more consumers to participate in channel consumption. The third place of smart cashier means avoiding the checkout crowd. It is also the starting point for no one to overtake business. The cloud function that consumers and the Internet platform expect can be used to simplify the labor cost without card withdrawal, payment and transfer. And simultaneous extensions can be used across international mobile payment services.

At present, the community O2O strategy is difficult to achieve, mainly for Taiwan's convenience and super-business density. The active community O2O needs to cooperate with upstream and downstream suppliers to achieve resource sharing. After the customer is introduced into the physical store, consumers can't buy it. The required products can be immediately connected to the mobile device or IBON machine to provide shopping, providing fast delivery or home delivery to the government distribution service strategy, consumers in the community shopping rate increase, and further promote community O2O consumption dependence.

Intelligent cashiers are the main reason for the reduction of personnel costs. The choice of "machines" rather than "people" has a close interaction between employees and consumers, affecting consumers' offline storefront service and line marketing expertise, directly affecting the perception of service. Indirectly affecting the operational quality of retail enterprises, employees' education and training are highly valued; traditional selection, education, retention, and talents require time. The Internet era pays attention to speed, and education and training enhances the quality of employees. The development direction is trained by work. The rotation of the work content or the senior staff or managers to lead the staff, learning the different areas of work to develop employee service, comprehensive work execution and personal work characteristics, will be time-consuming and labor-intensive and eliminated by the information automation era, Therefore, the final main reason for sorting.

At the end of the rankings is the ranking of 11 employees. Its factors are internal level projects. This factor ranks the response expert's recognition of the factor and one of the medium and long-term strategies for the future. The key to the success of cloud-based super-commercial integration is to increase consumer purchasing rate and dependence, and to purchase full-channel retail merchandise when going out or not, and to be able to get goods in close proximity to physical businesses or at home quickly and at specific times. The quality of employees is limited by automated cash register machines, consumers can purchase goods, can purchase goods anytime, anywhere, and can practice any physical store can quickly pick up the goods, so the community O2O and staff quality, seamless retail, shopping for consumers The interaction rate is low, and the importance of identity is low.

Based on the above analysis, the data of 18 professional managers and operational supervisors interviewed and evaluated the results, the respondents most concerned about the development trend of virtual and real development to develop APP software. In the era of Internet big data, smart mobile devices are commonly used and unlimited networks. Under the coverage of the road, it becomes the most important link between online virtual stores and offline entities to enhance the purchase rate of consumers. In the successful business strategy of retail 4.0, the development of APP software links online and offline stores and the second place in eleven facets. The full-channel retail model is launched, connected to the whole market, and it can be used in any space position at any time. It can realize consumption behavior arbitrarily. Through the third-place intelligent cash register, high labor cost and low manpower, the entity super-business manpower is facing the biggest problem for the current situation. In combination with the effective use of third-party payment methods for smart cashier results, the future will significantly improve labor costs and significantly improve operational performance.

Level 1 goal	Level 2 aspects			Level 3 criteria		Final weights	Ranking	Conformance testing
KSF of O2O Strategies of 7–11 in Taiwan	External	26.6%	2	Full-path retailing pattern	47.5%	12.7%	2	C.I. = 0.014 C.R. = 0.025
				Segment marketing	27.4%	7.3%	6	
				Social media	25.1%	6.7%	8	
	Internal	16.8%	4	Innovation management	38.1%	6.4%	9	C.I. = 0.055 C.R. = 0.095
				Employee manpower	27.4%	4.6%	11	
				Information sharing	34.5%	5.8%	10	
	Technology	34.2%	1	Mobile app development	76.4%	26.1%	1	**
				Automatic cashier	23.6%	8.1%	3	
	Government	22.4%	3	Government policy	32.6%	7.3%	7	C.I. = 0.009 C.R. = 0.015
				finance technology	34.5%	7.7%	4	
				Third-party payment	32.9%	7.4%	5	

4   Conclusion

The cloud super-business virtual integration development APP interview questionnaire, the success of the key factors evaluation is the highest degree of acceptance, is the integration of science and technology information technology, the next road is based on the retail 4.0 thinking spindle, cloud super-business and physical business links, through APP software development, Extend the diversified marketing strategy, APP built-in store information combined with software push function, APP members provide consumer accumulated bonus points by real-name system, non-members to issue coupons, attract customers to the store to consume shopping, and improve consumer loyalty Degree, platform cooperation mode combined with upstream and downstream partners, strategic alliance cooperation to reduce costs [12].

The relationship between cloud super-business and big data is the highest in the external facet in the full-channel mode, and the second in the eleven facets. Unlimited networks are covered by the entire channel in the market. Consumers rely on mobile smart devices to shop in online and offline mode anytime, anywhere, and full-channel mode shopping has begun on the market. With the integration of information technology development, the entity super-business can connect to the ibon machine through the smart mobile device network, diversify the O2O channel trading platform, and the intangible store combines IT to develop all-round shopping and social activities. The customer consumption marketing model is not affected.

Financial supervision ranks the highest in government regulations. The government's open service industry can use third-party payment stored value services. Financial institutions provide identity certification and stored value limits. They are subject to high financial supervision and have no management costs and risks. If the open e-commerce provider provides the stored value service function, it needs to first collect a large amount of money from the consumer. If the business is not good, it will affect the consumer rights (no deposit insurance protection) and prevent money laundering. Most of the national laws and regulations are designed with reference to the Uniform Money Services Act set by the United States Unified State Law Commission, so that non-bank institutions that meet certain qualifications are licensed by the competent authority. It is able to operate part of the banking business; the "Management Measures for Payment Services of Non-financial Institutions" in mainland China is included in various financial payment financial supervision issues. Paypal, Alipay and other international third-party payment and storage companies are non-financial industries. After development, governments have established special laws. Domestically, for the financial industry, the stored value business has the basic source management, the non-financial third-party payment industry, the development of management norms, with reference to foreign development experience, can also avoid the ills that have emerged abroad.

References

1. APCA, Online Payments: What's Next? In: A payments industry discussion paper (2009)
2. Chen, J.E., Pan, S.L., Ouyang, T.H.: Routine reconfiguration in traditional companies'e-commerce strategy implementation: a trajectory perspective. Inf. Manag. **51**(2), 270–282 (2014)
3. Hofer, C.W., Schendel, D.: Strategy formulation: Analytical concepts 1978: West Publ (1978)
4. Althoff, T., Jindal, P., Leskovec, J.: Online actions with offline impact: how online social networks influence online and offline user behavior. In: Proceedings of the Tenth ACM International Conference on Web Search and Data Mining. ACM (2017)
5. Chang, C.-Y.: The Mysterious Third-Party on Mobile Phone (2016)
6. Sun, Xiaohua, Qiu, Jie, Zhang, Lei: SoLoMo user experience study using a pivoted parallel coordinates. In: Rau, P.L.P. (ed.) CCD 2013. LNCS, vol. 8024, pp. 336–345. Springer, Heidelberg (2013). https://doi.org/10.1007/978-3-642-39137-8_38
7. Vuckovac, D., et al.: From Shopping Aids to Fully Autonomous Mobile Self-checkouts-A Field Study in Retail (2017)
8. Liao, C., et al.: Factors influencing online shoppers' repurchase intentions: the roles of satisfaction and regret. Inf. Manag. **54**(5), 651–668 (2017)
9. Li, Q., et al.: The impact of big data analytics on customers' online behaviour. In: Proceedings of the International Multi Conference of Engineers and Computer Scientists (2017)

10. Jui-Mei, Y.: Key factors of bank evaluation: a case study of small and medium enterprises (2016)
11. Lazar, J., Preece, J.: Classification schema for online communities. In: AMCIS 1998 Proceedings, p. 30 (1998)
12. Grewal, D., Roggeveen, A.L., Nordfält, J.: The future of retailing. J. Retail. **93**(1), 1–6 (2017)

Human-Computer Interaction in Physical Retail Environments and the Impact on Customer Experience: Systematic Literature Review and Research Agenda

Gabriele Obermeier[(⊠)] and Andreas Auinger[(⊠)]

University of Applied Sciences Upper Austria, Steyr, Austria
{gabriele.obermeier,andreas.auinger}@fh-steyr.at

Abstract. Shopping in the traditional retail environment is increasingly being influenced by technologies enabling human-computer interaction. Scientists, as well as retailers, are interested in examining the effects of interactive in-store technologies on customer behavior. An abundance of researchers have examined customer acceptance of interactive technologies, but little is known about its effects on the customer's experience and its consequences, such as satisfaction, loyalty, and purchase intention. Following the guidelines for a systematic literature review, this article gives an overview of empirical studies conducted on interactive technologies in traditional brick-and-mortar retail stores. Based on that review, this paper provides a research agenda for future work on interactive in-store technologies and their impact on customer experience and suggests possible research methods for empirical studies in the field of human-computer interaction.

Keywords: Customer experience · Interactive technology · Digital retail · Research methods

1 Introduction

In recent years, the retail industry has experienced increased pressure from competitors, not only in the traditional retail environment but also from online market players. As the online and offline retail worlds converge, traditional brick-and-mortar stores "will change into connected stores, serving as places for inspiration, experiences, showcases, and service centers" (p. 17) as Jongen [1] claims. According to a recent study by Capgemini Consulting [2], customers expect the same customer experience from traditional retail stores as from online shops. KPMG [3] state in their 2018 retail industry trend report that "[t]he customer experience is more important than ever as retailers are striving to differentiate themselves in a challenging and crowded market" (p. 4). The topic of technologies in the retail industry has been even more discussed in research and practice since Amazon's announcement of plans to open more than 3,000 self-service stores by 2021 [4]. In science, Grewal et al. [5] reveal the main topics of the future of retail, and Priporas et al. [6] conceptualize a future agenda for digital retailing. All parties agree on the central aspect: Customers demand a superior and engaging

---

The original version of this chapter was revised: This chapter was mistakenly published as a regular chapter instead of open access. The correction to this chapter is available at https://doi.org/10.1007/978-3-030-22335-9_26

F. F.-H. Nah and K. Siau (Eds.): HCII 2019, LNCS 11588, pp. 51–66, 2019.
https://doi.org/10.1007/978-3-030-22335-9_4

experience in an interactive retail environment [6–12]. According to Roy et al. [11], the digital retail environment can be defined as "[a]n interactive and connected retail system which supports the seamless management of different customer touchpoints to personalize the customer experience across different touchpoints and optimize performance over these touchpoints" (p. 259).

Retailers and brands increasingly use technology to provide an engaging shopping experience in the physical retail environment [13]. For example, self-service checkout terminals can be found in almost every supermarket branch. This allows users to quickly scan and pay for products on their own [7] or easily retrieve detailed product information by scanning the product's barcode [9]. Willems et al. [12] address three major benefits of technology in retail stores: beyond (1) time and cost savings, customers gain (2) utilitarian as well as (3) hedonic shopping value. First, using self-service technologies helps customers to save time because they can proceed without spending time waiting for a salesperson or queuing at the service counter [9, 11]. Moreover, it is possible to monitor and control expenditure in the store [8]. Second, customers derive utilitarian benefits from a shopping trip when accomplishing an intended task [10], such as gaining more knowledge about the product and comparing different variations [12]. Third, interactive in-store retail technology in combination with fun and engaging tools enhance the customer's hedonic shopping value. For example, smart mirrors with augmented reality [10] or monitors with gamification mechanisms [14] provide such appealing experiences.

An abundance of researchers has examined the user acceptance of new technologies in a digital retail environment by using well-known theories, such as the theory of reasoned action (TRA) [15] or the technology acceptance model (TAM) [16, 17]. For example, Roy et al. [11] investigated the moderating effect of technology readiness on the customer's attitude and behavioral intentions when using smart technologies, such as smart checkouts, personal shopping assistance, and augmented reality. Other researchers examined the application, functionality, and adoption of RFID (Radio Frequency Identification) equipped retail stores in a complex field study [18]. Willems et al. [12] extensively reviewed and summarized 54 digital retail technologies from various manufacturers along the customer's path of purchase.

Following Parasuraman's [19] pyramid model of marketing services, retailers need to consider that technology mediates nearly any communication between the three dimensions involved in the physical retail environment: the company, its employees, and the customers. Human-computer interaction is intensively discussed in the literature of retailing, consumer services, business, and information systems. However, empirical findings are limited considering the impact of interactive technologies in physical retail stores on the customer's experience and its consequences, such as customer satisfaction [7, 10, 14, 20, 21], loyalty [22], intention to reuse [9], (re)patronage [10, 14, 23–25], word-of-mouth [26], and purchase intention [27]. In consideration of these criteria, this paper presents a systematic literature review based on 15 identified empirical studies.

The structure of this paper is organized as follows: Sect. 2 presents the methodology of this work, which is based on the guidelines for systematic literature reviews of vom Brocke et al. [28]. In the following Sect. 3, we conduct the review by defining the review scope, describing the literature search, and how the studies are analyzed and synthesized. Afterward, Sect. 4 presents the results of the systematic literature review, categorized by technology usage, research methods, and the applied retail context. The same classification is adopted to discuss the future agenda and further research possibilities (Sect. 5). Finally, the conclusion can be found in Sect. 6.

2 Methodology

This work follows the guidelines for conducting systematic literature reviews in the field of information systems (IS) proposed by vom Brocke et al. [28]. The authors claim that a literature analysis must be "comprehensibly described" as researchers should be able to use the same data for their own research purposes. By analyzing previous work of IS researchers, vom Brocke et al. [28] found that most of the reviewed publications leave gaps in the process documentation. Therefore, the guidelines on systematic literature reviews have been developed and are now used in this present work. The authors define five phases to the literature review: (1) scoping the review, (2) conceptualizing the topic, (3) searching appropriate literature, (4) analyzing and synthesizing identified literature, and (5) stating the review's contributions to a research agenda.

In the first phase, researchers should define the scope of their literature review. The use of the six characteristics of Cooper's [29] taxonomy, which highlight some of the central aspects of the review, is recommended. In the second phase, vom Brocke et al. [28] state that researchers must provide key definitions relevant to the topic. Therefore, we describe the concepts of customer experience and interactive technologies in physical retail stores. The third phase reveals the exact process of the peer-reviewed literature search and provides the keywords used in digital libraries. Moreover, this phase outlines the including and excluding criteria as well as the total number of recognized publications. After we have identified the relevant literature, we applied phase four and analyzed the studies in relevance to the technologies, the research methods and the retail context. The fifth phase of vom Brocke et al.'s [28] guidelines comprises the research agenda and presents several approaches and questions for future research.

This present work contains all five phases of the systematic literature review of vom Brocke et al. [28] and accumulates the current state of empirical research on interactive technologies in traditional brick-and-mortar stores.

3 Systematic Literature Review

The following section will outline in detail the focus of our systematic literature review by defining the review scope and the key terms, describing the literature search process and how we conducted the analysis.

3.1 Definition of the Review Scope

We defined the taxonomy of our search query with reference to Cooper [29], who proposed to classify the review to the following six major characteristics which are shown in Table 1: goal, focus, organization, perspective, audience, and coverage. (1) Our *goal* is to integrate and summarize empirical studies (journals and conference proceedings) on the customer's experience arising from the use of interactive retail technologies. (2) Therefore, the *focus* is on the research methodology (qualitative, quantitative, or mixed) and the different physical retail environments (e.g., supermarket, fashion store) in which the studies have been applied. (3) The *organization* of the review follows a conceptual process in which the studies are initially organized according to the technologies' application scenario (e.g., self-service, shopping assistance, store atmospherics). Afterward, we categorized the reviewed articles by the research methods used (e.g., laboratory or field experiments, surveys). (4) A neutral *perspective* is chosen to summarize and synthesize relevant empirical studies, but no critical assessment of the research is conducted. (5) The relevant *audience* for this paper primarily consists of researchers in the field of IS and human-computer interaction. (6) Finally, we *cover* an exhaustive literature review on empirical studies examining the use of interactive technologies in physical retail environments in terms of customer experience and its consequences, such as purchase intention and loyalty.

Table 1. Scope of Review (highlighted in Grey) using the Taxonomy proposed by Cooper [29]

Characteristic	Categories			
(1) **goal**	Integration	Criticism		Central issues
(2) **focus**	Research outcomes	Research methods	Theories	Applications
(3) **organization**	Historical	Conceptual		Methodological
(4) **perspective**	Neutral representation		Espousal of position	
(5) **audience**	Specialized scholars	General scholars	Practitioners/politicians	General public
(6) **coverage**	Exhaustive	Exhaustive and selective	Representative	Central/pivotal

3.2 Conceptualization of Topic

Following the guidelines of vom Brocke et al. [28], the key terms and the theoretical background of customer experience and interactive technologies will be provided.

Customer Experience. In the 1960s, researchers started to investigate the customer's decision-making process and the phenomena influencing customerbehaviorin physical retail stores [30]. Holbrook and Hirschman [31] were among the first to recognize the consumer's "pursuit of fantasies, feelings, and fun" (p. 132), discussing emotionally rather than rationally driven customer choices. Ever since, however, marketing literature appears to develop from understanding the customer's behavior to creating a customer-centric experience [30]. The work of Verhoef et al. [32] defines customer experience as a multidimensional construct that is "holistic in nature and involves the customer's cognitive, affective, emotional, social and physical responses to the retailer" (p. 32). Furthermore, the authors argue that "[t]his experience is created not only by those elements which the retailer can control (e.g., service interface, retail atmosphere, assortment, price) but also by elements that are outside of the retailer's control (e.g., influence of others, purpose of shopping)" (p. 32). Several researchers have investigated that the customer experience influences satisfaction and loyalty, both being crucial preconditions for a higher rate of shopping visits, higher spending and the retailer's growth [8, 30]. Recently, the consideration of technology in multi- and omnichannel environments has played a major role in enabling retailers to provide a superior customer retail experience [8, 30].

Interactive Technologies. The use of interactive technologies in the retail sector describes the communication between the customer and the retailer (the company and its employees) based on internet-enabled devices. The goal is to respond to customer needs by providing the requested service without any human interference [33]. Researchers intensively investigate self-service technologies such as order terminals and checkout systems, which allow users to experience service support or accomplish tasks without the involvement of service employees [34]. Interactive technologies offer a more engaging and superior shopping experience for customers in retail stores and beyond, by connecting channels with each other, such as interactive fitting rooms that would link to social networks [35]. Poncin et al. [10] claim that new digital technologies are key to enhancing the appearance of physical retail stores and lead to higher visitor rates as well as increased sales. Therefore, the use of interactive technologies results in an enhanced customer retail experience [10], strengthens customer engagement and generates a competitive advantage [36].

3.3   Literature Search

The search query covered interactive technologies (using the keywords "technology" or " technologies" or "smart" or "interactive" or "digital") in the context of customer experience (using the keywords "experience" and ("shopping" or "retail" or "customer" or "customers" or "consumer" or "consumers"). We included all types of English publications (e.g., research articles, proceedings papers, etc.) in the field of information and communication technology and business, the latter comprising the subcategory of marketing [12]. Based on the approach of Willems et al. [12] and due to the high-speed development of technologies, the ideal timeframe to review innovative in-store technologies covers 8.5 years, hence this present review contains scientific publications from July 2010 until December 2018. The search was conducted in the libraries of ScienceDirect (total number of results: 403; the number of results after the first review: 50; the number of results after the second review: 20), Web of Science (199; 55; 21) and Springer's disciplines of business and management (600;20;0) and computer science (263;14;0). In order to identify retail-related publications, we first reviewed the title and keywords and second, excluded duplicates and analyzed the abstracts of 133 remaining publications. Subsequently, we used these publications to conduct a forward and backward search according to vom Brocke et al. [28]. Finally, we identified 15 studies that met our criteria, having investigated the use of interactive technologies and their influence on the customer's experience in brick-and-mortar retail stores.

3.4 Literature Analysis and Synthesis

According to the guidelines of systematic literature reviews, we organize and systematically analyze the papers collected in the literature review on the technologies' application scenario, methodology and research design, as well as on the retail context.

Application Scenario. We classify the identified empirical studies by the application scenario. First, we summarize self-service checkout technologies. Second, we group shopping assistance technologies, such as smart fitting rooms and self-scanning systems. The third group comprises all technologies influencing the store's atmosphere, such as smart mirrors and interactive window displays.

Methodology and Research Designs. The consideration of research methodologies (qualitative, quantitative, and mixed) and designs (e.g., experiments, focus groups, and surveys), which have been used to conduct research on the interaction with technologies in physical retail stores.

Retail Context. Finally, the literature review will show in which retail contexts the empirical investigations were conducted, such as supermarkets, fashion, or do-it-yourself (DIY) retail stores.

4 Results in the HCI Context

In this section, we provide the results of our systematic literature review. We follow the procedure proposed by vom Brocke et al. [28]. First, we describe the studies used in terms of interactive technologies and their influence on the customer experience in brick-and-mortar retail stores. Second, we report the research methodology used and third, the retail context in which the 15 empirical studies were conducted.

4.1 Interactive Technologies and Their Impact on Customer Experience

Self-service Checkout Technologies. The majority of the identified papers focus on the evaluation of self-service checkout technologies. Retailers increasingly implement checkout terminals in their physical retail environments, which allow customers to quickly scan and pay for products on their own instead of queuing at the cashier desk [7, 9, 20]. In addition to the speed advantage, researchers involve further attributes to determine the perceived service quality of self-checkouts [23, 37]. These attributes include the ease of use, reliability, fun/entertainment, and perceived control. Another approach to measuring the service quality of self-checkout systems is to use standard scales, such as the SSTQUAL [22], which consists of seven dimensions (functionality, enjoyment, security, assurance, design, convenience, and customization). Reliability (individual and as a part of functionality) has been identified as a main [22] and even the most important [23, 37] driver of the customer's perceived service quality of self-service checkout technologies. Consequently, service quality positively influences customer loyalty [22], purchase intention [37], intention to reuse [9, 38], and repatronage intention [23], directly as well as through the mediating effect of customer satisfaction. On the other hand, if customers are forced to use self-service checkout systems and gain the feeling of unfairness and dissatisfaction (due to no/little technology readiness or the need for human interaction), customers will be more likely to spread negative word of mouth, reduce future spending, and develop intentions to become the competitor's customer [26]. Therefore, researchers suggest that employees should personally help to introduce new technologies to customers in order to create a positive customer experience, which will in turn, lead to higher satisfaction with the self-service checkout technology as well as with the store [7]. Satisfaction is considered one of the main drivers of the retailer's revenue performance, store appeal, patronage, positive word-of-mouth, and customer loyalty [7, 12, 38, 39].

Shopping Assistance. Self-scanning devices can be used with barcodes of products in order to receive enhanced product information, ratings from other customers, and recommendations for complementary products [7]. Moreover, the additional decision support features allow customers to manage and control their spending in the store [7], gain detailed product information, compare prices, check recommendations and ratings by other consumers [9, 13]. The advantages of self-service technologies enhance customer experience and subsequently overall satisfaction with the store [7]. However, retailers need to consider that the interpersonal service quality and the service quality of the self-scanning technology moderates the relationship between the customer and retail patronage [25]. This can be critical when the need for human interaction and technology anxiety are high.

Smart fitting rooms can support product choices by providing additional product information and recommendations [27]. The technology in the background of smart fitting rooms is the combination of RFID chips attached to the price tags of fashion articles and sensors installed in fitting rooms [18, 27]. The sensors are able to detect the products and display detailed information on the monitor, such as the brand's name and logo, as well as the price of the product [27]. If retailers provide details of their security policy, customers appreciate the possibility to enter personal data at the monitor for an enhanced and more personalized experience. This study shows, that especially in the case of low-quality brands, it is advisable to provide data security disclosure. Moreover, higher interaction and fewer security concerns lead to higher satisfaction and result in stronger purchase intentions [27].

Multimedia kiosks in physical retail stores deliver entertaining information and allow customers to perform transactions [21]. Research shows that customers gain the feeling of perceived control and convenience by performing tasks on their own, which consequently results in satisfaction and the intention to reuse the technology [21].

Store Atmospherics. Smart mirrors are considered as store atmospherics and are based on the technology of augmented reality [40]. A human-sized touch-screen monitor pictures the person standing in front of it. Customers are able to virtually try on digital clothing items by selecting and moving them on the touch-screen [41]. The holistic perception of a play store atmosphere can be supported by game terminals and magic mirrors where children can engage in an interactive playing scenario [10]. The positive evaluation of store atmospherics influences the customer's perceived shopping value and positive emotions, which result in higher customer satisfaction and greater likelihood of future patronage and recommendation [10]. The gamification aspect also works for adults by stimulating positive feelings and enhancing the experience at the moment of play [14]. The results of the study showed, that the combination of gamification and augmented reality affects the likelihood of future patronage but cannot enhance the quality of the overall experience.

Besides in-store atmospherics, researchers examined the effect of exterior atmospherics by installing interactive window displays [42]. The main purpose of installing interactive screens in the shop window is to attract the customer's attention and to

Table 2. Results of the literature review conducted in accordance with the guidelines of vom Brocke et al. [28]

#	Authors	Year	Interactive technology	Group (Sec. 3)	Methodology	Research design	Retail context
1	Djelassi et al.	2018	Self-scanning & checkout	1 & 2	Quan	Field experiment	Supermarket chain
2	Fernandes, Pedroso	2017	Self-checkout	1	Quan	Field experiment	Supermarket chain
3	Kallweit et al.	2014	Self-scanning	1 & 2	MM	Lab. experiment	DIY store
4	Lecointre-Erickson et al.	2018	Interactive window display	3	Quan	Survey	Tourist bureau
5	Lee, Yang	2013	Self-scanning	2	Quan	Survey	Grocery store
6	Mukherjee et al.	2018	Smart fitting room	2	Quan	Lab. experiment	Fashion store
7	Orel, Kara	2014	Self-checkout	1	Quan	Interview	Supermarket chain
8	Pantano	2016	Interactive window displays	3	Qual	Focus group interview	Retail stores
9	Penttinen et al.	2014	Self-checkout	1	Quan	Survey	Supermarket chain
10	Poncin, Mimoun	2014	Magic mirror, game terminals	3	Quan	Lab. experiments	Toy store
11	Poncin et al.	2017	Augmented reality	3	MM	Lab experiment	Store for accessories
12	Siah, Fam	2018	Self-checkout	1	Quan	Survey	Supermarket chain
13	Wang et al.	2013	Self-checkout	1	Quan	Survey	Grocery store
14	Wang	2012	Multimedia kiosks	2	Quan	Field study	Convenience store chain
15	White et al.	2012	Self-checkout	1	Quan	Survey	Grocery store

motivate them to enter the store. Once the customer recognizes the display, it provides hedonic impressions (e.g., pictures and videos of white beaches) and presents utilitarian information (e.g., text descriptions of a travel destination), as well as insights into what the customer can expect in the store [42]. Obviously, the retail context is significant, as interactive window displays have a strong negative effect on perceived pleasure in terms of tourist travel bureaus, which sell local goods [24]. However, for tourist travel shop contexts only, the study found that customers are seeking for a high-contact and task-oriented shopping experience.

4.2 Methodology and Research Designs

We reviewed 15 empirical studies about interactive technologies and their influence on the customer experience in brick-and-mortar retail stores. As shown in Table 2, twelve publications used a quantitative questionnaire (quan), two used a mixed methods approach (MM) and one author conducted a focus group interview, which is considered a qualitative method (qual). Most of the studies used online or offline surveys, laboratory or field experiments as research design.

4.3 Retail Context

The results of the literature review indicate that nine of 15 studies conducted their research in food retail environments. In the case of non-food retail scenarios, researchers used laboratory environments or surveys. No field experiment has yet been conducted in a non-food retail store, such as a fashion, decoration, or sports shop.

5 Discussion and Research Agenda

The research agenda of this systematic literature review provides an overview of empirical studies which have examined technologies used for human-computer interaction in brick-and-mortar retail stores. In the following section, we demonstrate research gaps and promote various possibilities for further research.

5.1 Interactive Technologies

From the practitioners' and researchers' perspectives, we see a high level of interest in the examination of customers behavior with interactive technologies in physical retail stores, as these usually require high expenditure and investment. Researchers should support retailers by examining how or even whether customer experience can be enhanced in specific retail environments through the installation of human-computer interaction enabling technologies. For example, interactive digital shopping walls allow customers to order products on a touch-screen monitor, which will later be delivered to the customer's home or prepared for in-store pick up [12]. Modern checkout-processes include mobile payment as well as biometric authentication payment technology, such as face recognition or fingerprint [12]. Amazon presented a cashierless self-service checkout system called "Amazon Go" [5]. In Amazon's case, store visitors identify themselves at the entrance by scanning a code in their smartphone app. Customers can pick up all the items they want and leave the store without any interference, either from a salesperson or a checkout terminal. According to Grewal et al. [5], this high-tech self-service technology, supported by a combined system of computer vision, sensor fusion, and deep learning technology, is what customers expect from shopping in the future. Artificial intelligence (AI), such as chatbots and AI-powered conversational interfaces, offers a whole new research field in the field of human-computer interaction and customer behavior. For example "Roberta" is a service-robot, working with chatbot technology, implemented to welcome customers, collect their inquiries as well as arrange appointments with a human service manager in the retail store [43].

Further investigation of the impact of interactive in-store technologies is recommended for several reasons. First, retailers are aware of the need for action to enable a superior and engaging customer experience in traditional brick-and-mortar stores. Therefore, scientifically proven results on the effects of technology on customer behavior are highly relevant for retailers. Second, the field of human-computer interaction in retail stores offers various research possibilities due to the number of different interactive technologies and retail sectors. Third, influence factors such as age, gender, countries, technology readiness, education, and motivation to shop, can determine in which retail environment the application of interactive technologies is recommended or discouraged.

5.2 Methodology and Research Designs

The great majority of the empirical studies in this review used quantitative questionnaires to measure the customer's post-purchase experience evoked by using interactive technology in physical retail stores. Most of these studies were conducted in a laboratory or field experiment, as well as in online or offline survey scenarios. Quantitative questionnaires deliver numerical results, which researchers can easily use to calculate the influence of one variable on another, generalize and compare results, reuse the data for other research purposes, etc. [44]. However, on the other hand, quantitative results neither provide a deep insight into the topic nor reveal strong evidence for causal relationships [44]. Moreover, the feedback is based on the customer's self-assessment of the human-computer interaction. Due to possible judgment errors, the self-evaluation might lead to deviations between the actual behavior and the answers given in the questionnaire [45]. Therefore, we suggest considering alternative measurement techniques from the field of Neurobiological Information Systems (NeuroIS), such as the ones below. These methods are usually applied in experimental settings [46] and allow researchers to identify responses to stimuli based on the nervous system [47].

- Eyetracking records the customer's eye movements and where they focus on. The results are usually aggregated and displayed on a heat map, which reveals which points were of high or low interest. Additionally, eyetracking can be combined with observation data or the "think aloud" technique in which participants comment on what they are doing, during or after the experiment. [48]

- Electrodermal (or galvanic skin response) measurement is a technique from the field of psychophysiology. It measures the sweat glands in the palms of the hands and soles of the feet. It is possible to examine various activities with the electrodermal measurement method: arousal, stress, coping, information processing or decision-making. [49]
- Electroencephalography (EEG) measures the electrical brain activation from the surface of the scalp. [50] A similar technique is called "functional magnetic resonance imaging" which measures brain activity by recognizing which areas are more active than others according to bloodstreams [47]. The measurement technique of EEG is often applied to investigate the performance of cognitive tasks with human-computer interaction system of an individual and serves as knowledge basis for the development of such systems [51].

According to Riedl and Léger [46] "[i]t is very common to use psychometric measures (i.e. surveys) in addition to neurophysiological measures in NeuroIS studies" (p. 108). Although one could assume that neurobiological measurements are more objective or reliable, they also have their weaknesses. This is, for example, highlighted by Riedl et al. [52] who state, that we should not assume that "neurobiological measurements are (necessarily) stable across repeated measurement and hence (perfectly) reliable [as] they are not" (p. xi). Various circumstances might influence the body's measured values, such as situational factors (e.g., the participant is nervous because of the laboratory environment) or the experience and skill of the respective experimenter [52]. Other constructs which need to be considered with neurobiological measurements in empirical research of information systems are validity, sensitivity, diagnosticity, objectivity, and intrusiveness as proposed and discussed in detail by Riedl et al. [52]. Besides the neurobiological approach, researchers use cardiovascular or biochemical methods to examine phenomena in empirical studies. Cardiovascular measures assess the participant's heart rate or blood pressure, which can be indicative of a stressful situation, whereas biochemical methods ascertain the hormone levels (e.g., cortisol) in saliva, blood or urine [53].

Technology development in the retail environment also leads to new measurement techniques for customer behavior in retail stores and evaluates implications to enhance the customer's experience. Various customer tracking possibilities are enabled through the customer's smartphone and near field communication (NFC) technology, global positioning systems (GPS) or wireless internet connection (Wi-Fi) in the local area network (LAN) [33]. These technologies are already commonly used in many retail stores and provide information on the customer's behavior. Attention estimation measure methods use camera or sensor (e.g., infrared) technology to assess if customers are in the state of "ignoring", "watching" or "ready to interact" with a stimulus [54]. Video observation is increasingly used to detect in-store shopping behaviors, such as walking (e.g., direction, speed, paths, stopping, queuing, etc.), the product choice (browsing, touching, holding, buying, etc.), socializing (people on the phone, with personnel or other customers, etc.), assistance behaviors (smartphone consultation, using hand-held scanners, using a shopping list, etc.), or other behaviors (redeeming coupons, eating, parking carts and baskets, etc.) [55]. Emotion recognition by the customer's facial expression is based on video technology, such as Microsoft's Kinect v2 [56] or Noldus' FaceReader [57]. These devices are able to recognize the customer's head pose and emotions, such as happiness, anger, surprise, or a neutral facial expression [57]. The data are used to inform managerial decisions, for example towards the products, layout, and atmospherics in the physical retail store [56, 57].

These gaps should be addressed in future works by combining both, technology-based and traditional research methods, to gain a holistic view of the effects of human-computer interaction in physical retail stores. "Roberta" the before mentioned service-robot does not collect the customer's inquiries, but analyses the environment with integrated cameras and sensors [43]. Future research could investigate the customer's behavior by analyzing the data logs of chatbot "Roberta" and combining them with a quantitative questionnaire after the customer's experience in the store.

5.3   Retail Context

So far researchers have not yet examined interactive retail technologies in a non-food store field experiment. It can be assumed that most studies used self-checkout systems in a food store environment as this application scenario is already well established in practice. Future research questions should focus on the in-store human-computer interaction in different retail contexts, especially those that face increasing pressure coming from online commerce, such as fashion, active wear, sports equipment, cosmetics, and accessories.

6   Conclusion

The field of human-computer interaction has seen that investigating interactive technologies in a physical retail environment results in a better understanding of the customer's experience and its consequences. These consequences refer to constructs such as customer satisfaction, loyalty, intention to reuse, patronage, word-of-mouth, and purchase intention. Our systematic literature review reveals first, that researchers should focus on the examination of interactive in-store technology to support retailers in their decisions on the appropriate choices in their physical retail stores. Second, the identified studies are mainly concerned with self-service checkout services examined by the customer's self-assessment through quantitative questionnaires. We propose to extend the scientific literature on the customer's in-store experience by using neuro-biological, cardiovascular or biochemical measure methods complementary to traditional research methods in laboratory experiments, such as surveys or interviews. Moreover, using technologies (e.g., video cameras) to observe the customer's behavior with in-store technologies (e.g., smart mirrors) could also offer a deeper insight into the customer's perception of the experience in physical retail environments. Finally, our work proposes to cover many different retail scenarios, beyond food retail, such as fashion and cosmetics. In summary, researchers are encouraged to conduct studies on retail technologies by applying it to different technologies, research methods, and retail industries.

Acknowledgments. The present work was conducted within the training network project PERFORM funded by the European Union's Horizon 2020 research and innovation program under the Marie Skłodowska-Curie grant agreement No. 76539. This study reflects only the authors' view, the EU Research Executive Agency is not responsible for any use that may be made of the information it contains.

References

1. Jongen, W.: The End of Online Shopping: The Future of New Retail in an Always Connected World. World Scientific Books (2018)
2. Capgemini Consulting: Making the Digital Connection: Why Physical Retail Stores Need a Reboot (2017). https://www.capgemini.com/wp-content/uploads/2017/01/report-making-the-digital-connection.pdf
3. KPMG International Cooperative: Global retail trends (2018). https://assets.kpmg.com/content/dam/kpmg/xx/pdf/2018/03/global-retail-trends-2018.pdf
4. Spencer Soper: Amazon Will Consider Opening Up to 3,000 Cashierless Stores by 2021 (2018). https://www.bloomberg.com/news/articles/2018-09-19/amazon-is-said-to-plan-up-to-3-000-cashierless-stores-by-2021
5. Grewal, D., Roggeveen, A.L., Nordfält, J.: The future of retailing. J. Retail. **93**(1), 1–6 (2017)
6. Priporas, C.-V., Stylos, N., Fotiadis, A.K.: Generation Z consumers' expectations of interactions in smart retailing: a future agenda. Comput. Hum. Behav. **77**, 374–381 (2017)
7. Djelassi, S., Diallo, M.F., Zielke, S.: How self-service technology experience evaluation affects waiting time and customer satisfaction? A moderated mediation model. Decis. Support Syst. (2018). https://doi.org/10.1016/j.dss.2018.04.004
8. Grewal, D., Levy, M., Kumar, V.: Customer experience management in retailing: an organizing framework. J. Retail. (2009). https://doi.org/10.1016/j.jretai.2009.01.001
9. Kallweit, K., Spreer, P., Toporowski, W.: Why do customers use self-service information technologies in retail? The mediating effect of perceived service quality. J. Retail. Consum. Serv. (2014). https://doi.org/10.1016/j.jretconser.2014.02.002
10. Poncin, I., Ben Mimoun, M.S.: The impact of "e-atmospherics" on physical stores. J. Retail. Consum. Serv. (2014). https://doi.org/10.1016/j.jretconser.2014.02.013
11. Roy, S.K., Balaji, M.S., Sadeque, S., Nguyen, B., Melewar, T.C.: Constituents and consequences of smart customer experience in retailing. Technol. Forecast. Soc. Change (2017). https://doi.org/10.1016/j.techfore.2016.09.022
12. Willems, K., Smolders, A., Brengman, M., Luyten, K., Schöning, J.: The path-to-purchase is paved with digital opportunities: an inventory of shopper-oriented retail technologies. Technol. Forecast. Soc. Change (2017). https://doi.org/10.1016/j.techfore.2016.10.066
13. Lazaris, C., Vrechopoulos, A.: Human-computer vs. consumer-store interaction in a multichannel retail environment: some multidisciplinary research directions. In: Nah, F.F.-H. (ed.) HCIB 2014. LNCS, vol. 8527, pp. 339–349. Springer, Cham (2014). https://doi.org/10.1007/978-3-319-07293-7_33
14. Poncin, I., Garnier, M., Ben Mimoun, M.S., Leclercq, T.: Smart technologies and shopping experience: are gamification interfaces effective? The case of the Smartstore. Technol. Forecast. Soc. Change (2017). https://doi.org/10.1016/j.techfore.2017.01.025
15. Ajzen, I., Fishbein, M.: Understanding Attitudes and Predicting Social Behavior. Prentice Hall, Englewood Cliffs (1980)

16. Davis, F.D.: User acceptance ôf information technology: system characteristics, user perceptions and behavioral impacts. Int. J. Man-Mach. Stud. **38**(3), 475–487 (1993)
17. Davis, F.D., Bagozzi, R.P., Warshaw, P.R.: User acceptance of computer technology: a comparison of two theoretical models. Manage. Sci. **35**(8), 982–1003 (1989)
18. Landmark, A.D., Sjøbakk, B.: Tracking customer behaviour in fashion retail using RFID. Intl. J. Retail. Distrib. Manag. (2017). https://doi.org/10.1108/ijrdm-10-2016-0174
19. Parasuraman, A., Grewal, D.: The impact of technology on the quality-value-loyalty chain: a research agenda. J. Acad. Mark. Sci. **28**(1), 168–174 (2000)
20. Penttinen, E., Rinta-Kahila, T., Ronkko, M., Saarinen, T.: Triggering intention to use to actual use – empirical evidence from self-service checkout (SCO) systems. In: 2014 47th Hawaii International Conference on System Sciences (HICSS), Waikoloa, HI, 06.01.2014– 09.01.2014, pp. 3347–3355. IEEE (2014). https://doi.org/10.1109/hicss.2014.414
21. Wang, M.C.-H.: Determinants and consequences of consumer satisfaction with self-service technology in a retail setting. Manag. Serv. Qual. (2012). https://doi.org/10.1108/09604521211218945
22. Orel, F.D., Kara, A.: Supermarket self-checkout service quality, customer satisfaction, and loyalty: Empirical evidence from an emerging market. J. Retail. Consum. Serv. (2014). https://doi.org/10.1016/j.jretconser.2013.07.002
23. Fernandes, T., Pedroso, R.: The effect of self-checkout quality on customer satisfaction and repatronage in a retail context. Serv. Bus. (2017). https://doi.org/10.1007/s11628-016-0302-9
24. Lecointre-Erickson, D., Daucé, B., Legohérel, P.: The influence of interactive window displays on expected shopping experience. Int. J. Retail. Distrib. Manag. (2018). https://doi.org/10.1108/ijrdm-05-2017-0111
25. Lee, H.-J., Yang, K.: Interpersonal service quality, self-service technology (SST) service quality, and retail patronage. J. Retail. Consum. Serv. (2013). https://doi.org/10.1016/j.jretconser.2012.10.005
26. White, A., Breazeale, M., Collier, J.E.: The effects of perceived fairness on customer responses to retailer sst push policies. J. Retail. (2012). https://doi.org/10.1016/j.jretai.2012.01.005
27. Mukherjee, A., Smith, R.J., Turri, A.M.: The smartness paradox: the moderating effect of brand quality reputation on consumers' reactions to RFID-based smart fitting rooms. J. Bus. Res. (2018). https://doi.org/10.1016/j.jbusres.2018.07.057
28. vom Brocke, J., Simons, A., Niehaves, B., Riemer, K., Plattfaut, R., Cleven, A.: Reconstructing the giant: on the importance of rigour in documenting the literature search process. In: ECIS (European Conference on Information Systems), vol. 9, pp. 2206–2217 (2009)
29. Cooper, H.M.: Organizing knowledge syntheses: a taxonomy of literature reviews. Knowl. Soc. **1**(1), 104–126 (1988)
30. Lemon, K.N., Verhoef, P.C.: Understanding customer experience throughout the customer journey. J. Mark. (2016). https://doi.org/10.1509/jm.15.0420
31. Holbrook, M.B., Hirschman, E.C.: The experiential aspects of consumption: consumer fantasies, feelings, and fun. J Consum. Res. (1982). https://doi.org/10.1086/208906
32. Verhoef, P.C., Lemon, K.N., Parasuraman, A., Roggeveen, A., Tsiros, M., Schlesinger, L. A.: Customer experience creation: determinants, dynamics and management strategies. J. Retail. (2009). https://doi.org/10.1016/j.jretai.2008.11.001
33. Varadarajan, R., et al.: Interactive technologies and retailing strategy: a review, conceptual framework and future research directions. J. Interact. Mark. (2010). https://doi.org/10.1016/j.intmar.2010.02.004

34. Meuter, M.L., Ostrom, A.L., Roundtree, R.I., Bitner, M.J.: Self-service technologies: understanding customer satisfaction with technology-based service encounters. J. Mark. (2000). https://doi.org/10.1509/jmkg.64.3.50.18024
35. Blázquez, M.: Fashion shopping in multichannel retail: the role of technology in enhancing the customer experience. Int. J. Electron. Commerce (2014). https://doi.org/10.2753/jec1086-4415180404
36. Bustamante, J.C., Rubio, N.: Measuring customer experience in physical retail environments. J. Serv. Manag. (2017). https://doi.org/10.1108/josm-06-2016-0142
37. Siah, J.W., Fam, S.-F.: Self-checkout service quality and purchasing intention in Malaysia. J. Fundam. Appl. Sci. 10(6S), 2669–2682 (2018)
38. Wang, C., Harris, J., Patterson, P.: The roles of habit, self-efficacy, and satisfaction in driving continued use of self-service technologies: a longitudinal study. J. Serv. Res. (2013). https://doi.org/10.1177/1094670512473200
39. Hunneman, A., Verhoef, P.C., Sloot, L.M.: The moderating role of shopping trip type in store satisfaction formation. J. Bus. Res. (2017). https://doi.org/10.1016/j.jbusres.2017.05.012
40. Beck, M., Crié, D.: I virtually try it ... I want it! Virtual fitting room: a tool to increase on-line and off-line exploratory behavior, patronage and purchase intentions. J. Retail. Consum. Serv. 40, 279–286 (2018)
41. Poushneh, A.: Augmented reality in retail: a trade-off between user's control of access to personal information and augmentation quality. J. Retail. Consum. Serv. 41, 169–176 (2018)
42. Pantano, E.: Engaging consumer through the storefront: evidences from integrating interactive technologies. J. Retail. Consum. Serv. (2016). https://doi.org/10.1016/j.jretconser.2015.09.007
43. Eberhardt, G.: Guten Tag, wie kann ich Ihnen behilflich sein? Über Welcome Agents im Einzelhandel (2018). https://www.ibm.com/de-de/blogs/think/2018/10/18/guten-tag-wie-kann-ich-ihnen-behilflich-sein-uber-welcome-agents-im-einzelhandel/
44. Recker, J. (ed.): Scientific Research in Information Systems: a Beginner's Guide, pp. 76–87. Springer, Heidelberg (2012). https://doi.org/10.1007/978-3-642-30048-6
45. Hufnagel, E.M., Conca, C.: User response data: tpotential for errors and biases. Inf. Syst. Res. 5(1), 48–73 (1994)
46. Riedl, R., Léger, P.-M.: Fundamentals of NeuroIS - Information Systems and the Brain. Springer, Heidelberg (2016). https://doi.org/10.1007/978-3-662-45091-8
47. Neben, T., Xiao, B.S., Lim, E., Tan, C.-W., Heinzl, A.: Measuring appeal in human computer interaction: a cognitive neuroscience-based approach. In: Davis, F.D., Riedl, R., vom Brocke, J., Léger, P.-M., Randolph, Adriane B. (eds.) Information systems and neuroscience. LNISO, vol. 10, pp. 151–159. Springer, Cham (2015). https://doi.org/10.1007/978-3-319-18702-0_20
48. Webb, N., Renshaw, T.: Eyetracking in HCI. Research Methods for Human-Computer Interaction, pp. 35–69 (2008)
49. Weinert, C., Maier, C., Laumer, S.: What does the skin tell us about information systems usage? A literature-based analysis of the utilization of electrodermal measurement for IS research. In: Davis, F.D., Riedl, R., vom Brocke, J., Léger, P.-M., Randolph, A.B. (eds.) Information Systems and Neuroscience. LNISO, vol. 10, pp. 65–75. Springer, Cham (2015). https://doi.org/10.1007/978-3-319-18702-0_9
50. Müller-Putz, G.R., Riedl, R., Wriessnegger, S.C.: Electroencephalography (EEG) as a research tool in the information systems discipline: foundations, measurement, and applications. Commun. Assoc. Inf. (37), 46 (2015)

51. Riedl, R.: Zum Erkenntnispotenzial der kognitiven Neurowissenschaften für die Wirtschaftsinformatik: Überlegungen anhand exemplarischer Anwendungen. Neuro. Psychoanal. Econom. **4**(1), 32–44 (2009)
52. Riedl, R., Davis, F.D., Hevner, A.R.: Towards a NeuroIS Research Methodology: Intensifying the Discussion on Methods, Tools, and Measurement. JAIS (2014). https://doi.org/10.17705/1jais.00377
53. Vogel, J., Auinger, A., Riedl, R.: Cardiovascular, neurophysiological, and biochemical stress indicators: a short review for information systems researchers. In: Davis, F.D., Riedl, R., vom Brocke, J., Léger, P.-M., Randolph, A.B. (eds.) Information Systems and Neuroscience. LNISO, vol. 29, pp. 259–273. Springer, Cham (2019). https://doi.org/10.1007/978-3-030-01087-4_31
54. Narzt, W.: A comparison of attention estimation techniques in a public display scenario. In: Nah, F.F.-H., Tan, C.-H. (eds.) HCIBGO 2017. LNCS, vol. 10293, pp. 338–353. Springer, Cham (2017). https://doi.org/10.1007/978-3-319-58481-2_26
55. Larsen, N.M., Sigurdsson, V., Breivik, J.: The use of observational technology to study in-store behavior: consumer choice, video surveillance, and retail analytics. Behav. Anal. (2017). https://doi.org/10.1007/s40614-017-0121-x
56. Le, H.T., Vea, L.A.: A customer emotion recognition through facial expression using Kinect Sensors v1 and v2. In: Unknown (ed.) Proceedings of the 10th International Conference on Ubiquitous Information Management and Communication - IMCOM 2016. The 10th International Conference, Danang, Viet Nam, 04.01.2016–06.01.2016, pp. 1–7. ACM Press, New York (2016). https://doi.org/10.1145/2857546.2857628
57. Noldus Information Technology: FaceReader (2019). https://www.noldus.com/human-behavior-research/products/facereader

Modifying e-Service Quality for Automotive Repair Shops

Canveet Randhawa and Norman Shaw[(✉)]

Ryerson University, Toronto, Canada
norman.shaw@ryerson.ca

Abstract. Third party automotive repair shops compete with auto dealerships. Lacking the brand recognition, they need to develop strategies that will enhance customer loyalty. Extant literature has shown that service quality is an antecedent of loyalty. The measurement of service quality is context sensitive and scales have been developed for e-servqual, to measure the service quality delivered by websites. This study adapts the measurement of e-servqual for the context of third party automotive repair shops. The research model is extended to include the physical surroundings, represented by the construct, servicescape. Data is collected from customers who are servicing their cars. The analysis shows that service quality, trust and reputation have a significant influence on customer loyalty.

Keywords: Third-party · Automotive repair shops · Servqual · Servicescape · Customer loyalty

1 Introduction

In the automotive industry, loyalty to a vehicle brand, such as GM or Ford, is often retained through generations with offspring more likely to purchase the same brand as their parents [1]. Loyalty to the automotive dealership for repair and service, however, significantly declines after a vehicle's warranty period expires and many people turn to independent service and repair shops that provide fluid changes and other services recommended by the vehicle manufacturer [2].

Service suppliers include dealerships, third-party auto repair and service shops, self-employed mechanics, car care centers and garages [3]. The majority of third-party shops (i.e. those businesses not affiliated with a vehicle manufacturer) are individually or family owned [3]. These shops are keen to build customer loyalty not only to sustain themselves but also to ensure growth and profitability [4]. Customer loyalty refers to behaviors where customers repeatedly obtain a particular service from only one service provider. The reasons for staying include satisfaction with services, reasonable costs, familiarity with employees, trust and ease of use [5]. In Canada, nearly half of all Canadians have their vehicles serviced at local third-party shops with 70% repeatedly returning to the same shop for services [6].

Regardless of the type of automotive service shop, customers universally fear this segment of the automobile industry due to the number of scams that are reported in the media [7]. Scott [7] argues that customers are becoming increasingly vigilant in their

© Springer Nature Switzerland AG 2019
F. F.-H. Nah and K. Siau (Eds.): HCII 2019, LNCS 11588, pp. 67–81, 2019.
https://doi.org/10.1007/978-3-030-22335-9_5

selection due to trust issues. Many automotive repair and service centers aim to provide credible and reliable services, and thereby increase customer loyalty, but there are limited studies on the actual perception of customers using third-party automotive service shops. Although surveys have shown that women (76%) are more likely than men (66%) to return to the same service center year over year, the factors which influence this loyalty in the Canadian automotive service sector is unknown [6].

The aim of this research is to address the current gaps in knowledge by identifying the main factors that influence customer loyalty to third-party automotive repair shops and provide strategies so customer loyalty and retention can be improved. The research question is what factors influence customer loyalty in the context of third party automotive service shops.

The structure of this paper is as follows. The next section is a review of the literature that aims to put the present study in context and outline the research gaps that this study will fill. Section three explains the research methodology, which is followed by the results in section four. Section five is a discussion, including limitations and suggestions for future research. The final section is the conclusion.

2 Literature Review

Third-party automotive shops co-exist and compete with car dealerships and automotive service chains such as Midas, Wal-Mart and Canadian Tire. Most of these third-party shops have maintained their businesses because customers are comfortable with receiving services from a shop where they are recognized, the service is reliable, the parts are dependable, and customer demands are met [8]. Generally, third-party automotive shops are more interactive with their clients and directly reveal the price they charge for a given automotive service. Furthermore, automotive service shops have kept pace with improvements in technologies offering these to their customers [9].

Chain service centers and car dealerships have an advantage over third-party shops in that they are certified by the major automobile manufacturers. Third-party shops, however, have an advantage in terms of customer recognition and trust due to personal interactions over the course of many encounters [10]. The customer is valuable for all businesses and thus customer loyalty should not be taken for granted. The intention of this literature review is to outline some factors that influence customer loyalty towards third-party automotive shops.

2.1 Service Quality

Service quality can be defined as a consumer's expectation for a given service. It is positive when expectations are met and negative when the reverse occurs [11]. Service quality consists of a broad spectrum of factors, all of which make a customer feel satisfied and increase the possibility of them returning [11]. These include reliability, responsiveness to a customer's needs, competence in carrying out the necessary work, and employing people who are approachable, courteous, trustworthy and who exhibit strong communication skills [11].

In a study conducted by Yee and Faziharudean [12], their measure of service quality was geared towards a virtual website. They modified ES-QUAL [13] adding questions related to web design, quickness of loading pages, ease of navigation, and promptness of customer service. These measures can be applied to the context of this study. For example, quickness of loading pages is equivalent to waiting time prior to service; and ease of navigation is equivalent to clarity of service provided.

The quality of service that customers receive from auto service shops directly influences customer loyalty [14]. Quality, in this case, means that customers have their vehicles serviced with care, quality parts are used and customers leave feeling satisfied having received good value [15, 16]. Service quality is important to all service organizations and it is key for developing client loyalty. It is in the interest of any business organization to evaluate the quality of services often, as this can impact customer loyalty. In one study, the authors evaluated a loyalty model by surveying 495 customers of 15 Nissan, Toyota and Mitsubishi repair centers [14]. They discovered that the service quality affected consumer loyalty more than the price of the service. Hence, our first hypothesis:

H1: Service Quality positively influences Customer Loyalty in third-party automotive shops.

2.2 Perceived Value

Perceived value can be defined as a customer's perception of the differences between the service they receive and the sacrifice they make to obtain the service [17]. Sacrifices include the effort to research potential service providers, duration of time spent in the shop, inconvenience of not having use of the vehicle during the service and the financial outlay for the service. When a consumer feels that the offering's value is fair and equitable, and is similar or better to a competitor's, the perceived value is higher, leading to loyalty and repeat business [18].

For automotive repair shops, similar services are offered by various companies and, together with an explosion of Internet reviews that describe services and costs, customers can compare and be more aware of the value received for their expenditure. In urban areas, drivers have multiple alternatives [19, 20], leading to low switching costs, which makes it ever more important for service shops to focus on factors that will increase customer loyalty [21]. For example, when businesses sell their replacement parts at fair prices and make honest service recommendations, customers will deem that they have received fair value. An emotional bond develops and customers will hesitate to switch to a different provider [21]. Our next hypothesis is:

H2: Perceived Value positively influences Customer Loyalty in third-party automotive shops.

2.3 Trust

Trust is defined as "a psychological state comprising the intention to accept vulnerability based on positive expectations of the intentions or behaviors of another" [22]. This is directly applicable to the vulnerability that customers experience when they give their car for service, due to media reports about shops who defraud customers [23, 24]. Examples include charging for new premium parts but using older lower quality ones, overcharging for labour and recommending services that are not required [7, 25]. Underlying the importance of trust in the automotive service business is that the customer cannot return the oil or the filter that has been replaced [26].

Generally speaking, women are less confident in their knowledge about automobile repairs and services, with some service centers taking advantage by overcharging them [27]. However, once trust is gained, female customers are more loyal than their male counterparts [6]. Women place more emphasis on the social skills that reflect how they are treated [21, 28]. Trust, therefore, is critical to cultivate and sustain. It leads to loyal customers who repeatedly patronize the business and recommend the shop to friends [29].

H3: Trust positively influences Customer Loyalty in third-party automotive shops.

2.4   Consumer Habit

Nearly half of people's behavior is repeated daily and is "a specific form of automaticity in which responses are directly cued by the context" [30]. This tendency to repeat behavior is further compounded because of time pressures, so that when customers are comfortable with a particular business, they may readily form habitual behavior to frequent that business [31].

Consumer habit is behavior that is automated and repeated [32]. Habit formation requires an initial investment of research: the service shop has to be found in a convenient location and a trial appointment set up with associated risks of unsatisfactory quality of service. When a business earns trust at this first encounter, repeat visits are encouraged because their customers do not need to expend additional energy to search for and try the services of another establishment [33]. Habitual behavior is therefore reinforced [34].

Darley, Luethge and Thatte [35] have noted that habit results from behavioral preferences while Rai and Srivastava [36] have noted that habitual behavior allows for the continuation of the same purchase intents, ideally strengthening the position on each occasion [35, 36].

H4: Habit positively influences Customer Loyalty in third-party automotive shops.

2.5   Reputation

Reputation can be defined as "a concept related to image, but one that refers to value judgments among the public about an organization's qualities, formed over a long period, regarding its consistency, trustworthiness, and reliability [37]. The reputation of a business often precedes it before a consumer sets foot into the premise or agrees to the services. A positive reputation is difficult to build and requires consistent effort, over the long term, to maintain trustworthy service of high quality. Once built, reputation is able to withstand adverse publicity or a finite lag in quality of service [38].

Previous literature suggests that the third-party automobile service industry is heavily reliant on positive word-of-mouth, which necessitates the importance of a good reputation, while a bad reputation can reduce the number of loyal customers [39]. Third-party automotive shops are able to build and maintain their reputation through their close interactions with their clients, which in turn wins them loyalty [40]. A good reputation protects a business from those rare occasions when there is a service failure and customers are dissatisfied [41]. By having a reputable business, loyalty is created and this in turn brings an increased number of customers while also retaining the present ones.

H5: Reputation positively influences Customer Loyalty in third-party automotive shops.

2.6   Servicescape

Servicescape describes the physical attributes associated with a business: for example, its location, its physical layout, the cleanliness of the premises, odor, the lighting conditions and sounds [42]. In the context of a third-party automotive shop, servicescape refers to the appearance and layout of the service bays, the location, the sounds and the associated industrial smell. This environment where the service takes place can play a significant role in explaining people's behavior [42].

Traditionally, the basics of marketing products or services has been described by the four P's: product, price, promotion, and place [16]. Using this model for an independent garage, the product is the entire experience, from the time the customers see the shop, enter it, interact with the employees and then depart with their vehicle serviced. Servicescape is an integral component, where a customer's reaction is stimulated cognitively, emotionally and physiologically (Wakefield and Blodgett 1994). Bitner [42] suggests that organizations should think of their physical environment as a resource that could further their goals.

Servicescape can help to positively alter perceptions and behaviours of customers [43], encouraging them to approach and frequent the business [44]. Clients may still perceive an overall positive experience, even when the service itself may be less than adequate [45]. Servicescape influences a customer's belief about whether a firm is successful or unsuccessful, trustworthy or untrustworthy [45, 46] and, as such, it can play a critical role in customer loyalty [47].

H6: Servicescape positively influences Customer Loyalty in third-party automotive shops.

2.7   Research Model

Yee and Faziharudean [12] investigated the factors that influence customers' loyalty towards banking websites. They found that service quality, perceived value, trust, habit and reputation influenced customer loyalty. In this study, we have adopted their model and extended it with the construct of servicescape. See Fig. 1.

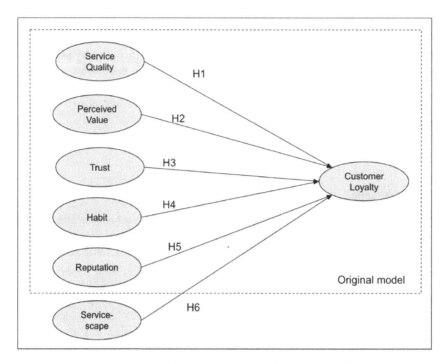

Fig. 1. Extended conceptual model adapted from [12].

3 Research Methodology

3.1 Survey Instrument

For the purpose of collecting data for this study, an online survey was constructed with a software tool [48]. The questions asked for opinions and judgements about service quality, perceived value, trust, habit, reputation, and servicescape. A 7-point Likert Scale was used, ranging from strongly disagree (= 1) to strongly agree (= 7) and is more sensitive to measuring a respondent's actual views as compared to a 5-point item scale [49].

3.2 Sampling

Prior to administering the survey to customers, approval was sought and received from the Research Ethics Board of Ryerson University. Recruitment was done in-person by approaching customers who were visiting a third-party repair shop in order to have services performed on their vehicle. An Apple iPad was provided to each customer to take the survey. All of the customers who were approached were provided an instant $10 discount on their invoice, whether they chose to participate or not.

The sampling procedure utilized convenience sampling, which is a non-probability sampling strategy used to obtain a reasonable response rate [50]. The population of interest are consumers who visit third-party automotive repair shops for services.

For this study, the locations selected were two of the most significant players in the automotive repair and service business, Jiffy Lube and Pennzoil, both of which are owned by Royal Dutch Shell. To ensure a representative sample size and statistically significant data set (one in which type I and type II errors are reduced), 306 surveys were distributed [50]. Convenience sampling and the use of iPads allowed the data to be obtained in a timely, cost-effective manner.

The respondent size of 300 people represented a statistically significant sample of the customers visiting the service shops [51, 52]. Specifically, given that there are six exogenous variables with paths to the endogenous variable, customer loyalty, 130 observations are required to achieve a statistical power of 80% for detecting R^2 values of at least 0.1 [53]. Therefore, a sample size of 306 participants in this study is adequate to realize a statistically significant result.

3.3 Operationalization of Variables

All constructs were operationalized based on extant literature. A major source was the work done by Yee and Faziharudean [12]. They had adopted ES-QUAL [13]. In the context of this study, service quality was operationalized in a similar manner. For example, "ease of navigation" became "how easy was it to find our location?", and "quickness of loading pages" became "was the wait time acceptable?". Asking if "the service is performed properly the first time" [12] is as applicable to a website as it is to the repair shop. The indicator asking if the website projects an image of reliability and trustworthiness [12] became "do the employees and environment of the service center project an image of reliability and trustworthiness?"

3.4 Data Analysis

In this study, SmartPLS was used to analyze the data [54]. Smart PLS is a software application used for Partial Least Squares Structural Equation Modeling (PLS-SEM). There are two steps performed in SmartPLS analysis: confirmation of the measurement model and the calculation of the coefficients in the path model [55]. Four assessments were conducted: composite reliability, outer loadings of indicators, the average variance extracted (AVE) and the Fornell - Larcker criterion [56]. The composite reliability examines the internal consistency; outer loadings show the indicator reliability for each construct; AVE examines convergent validity; the Fornell - Larcker criterion and the Heterotrait - Monotrait ratio of correlations (HTMT) examines discriminant validity. The second part of the analysis was the calculation of the path coefficients followed by bootstrapping with 5000 samples to calculate the t-statistic and p-values for each path.

4 Results

4.1 The Sample

306 total customers were approached. After cleaning the raw data, 16 surveys were discarded, resulting in 290 completed surveys, representing a response rate of 94.7%.

This high response rate was due to the business being local and family owned, with the researcher interacting with the customers. In addition, participants could take the survey while their car was being serviced so there was no extra time involved. Surveys with low response rates are not necessarily inaccurate as compared to surveys with higher response rates [57].

Of the 290 surveys, 51.2%, (n = 152) were male and 48.8%, (n = 145) were female. The majority (54.2%) were between the ages of 18–40. The next largest group was those between the ages of 41–52 (27.6%) with the remainder (18.2%) being over 52.

4.2   Testing the Measurement Model

Outer Loadings
The SmartPLS algorithm calculates the outer loadings of each variable. All indicators were convergent, as their correlation coefficients were greater than 0.708 [58].

Internal Consistency and Validity
Cronbach's alpha is a tool that assesses how closely related a set of items or variables are as a group [59]. A Cronbach's alpha value of 0.70 or higher is considered acceptable in most research studies [60]. In the present study, the Cronbach's value ranged from 0.716 to 0.954 (Table 1). Composite reliability is another measure of internal consistency. This measurement takes into account different outer loadings of the indicator variables of each specific construct [61]. Values greater than 0.70 are considered adequate in exploratory research [53]. The Average Variance Extracted (AVE) is a measure of the variance explained by the latent variables relative to the variance due to error measurement. The threshold for an adequate AVE is 0.50 [53]. Results are shown in Table 1.

Table 1. PLS construct reliability and validity

Latent variable	Cronbach's alpha	Composite reliability	AVE
Service Quality (SQ)	0.874	0.908	0.664
Perceived Value (PV)	0.954	0.970	0.916
Habit (HB)	0.949	0.967	0.908
Servicescape (SS)	0.716	0.839	0.635
Trust (TR)	0.765	0.625	0.531
Customer Loyalty (CL)	0.854	0.901	0.696
Reputation (RP)	0.899	0.937	0.832

Discriminant Validity
It is necessary to assess the discriminant validity in all research pertaining to latent variables to prevent multicollinearity issues. The Fornell and Larcker criterion is the most widely used method [56]. For our empirical data, the AVE square root of every construct was more than the highest correlation construct with any other in the model [56], thereby supporting discriminant validity.

We also conducted the Heterotrait - Monotrait Ratio (HTMT) criterion test as it has been shown to outperform the Fornell-Larcker test [53]. The calculation results in HTMT values less than 1, which also supports the discriminant validity among the constructs [53].

4.3 Testing the Path Model

The PLS algorithm calculates the path coefficients and the coefficient of determination, denoted as R^2, which is the most commonly used measurement to evaluate the structural model [53]. The higher the R^2 value of endogenous constructs, the better the construct is explained by the latent variables in the path model. R^2 ranges between 0 and 1 with higher values indicating that more of the variance is explained by the independent variables [53]. R^2 for Intention to use is 0.402, which is moderately strong [53].

The significance of each path was calculated via a bootstrap, where randomly drawn observations are created from the original data set, with replacement. This was repeated for 5,000 sub-samples. Three paths were significant and the results are summarized in Table 2.

Table 2. Summary of results

Number	Path	Coefficient	t value
H1	**SQ --> CL**	**0.219**	**2.435 ***
H2	PV --> CL	0.143	1.902
H3	HB --> CL	0.070	1.056
H4	SS --> CL	0.082	1.013
H5	**TR--> CL**	**0.176**	**2.525 ***
H6	**RP --> CL**	**0.209**	**2.646 ****

*Significance: * p<0.05; ** p<0.01*

4.4 Summary of Results

Table 2 summarizes the paths and their significance, showing which hypotheses were supported.

5 Discussion

This study explored the influence of service quality, perceived value, trust, reputation, habit and servicescape on customer loyalty, with empirical data collected from two third-party automotive service shops. The data illuminated which of the six factors motivate customers to remain loyal. Statistical analysis of the data indicated that three hypotheses are supported, while three hypotheses are rejected at the significance level of $p < 0.05$.

Service quality significantly influences the level of customer loyalty. Customers will be loyal to automotive shops which are reliable, responsive to a customer's needs, competent in carrying out the necessary work, and have employees who are approachable, courteous, exhibit strong communication skills and trustworthy. Service quality, in this case, means that customers have their vehicles serviced with care, quality parts are used resulting in customers feeling satisfied [12]. Taking clients' complaints or grievances seriously is also part of perceived service quality [11].

Perceived value did not have a significant effect on customer loyalty. When the exact services a consumer wants are readily available at numerous shops with nearly equivalent pricing, such as an oil change, other non-monetary factors have greater influence [44, 46, 47].

Consumer habits do not directly relate to loyalty as behavior is automated and repeated without regarding the quality of parts, services, or prices [30]. This tendency can be seen in the repeated purchase of the same vehicle brand across generations and the same brands across different shopping episodes or locations [1]. Rather than habit influencing customer loyalty, it may well be that customer loyalty is an antecedent of habit. Loyal customers will show habitual behavior, frequenting the same automotive repair shop.

Of surprise is that servicescape did not significantly influence loyalty. Servicescape is determined by a number of factors like accessibility, parking space, building, its design and color, lighting, air quality, temperature, noise, cleanliness, smell, layout of furnishings, signs, symbols (such as flags), employee uniforms, and a myriad of other things [43]. Some reasons for this result could be that customers know they are going to an automotive shop and they do not expect a clean, quiet environment. They may even be less inclined to visit a shop which has a more refined atmosphere, as they may feel that prices are inflated because of money being diverted towards superfluous servicescape items rather than the service itself.

Trust has a direct impact on customer loyalty. When customers first enter the premises of a business, they are vulnerable, but if the shop meets or exceeds their expectations, then trust will be established [23]. Trust can be further built by treating customers well, explaining clearly what service needs to be performed and returning the vehicle on time with no surprise charges. Paying careful attention to the needs of customers, who are likely to know less about automobile repairs than the employees, will lead to satisfied customers [27]. With greater trust, there is greater loyalty with more likelihood of returning customers.

Reputation has a significant influence on customer loyalty. Clients prefer giving their car to a company that has a good reputation [37, 39], which in turn gives the repair shop an advantage when competing with other shops that offer cheaper services of a similar nature but whose reputation is less stellar [41]. By having a reputable business, loyalty is encouraged bringing an increased number of customers while also retaining the present ones.

5.1   Theoretical Implications

The concept of service quality, which is directly linked to customer satisfaction and loyalty, has evolved over the last years. Scholars have adapted the construct to study different industrial sectors and business types. We adapted the website construct of es-servqual and successfully applied it to the context of third party automotive repair shops. We extended the model of Yee and Faziharudean [12] with the construct of servicescape, which includes factors such as lighting conditions, color, noise, and numerous other sensory stimuli. The study has broadened the understanding of factors that influence loyalty within the context of third-party auto repair shops.

5.2 Implications for Business

For third-party auto-repair and service shops, there are significant benefits of this research. Due to increased competition between many third-party shops and other similar service providers, customer loyalty is a priority [10]. The study highlighted service quality, trust and reputation as key, implying that managers in the automotive industry should build their retention strategies around these elements. A trusting relationship can be built by being honest, loyal, sincere and keeping promises. Findings in a study conducted by Dasu and Chase [62] found that service providers need to recognize how factors, such as emotions, trust and control, shape how customers perceive their service experience. They found that "ETCs" (emotions, trust and control) can influence customer assessments of service experiences and their loyalty. This study confirms that trust, service quality and reputation are important factors in gaining customer loyalty. Third-party service shops can mitigate defection rates and increase customer retention by modifyingtheir practices in light of these findings.

5.3 Future Research

The study has highlighted trust and good reputation to be among the key factors influencing customer loyalty in the automotive repair business. Future research could focus on the antecedents of trust and reputation in the automotive business, with additional data collected to determine the moderating role of gender. Considering that in this study, the research focused on third-party automotive shops in Canada, further research could be done to investigate factors influencing loyalty in other services in other cultures [63].

5.4 Limitations

The study employed a quantitative design where structured closed ended questions were used to gather data. An important limitation to this study could be that participants were about to have their car serviced and therefore might be biassed to provide more positive answers. The sample was from two similar businesses, owned and operated by the same family. The sample may not be representative of other third party shops managed in a different manner. Vehicle owners may be influenced by the condition of the car, or the incentive to participate. These factors would limit the generalizability of the results.

6 Conclusion

This study addresses the current gaps in knowledge by identifying the main factors that influence customer loyalty for third-party automotive repair shops. Among the six independent variables, service quality, trust and reputation were found to be the significant predictors of customer loyalty. Customers want assurance that the repairs will last a reasonable time without problems. In many cases, customers compare available offerings in the market and settle for what they perceive to be quality service at the lowest price. Repair shops must therefore emphasize the quality of their service by delivering according to customers' expectation. There is less need to invest in the physical surroundings, as represented by the construct of servicescape. Consumers understand they are in an automotive shop and they expect the surroundings to reflect this. Establishing a good reputation by building trust through excellent quality of service will lead to increased customer loyalty.

References

1. Anderson, S.T., et al.: The intergenerational transmission of automobile brand preferences. J. Ind. Econ. **63**(4), 763–793 (2015)
2. Nadzri, W.N.M., et al.: The antecedents of brand experience within the national automotive industry. Procedia Econ. Financ. **37**, 317–323 (2016)
3. Peter Pauper Press: Auto Log Book. Peter Pauper Press, New York (2015)
4. Bowen, J.T., Chen, S.-L.: The relationship between customer loyalty and customer satisfaction. Int. J. Contemp. Hosp. Manag. **13**(5), 213–217 (2001)
5. De Ruyter, K., Bloemer, J.: Customer loyalty in extended service settings: the interaction between satisfaction, value attainment and positive mood. Int. J. Serv. Ind. Manag. **10**(3), 320–336 (1999)
6. Canada Post: Marketing Research Group Fact Sheet: Automotive industry and Aftermarket (2008). https://www.canadapost.ca/cpo/mr/assets/pdf/business/autoindustryaftermarket_en.pdf
7. Scott, G.G., Watch out for third party auto repair scams. Huffington Post (2014)
8. Devaraj, S., Matta, K.F., Conlon, E.: Product and service quality: the antecedents of customer loyalty in the automotive industry. Prod. Oper. Manag. **10**(4), 424–439 (2001)
9. Biery, M.E.: Auto Repair Shops' Growth Stalls, Forbes (2014). https://www.forbes.com/sites/sageworks/2014/01/26/auto-repair-shops-financial-analysis/#307b72a421c0
10. Gurski, D.: Customer Experiences Affect Customer Loyalty: An Empirical Investigation of the Starbucks Experience Using Structural Equation Modeling. Anchor Academic Publishing (aap_verlag) (2014)
11. Parasuraman, A., Zeithaml, V.A., Berry, L.L.: SERVQUAL: a multiple-item scale for measuring consumer perc. J. Retail. **64**(1), 12 (1988)
12. Yee, B.Y., Faziharudean, T.: Factors affecting customer loyalty of using Internet banking in Malaysia. J. Electron. Bank. Syst. **21** 2010
13. Parasuraman, A., Zeithaml, V.A., Malhotra, A.: ES-QUAL: a multiple-item scale for assessing electronic service quality. J. Serv. Res. **7**(3), 213–233 (2005)
14. Bei, L.-T., Chiao, Y.-C.: An integrated model for the effects of perceived product, perceived service quality, and perceived price fairness on consumer satisfaction and loyalty. J. Consum. Satisf. Dissatisfaction Complain. Behav. **14**, 125 (2001)

15. Cronin Jr, J.J., Brady, M.K., Hult, G.T.M.: Assessing the effects of quality, value, and customer satisfaction on consumer behavioral intentions in service environments. J. Retail. **76**(2), 193–218 (2000)
16. Boulding, W., et al.: A dynamic process model of service quality: from expectations to behavioral intentions. J. Mark. Res. **30**(1), 7–27 (1993)
17. Woodruff, R.B.: Customer value: the next source for competitive advantage. J. Acad. Mark. Sci. **25**(2), 139 (1997)
18. Agbor, J.M.: The Relationship between Customer Satisfaction and Service Quality: a study of three Service sectors in Umeå (2011)
19. Parasuraman, A.: Reflections on gaining competitive advantage through customer value. J. Acad. Mark. Sci. **25**(2), 154 (1997)
20. Yang, Z., Peterson, R.T.: Customer perceived value, satisfaction, and loyalty: the role of switching costs. Psychol. Mark. **21**(10), 799–822 (2004)
21. Reichheld, F.F., Teal, T.: The Loyalty Effect: The Hidden Force Behind Growth, Profits, and Lasting Value. Harvard Business School Press, Boston (1996)
22. Rousseau, D.M., et al.: Not so different after all: a cross-discipline view of trust. Acad. Manag. Rev. **23**(3), 393–404 (1998)
23. Singh, J., Sirdeshmukh, D.: Agency and trust mechanisms in consumer satisfaction and loyalty judgments. J. Acad. Mark. Sci. **28**(1), 150–167 (2000)
24. Aviva: The evidence: Auto repair fraud (2017). https://www.avivacanada.com/fightfraud/the-evidence
25. Pedersen, K., Wesley, A.: 'You have to upsell them': marketplace exposes how dealerships push maintenance you don't need (2017). https://www.cbc.ca/news/business/marketplace-dealerships-service-upselling-1.4300557
26. Janakiraman, N., Syrdal, H.A., Freling, R.: The effect of return policy leniency on consumer purchase and return decisions: a meta-analytic review. J. Retail. **92**(2), 226–235 (2016)
27. Busse, M.R., Israeli, A., Zettelmeyer, F.: Repairing the damage: the effect of price knowledge and gender on auto repair price quotes. J. Mark. Res. **54**(1), 75–95 (2017)
28. Payne, A., Frow, P.: A strategic framework for customer relationship management. J. Mark. **69**(4), 167–176 (2005)
29. Doney, P.M., Cannon, J.P.: An examination of the nature of trust in buyer-seller relationships. J. Mark. **61**, 35–51 (1997)
30. Wood, W., Neal, D.T.: The habitual consumer. J. Consum. Psychol. **19**(4), 579–592 (2009)
31. Seetharaman, P.: Modeling multiple sources of state dependence in random utility models: a distributed lag approach. Mark. Sci. **23**(2), 263–271 (2004)
32. Limayem, M., Hirt, S.G., Cheung, C.M.: How habit limits the predictive power of intention: the case of information systems continuance. MIS Q., 705–737 (2007)
33. Aarts, H., Verplanken, B., Van Knippenberg, A.: Predicting behavior from actions in the past: repeated decision making or a matter of habit? J. Appl. Soc. Psychol. **28**(15), 1355–1374 (1998)
34. Tobias, R.: Changing behavior by memory aids: a social psychological model of prospective memory and habit development tested with dynamic field data. Psychol. Rev. **116**(2), 408 (2009)
35. Darley, W.K., Luethge, D.J., Thatte, A.: Exploring the relationship of perceived automotive salesperson attributes, customer satisfaction and intentions to automotive service department patronage: the moderating role of customer gender. J. Retail. Consum. Serv. **15**(6), 469–479 (2008)
36. Rai, A.K., Srivastava, M.: Customer loyalty attributes: a perspective. NMIMS Manag. Rev. **22**(2), 49–76 (2012)

37. Bennett, R., Rentschler, R.: Foreword by the guest editors. Corp. Reput. Rev. **6**(3), 207–210 (2003)
38. Whitmeyer, J.M.: Effects of positive reputation systems. Soc. Sci. Res. **29**(2), 188–207 (2000)
39. Loureiro, S.M.C., Sarmento, E.M., Le Bellego, G.: The effect of corporate brand reputation on brand attachment and brand loyalty: Automobile sector. Cogent Bus. Manag. **4**(1), 1360031 (2017)
40. Srinivasan, S.S., Anderson, R., Ponnavolu, K.: Customer loyalty in e-commerce: an exploration of its antecedents and consequences. J. Retail. **78**(1), 41–50 (2002)
41. Sengupta, A.S., Balaji, M., Krishnan, B.C.: How customers cope with service failure? A study of brand reputation and customer satisfaction. J. Bus. Res. **68**(3), 665–674 (2015)
42. Bitner, M.J.: Servicescapes: the impact of physical surroundings on customers and employees. J. Mark. **56**, 57–71 (1992)
43. Wakefield, K.L., Blodgett, J.G.: The effect of the servicescape on customers' behavioral intentions in leisure service settings. J. Serv. Mark. **10**(6), 45–61 (1996)
44. Lin, I.Y.: Evaluating a servicescape: the effect of cognition and emotion. Int. J. Hosp. Manag. **23**(2), 163–178 (2004)
45. Reimer, A., Kuehn, R.: The impact of servicescape on quality perception. Eur. J. Mark. **39**(7/8), 785–808 (2005)
46. Kim, W.G., Moon, Y.J.: Customers' cognitive, emotional, and actionable response to the servicescape: a test of the moderating effect of the restaurant type. Int. J. Hosp. Manag. **28**(1), 144–156 (2009)
47. Harris, L.C., Ezeh, C.: Servicescape and loyalty intentions: an empirical investigation. Eur. J. Mark. **42**(3/4), 390–422 (2008)
48. Qualtrics: Panel Management (2017). http://www.qualtrics.com/panel-management/
49. Finstad, K.: Response interpolation and scale sensitivity: evidence against 5-point scales. J. Usability Stud. **5**(3), 104–110 (2010)
50. Delice, A.: The sampling issues in quantitative research. Educ. Sci. Theory Pract. **10**(4), 2001–2018 (2010)
51. Leung, L.: Validity, reliability, and generalizability in qualitative research. J. Fam. Med. Prim. Care **4**(3), 324 (2015)
52. Saunders, M.N.: Research Methods for Business Students, 5th edn. Pearson Education, New Delhi (2011)
53. Hair, J.F., et al.: A Primer on Partial Least Squares Structural Equation Modeling (PLS-SEM). Sage Publications, Thousand Oaks (2016)
54. Ringle, C.M., Wende, S., Becker, J.-M.: SmartPLS3. SmartPLS, Bönningstedt (2015). http://www.smartpls.com/
55. Chin, W.W.: Bootstrap cross-validation indices for PLS path model assessment. In: Esposito, V., Chin, W., Henseler, J., Wang, H. (eds.) Handbook of Partial Least Squares. Springer Handbooks of Computational Statistics, pp. 83–97. Springer, Heidelberg (2010). https://doi.org/10.1007/978-3-540-32827-8_4
56. Fornell, C., Larcker, D.F.: Evaluating structural equation models with unobservable variables and measurement error. J. Mark. Res. **18**, 39–50 (1981)
57. Visser, P.S., et al.: Mail surveys for election forecasting? An evaluation of the Columbus Dispatch poll. Public Opin. Q. **60**(2), 181–227 (1996)
58. Henseler, J., Sarstedt, M.: Goodness-of-fit indices for partial least squares path modeling. Comput. Stat., 1–16 (2013)
59. Cronbach, L.J., Meehl, P.E.: Construct validity in psychological tests. Psychol. Bull. **52**(4), 281–302 (1955)

60. Santos, J.R.A.: Cronbach's alpha: a tool for assessing the reliability of scales. J. Ext. **37**(2), 1–5 (1999)
61. Bollen, K.A.: Evaluating effect, composite, and causal indicators in structural equation models. MIS Q. **35**(2), 359–372 (2011)
62. Dasu, S., Chase, R.B.: Designing the soft side of customer service. MIT Sloan Manag. Rev. **52**(1), 33 (2010)
63. Arora, P., Narula, S.: Linkages between service quality, customer satisfaction and customer loyalty: a literature review. IUP J. Mark. Manag. **17**(4), 30 (2018)

Smartphones as an Opportunity to Increase Sales in Brick-and-Mortar Stores: Identifying Sales Influencers Based on a Literature Review

Robert Zimmermann[1(✉)], Andreas Auinger[1], and René Riedl[1,2]

[1] University of Applied Sciences Upper Austria, Steyr, Austria
{robert.zimmermann,andreas.auinger,
rene.riedl}@fh-steyr.at
[2] Johannes Kepler University, Linz, Austria
rene.riedl@jku.at

Abstract. The increasing popularity of smartphones, the constant rise of e-commerce turnover and plungingdepartment storesales have a significant impact on brick-and-mortar stores revenue. Nevertheless, brick-and-mortar revenue still makes up 90% of total retail revenue. This gives rise to the question of how smartphones affect sales in brick-and-mortar stores. In order to investigate the impact of smartphones on brick-and-mortar store sales, this article presents the results of a literature review, summarizing statements about the impact of smartphones on brick-and-mortar store sales into sales influencers. These sales influencerswere categorized into three main types of sales drivers, namely: Utilitarian drivers, cost and time reduction drivers and hedonic drivers. Subsequently, the categorized statements were evaluated according to their potential positive or negative influence on sales. The resulting overview provides information about the current status of research in the field of smartphones as sales influencers in brick-and-mortar stores. It reveals extensively as well as partially researched sales influencers. Hence, the overview also acts as call for future research, encouraging research progression in the field of smartphone influenced sales in brick-and-mortar stores. It can be concluded that, according to the current literature, smartphones have the potential to increase sales in brick-and-mortar stores. However, the variety of sales influencers identified suggests that research is scattered. Hence, future research is needed to analyse how strongly each individual sales influencer affects sales in brick-and-mortar stores.

Keywords: Smartphone · Brick-and-mortar stores · Sales

1 Introduction

By the year 2018 the smartphone has become part of the everyday lives of 2.6 billion people [1]. E-commerce revenue of 2018 grew 15% worldwide compared to 2017 summing up to €1,617,053 million [2] from which 63.5% were made through mobile retail [3]. In comparison, department store revenue peaked in 2001 and plunged by 36% until 2018 [4–6]. The emergence of the smartphone as an omnipotent device which for example allows for instant information search, social interactions and online

---

The original version of this chapter was revised: This chapter was mistakenly published as a regular chapter instead of open access. The correction to this chapter is available at https://doi.org/10.1007/978-3-030-22335-9_26

© The Author(s) 2019
F. F.-H. Nah and K. Siau (Eds.): HCII 2019, LNCS 11588, pp. 82–98, 2019.
https://doi.org/10.1007/978-3-030-22335-9_6

shopping [7], made some authors forecast the end of traditional retail [8, 9] and even its complete disappearance [10, 11]. However, business frombrick-and-mortar stores still accounts for 90% of total retail revenue [12], wherefore it is unlikely to suffer a major decline of importance in the near future. Nevertheless, smartphones are disrupting brick-and-mortar store business. For example, it is argued that showrooming effects can have a strong impact on brick-and-mortar store sales, or that an informed customer will switch from an in-store offer to an online offer as soon as the price is lower (e.g. [13–15]). However, it is also argued thatthe use of smartphones can drive brick-and-mortar store sales by providing an augmented personalized customer experience or that mobile payments can lead to a more streamlined and efficient shopping experience [16–19]. To investigate these conflicting arguments we conducted a literature review, which identifies how the use of smartphones in brick-and-mortar stores can affect their sales. Consequently, the guiding research questions of this paper are:

I: Which smartphone-based factors affect sales in brick-and-mortar stores?
II: Where is additional research needed to complement the understanding of smartphone related influence on sales in brick-and-mortar stores?

This literature review is based on the concept of Vom Brocke et al. [20] and accordingly structured in the following way: First, the "Scope" of the literature review is presented, followed by the underlying "Search Process" and a comprehensive "Literature Analysis and Synthesis". Afterwards, the results of the literature analysis and synthesis are "discussed", a concluding call for future research is madeand the "Limitations" of the literature review are outlined. The paper ends with a conclusion.

2 Literature Review

2.1 Scope

The focus of this literature review is to identify research outcomes of previous studies, which dealt with the use of smartphones in brick-and-mortar stores and their influence on brick-and-mortar store sales. We summarize previous research and present an overview of possible influencers, which influence sales in brick-and-mortar stores. In the context of Vom Brocke et al. [20], we hereby take a neutral perspective, as we collect rather than criticize available literature. The literature review aims at specialist scholars who are looking for future research opportunities and practitioners who want to have an overview of sales enhancing techniques using smartphones in brick-and-mortar stores. We give an exhaustive coverage of the literature, as we want to summarize the current status of smartphone based sales enhancing techniques in brick-and-mortar stores.

2.2 Search Process

To identify literature, which deals with the topic of how to influence sales in brick-and-mortar stores with the use of smartphones, the databases DBIS, Science Direct, Business Source Premier and Web of Science were used. All databases were screened using the keyword string "(Smartphone* AND (Brick and Mortar) AND Sales)" in all search fields (DBIS: "All Fields"/Science Direct: "Articles with these terms"/Business Source Premier: "TX All Text"/Web of Science: "TS="). Additionally, the timeframe was set to cover the period from 2007 to 2018. This timeframe was chosen because of the significant shift in smartphone technology brought about by the launch of the iPhone in 2007. Also, the database option of including only academic journals was used. The search was executed in November 2018 and revealed the following number of articles per database: DBIS (155), Science Direct (112), Business Source Premier (108), Web of Science (0). Next, the search results were checked for promising titles and if one was identified, the abstract was read to evaluate if the paper contains information about the influence of smartphones on sales in brick-and-mortar stores. When this condition was met, the paper was included in the final set of papers. To discover additional literature the included papers were used in citation mining including forward and backward search bringing the final number of included papers to 26.

2.3   Literature Analysis and Synthesis

Analysis. To analyze the 26 papers, they were screened for statements indicating an influence of smartphones on sales in brick-and-mortar stores. Afterwards, these statements were rated according to whether they propose a positive (+), neutral (0) or negative (-) influence on sales. They were then summarized into multiple sales influencers (SI) to give a more condensed overview of the various possibilities to influence sales in brick-and-mortar stores with the use of smartphones. Additionally, the statements were assigned to three sales drivers (SD), to allow for a top-level overview of their influence on sales in brick-and-mortar stores. The sales drivers are based on shopper values identified by Willems et al. [13] and consequently split up into Utilitarian Drivers (UD), Cost and Time reduction Drivers (CTrD) and Hedonic Drivers (HD). They are described below and their corresponding sales influencers and the underlying statements are presented in Tables 1, 2, 3. Each statement could be assigned to multiple sales influencers if the statement fitted into more than one description. We paraphrased the original statements to give a more condensed summary of information.

Utilitarian Drivers. Utilitarian drivers describe opportunities, which can affect sales by influencing the customer's shopping experience with the use of a smartphone by providing additional product information, the possibility to compare products or the option for personalization or customization.

Cost and Time Reduction Drivers. This category contains all influences on sales, which present their value by either reducing costs or saving time for the customer or the retailer when using a smartphone in a brick-and-mortar store.

Hedonic Drivers. Hedonic drivers affect sales by altering the customer experience with the use of smartphones in brick-and-mortar stores by providing social interactions, additional experiences and the non-shopping related or playful use of phones.

Table 1. Literature review – utilitarian drivers.

SalesInfluencer	Utilitarian DriversInfluence - Statement
Showrooming	(-) Young adults use smartphones when bargain hunting. They try products in-store to make sure they fit properly, then purchase them online at a lower price [15]
Retailer App	(+) Using an app enables retailers to send personalized promotions, provide in-store navigation and in-store pick up options, thus enabling retailers to increase sales and cut labor costs. Perceived ease of use, usefulness and adoption likelihood are regarded highly by customers [17]
MobileScanning	(0) Mobile scanning is not perceived as more enjoyable nor as having a greater utilitarian benefit compared to fixed scanning. The authors also found that mobile unassisted scanning with a fixed unassisted checkout was a preferred service mode, while there was evidence that mobile assisted scanning with mobile assisted payment was the least preferred checkout mode [21]
Personalized Mobile Coupons	(+) Personalized coupons sent to mobile phones which offer price reductions lead to an increase in-store revenue [22] (+) Mobile coupons based on a personalized shopping list that require shoppers to travel farther from their planned path result in a substantial increase in unplanned spending compared to coupons for an unplanned category near their planned path [23]
Personalized Offers	(+) Exclusive offers for customers based on their previous purchase behavior have limited positive impact on the purchase decision [24]
LocationTargetedMobile Ads	(+) Product ads received close to the actual product have an high impact on the purchase decision [24]
Location Based Information	(0) Location based information services are perceived as useful by customers [25]
Information Search Differences by Product Type	(0) High involvement product categories attract higher smartphone use for decision support in retail [16]
Information Search Differences by Gender	(0) Young adult men have a significantly higher tendency than young adult women to conduct smartphone searches for product information and price of electronics. Young adult women ask for advice regarding clothing with their smartphone significantly more often than young adult men [16]
In-StoreGuidance	(+) Providing customers with a personalized shopping route based on their shopping list can lead to an increase in brick-and-mortar revenue if the provided route is optimized by incorporating customers previous shopping behavior [22] (+) If consumers using smartphones are presented a hyper relevant shopping experience through "In-Store Guidance" retailers can capture millions in extra revenue [18]

(continued)

Table 1. (*continued*)

SalesInfluencer	Utilitarian DriversInfluence - Statement
Location Based Promotions	(-) The majority of customers do not like to be bothered with location based promotions [26]
InformationSearch	(-) Consumers using mobile technology in a shopping related way in-store, purchase fewer unplanned items and fail to purchase more planned items [27]
	(-) Young adults use their smartphone to obtain information about their desired products which makes them feel more knowledgeable and competent, to the point where they feel they have more knowledge about products than the shop assistants. This allows them to challenge the "sales pitch," and empowers them in their relationships with retailers [15]
	(-) Using mobile phones in a task related manner leads to fewer unplanned purchases [28]
	(0) Consumers recognize differences in online and offline prices which influences their evaluation of the shop's price competence, their trust in the shop and their patronage of it [29]
	(+) Shopping related mobile phone use causes consumers to become distracted from their shopping task. Once distracted, they spend more time in the store, attend to shelf information more, and divert from their normal path more often, which ultimately increases the amount they purchase. This effect gets stronger with increasing customer age [30]
	(+) Mobile devices connected to inventory management can be used by staff to reduce stock outs and also to inform the customer about in-store stock levels, therefore, improve customer experience and leads to an increase in sales [31]
	(+) Providing customers with local information such as item availability at a nearby store or local store hours, fills in information gaps that keep consumers away from stores [7]
	(+) Mobile technology provides customers with increased access to information about product, location, special events and promotions which keeps them from looking elsewhere and makes them stay in-store, thus increasing in-store sales [31]
	(+) The more searching consumers do on their phones, the more they experience an increase in perceived control over the buying process, which fosters their purchase intention [32]
Location Targeted Mobile Coupons	(+) Location of mobile coupon delivery significantly influences redemption rate - the closer the more redemptions [33]
Customized Mobile Coupon Expiry Length	(+) Expiry length influences the redemption rate of mobile coupons - the shorter the more redemptions [33]
Customized MobileCoupon Delivery Day	(+) Day of the week affects mobile coupon redemption rate - Monday and Tuesday morning having the highest impact [33]

(*continued*)

Table 1. (*continued*)

SalesInfluencer	Utilitarian DriversInfluence - Statement
Competitive Locational Coupon Targeting	(+) Competitive locational targeting produced increasing returns to promotional discount [34]
Coupons Locational Targeting own Retail Store	(-) Targeting retailers' own location produced decreasing returns to discounts, indicating saturation effects and profit cannibalization [34]
Proximity Marketing	(0) Using proximity marketing enables retailers to send personalized real time promotions, thus enabling retailers to increase redemptions of proximity offers. Perceived ease of use and usefulness are regarded highly by customers. Nevertheless adoption likelihood is only average [17]
Product Recommendations	(+) If consumers using smartphones are presented a hyper relevant shopping experience through "Product Recommendations" retailers can capture millions in extra revenue [18]
ReadingReviews	(+) If consumers using smartphones are presented a hyper relevant shopping experience through "Reviews" retailers can capture millions in extra revenue [18]
Mobile Recommendation Agent	(+) Mobile Recommendation Agents (MRA) and corresponding infrastructures might increase the sales volume of retail stores through an increase of consumer frequency – predicted by consumers' intention to prefer MRA-enabled retail stores – and the potential of product purchases – predicted by the consumers' intention to purchase a product after using the MRA [35]

Synthesis. Looking at each individual paper, 20 dealt with utilitarian drivers, 14 with cost and time reduction drivers and 12 with hedonic drivers. The papers stretched along the following timeline: No paper published in 2007, in the years 2008–2013 one paper a year, in the years 2014 and 2015 four papers each, in 2016 two papers, in the year 2017 seven papers and in the year 2018 four papers were published.

From the 26 papers included in this literature review we could extract 56 statements about the influence of smartphones on sales in brick-and-mortar stores, of which 39 presented a positive, 8 a neutral and 9 a negative influence on sales in brick-and-mortar stores. Most statements belonged to the category of utilitarian drivers (total: 31/negative: 6/neutral 6/positive 19), followed by cost and time reduction drivers (total: 25/negative: 5/neutral 1/positive 19) and hedonic drivers (total: 23/negative: 2/neutral 3/positive 18) (see also Fig. 1).

The 56 statements were condensed into 29 sales influencers. The number of papers dealing with each individual sales influencer as well as each paper's predicted influence regarding sales in brick-and-mortar stores can be seen in Table 4.

Table 2. Literature review – cost and time reduction drivers.

SalesInfluencer	Cost and Time reduction DriversInfluence - Statement
Showrooming	(-) Showrooming decreases profit for online and offline retailers [14] (-) Showrooming enhances price competition, leading to lower profits [13] (-) Young adults use smartphones when bargain hunting. They try products in-store to make sure they fit properly, then purchase them online at a lower price [15]
MobileCoupons	(+) Mobile coupons work as a value driver for stores though their impact on the purchase decision is limited [24]
Face Value of MobileCoupons	(+) Face value dominates m-coupon effectiveness [33]
Product Type Customized MobileCoupons	(+) Product type influences mobile coupon effectiveness - the cheaper the product the more redemptions [33]
ScanandPay	(+) Using Scan and Pay enables retailers to reduce the number of cashiers and customer waiting time, thus enabling retailers to cut costs and improve customer experience. Perceived ease of use, usefulness and adoption likelihood are regarded high by customers [17] (+) Mobile check out increases both customer service levels (in terms of speeding up the process) as well as retailer internal performance [36]
MobilePayments	(+) Mobile Payments can lead to an improvement of customer experience by simplifying coupon redemption [31] (+) Mobile Payments can lead to an improvement of customer experience by reducing wait times. Mobile Payment reduces counters in brick-and-mortar stores freeing up floor space for more productive use [31]
Retailer App	(+) App users on average save 60 s while shopping. Purchasing time for app users is stable throughout the day, even in the presence of queues during morning and afternoon rush hours [19] (+) Using an app enables retailers to send personalized promotions, provide in-store navigation and in-store pick up options, thus enabling retailers to increase sales and cut labor costs. Perceived ease of use, usefulness and adoption likelihood are regarded highly by customers [17]
Personalized MobileCoupons	(+) Personalized coupons sent to mobile phones which offer price reductions lead to an increase in-store revenue [22] (+) Mobile coupons based on a personalized shopping list that require shoppers to travel farther from their planned path result in a substantial increase in unplanned spending compared to coupons for an unplanned category near their planned path [23]

(continued)

Table 2. (*continued*)

SalesInfluencer	Cost and Time reduction DriversInfluence - Statement
SpecialOffers	(+) If consumers using smartphones are presented a hyper relevant shopping experience through "Special Offers" retailers can capture millions in extra revenue [18]
Personalized Offers	(+) If consumers using smartphones are presented a hyper relevant shopping experience through "Targeted Offers" retailers can capture millions in extra revenue [18] (+) Exclusive offers for customers based on their previous purchase behavior have limited positive impact on the purchase decision [24]
Information Search	(+) Mobile technology provides customers with increased access to information about product, location, special events and promotions which keeps them from looking elsewhere and makes them stay in-store, thus increasing in-store sales [31]
Location Based Promotions	(-) The majority of customers do not like to be bothered with location based promotions [26]
Location Targeted Mobile Coupons	(+) Location of mobile coupon delivery significantly influences redemption rate - the closer the more redemptions [33]
Customized Mobile Coupon Expiry Length	(+) Expiry length influences the redemption rate of mobile coupons - the shorter the more redemptions [33]
Customized MobileCoupon Delivery Day	(+) Day of the week affects mobile coupon redemption rate - Monday and Tuesday morning having the highest impact [33]
Competitive Locational Coupon Targeting	(+) Competitive locational targeting produced increasing returns to promotional discount [34]
Coupons Locational Targeting own Retail Store	(-) Targeting retailers' own location produced decreasing returns to discounts, indicating saturation effects and profit cannibalization [34]
Proximity Marketing	(0) Using proximity marketing enables retailers to send personalized real time promotions, thus enabling retailers to increase redemptions of proximity offers. Perceived ease of use and usefulness are regarded highly by customers. Nevertheless adoption likelihood is only average [17]

Most papers (8/26 = 31%) conducted research about the sales influencer "Information Search". "Mobile Payment" was the second most covered sales influencer (5/26 = 19%). The sales influencers "Showrooming", "Distraction", "Scan and Pay" and "Personalized Mobile Coupons" were covered by three papers each (3/26 = 12%). The rest of the sales influencers were covered by either two (4 sales influencers; 7.7%) or one paper (19 sales influencers; 3.8%).

Table 3. Literature review – hedonic drivers.

SalesInfluencer	Hedonic DriversInfluence - Statement
Showrooming	(-) Young adults use smartphones when bargain hunting. They try products in-store to make sure they fit properly, then purchase them online at a lower price [15]
Scan and Pay	(+) If consumers using smartphones are presented a hyper relevant shopping experience through "Scan and Pay" retailers can capture millions in extra revenue [18]
MobilePayments	(0) Mobile payment scenarios do not entail greater privacy concerns compared to fixed payment [21] (+) If consumers using smartphones are presented a hyper relevant shopping experience through "Mobile Payments" retailers can capture millions in extra revenue [18] (+) Mobile payment, as an innovative payment option, leads to more positive overall price image judgments by customers, which contributes to a greater store loyalty [37] (+) Mobile payment significantly increases customers' willingness to pay when compared to cash payments [37] (+) All interviewed merchants view enhancement of the customer shopping experience as a primary benefit of mobile payments, although some are concerned their customers may find mobile commerce or payment applications burdensome or complex [38]
Retailer App	(+) Using an app enables retailers to send personalized promotions, provide in-store navigation and in-store pick up options, thus enabling retailers to increase sales and cut labor costs. Perceived ease of use, usefulness and adoption likelihood are regarded highly by customers [17]
MobileScanning	(+) If consumers using smartphones are presented a hyper relevant shopping experience through "Scan QR Code" retailers can capture millions in extra revenue [18] (0) Mobile scanning is not perceived as more enjoyable nor as having a greater utilitarian benefit compared to fixed scanning. The authors also argue that mobile unassisted scanning with a fixed unassisted checkout was a preferred service mode, while there was evidence that mobile assisted scanning with mobile assisted payment was the least preferred checkout mode [21]
SocialSharing	(0) Young adults use smartphones to ask for advice and feedback concerning their planned in-store purchases using their social media channels [15]
Distraction	(-) The non-shopping related use of mobile technology negatively impacts shoppers' ability to recall in-store stimuli [27] (+) Non-shopping related use of smartphones causes consumers to become distracted from their shopping task. Once distracted, they spend more time in the store, attend to shelf information more, and divert from their normal path more often, which ultimately increases the amount they purchase. This effect gets stronger with increasing customer age. This effect is also present but not as strong in shopping related smartphone use [30] (+) Using mobile phones in a task unrelated manner leads to more unplanned purchases [28]

(continued)

Table 3. (*continued*)

SalesInfluencer	Hedonic DriversInfluence - Statement
	(+) Task unrelated device use plays in consumers' reliance on in-store signage and promotion signals during decision-making [28]
Personalized Mobile Coupons	(+) Shoppers are more likely to shop in brick-and-mortar stores that provide personalized coupons and exclusive offers [7]
SpecialOffers	(+) If consumers using smartphones are presented a hyper relevant shopping experience through "Special Offers" retailers can capture millions in extra revenue [18]
Personalized Offers	(+) If consumers using smartphones are presented a hyper relevant shopping experience through "Targeted Offers" retailers can capture millions in extra revenue [18]
Information Search	(+) The more searching consumers do on their phones, the more they experience an increase in perceived control over the buying process, which fosters their purchase intention [32]
In-StoreGuidance	(+) If consumers using smartphones are presented a hyper relevant shopping experience through "In-Store Guidance" retailers can capture millions in extra revenue [18]
Product Recommendations	(+) If consumers using smartphones are presented a hyper relevant shopping experience through "Product Recommendations" retailers can capture millions in extra revenue [18]
ReadingReviews	(+) If consumers using smartphones are presented a hyper relevant shopping experience through "Reviews" retailers can capture millions in extra revenue [18]
Mobile Recommendation Agent	(+) Mobile Recommendation Agents (MRA) and corresponding infrastructures might increase the sales volume of retail stores through an increase of consumer frequency – predicted by consumers' intention to prefer MRA-enabled retail stores – and the potential of product purchases – predicted by the consumers' intention to purchase a product after using the MRA [35]

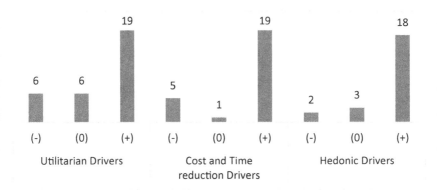

Fig. 1. Descriptive results of literature review – statements

Table 4. Overview sales influencer.

SI	$\sum$ UD statements	$\sum$ UD P.	$\sum$ CTrD statements	$\sum$ CTrD P.	$\sum$ HD statements	$\sum$ HD P.	$\sum$ P.
Information Search	(-)3 [15, 27, 28] (0)1 [29] (+)5 [7, 30–32]	8	(+)1 [31]	1	(+)1 [32]	1	8
Mobile Payments	N/A	0	(+)2 [31]	1	(0)1 [21] (+)4 [18, 37, 38]	4	5
Showrooming	(-)1 [15]	1	(-)3 [13–15]	3	(-)1[15]	1	3
Distraction	N/A	0	N/A	0	(-)1 [27] (+)3 [28, 39]	3	3
Scan and Pay	N/A	0	(+)2 [17, 36]	2	(+)1 [18]	1	3
Personalized Mobile Coupons	(+)2 [22, 23]	2	(+)2 [22, 23]	2	(+)1 [7]	1	3
Mobile Scanning	(0)1[21]	1	N/A	0	(0)1 [21] (+)1 [18]	2	2
In-Store Guidance	(+)2[18, 22]	2	N/A	0	(+)1 [18]	1	2
Retailer App	(+)1 [17]	1	+2 [17, 19]	2	(+)1 [17]	1	2
Personalized Offers	(+)1 [24]	1	(+)2 [18, 24]	2	(+)1 [18]	1	2
Coupons Locational Targeting Own Retail Store	(-)1 [34]	1	(-)1 [34]	1	N/A	0	1
Location Based Promotions	(-)1 [26]	1	(-)1 [26]	1	N/A	0	1
Information Search Differences by Gender	(0)1 [16]	1	N/A	0	N/A	0	1
Information Search Differences by Product Type	(0)1 [16]	1	N/A	0	N/A	0	1
Location Based Information	(0)1 [25]	1	N/A	0	N/A	0	1
Social Sharing	N/A	0	N/A	0	(0)1 [15]	1	1
Face Value of Mobile Coupons	N/A	0	(+)1 [33]	1	N/A	0	1
Location Targeted Mobile Ads	(+)1 [24]	1	N/A	0	N/A	0	1

(*continued*)

Table 4. (*continued*)

SI	$\sum$ UD statements	$\sum$ UD P.	$\sum$ CTrD statements	$\sum$ CTrD P.	$\sum$ HD statements	$\sum$ HD P.	$\sum$ P.
Mobile Coupons	N/A	0	(+)1 [24]	1	N/A	0	1
Product Type Customized Mobile Coupons	N/A	0	(+)1 [33]	1	N/A	0	1
Competitive Locational Coupon Targeting	(+)1 [34]	1	(+)1 [34]	1	N/A	0	1
Customized Mobile Coupon Delivery Day	(+)1 [33]	1	(+)1 [33]	1	N/A	0	1
Customized Mobile Coupon Expiry Length	(+)1 [33]	1	(+)1 [33]	1	N/A	0	1
Location Targeted Mobile Coupons	(+)1 [33]	1	(+)1 [33]	1	N/A	0	1
Mobile Recommendation Agent	(+)1 [35]	1	N/A	0	(+)1 [35]	1	1
Product Recommendations	(+)1 [18]	1	N/A	0	(+)1 [18]	1	1
Proximity Marketing	(+)1 [17]	1	(+)1 [17]	1	N/A	0	1
Reading Reviews	(+)1 [18]	1	N/A	0	(+)1 [18]	1	1
Special Offers	N/A	0	(+)1 [18]	1	(+)1 [18]	1	1

P. = Papers

3 Discussion and a Call for Future Research

3.1 Discussion

Looking at the overall results of the literature review we argue that this paper found more evidence that smartphones rather increase than decrease sales in brick-and-mortar stores, as far more positive (38) than negative statements (9) could be identified. However, no prediction can be made about how strongly each individual factor affects sales in brick-and-mortar stores. The research conducted on the various sales influencers is discussed below.

Extensively Researched Sales Influencer. Looking at the sales influencers in detail, only "Information Search" and "Mobile Payment" have been researchedextensively. "Information Search" was mostly analyzed from a utilitarian driver perspective (see Table 4). Additionally, the highest number of positive (5) but also negative statements (3) was found for this sales influencer. Grewal et al. [30] argues that "Information Search" can lead to distraction which makes customers divert from their normal shopping path and increases purchases (this effect gets stronger with increasing customer age). Paul et al. [31] indicate that "Information Search" leads to a more locked in shopping experience which drives sales rate. Rippé et al. [32] reasons that "Information Search" leads to a perceived increase in control which fosters purchase intention. In contrast, Bellini and Aiolfi [27] and Sciandra and Inman [28] claim, that the use of smartphones in a shopping related way leads to fewer planned and unplanned purchases because mobile device use consumes attentional resources and makes in-store communication strategies less effective. Fuentes and Svingstedt [15] argue that young adults who use their smartphone to obtain information become more knowledgeable and competent to the point where they can effectively challenge the "sales pitch" of shop assistants which leads to a reduction in revenue. Although "Information Search" is seen as positive, retailers should regard it as an ambivalent sales influencer. On the one hand, information search creates an informed and distracted customer who is locked into a perceived superior purchase experience and therefore buys more. Alternatively, it can lead to an over informed customer who has an increased bargaining power and does not rely on in-store stimuli. According to the reviewed literature, factors like gender, age or product categories are moderators [16]. For example, "Information Search" by younger customers is more likely to have a negative effect on sales whereas information search by older customers leads to an increase in sales. Therefore, it can be concluded, that the sales influencer "Information Search" can be viewed as having a sale enhancing effect on older customers and a sales decreasing effect on younger ones. Papers about "Mobile Payment" focused on a hedonic driver perspective. Six positive statements and one neutral statement could be identified, describing that "Mobile Payments" can enhance shopping experience [18, 31, 37, 38], lead to higher positive price image judgement and therefore store loyalty [37], increase the willingness to pay compared to cash payments [37] and do not inherit greater privacy concerns compared to fixed payment[21]. Therefore, mobile payments seem to have a strong influence on brick-and-mortar store sales rate. Although the sales influencers "Information Search" and "Mobile Payment" were researched by the highest number of papers in the conducted literature review this research focused mainly on one sales driver ("Information Search"/UD; "Mobile Payment"/HD). Therefore, we argue that even for these highly researched sales influencers more research, analyzing the sales drivers not yet covered, is needed to give a more comprehensive overview of their influence on sales.

Moderately Researched Sales Influencers. Moderate research has been carried out for the sales influencers "Showrooming", "Distraction", "Scan and Pay" and "Personalized mobile Coupons". Research about "Showrooming" was mainly conducted from a cost and time reduction perspective. According to literature "Showrooming" has a negative influence on sales as it is generally seen as a technique which decreases profit for retailers by enhancing price competition [13, 15, 27, 28]. However, it can be sale enhancing if it is avoided or mitigated by retailers. To counter "Showrooming" Mehra et al. [5] suggest price matching as a short term solution and an exclusivebrand strategy as a long term solution. Another way would be to cut internet access for instore customers but this would also have an unforeseeable impact on other sales influencers, which rely on an internet connection, wherefore it is not recommended. The sales influencer "Distraction" was analyzed from a hedonic driver perspective only. "Distraction" seems to have a mixed influence on sales. Grewal et al. [30] argue that distraction caused by non-shopping related phone use leads to extra time spent and distance walked in brick-and-mortar stores which ultimately leads to an increase in purchases (this effect gets stronger with increasing customer age). Sciandra and Inman [28] add that these distractions lead to more unplanned purchases and customer's reliance on in-store signage and promotion signals significantly improves. In sharp contrast, Bellini and Aiolfi [27] point out that non shopping related use of mobile technology negatively influences the ability of customers to recall in-store stimuli. Taking into account that according to Fuentes and Svingstedt [15] young adults use smartphones to ask for advice and feedback concerning their planed in-store purchases using their social media channels, we argue that young adults are more likely to miss or disregard in-store stimuli as they get distracted by checking their phones for new advice from their peers. Summing it up, the sales influencer "Distraction" is sale enhancing for older customers or customers who do not rely on social advice and feedback and sales diminishing for younger customers or customers who do rely on social advice and feedback. The sales influencer "Scan and Pay" was analyzed mainly from a cost and time reduction perspective. However, one paper also analyzed this aspect from a hedonic driver perspective. As all statements about "Scan and Pay" were positive, and therefore it seems to have a sale enhancing effect. According to literature, this works by enabling retailers to reduce the number of cashiers and customer waiting time, thus enabling retailers to cut costs and improve customer experience. Perceived ease of use, usefulness and adoption likelihood are regarded highly by customers [17]. Additionally, "Scan and Pay" does increase both customer service levels (in terms of speeding up the process) as well as retailer internal performance [36], while also making the shopping experience hyper relevant [18]. "Personalized Mobile Coupons" was mainly researched from a utilitarian driver and cost and time reduction driver perspective, though one paper analyzed it from a hedonic driver perspective. According to literature it positively influences sales in a hedonic way as shoppers prefer shopping in brick-and-mortar stores that provide personalized coupons[7], as well as in utilitarian and cost and time saving ways by offering discounts, based on previous shopping behavior, which require shoppers to travel farther through the retail store [22, 23]. Moderate research about the mentioned sales influencers was published and that research focused mainly on analyzing one type of sales driver. Therefore, we argue that more research needs to carried out to cover the non-addressed sales drivers to obtain a deeper understanding of how these factors can influence sales in brick-and-mortar stores.

Partially Researched Sales Influencers. For all not yet mentioned sales influencers only limited research was found, and therefore it is too early to draw conclusions regarding their impact on brick-and-mortar store sales rate. However, for all sales influencers in this category, with the exception of "Coupons Locational Targeting Own Retail Store and "Location Based Promotions", only positive statements about the influence of smartphones on sales in brick-and-mortar stores could be identified. This substantiates the conclusion that smartphones influence sales rather in a positive than a negative way.

Additional Findings. As 20 of the 26 papers analyzed utilitarian drivers and made 31 of the 56 identified statements (6 negative, 6 neutral 19 positive), we observe an imbalance if compared to cost and time reduction (14 papers/25 statements/5 negative, 1 neutral, 19 positive) and hedonic drivers (12 papers/23 statements/2 negative, 3 neutral, 18 positive). In the years 2007 to 2013 only little research was carried out, whereas after 2014 the quantity of research increased significantly peaking in 2017 with 7 published papers. This is correlated with the rising importance of smartphones in retail in general [3, 40] and the constant growth of e-commerce [2].

3.2   Call for Future Research

Future Research Implications. Summarizing the literature review, we conclude that additional research is needed for all identified sales influencers and sales drivers. Even the extensively researched sales influencers "Information Search" and "Mobile

Payment" have only been examined from either a utilitarian driver or a hedonic driver perspective, whereas even for these sales influencers additional research is needed to better understand their influence on sales in brick-and-mortar stores. Future researchers can use our overview created in Table 4 to identify possible research opportunities for each individual sales influencer. Additionally, we propose that some kind of unifying research is needed which makes it possible to predict the influence of each individual sales influencer on sales in brick-and-mortar stores.

Limitations. Although an extensive literature review with forward and backward search has been conducted, it cannot be guaranteed that all relevant literature has been found. Therefore, while we consider our review as comprehensive, it may not be necessarily exhaustive. In addition, in the present paper we did not take into account all specific store settings, product types, gender implications or other very specific variables. Therefore, one has to be careful when applying results of the extracted statements in different settings.

4   Conclusion

This paper raised the questions "Which smartphone-based factors affect sales in brick-and-mortar stores?" and "Where is additional research needed to complement the understanding of smartphone related influence on sales in brick-and-mortar stores?". Concerning the first research question, 29 sales influencers, which have an influence on sales in brick-and-mortar stores could be identified in literature. Additionally, we come to the conclusion that, in general, smartphones tend to increase sales in brick-and-mortar stores as this paper identified 56 statements from which 39 presented a positive, 8 a neutral and 9 a negative influence on sales. However, as the analyzed papers and their underlying research methods are not comparable we cannot make any prediction on how strongly each individual sales influencer influences sales in brick and mortar stores. Looking at the second research question, we conclude that additional research is needed for every identified sales influencer. This is because either limited research was done for most sales influencers or if the quantity of research was extensive, it was done from one of the three presented sales driver perspectives only.

Acknowledgments. This study has been conducted within the training network project PER-FORM funded by the European Union's Horizon 2020 research and innovation program under the Marie Skłodowska-Curie grant agreement No. 76539. Note: This research reflects only the authors' view. The Agency is not responsible for any use that may be made of the information it contains.

References

1. eMarketer: Smartphone-Nutzer weltweit 2012-2021 | Statista. Prognose zur Anzahl der Smartphone-Nutzer weltweit von 2012 bis 2021 (in Milliarden). https://de.statista.com/statistik/daten/studie/309656/umfrage/prognose-zur-anzahl-der-smartphone-nutzer-weltweit/. Accessed 6 Dec 2018
2. Statista: eCommerce - worldwide | Statista Market Forecast. https://www.statista.com/outlook/243/100/ecommerce/worldwide?currency=eur. Accessed 22 Jan 2019

3. eMarketer and InternetRetailing: Mobile retail commerce sales as percentage of retail e-commerce sales worldwide from 2016 to 2021. https://www.statista.com/statistics/806336/mobile-retail-commerce-share-worldwide/. Accessed 22 Jan 2019
4. Wolf, R.: Here's which brick-and-mortar retailers are getting hit the hardest. https://www.businessinsider.com/brick-and-mortar-retailers-getting-hit-the-hardest-2018-5?IR=T. Accessed 22 Jan 2019
5. US Census Bureau: Department store sales (excluding leased departments) in the United States from 1992 to 2016 (in billion U.S. dollars). https://www.statista.com/statistics/197712/annual-department-store-sales-in-the-us-since-1992/. Accessed 22 Jan 2019
6. ICSC: Sales growth of department stores in Western Europe from 2012 to 2017, by country. https://www.statista.com/statistics/911107/department-store-sales-growth-western-europe/. Accessed 22 Jan 2019
7. Google: Digital Impact on In-Store Shopping: Research Debunks Common Myths. https://think.storage.googleapis.com/docs/digital-impact-on-in-store-shopping_research-studies.pdf. Accessed 3 Dec 2018
8. Helm, S., Kim, S.H., van Riper, S.: Navigating the 'retail apocalypse': a framework of consumer evaluations of the new retail landscape. J. Retail. Consum. Serv. (2018)
9. Peterson, H.: A tsunami of store closings is about to hit the US — and it's expected to eclipse the retail carnage of 2017. https://www.businessinsider.de/store-closures-in-2018-will-eclipse-2017-2018-1?r=US&IR=T. Accessed 23 Jan 2019
10. Winthrop, B., Komisar, R.: I F**king Love that Company. How a New Generation of Brand Builders is Defining the Post-Amazon world. Paramount Market Publishing, Inc., Ithaca (2015)
11. Townsend, M., Surane, J., Orr, E., Cannon, C.: America's 'Retail Apocalypse' Is Really Just Beginning. https://www.bloomberg.com/graphics/2017-retail-debt/. Accessed 23 Jan 2019
12. Dennis, S.: E-Commerce May Be Only 10% Of Retail, But That Doesn't Tell The Whole Story. https://www.forbes.com/sites/stevendennis/2018/04/09/e-commerce-fake-news-the-only-10-fallacy/#22b6767539b4. Accessed 6 Dec 2018
13. Mehra, A., Kumar, S., Raju, J.S.: Competitive strategies for brick-and-mortar stores to counter "showrooming". Manag. Sci. **64**, 3076–3090 (2018)
14. Basak, S., Basu, P., Avittathur, B., Sikdar, S.: A game theoretic analysis of multichannel retail in the context of "showrooming". Decis. Support Syst. **103**, 34–45 (2017)
15. Fuentes, C., Svingstedt, A.: Mobile phones and the practice of shopping: a study of how young adults use smartphones to shop. J. Retail. Consum. Serv. **38**, 137–146 (2017)
16. Eriksson, N., Rosenbröijer, C.-J., Fagerstrøm, A.: Smartphones as decision support in retail stores – the role of product category and gender. Procedia Comput. Sci. **138**, 508–515 (2018)
17. Inman, J.J., Nikolova, H.: Shopper-facing retail technology: a retailer adoption decision framework incorporating shopper attitudes and privacy concerns. J. Retail. **93**, 7–28 (2017)
18. Bradley, J., Macaulay, J., O'Connell, K., Delaney, K., Pinto, A., Barbier, J.: Winning the New Digital Consumer with Hyper-Relevance. In Retail, Insight Is Currency and Context Is King. https://www.startitup.sk/wp-content/uploads/2015/11/ioe-retail-whitepaper.pdf. Accessed 24 Nov 2018
19. Vuckovac, D., Fritzen, P., Fuchs, K., Ilic, A.: From Shopping aids to fully autonomous mobile self-checkouts - a field study in retail. In: Wirtschaftsinformatik 2017 Proceedings, pp. 927–941 (2017)
20. vom Brocke, J., Simon, A., Niehaves, B., Reimer, K., Plattf, R., Cleven, A.: Reconstructing the giant: on the importance of rigour in documenting the literature search process
21. Aloysius, J.A., Hoehle, H., Venkatesh, V.: Exploiting big data for customer and retailer benefits. Int. J. Oper. Prod. Manag. **36**, 467–486 (2016)
22. Klabjan, D., Pei, J.: In-store one-to-one marketing. J. Retail. Consum. Serv. **18**, 64–73 (2011)

23. Hui, S.K., Inman, J.J., Huang, Y., Suher, J.: The effect of in-store travel distance on unplanned spending: applications to mobile promotion strategies. J. Mark. **77**, 1–16 (2013)
24. Bues, M., Steiner, M., Stafflage, M., Krafft, M.: How mobile in-store advertising influences purchase intention: value drivers and mediating effects from a consumer perspective. Psychol. Mark. **34**, 157–174 (2017)
25. Choi, S.: What promotes smartphone-based mobile commerce? Mobile-specific and self-service characteristics. Internet Res. **28**, 105–122 (2018)
26. Rudolph, T., Bassett, M., Weber, M.: Konsumententrends im Schweizer Lebensmitteldetailhandel (2015)
27. Bellini, S., Aiolfi, S.: The impact of mobile device use on shopper behaviour in store: an empirical research on grocery retailing. IBR **10**, 58 (2017)
28. Sciandra, M., Inman, J.: Digital distraction: consumer mobile device use and decision making. SSRN J. (2016)
29. Broeckelmann, P., Groeppel-Klein, A.: Usage of mobile price comparison sites at the point of sale and its influence on consumers' shopping behaviour. Int. Rev. Retail. Distrib. Consum. Res. **18**, 149–166 (2008)
30. Grewal, D., Ahlbom, C.-P., Beitelspacher, L., Noble, S.M., Nordfält, J.: In-store mobile phone use and customer shopping behavior: evidence from the field. J. Mark. **82**, 102–126 (2018)
31. Paul, A., Asmundson, P., Goswami, D., Mawhinney, T., Nannini, J.: Mobile retailing - are you ready for radical change? (2012)
32. Rippé, C.B., Weisfeld-Spolter, S., Yurova, Y., Dubinsky, A.J., Hale, D.: Under the sway of a mobile device during an in-store shopping experience. Psychol. Mark. **34**, 733–752 (2017)
33. Danaher, P.J., Smith, M.S., Ranasinghe, K., Danaher, T.S.: Where, when, and how long: factors that influence the redemption of mobile phone coupons. J. Mark. Res. **52**, 710–725 (2015)
34. Fong, N.M., Fang, Z., Luo, X.: Geo-conquesting: competitive locational targeting of mobile promotions. J. Mark. Res. **52**, 726–735 (2015)
35. Kowatsch, T., Maass, W.: In-store consumer behavior: how mobile recommendation agents influence usage intentions, product purchases, and store preferences. Comput. Hum. Behav. **26**, 697–704 (2010)
36. Andriulo, S., Elia, V., Gnoni, M.G.: Mobile self-checkout systems in the FMCG retail sector. A comparison analysis. Int. J. RF Technol. Res. Appl. **6**, 207–224 (2014)
37. Falk, T., Kunz, W.H., Schepers, J.J.L., Mrozek, A.J.: How mobile payment influences the overall store price image. J. Bus. Res. **69**, 2417–2423 (2016)
38. Hayashi, F., Bradford, T.: Mobile payments: merchants' perspectives. Econ. Rev. **Q II**, 33–58 (2014)
39. Grewal, D., Roggeveen, A.L., Nordfält, J.: The future of retailing. J. Retail. **93**, 1–6 (2017)
40. Gartner: Number of smartphones sold to end users worldwide from 2007 to 2017 (in million units). https://www.statista.com/statistics/263437/global-smartphone-sales-to-end-users-since-2007/. Accessed 23 Jan 2019

eBanking and Digital Money

The Value of Bank Relationship: Evidence from China

Chyi-Lun Chiou[(✉)]

Fu Jen Catholic University, New Taipei City 24205, Taiwan
clchiou@mail.fju.edu.tw

Abstract. This study investigates the influence of bank relationship on the firm's preference on liquidity. We address whether previous bank relationship affects firm value by examining how the value of cash holdings varies with bank relationship. Furthermore, we conduct how financial frictions alter the association between bank relationship and firm value. Using a sample of Chinese listed companies approved bank loans over the period 2008–2017, we find two supportive evidences on bank relationship. First, the marginal value of cash holdings decreases with the depth of bank relationship. Second, the negative impact of the bank relationship on the marginal value of cash holdings is more apparent for financial unconstrained companies. The results suggest that bank relationship is useful to alleviate the information asymmetry problem between the borrower and outside investors and thereby decreases a firm's need and valuation of liquidity. The investigation of bank relationship under distinct financial friction scenarios further supports the unique role of banks in dealing with information asymmetry. Compared to financial unconstrained companies, financial constrained firms is more vulnerable to holdup problem making them hard to experience the benefit of bank relationship. In sum, our study contributes to the literature of the value of bank relationship by showing that the marginal value of cash holdings decreases with close tie with banks because of the ease in information asymmetry.

Keywords: Bank relationship · Information asymmetry · Marginal value of cash holdings

1 Introduction

The literature has long recognized banks as the key channel in resolving information asymmetry in financial markets (Campbel and Kracaw 1980; Diamond 1984; Ramakrishnan and Thakor 1984). The uniqueness of banks hinges on their advantage in gathering private information during the lending process and the capability of monitoring borrowers after loans are approved (Diamond 1984; James 1987). The releasing of private information during the lending process can alleviate the information asymmetry problem between the borrower and outside investors and enhance a firm's ability in obtaining external financing. This study attempts to detect the bank relationship from another channel by examining its impact on liquidity preference.

© Springer Nature Switzerland AG 2019
F. F.-H. Nah and K. Siau (Eds.): HCII 2019, LNCS 11588, pp. 101–118, 2019.
https://doi.org/10.1007/978-3-030-22335-9_7

Specifically, we investigate the impact of lending relationship on the value of cash holdings. We expect that banks can alleviate information asymmetry and financial frictions of the borrowers, and thereby reduce their evaluation on liquidity.

We conduct bank relationship by analyzing the value of cash holdings for two reasons. First, cash holdings construct a significant proportion of balance sheet. The average cash to total asset ratio is around 15% in the well-developed counties such as the United States (Bates et al. 2009) as well as in the emerging markets like China (Kusnadi et al. 2015). Given the magnitude of corporate cash holdings, this is a potentially important channel through which bank relationship can affect firm value. Second, theoretical research argues that cash and line of credit are two main sources of funds for precautionary hedge against the unfavorable capital market friction (Lins et al. 2010). These two liquidity funds are applied to hedge against different risks. Cash is viewed as buffer to protect firms from unexpected cash flow shock in the bad time, while line of credit ensures a firm's capability to take profitable investment in good times. Although cash and line of credit offered by banks are not purely substitute (Lins et al. 2010), the investigation of bank relationship by means of cash is reasonable (Hu et al. 2016).

In spite of the well-documented on bank relationship, very little is known about the direct impact of bank relationship on firm value. In this study we count on evidence form by the listed companies in China to conduct this issue. The Chinese setting provides an ideal laboratory to study bank relationship in the presence of financial constraints and bank-based financial system. The banking system is dominated by state-owned banks in China where the government rules the economic development and the firm's investments by disciplining the lending policy of the commercial banks (Chang et al. 2014). Although the Chinese financial markets is on the path of deregulation and expansion, many companies, including small and median size companies and non-state owned companies, still have trouble in raising external funds. Since the external financing is mainly composed by banking system in this market, the bargaining power of banks is apparent in China and explains why banks may generate significantly impact on the valuation of borrowing company.

We employ two competing theories, the information asymmetry argument and holdup argument, to examine the impact of bank relationship on firm value. This study employs three variables in terms of previous bank loan records to identify the depth of bank relationship, and detect change in firm value by analyzing the marginal value of cash holdings. The main finding is that the marginal value of cash holdings decreases with bank relationship. Furthermore, the negative relationship between bank relationship and the value of cash holdings is more prominent for financial unconstrained firms. The results are consistent with the information asymmetry theory that firms view cash as a buffer to against unexpected shocks on cash flows and suggest that firms with bank relationship prefer less cash holdings because they have less concern on obtaining external financing. The aforementioned statements can well explain the behavior of financial unconstrained firms. However, the potential holdup problem enlarges the damage of lack of liquidity and leads the negative impact of bank relationship on firm value to be less pronounced for financial constrained firms.

The reminder of this study is organized as follows. Section 2 develops two hypotheses about the association between bank relationship and the value of cash holdings. Sections 3 describes the sample and the methodology. Section 4 displays the empirical results of the analysis. Section 5 concludes the paper.

2 Literature Review

2.1 Pros and Cons of Lending Relationship

Financial intermediations such as banks play an important role in diminishing the information asymmetry between borrowers and outsider investors. Banks can generate economies of scale in gathering information and supervising the borrowers in the lending process (Diamond 1984; James 1987). The cumulated information obtained in the previous banking transactions such as granting loans or other financial services allows borrowers to build close tie with banks. The close relationship allows banks experience lower operation costs and monitoring costs when lend to borrowers they are familiar with. Accordingly, it is argued that close bank relationship results in lower cost of bank debt (Berger and Udell 1995; Diamond 1991).

However, researchers also notice that keeping a close relationship with the current lenders is costly (Santos and Winton 2008; Schenone 2010). Given that the firm-specific information revealing in the lending process is hard to share with or transfer to other outsiders, it is difficult for firms to switch to another lenders. Furthermore, firms seeking for new lenders may be classified as lemon because of the adverse selection problem. Therefore, firms are forced to grant loans from the bank they are familiar with when they are in need. Lending bank may receive information rent by charging higher cost of debt (Schenone 2010) or asking for stricter covenants with bank loan deals (Prilmeier 2017). It is called the holdup problem of maintaining close tie with bank.

Previous studies document that relationship banks' information advantage can be explored by the bank loan rates, the amount of credit granted from the relation banks, or the choice between private and public debt (Berger and Udell 1995; Diamond 1991; Rajan 1992). They assert that lending banks extract information rent from the borrowers by setting higher cost of bank debt. Meanwhile, firms choose to issue public debts rather than private bank debt to prevent the holdup costs caused by lending relationship. Given the relevance of holdup costs, how to reflect such costs in an appropriate way is critical, particularly, for companies in developing financial markets where the majority of external funds are provided by banks and the monopoly power of banks is apparent.

Building lending relationship is a value creation or destruction policy would depend on the net impact of these offsetting factors. If the value of a relationship tends to increase over time or more and more borrowers choose to lock into one specific bank, the extra cash holdings should be valueless. On the other hand, if relationship becomes less valuable and if the switching costs arise gradually, we should observe that the marginal value of cash holdings increases with relationship. Keeping a close tie with banks is to reduce the financial constraints when firms need external funds to finance their new projects or repay their debt obligation. If firms find banking relationship has nothing to do with the cheaper source of funds, they have to search other channel to reduce their reliance on the lending relationship. Houston and James (1996) and Santos and Winton (2008) suggest that building multiple bank relationship or borrowing from public debt markets are alternative choices for firms locked-in close lending relationship.

2.2   Liquidity Demand

This study focuses on the information provision function of banks and lock-in issue arising from lending banks in addressing the influence of bank relationship on firms' preference on liquidity. The conventional theorem of liquidity preference can be traced back to the original work of Keynes (1936). From the perspective of shareholder wealth maximization, Opler et al. (1999) summarize two incentives of cash holdings proposed by Keynes (1936): transaction cost motive and precautionary motive. The transaction motive for holding cash arises from the cost of acquiring cash, including raising funds in the capital markets, liquidating existing assets, reducing dividends and investment, renegotiating existing financial contracts. For example, Opler et al. (1999) suggest that firms with specific asset have higher levels of liquid assets.

The precautionary motive, otherwise, emphasizes that holding liquid assets allows the firm to finance its activities and investments without any access of external funds. Hence, holding liquidity assets prevents the possibility of financial constraints when firms need to finance their profitable projects. Following the argument of preference for liquidity asset, I propose that building close tie with banks may decrease the value of cash holdings because of the alleviating financial constraints arising from the less concerns on information asymmetry. However, the marginal value of cash holding is more valuable for firms with lending relationship when the holdup problem worsens and encourages firms to retain more cash to escape from the possible expropriation form by relation banks.

2.3   Hypotheses

In the world of perfect capital markets as stated by Modigliani and Miller (1958), firms can receive sufficient funds from the capital markets to finance their profitable investment projects. The necessity of maintaining internal funds is unclear. However, in practice firms deal with different kinds of external financing constraints due to the information asymmetry problems. Managers are forced to manage their liquidity in an efficient way to ensure the ability to repay debt obligations or to invest profitable projects.

In literature information asymmetry make it harder to raise external funds (Myers and Majluf 1984). When shareholders believe that some value-increasing projects would be forgone due to the financial constraints, they would persuade a company to maintain its financial slackness by hoarding cash at hand (Opler et al. 1999). Faulkender and Wang (2006) argue that if the cash hoarding policy is valuable to the company as well as to shareholders, then a dollar of cash may be worth more than a dollar. In brief, referring to the possible damages or costs from cash flows shortage, shareholders will increase their preference and valuation for liquidity.

Being the most important part of financial intermediations, banks possess the advantage in resolving adverse selection and moral hazard problem in lending process (Diamond 1984; Fama 1985). The critical debate of bank relation is the question of whether the existence of bank relation increases firm value. The uniqueness of bank should rely on the fact that building sustainable relation with a specific bank is beneficial to shareholders. Fama (1985) states that, being the insider lenders, banks can access some proprietary information that are not available to the lenders of arm-length's debts. Lending banks could be the membership of board of directors of the borrowing firm and have the right to guild and monitor the company's decisions. The early evidence of James (1987) supports the argument of Fama (1985) that bank relation is of value. Based on the event study around the bank loans announcement, James finds a significant and positive effect on the stock values of the borrowing firm.

While banks are capable of resolving information asymmetry between borrowers and outsiders, they may use such information advantage to create their own benefits by charging higher loan rates, or intervening borrower's decision making in an inappropriate way. To prevent the possible holdup problem, borrowers may hoard cash in hand and reduce their reliance on bank funds. In this study I attempt to use Chinese companies as my research target to verify my propositions. Khurana et al. (2006) argue that the influence of financial constraints on the external financing is associated with the development of financial markets. Their cross countries evidence reveals that the sensitivity of cash holdings to cash flows decreases with the development of financial markets. Accordingly, we expect that in a less than well-developed financial market such as China, the impact of financial constraints on liquidity will be enlarged.

In this study I address the value of lending relationship by conducting the marginal value of cash holding. The remarkable reward of cash holdings is to be released from the financial constraints set by external capital markets. Referring to the value creation function from reducing information asymmetry, I extend the previous the study of bank loan announcement effect by directly examining the value of bank relation. We propose that bank relationship is associated with lower value of cash holdings due to the ease in information asymmetry. However, the holdup costs associated with close tie with banks encourages firms to retain more cash and increases their evaluation on the excess cash holdings. We expect that financial constrained firms are vulnerable to the holdup problem due to their limitation in finding other channel of external financing. Therefore, in line with the pros and cons of lending relationship, the value of additional cash for financial constrained firms would be less sensitive to the depth of bank relationship. The proposed hypotheses are as follows:

H1: The marginal value of cash holdings decreases with bank relationship.
H2: The negative impact of bank relationship on the marginal value of cash holdings is more pronounced for financial unconstrained firms.

3 Methodology

3.1 The Sample

The required accounting information and stock returns are collected from the China Stock Market & Accounting Research database (CSMAR), including bank loan information, financial statements information, and stock returns. The benchmark returns for the 125 portfolios formed by size, book-to-market ratio of equity, and momentum are also received from CSMAR. The sample covers from 2008 to 2017. We exclude all financial firms and utility firms in the analysis. In addition, we also require firm-year observations should have nonnegative net assets, nonnegative market value of equity, and nonnegative dividends. Since Chinese firms' fiscal reporting calendar is the same as the year/quartet calendar, we use the December financial reports for the analysis (Qian and Yeung 2015). Due to the limitation of bank loans information, the bank loan initiation is available after 1997. Moreover, we only account for the approved loans as our research target. All variables are winsorized at the 1st and 99th percentiles to mitigate the influence of outliers. After the aforementioned adjustments, we obtain a final sample of 3,301 firm-year observations.

3.2 Dependent Variable

In line with the long-run event study framework of Faulkender and Wang (2006), the dependent variable is the excess stock return $(r_{it} - R_{it}^B)$ where r_{it} is the stock return for firm i during fiscal year t and R_{it}^B is stock i's benchmark return at year t. We apply the 125 Fama and French portfolio form on size, book-to-market, and momentum as our benchmark portfolio. A stock's benchmark return at a given year is the return of the portfolio to which the stock belongs to at the fiscal year. To avoid the possible noise from trading suspension, monthly returns with less than 10 trading days during a month or observations with two missing monthly returns in a given year are excluded. The excess return is then defined as the cumulative abnormal returns during a fiscal year.

3.3 Bank Relationship

In literature the measurement of bank relation is multiple (Chang et al. 2014). Since the bank loans information is collected from the announcement of bank loans recorded by the borrowing firm, any approved loan deal represents a successful relation building. Accordingly, bank relationship is defined based on a firm's previous bank loan records. In this study bank loans refers to the lending activities offered by the commercial banks. Loans form by other financial intermediations or syndicated loans are excluded from the analysis.

To verify whether bank relationship is valuable to stockholders, we adopt three proxies for the depth a relationship. The first proxy is based on whether a firm is owned or controlled by the state. We introduce a dummy variable, d_SOE, that equal to one when the firm is classified as state-owned company, and zero otherwise. In China the bank relationship were mandated by the government rather than being driven by economic principles. Many of bank loans initiated by state-owned banks to state-owned enterprise (SOEs) are based on political and policy considerations. To fulfill the duty of SOEs in maintaining social stability by providing consistent disposable income and lowering unemployment rate, state-owned banks provide loans to SOEs even though these companies are unprofitable, non-competitive, or with high default risk. Because the identity of SOEs and state-owned banks were mandated by the Chinese government, such firm-bank relationship is totally exogenous, and is therefore not subjected to the doubt-matching endogeneity problem widely seen in the literature (Chang et al. 2014).

Our second proxy is based on the duration of the bank relationship (*duration*). We utilize the loan approved information offered by the dataset and identify the year when a firm obtained its very first bank loan. The duration variable is then calculated as the difference between the current valuation year and the earliest loan year recorded. Furthermore, we use dummy variable (*d_duration*) to represent a firm has a close tie with bank that equals to one when duration is more than 7 year (sample median in the sample period), and zero otherwise.

The third proxy of bank relationship is the number of lending banks that a firm has received loans five years before the valuation year (*num_bank*). We define a firm has weak relation with one specific bank when it has built relation with different banks. We introduce a dummy variable to represent the multiple bank relation, *d_mulbank*, that equals to one when the company has multiple bank relation, and zero if it only receives loans from single lending bank. Multiple bank relation implies the firm has alternatives in choosing which banks to cooperate with and thereby indicates a weak loyalty of the borrower. In addition, firms with multiple bank relationships are better to absorb financial shocks and have a lower probability of financial distress which lead to firm less reliance on banking. Using the number of bank as an inverse measure of bank relationship, Bonfim et al. (2018) find that conducting another new bank allows borrowing companies to generate lower bank loan rate by 14 to 28 basis points because of the increasing bargaining power of borrowers.

3.4 Control Variables

Referring to the setting of Faulkender and Wang (2006), the control variables can be defined as follows. The market value of equity is defined as the number of shares multiplied by the stock's price at the fiscal year-end.[1] Cash holdings (C_t) is cash plus marketable securities. Earnings (E_t) are calculated as income before tax. Interest expense (I_t) is equal to zero if missing. Net financing (NF_t) is defined as total equity issuance plus debt issuance minus debt redemption.[2] R&D expenditure (RD_t) is equal to zero if missing. Dividend (D_t) is total cash dividends paid to common shareholders, which equals to zero if missing. Leverage (L_t) is defined as market debt ratio, calculated as total debt over the sum of total debt and the market value of equity. To prevent the results

---

[1] The market value of equity refers to the value of all issued shares.

[2] Debt issuance includes the issuance of corporate bonds and funds granted from banks or other financial intermediations.

being dominated by large companies, all firm-specific variables, except for leverage (L_t), are deflated by the 1-year lagged market value of equity, M_{t-1}.

3.5 The Model

In this study we employ the regression framework offered by Faulkender and Wang (2006) to detect the value of cash holdings and investigate how firm value varies with bank relation. The primary regression model setting is shown as follows.

$$
\begin{aligned}
r_{i,t} - R_{i,t}^B = &\beta_0 + \beta_1 \frac{\Delta C_{i,t}}{M_{i,t-1}} + \beta_2 d\_BR_{i,t-1} \times \frac{\Delta C_{i,t}}{M_{i,t-1}} + \beta_3 d\_BR_{i,t-1} + \beta_4 \frac{\Delta E_{i,t}}{M_{i,t-1}} + \beta_5 \frac{\Delta NA_{i,t}}{M_{i,t-1}} \\
&+ \beta_6 \frac{\Delta RD_{i,t}}{M_{i,t-1}} + \beta_7 \frac{\Delta I_{i,t}}{M_{i,t-1}} + \beta_8 \frac{\Delta D_{i,t}}{M_{i,t-1}} + \beta_9 \frac{C_{i,t-1}}{M_{i,t-1}} + \beta_{10} L_{i,t} + \beta_{11} \frac{NF_{i,t}}{M_{i,t-1}} \\
&+ \beta_{12} \frac{C_{i,t-1}}{M_{i,t-1}} \times \frac{\Delta C_{i,t}}{M_{i,t-1}} + \beta_{13} L_{i,t} \times \frac{\Delta C_{i,t}}{M_{i,t-1}} + Industry\_effect + Year\_effect + \varepsilon_{i,t}
\end{aligned}
$$

$$(1)$$

We introduce two variables into the framework, including bank relationship ($d\_BR_{i,t-1}$) and the interaction term of bank relationship and the change in cash holdings ($d\_BR_{i,t-1} \times \Delta C_{i,t}$), and employ this interaction term to detect the impact of bank relationship on the marginal value of cash holdings. $d\_BR_{i,t-1}$ is a dummy variable that equals to one for close bank relation and zero for weak relation when we introduce SOEs and duration in identifying close bank relation. However, we also use the number of lending banks to measure bank relation and define an inverse measure of bank relation, $d\_mulbank$. The inclusion of $d\_BR_{i,t-1}$ in the regression model ensures that the estimated coefficient of the interaction term is the result of the interaction, and not due to bank relation itself. In addition, we employ industry effects and year effects in the analysis to control for unobservable industry characteristics and time effects.

4 Empirical Results

4.1 Preliminary Results

Table 1 reports the summary statistics of the major variables used in this study. The mean (median) value of excess return ($r_t - R_t^B$) on the sample is −16.5% (−16.0%) which is lower that found in Faulkender and Wang (2006). One possibility is that the momentum effect is included in the calculation of benchmark return, while most papers use 25 portfolio formed on size and book-to-market as their benchmark.

The median value of cash change (ΔC_t) is 0.005 which implies that half of the observations attempt to increase their cash holdings. The mean cash holdings level (C_{t-1}) is equilibrium to 15.60% of market equity value at the beginning of the fiscal year, similar to that found in the U.S. of 17.3% shown by Faulkender and Wang (2006). It is noteworthy that the average leverage ratio (L_t) in Chinese listed companies is 35.70%, which is higher than that shown in the U.S of 27.78%. This indicates that Chinese companies utilize more debt financing in support of their business.

Table 1. Summary statistics.

Variables	Mean	SD	Q1	Median	Q3
Dependent var.					
$r_t - R_t^B$	-0.165	0.440	-0.359	-0.160	0.0402
Bank rel.					
d_SOE	0.553	0.497	0	1	1
num_bank	1.106	1.814	0	1	1
$duration$	7.633	4.328	4	7	11
Control var.					
ΔC_t	0.022	0.099	-0.021	0.005	0.042
ΔE_t	0.006	0.055	-0.011	0.004	0.020
ΔNA_t	0.147	0.310	0.003	0.062	0.184
ΔRD_t	0.0002	0.001	0	0	0
ΔI_t	0.002	0.009	-0.001	0.0004	0.004
ΔD_t	0	0.002	0	0	0
C_{t-1}	0.156	0.168	0.046	0.097	0.201
L_t	0.357	0.213	0.181	0.325	0.517
NF_t	0.076	0.181	-0.006	0.022	0.103

The mean and median changes in R&D expense and interest expense are close to zero, implying that the distribution of the change in R&D expenses as well as interest expense are relatively symmetric. One common feature of Chinese and U.S companies is that they intend to maintain a constant dividend payout policy because both the mean and median value of changes in dividends are close to zero. In addition, the positive value at the mean and the median of the changes in earnings also reflects the fact that on average Chinese companies experience increasing in profitability over time.

This table displays summary statistics for variables used in this study. $r_t - R_t^B$ is the annul excess return in which r_t is the annual stock return of firm i at time t (fiscal year-end) and the stock benchmark return, R_t^B, refers to the 125 portfolios return formed by size, book-to-market value of equity, and momentum. Bank relationship is measured by three different proxies. A dummy variable, d_SOE, that equal to one when the firm is classified as state-owned company, and zero otherwise. Next, we measure the duration of bank relation by calculating the difference between the current valuation year and the earliest loan year recorded. The third proxy of bank relationship is the number of banks that a firm has received loans five years before the valuation year (num_bank). ΔX_t indicates the change in the variable X from year $t-1$ to t that is standardized by market value of equity at year end $t-1$, M_{t-1}. Cash holdings, C, equals cash plus cash equivalents. E is income before tax. NA stands for net assets, defined as total assets minus cash holdings. RD represents R&D expenses. I is interest expenses. D is total common dividends paid. L stands for leverage ratio, calculated as total debt over the sum of total debt and the market value of equity. NF stands for net new equity issues plus net debt issues.

Table 2. Correlation analysis.

	(1) $r_t - R_t^B$	(2) d_SOE	(3) duration	(4) num_bank	(5) ΔC_t	(6) ΔE_t	(7) ΔNA_t	(8) ΔRD_t	(9) ΔI_t	(10) ΔD_t	(11) C_{t-1}	(12) L_t	(13) NF_t
(2)	-0.04 (0.03)	1.00											
(3)	0.00 (0.94)	0.13 (0.00)	1.00										
(4)	-0.01 (0.71)	-0.05 (0.00)	-0.33 (0.00)	1.00									
(5)	0.08 (0.00)	-0.01 (0.62)	0.00 (0.85)	0.04 (0.01)	1.00								
(6)	0.21 (0.00)	-0.02 (0.26)	0.02 (0.29)	0.02 (0.32)	0.21 (0.00)	1.00							
(7)	0.05 (0.00)	0.01 (0.43)	-0.03 (0.08)	0.08 (0.00)	0.32 (0.00)	0.24 (0.00)	1.00						
(8)	0.02 (0.21)	-0.03 (0.06)	0.03 (0.14)	-0.02 (0.30)	0.00 (0.99)	0.04 (0.04)	0.05 (0.00)	1.00					
(9)	-0.02 (0.26)	0.02 (0.18)	-0.02 (0.25)	0.04 (0.04)	0.15 (0.00)	-0.02 (0.16)	0.41 (0.00)	0.02 (0.39)	1.00				
(10)	0.05 (0.01)	-0.01 (0.66)	-0.01 (0.65)	-0.01 (0.67)	0.02 (0.39)	0.04 (0.01)	0.06 (0.00)	0.01 (0.43)	-0.01 (0.58)	1.00			
(11)	0.11 (0.00)	0.11 (0.00)	0.03 (0.11)	0.09 (0.00)	0.59 (0.00)	0.18 (0.00)	0.45 (0.00)	0.08 (0.00)	0.20 (0.00)	0.03 (0.04)	1.00		
(12)	0.03 (0.15)	0.19 (0.00)	0.05 (0.00)	0.11 (0.00)	0.23 (0.00)	0.11 (0.00)	0.49 (0.00)	0.05 (0.01)	0.31 (0.00)	0.03 (0.07)	0.63 (0.00)	1.00	
(13)	0.00 (0.93)	-0.01 (0.64)	-0.04 (0.04)	0.07 (0.00)	0.45 (0.00)	0.04 (0.02)	0.68 (0.00)	0.06 (0.00)	0.35 (0.00)	0.01 (0.45)	0.47 (0.00)	0.42 (0.00)	1.00

Few findings are revealed in the investigation of the three measures of bank relationship. First, more than half of the observations in our sample are classified as stated-owned companies since the median value of *d_SOE* is one, consistent with the advantage of SOEs in bank financing. Next, most companies maintains relationship with one single specific bank since the median value and the third quarter of the number bank (*num_bank*) is one. Third, the mean and median bank relation duration (*duration*) are close to 7, implying that the distribution of duration is relatively symmetric. In brief, the sample is consistent with the understanding that Chinese listed companies have built close tie with banks, particularly for SOEs.

This table displays the pairwise correlation among the variables. Variables definitions are shown in Table 1. *p*-value are reported in the parentheses.

Table 2 reports the correlation analysis among the variables conduct in this study. The correlation coefficient between the number of lending bank (*num_bank*) and duration (*duration*) is −0.33, suggesting that multiple banks is associated with a short-term cooperative relationship with bank. In addition, the number of lending bank (*num_bank*) is negative with the dummy variable of stated-owned companies (*d_SOE*), indicating that multiple bank relation is uncommon among SOEs. Both evidences reveals that multiple bank relationship is a signal of weak bank relation. Most importantly, we find that the three measure of bank relation experience weak correlation with other variables, including the dependent variable and the control variables. However, we do find cash holdings is highly correlated with leverage, suggesting that bank financing provides a significant contribution to a firm's liquidity assets.

4.2 Regression Results

We apply the valuation framework proposed by Faulkender and Wang (2006) to detect the dollar change in shareholder value and examine factors contribute to this value. To highlight the advantage of bank relation in dealing with information asymmetry, I further divide the sample into two subsets, financial constrained and financial unconstrained companies, and reexamine whether the value effect of bank relation varies with financial frictions.

Table 3 displays the regression result of the marginal value of cash holdings for the whole sample. Model 1 of Table 3 shows the results from the benchmark model of Faulkender and Wang (2006). The initial coefficient estimate corresponding to the change in cash holdings (ΔC_t) reveals that for shareholders an additional dollar of cash is only worth $0.67 if the firm has zero cash and no leverage at the beginning of the fiscal year. This is consistent with the argument in the literature that there are pros and cons in cash holdings. However, this value is less than that found in Faulkender and Wang (2006) of $1.466. One possible explanation is associated with the fact that the magnitude of agency costs of extra cash holdings is larger in China than that in the U.S. where the governance mechanism is well-developed. The sign of coefficients on other independent variables are consistent with the finding of Faulkender and Wang (2006). However, we do find in China shareholders are insensitive to the change in R&D expense and the change in net financing while both factors have significant impact on firm value in the US.

The estimated coefficient corresponding to the interaction of the level of cash holdings with the change in cash ($C_{t-1} \times \Delta C_t$) is statistically insignificant, indicating that a firm's current cash position doesn't alter the value of additional dollar of cash. Meanwhile, the coefficient on the interaction of the level of cash holdings with the leverage ratio ($L_t \times \Delta C_t$) is also negative and statistically significant at 1%. That implies the phenomenon of higher leverage impairing the value of extra cash holdings still works in China. The reported R^2 is about 0.17 and is similar with the previous studies (Faulkender and Wang 2006). Meanwhile, Chinese stock markets are more sensitive to the change in earnings and one additional increasing in earnings is valued at \$1.37, compared to that of \$0.53 in the U.S. This implies shareholders might overreact to the increase in earnings. In brief, my dataset and model setting is comparable with that of Faulkender and Wang (2006).

Next, I detect Hypothesis 1 that bank relation is of value through Model 2 to 4. We introduce a new interaction term between bank relation and the change in cash ($d\_BR_{t-1} \times \Delta C_t$) to test Hypothesis 1. The interaction measures the difference in the value of cash between with and without bank relationship firms. The expected sign on this new interaction term is negative if the advantage of bank relation in curing information asymmetry reduces the borrower's reliance on internal funds and preference on liquidity. Model 2 of Table 3 displays the regression result of the inclusion of the interaction term, $d\_BR_{t-1} \times \Delta C_t$, in which bank relation is defined by a dummy variable of SOEs (d_SOE). The estimated coefficient on $d\_BR_{t-1} \times \Delta C_t$ is -0.32 and is statistically significant at the 10% level. This result indicates that the value of one extra dollar holding does vary with bank relation. Model 3 of Table 3 uses the duration dummy to represent bank relationship in which longer duration indicates with close tie with bank ($d\_duration$). The estimated coefficient on $d\_BR_{t-1} \times \Delta C_t$ is negative with value of -0.28 but is less than statistically significant ($t - value = -1.52$). In Model 4 of Table 3 bank relation is proxied by the number of bank a firm has received loans from. We use the dummy variable of multiple bank to represent close bank relation ($d\_mulbank$). We find that the interaction term of bank relation, $d\_BR_{t-1} \times \Delta C_t$, is statistically significant with positive sign because $d\_mulbank$ is an inverse measure of close bank relationship. In brief, our evidences is consistent with Hypothesis 1a that close bank relationship decreases the marginal value of cash holdings due to the lending bank's uniqueness in resolving information asymmetry between the borrowing company and financial markets.

This table presents the regression result of bank relation on the value of cash holdings. Model (1) is the benchmark analysis of Faulkender and Wang (2006). The ordinary least squares regression analysis is applied in Model (1) through Model (4). We conduct the fixed effect regression analysis in Model (5) to Model (7). In Model (2) and (5) bank relationship is measured by a dummy variable, d_SOE, that equals to one when the borrower is SOE and is zero, otherwise. In Model (3) and (6) bank relationship is associated with the duration of bank relationship. A dummy variable, $d\_duration$, represents a firm has a close tie with bank that equals to one when the duration of bank relationship ($duration$) is more than 7 year (sample median in the sample period), and zero otherwise. In Model (4) and (7) bank relationship is measured by the number of bank that a firm has cooperated with. We define a dummy variable to stand for multiple bank relation, $d\_mulbank$, that equals to one for multiple bank

Table 3. Regressionresults for the value of bank relation: Whole sample.

	(1) Bench-mark	(2) d_BR_{r-1} $=d\_SOE$	(3) $d\_BR_{r-1}=$ $d\_duration$	(4) $d\_BR_{r-1}=$ $d\_mulbank$	(5) d_BR_{r-1} $=d\_SOE$	(6) $d\_BR_{r-1}=$ $d\_duration$	(7) $d\_BR_{r-1}=$ $d\_mulbank$
ΔC_t	0.67**	0.78***	0.85***	0.60**	0.56**	0.64**	0.33
	(2.57)	(2.92)	(2.91)	(2.30)	(1.99)	(2.14)	(1.20)
$d\_BR_{r-1}\times\Delta C_t$		-0.32*	-0.28	0.39*	-0.35*	-0.35*	0.49**
		(-1.67)	(-1.52)	(1.96)	(-1.85)	(-1.82)	(2.40)
d_BR_{r-1}		-0.040**	0.015	-0.034**	-0.079	-0.0030	-0.029
		(-2.54)	(1.06)	(-2.13)	(-1.22)	(-0.11)	(-1.16)
ΔE_t	1.37***	1.35***	1.38***	1.38***	1.22***	1.24***	1.23***
	(7.47)	(7.36)	(7.56)	(7.54)	(6.58)	(6.69)	(6.70)
ΔNA_t	0.036	0.037	0.041	0.037	-0.012	-0.0079	-0.016
	(0.86)	(0.88)	(0.97)	(0.90)	(-0.27)	(-0.19)	(-0.37)
ΔRD_t	4.72	4.35	4.44	4.07	-0.63	-0.92	-1.57
	(0.78)	(0.72)	(0.73)	(0.67)	(-0.09)	(-0.12)	(-0.21)
ΔI_t	-2.36**	-2.41***	-2.29**	-2.38**	-3.06***	-2.98***	-3.07***
	(-2.55)	(-2.62)	(-2.48)	(-2.57)	(-3.23)	(-3.17)	(-3.22)
ΔD_t	7.40*	7.31*	7.49*	7.23*	8.45*	8.43*	8.06*
	(1.78)	(1.76)	(1.81)	(1.72)	(1.91)	(1.90)	(1.79)
C_{t-1}	0.29***	0.31***	0.29***	0.29***	0.42***	0.43***	0.44***
	(4.27)	(4.60)	(4.28)	(4.26)	(3.80)	(3.88)	(3.90)
L_t	-0.012	0.0100	-0.013	-0.0069	0.46***	0.46***	0.46***
	(-0.23)	(0.19)	(-0.26)	(-0.13)	(4.72)	(4.78)	(4.79)
NF_t	-0.078	-0.096	-0.088	-0.074	-0.14*	-0.14*	-0.12
	(-1.11)	(-1.38)	(-1.24)	(-1.07)	(-1.87)	(-1.88)	(-1.62)
$C_{t-1}\times\Delta C_t$	0.45	0.36	0.46	0.42	0.55	0.56	0.51
	(0.98)	(0.80)	(1.02)	(0.91)	(1.10)	(1 13)	(1.01)
$L_t\times\Delta C_t$	-1.40**	-1.22**	-1.42**	-1.46***	-1.09*	-1.24**	-1.29**
	(-2.50)	(-2.21)	(-2.54)	(-2.65)	(-1.90)	(-2.16)	(-2.27)
_cons	-0.33***	-0.31***	-0.34***	-0.32***	-0.38***	-0.29***	-0.42***
	(-4.18)	(-3.98)	(-4.29)	(-4.18)	(-5.29)	(-7.56)	(-6.48)
Industry effect	Y	Y	Y	Y			
Firm effect					Y	Y	Y
Year effect	Y	Y	Y	Y	Y	Y	Y
Obs.	3301	3301	3301	3301	3301	3301	3301
R^2	0.169	0.172	0.170	0.171	0.187	0.186	0.187

relation, and zero when the firm only has received loans from one specific bank. The definition of all other control variables are shown in Table 1. Both industry fixed effect and year effect are controlled in the regression analysis. t-statistics are calculated based on robust standard errors adjusted for firm-level clustering. ***, **, and * denote the significance level of 1%, 5%, and 10%, respectively.

To account for the potential endogeneity problem arising from bank relationship, we apply fixed effect regression model to reexamine the impact of bank relationship on the value of cash holdings. We introduce a two-way fixed effect estimation to account for the omitted variable problem. Fixed firm effects and year effects are used to control for unobservable firm characteristics and time effects. The results are reported in Model

5 to 7 of Table 3. In Model 7 of Table 3 we find that the coefficient of the interaction term, $d\_BR_{t-1} \times \Delta C_t$, is 0.49 and is statistically significant at 5% level, implying that multiple bank relation, an indicator of weak borrower-bank connection, is associated with higher value on additional cash position. These results are consistent with the interpretation that bank relationship reduces the value of cash holdings controlling for the potential endogeneity problem. In brief, the aforementioned finding is in support of our hypothesis that the value of additional cash decreases with lending relationship.

Furthermore, I detect whether financial constraint alters the impact of bank relation on the value of liquidity. With the presumption that small firms and younger firms are more vulnerable to capital market imperfections (Denis and Sibilkov 2010), we define a firm is financial constrained when the firm age is less than 19 years (the median value of the sample) or when the firm is ranked in the bottom quarter of the size distribution. Firm size is calculated based on book value of total assets. Tables 4 and 5 display the fixed effect regression result of financial unconstraint and financial constraint firms, respectively.

In Model 1 to Model 3 of Table 4 the financial constraint is proxy by firm age, while we use firm size to classify unconstrained firms in Model 4 to Model 6 of Table 4. We find that in Model 1 of Table 4 the estimated coefficient on the interaction term $d\_BR_{t-1} \times \Delta C_t$ is −0.87 and statistically significant at 1% level, suggesting that bank relation, proxy by d_SOE, has significant negative impact on the marginal value of cash holdings for financial unconstraint firms. When we apply $d\_duration$ (Model 2) and $d\_mulbank$ (Model 3) in measuring the depth of bank relation, we also find the estimated coefficient of $d\_BR_{t-1} \times \Delta C_t$ have expected negative sign and positive sign, respectively. The investigation of the performance on $d\_BR_{t-1} \times \Delta C_t$ using firm size as an alternative measure of financial constraint shown in Model 4 to Model 6 of Table 4 also reveals similar results. The finding is in line with the prediction of Petersen and Rajan (1994) that bank relationship is associated the information disclosure and allows firms with less financial frictions to reduce their reliance on internal funds.

By contrast, there is less apparent evidence indicating the impact of bank relation on liquidity value for financial constraint firms. In Model 1 of Table 5 the estimated coefficient of the interaction term $d\_BR_{t-1} \times \Delta C_t$ is 0.33 and statistically insignificant. The investigation of financial constrained firms on the interaction term $d\_BR_{t-1} \times \Delta C_t$ is insignificant in all setting of Table 5 except for Model 3. This suggests that the potential holdup costs reduces the benefit of lending relationship making cash holdings as neutral to financial constrained firms.

This table displays the fixed effect regression result of bank relation on the marginal value of cash holdings for companies with the ease in the external financing. It is presumed that companies with age (Model 1 to 3) or large size (Model 4 to 6) are financial unconstrained. In Model (1) and (4) bank relationship is measured by a dummy variable, d_SOE, that equals to one when the borrower is SOE and is zero, otherwise. In Model (2) and (5) bank relationship is associated with the duration of bank relationship. A dummy variable, $d\_duration$, represents a firm has a close tie with bank that equals to one when the duration of bank relationship (*duration*) is more than

Table 4. Fixed effect regression for the impact of bank relation on marginal value of cash holdings: Subsample of financial unconstrained firms.

	Elder Companies			Large Companies		
	(1) $d\_BR_{t-1} =$ d_SOE	(2) $d\_BR_{t-1} =$ $d\_duration$	(3) $d\_BR_{t-1} =$ $d\_mulbank$	(4) $d\_BR_{t-1} =$ d_SOE	(5) $d\_BR_{t-1} =$ $d\_duration$	(6) $d\_BR_{t-1} =$ $d\_mulbank$
ΔC_t	0.74**	1.03***	0.35	1.04	1.20	0.66
	(2.21)	(2.67)	(1.00)	(1.47)	(1.49)	(0.95)
$d\_BR_{t-1} \times \Delta C_t$	-0.87***	-0.78***	0.37	-0.64**	-0.27	0.48*
	(-3.61)	(-2.95)	(1.23)	(-2.11)	(-0.95)	(1.85)
d_BR_{t-1}	-0.18**	-0.053	-0.021	0.10	-0.056	-0.032
	(-2.29)	(-1.15)	(-0.56)	(0.77)	(-0.98)	(-0.67)
ΔE_t	1.37***	1.36***	1.34***	1.44***	1.44***	1.45***
	(5.84)	(5.74)	(5.68)	(5.32)	(5.42)	(5.31)
ΔNA_t	-0.026	-0.0054	-0.029	-0.030	-0.024	-0.033
	(-0.46)	(-0.10)	(-0.50)	(-0.42)	(-0.35)	(-0.47)
ΔRD_t	-23.0*	-25.4**	-26.3**	2.34	-0.51	-2.12
	(-1.76)	(-2.00)	(-2.06)	(0.21)	(-0.04)	(-0.18)
ΔI_t	-3.81***	-3.76***	-3.90***	-1.14	-1.34	-1.30
	(-2.84)	(-2.90)	(-2.90)	(-0.89)	(-1.04)	(-1.01)
ΔD_t	7.03	4.07	4.63	6.10	4.27	3.48
	(1.61)	(0.89)	(1.00)	(0.95)	(0.68)	(0.55)
C_{t-1}	0.45***	0.50***	0.50***	0.65***	0.64***	0.65***
	(2.87)	(2.96)	(2.94)	(3.77)	(3.67)	(3.74)
L_t	0.45***	0.46***	0.44***	0.76***	0.80***	0.81***
	(3.38)	(3.47)	(3.23)	(4.67)	(4.81)	(5.01)
NF_t	-0.037	-0.047	-0.0070	-0.14	-0.15	-0.13
	(-0.40)	(-0.49)	(-0.07)	(-1.12)	(-1.13)	(-1.03)
$C_{t-1} \times \Delta C_t$	0.15	-0.0010	0.16	-0.035	0.029	0.036
	(0.27)	(-0.00)	(0.27)	(-0.05)	(0.04)	(0.05)
$L_t \times \Delta C_t$	-0.71	-1.07*	-1.14	-1.23	-1.90	-1.60
	(-1.03)	(-1.66)	(-1.62)	(-1.02)	(-1.57)	(-1.37)
_cons	-0.15**	-0.27**	-0.20	-0.69***	-0.71***	-0.64***
	(-2.13)	(-2.19)	(-1.58)	(-4.31)	(-6.73)	(-4.91)
Firm effect	Y	Y	Y	Y	Y	Y
Year effect	Y	Y	Y	Y	Y	Y
Obs.	1434	1434	1434	830	830	830
R^2	0.211	0.205	0.196	0.203	0.198	0.199

7 year (sample median in the sample period), and zero otherwise. In Model (3) and (6) bank relationship is measured by the number of bank that a firm has cooperated with. We define a dummy variable to stand for multiple bank relation, $d\_mulbank$, that equals to one for multiple bank relation, and zero when the firm only has received loans from one specific bank. The definition of all other control variables are shown in Table 1. Year effect is controlled in the regression analysis. t-statistics shown in parentheses are calculated based on robust standard errors adjusted for firm-level clustering. ***, **, and * denote the significance level of 1%, 5%, and 10%, respectively.

Table 5. Fixed effect regression for the impact of bank relation on marginal value of cash holdings: Subsample of financial constrained firms.

	Young Companies			Small Companies		
	(1) $d\_BR_{r-1} =$ d_SOE	(2) $d\_BR_{r-1} =$ $d\_duration$	(3) $d\_BR_{r-1} =$ $d\_mulbank$	(4) $d\_BR_{r-1} =$ d_SOE	(5) $d\_BR_{r-1} =$ $d\_duration$	(6) $d\_BR_{r-1} =$ $d\_mulbank$
ΔC_t	0.16	0.26	0.13	0.43	0.39	0.0054
	(0.36)	(0.59)	(0.31)	(0.66)	(0.55)	(0.01)
$d\_BR_{r-1} \times \Delta C_t$	0.33	0.050	0.57**	-0.92	-0.52	0.39
	(1.24)	(0.17)	(2.01)	(-1.57)	(-0.85)	(0.57)
d_BR_{r-1}	-0.0068	0.026	-0.020	0.12	0.030	-0.0019
	(-0.05)	(0.65)	(-0.51)	(0.84)	(0.43)	(-0.03)
ΔE_t	1.06***	1.05***	1.07***	1.65***	1.67***	1.66***
	(3.69)	(3.63)	(3.71)	(3.59)	(3.66)	(3.64)
ΔNA_t	-0.036	-0.035	-0.045	-0.052	-0.057	-0.077
	(-0.55)	(-0.53)	(-0.69)	(-0.32)	(-0.36)	(-0.49)
ΔRD_t	12.6	12.8	11.6	-5.82	-6.22	-6.15
	(1.33)	(1.34)	(1.22)	(-0.37)	(-0.39)	(-0.39)
ΔI_t	-2.46*	-2.54*	-2.41	-14.4***	-13.4***	-13.7***
	(-1.69)	(-1.74)	(-1.65)	(-3.21)	(-2.87)	(-3.05)
ΔD_t	9.21	8.86	9.46	-11.8	-12.2	-12.7
	(1.26)	(1.21)	(1.31)	(-0.75)	(-0.76)	(-0.78)
C_{t-1}	0.48***	0.48***	0.49***	0.44	0.32	0.30
	(2.75)	(2.76)	(2.75)	(0.93)	(0.70)	(0.65)
L_t	0.69***	0.68***	0.69***	0.62**	0.69**	0.68**
	(4.45)	(4.37)	(4.45)	(1.99)	(2.19)	(2.18)
NF_t	-0.24*	-0.24*	-0.23*	0.30	0.27	0.32
	(-1.89)	(-1.90)	(-1.75)	(1.04)	(0.88)	(0.99)
$C_{t-1} \times \Delta C_t$	1.07	1.03	0.99	0.60	0.44	0.33
	(1.18)	(1.14)	(1.13)	(0.34)	(0.24)	(0.17)
$L_t \times \Delta C_t$	-1.42	-1.28	-1.28	-1.72	-1.34	-1.21
	(-1.57)	(-1.42)	(-1.47)	(-0.87)	(-0.71)	(-0.63)
_cons	-0.39***	-0.42***	-0.39***	-0.32***	-0.28***	-0.28***
	(-4.06)	(-5.68)	(-7.09)	(-3.60)	(-4.14)	(-4.02)
Firm effect	Y	Y	Y	Y	Y	Y
Year effect	Y	Y	Y	Y	Y	Y
Obs.	1867	1867	1867	830	830	830
R^2	0.211	0.210	0.212	0.187	0.183	0.182

This table displays the fixed effect regression result of bank relation on the marginal value of cash holdings for companies having difficulty in external financing. It is presumed that young (Model 1 to 3) or small size (Model 4 to 6) companies are financial constrained. In Model (1) and (4) bank relationship is measured by a dummy variable, d_SOE, that equals to one when the borrower is SOE and is zero, otherwise. In Model (2) and (5) bank relationship is associated with the duration of bank relationship. A dummy variable, $d\_duration$, represents a firm has a close tie with bank that equals to one when the duration of bank relationship (*duration*) is more than 7 year (sample median in the sample period), and zero otherwise. In Model (3) and (6) bank relationship is measured by the number of bank that a firm has cooperated with. We define a dummy variable to stand for multiple bank relation,$d\_mulbank$, that equals to one for multiple bank relation, and zero when the firm only has received loans from one specific bank. The definition of all other control variables are shown in Table 1. Year effect is controlled in the regression analysis. t-statistics shown in parentheses are calculated based on robust standard errors adjusted for firm-level clustering. *** , ** , and * denote the significance level of 1%, 5%, and 10%, respectively.

5 Conclusion Remark

In literature banks play an important mechanism in resolving information asymmetry between borrowers and outsiders. The governance function of banks is also verified by exploring the abnormal return during bank loans announcement and the choice between private and public debts (Lin et al. 2011). However, some scholars notice when keeping a close tie with banks the borrower are more likely to be locked-in such relationship. In this study I count on the marginal value of cash holdings to verify whether the impact of lending relation varies with the concern of financial constraints. We contribute to the debate in this literature by offering an under-researched channel through which the depth of bank relationship can affect firm value: corporate cash holdings.

The impact of powerful banks has been verified on the setting of bank loan rates and cash holdings (Pinkowitz and Williamson 2001; Santos and Winton 2008; Schenone 2010). Scholars also point out that the impact of banking relationship diminishes with the access to external capital market and varies with business cycle. Accordingly, I further propose that the impact of lending relationship on the value of cash holdings alter with the severity of financial constraints. The conducting of Chinese listed companies' bank loans activities also offer us a unique venue to examine the pros and cons of lending relationship simultaneously.

Acknowledgments. The author gratefully acknowledged the financial support of the Ministry of Science and Technology, Taiwan, R.O.C. under Grant no. MOST 104-2410-H-030-012.

References

Bates, T.W., Kahle, K.M., Stulz, R.M.: Why do US firms hold so much more cash than they used to? J. Financ. **64**(5), 1985–2021 (2009)
Berger, A.N., Udell, G.F.: Relationship lending and lines of credit in small firm finance. J. Bus. **68**(3), 351–381 (1995)
Bonfim, D., Dai, Q., Franco, F.: The number of bank relationships and borrowing costs: the role of information asymmetries. J. Empir. Financ. **46**, 191–209 (2018)
Campbel, T.S., Kracaw, W.A.: Information production, market signalling, and the theory of financial intermediation. J. Financ. **35**(4), 863–882 (1980)
Chang, C., Liao, G., Yu, X., Ni, Z.: Information from relationship lending: evidence from loan defaults in China. J. Money Credit. Bank. **46**(6), 1225–1257 (2014)

Denis, D.J., Sibilkov, V.: Financial constraints, investment, and the value of cash holdings. Rev. Financ. Stud. **23**(1), 247–270 (2010)

Diamond, D.W.: Financial intermediation and delegated monitoring. Rev. Financ. Stud. **51**(3), 393–414 (1984)

Diamond, D.W.: Monitoring and reputation: the choice between bank loans and directly placed debt. J. Polit. Econ., 99, 689–721 (1991)

Fama, E.F.: What's different about banks? J. Financ. Intermediation **15**(1), 29–39 (1985)

Faulkender, M., Wang, R.: Corporate financial policy and the value of cash. J. Financ. **61**(4), 1957–1990 (2006)

Houston, J., James, C.: Bank information monopolies and the mix of private and public debt claims. J. Financ. **51**(5), 1863–1889 (1996)

Hu, H., Lian, Y., Su, C.-H.: Do bank lending relationships affect corporate cash policy? Rev. Account. Financ. **15**(4), 394–415 (2016)

James, C.: Some evidence on the uniqueness of bank loans. J. Financ. Econ. **19**(2), 217–235 (1987)

Keynes, J.M.: The General Theory of Employment, Interest and Money. McMillan, London (1936)

Khurana, I.K., Martin, X., Pereira, R.: Financial development and the cash flow sensitivity of cash. J. Financ. Quant. Anal. **41**(04), 787–808 (2006)

Kusnadi, Y., Yang, Z., Zhou, Y.: Institutional development, state ownership, and corporate cash holdings: evidence from China. J. Bus. Res. **68**(2), 351–359 (2015)

Lin, C., Ma, Y., Malatesta, P., Xuan, Y.: Ownership structure and the cost of corporate borrowing. J. Financ. Econ. **100**(1), 1–23 (2011)

Lins, K.V., Servaes, H., Tufano, P.: What drives corporate liquidity? An international survey of cash holdings and lines of credit. J. Financ. Econ. **98**(1), 160–176 (2010)

Modigliani, F., Miller, M.H.: The cost of capital, corporation finance and the theory of investment. Am. Econ. Rev. **48**(3), 261–297 (1958)

Myers, S.C., Majluf, N.S.: Corporate financing and investment decisions when firms have information that investors do not have. J. Financ. Econ. **13**(2), 187–221 (1984)

Opler, T., Pinkowitz, L., Stulz, R., Williamson, R.: The determinants and implications of corporate cash holdings. J. Financ. Econ. **52**(1), 3–46 (1999)

Petersen, M.A., Rajan, R.G.: The benefits of lending relationships: Evidence from small business data. J. Financ. **49**(1), 3–37 (1994)

Pinkowitz, L., Williamson, R.: Bank power and cash holdings: Evidence from Japan. Rev. Financ. Stud. **14**(4), 1059–1082 (2001)

Prilmeier, R.: Why do loans contain covenants? Evidence from lending relationships. J. Financ. Econ. **123**(3), 558–579 (2017)

Qian, M., Yeung, B.Y.: Bank financing and corporate governance. J. Corp. Financ. **32**, 258–270 (2015)

Rajan, R.G.: Insiders and outsiders: the choice between informed and arm's-length debt. J. Financ. **47**(4), 1367–1400 (1992)

Ramakrishnan, R.T.S., Thakor, A.V.: Information reliability and a theory of financial intermediation. Rev. Econ. Stud. **51**(3), 415–432 (1984)

Santos, J.A.C., Winton, A.: Bank loans, bonds, and information monopolies across the business cycle. J. Financ. **63**(3), 1315–1359 (2008)

Schenone, C.: Lending relationships and information rents: do banks exploit their information advantages? Rev. Financ. Stud. **23**(3), 1149–1199 (2010)

The Role of Mobile Money in Somalia's Remittance System

Mohamed Elmi[1,2(✉)] and Ojelanki Ngwenyama[1,2]

[1] Institute for Innovation and Technology Management,
Ryerson University, Toronto, Canada
{mohamed.elmi, ojelanki}@ryerson.ca
[2] University of Cape Town, Cape Town, South Africa

Abstract. Mobile money is rapidly transforming various sectors and economies worldwide. Somalia is one country that has been transformed by the emergence of mobile money. In 2017, the World Bank estimated that 73% of the Somali population over the age of 16 use mobile money services. Additionally, mobile money is the primary access point to financial services in the country. At the same time, Somalia relies heavily on the remittances to pay for children's education, social services and provides an investment funds for small businesses. The United Nations estimates that close to 40% of families in the country are dependent on the $1.4 billion remittances per year. Accordingly, remittances companies account for a large segment of the financial sector in Somalia. And yet, both the remittance and mobile money systems function in spite of a lack of a traditional financial system. Mobile money and the underlying technology is at the heart of the supports the daily existence of millions of Somalis. How this system functions and its role as the economic backbone of the country is little understood. Thus, the aim this paper is to analyze the crucial role served by mobile money in the delivery of the billions of remittance dollars into the country. This study is guided by the main question: What role does mobile money and the Somali diaspora in the Greater Toronto Area, through the remittance system, play in Somalia's remittance system?

Keywords: Electronic · Mobile and ubiquitous commerce · Mobile money · Remittances · Somalia

1 Introduction

Somalia has been without a functioning state apparatus since 1991, when President Siad Barre was ousted from office amid a civil war [1]. Ever since, the country has been mired in economic and social stagnation, in part due to the lack of a centralized government which has control over the recognized territory of the country [2]. Over this period, Somalia's social development indictors became some of the lowest in the world. Some of these indicators are attributed to the fact that parts of the country were still experiencing civil war conditions along with an insurgency inspired by the transnational ideology – Islamism of Al Qaida and the Islamic State [3–5]. As result of Somalia's economic and social stagnation, the country is very dependent on remittances from abroad to supplement any income they generated domestically. Remittance services play

© Springer Nature Switzerland AG 2019
F. F.-H. Nah and K. Siau (Eds.): HCII 2019, LNCS 11588, pp. 119–136, 2019.
https://doi.org/10.1007/978-3-030-22335-9_8

an important role throughout the global economy. The World Bank estimates that over $325 billion is transferred worldwide every year, with $40 billion remitted from developed countries to Africa [6]. Consequently, international agencies such as the United Nations, the African Development Bank and other international NGOs have postulated that the billions from remittances can be harnessed to effectively help developing countries such as Somalia economically and socially develop. The large Somali diaspora community, one study conservatively estimated at 1 million, contributes more than $1.4 billion in remittances into the country every year [7, 8]. Take for instance Somalis living in the United States alone remit around $215 million annually [9]. It has been estimated that, on average, residents in Somalia receive $3,000 per year [9], which is a large amount compared to the country's per capita GDP of $499 [10].

Electronic (or mobile) money has thrived in the country since it was introduced in 2009 by Telesom [11, 12]. This form of currency is increasingly replacing the hard currency through-out the region. Additionally, more people in Somalia have access to mobile money accounts than accounts in financial institutions [13, 14]. Prior to this, Somalia was a cash-heavy society in which large amounts of American dollars and local Shillings were used. This older Hawala system relied on the physical transfer of cash or equivalent goods [15]. The move to a mostly electronic form of money has allowed many in the country to move money easier [16]. An example of the money away from cash to mobile money is that 70% of Telesom's costumers buy airtime through mobile money rather through scratch cards. It is estimated that almost seven million transactions have taken place in March 2013, the last publically available data [11].

This paper examines the role the Somali diaspora plays in the country through extensive analysis of the remittance system and how technology such as mobile money is utilized in the money transfer process. Somalia relies heavily on the remittances sent by Somalis in the diaspora to pay for children's education, social services and provides an investment funds for small businesses. For instance, it has been estimated that close to 40% of families in the country as a whole rely on the $1.4 billion remittances per year [17]. Remittances are the second largest source of external funding in developing countries; however, in Somalia it is the largest source of foreign funding [18]. Oxfam [19] noted that the amount of money sent to Somalia in the form remittances exceeded the all the development aid, emergency assistance and FDI put together. Moreover, in 2017 remittances accounted for 26.7% of the national Gross Domestic Product (GDP), these figures increase during humanitarian emergencies serving as a financial cushion when needed most [7, 20]. Consequently, remittance enterprises account for a large segment of the financial sector in Somalia. And yet, the remittance system functions in spite of the lack of centralized, state-regulated financial system.

This study aims, through interviews and surveys, to better understand Hawala and how mobile money is utilized. By studying how they employ a modern tool such as the mobile banking, we also establish the role of ICT in the Somali money transfer sector. This study is guided by the main question: What role does technology and the diaspora, through the remittance system, play in the economic and social ecosystem of Somalia?

In order to answer this question, we begin this study by setting a baseline understanding of the Somali population in Canada and Greater Toronto Area (GTA). Once that was established, we then created an inventory of the Hawala business gathered from secondary sources and online business listings along with the Somali remittance sector worldwide. Next, a survey of 143 Somalis who have remitted internationally in 2017 was conducted. The survey was divided into four sections: inclusion criteria, reasons for remittances, technology used and demographics. Finally, small–sample interviews were conducted with members of Somali Money Transfer Organizations (MTOs) in the GTA to understand the business climate. The aim of the interviews was to get specific inputs from people with direct knowledge about the remittance system more generally and the technology utilized.

2 Context

Hawala, an informal money transfer system, plays an important role in several economies around the world [21–23]. Hawala comes from the Arabic word "transfer" [22]. While in Hindi it means "trust" [24]. The money transfer system operates similarly around the world and has a few meanings; examples include, hundi in Pakistan or padala in Philippines [25]. Although it originated centuries ago, the modern version of the Somali Hawala system, is traced to the partition of India and Pakistan when the legal transfer of money between the countries ended [26]. The Hawala system has often operated in areas that did not have access to formalized banks and financial institutions [27]. Hawala operates differently from other informal money transfer networks. A differentiating factor of the Hawala system is that it is characterized by the transfer of money without the immediate movement of currency. Specifically, the money does not physically leave the agents accounts immediately instead relying on a network of trust [28]. In short, the Hawala system is an informal channel to transfer funds from one location to another [22].

The system is proliferated for a few reason, these include the trust, speed and the reliability of the approach [29]. One reason for its relative success and endurance is that the system cuts down on the amount of bureaucracy required for sender to meet. Another reason is that the system is often preferred due its convenience, with locations and agents being easily accessible. Although the money transfer system is used to send money to Somalia, it can be reversed to assist in investment or cover unexpected expenses [25].

However, the Hawala system has come under heavy scrutiny as source financing for illicit behavior and terrorism. The Hawala system can offer anonymity of both the sender and the receiver. The system's opaqueness, speed and lack of records have risen concerns for being a conduit for criminal and terrorist financing. For example, fears that the Hawala sector was being used to fund terrorism led the United States government to close down one of the largest Somali money remittance companies in the US. In 2001 Al Barakat[1], which was based in the Dubai, UAE handling more than $140 million in remittances annually was suspended and had close to nine million dollars frozen [30, 31].

---

[1] In 2006, the U.S. government removed Al Barakat and all of its agents from terrorist financing list noting that there was no evidence in it involvement with terrorists.

Additionally, Western governments have placed heavy restrictions on banks that facilitate the Hawala brokers thus effectively driving them further underground [21]. For countries that rely on the Hawala system rather than the formal banks to transfer money, these restrictions have been criticized for hurting people dependent on the transfers [17].

Dubai, United Arab Emirates is home to a large number of the MTOs handling most money transfer transactions [24]. Dubai acts as a conduit for these funds to the Indian subcontinent and east Africa. The UAE is one of the Somalia's largest trading partners, most imports within Somalia pass though Dubai [31, 32]. In most cases, the United Arab Emirates (UAE) serves as the financial capital for Somali MTOs. After the September 11, 2001 attacks in New York, the UAE implemented regulations that ensured the all MTOs operating within the country were registered to curtail funds that might be used to finance terrorism. However, the UAE government stated "Regulations should be effective but not overly restrictive" [33]. The MTOs can send physical cash or wire a transfer to a bank account based in the UAE that act as clearing houses [7]. The money is then transferred as products that can then be exported to Somalia. The Hawala system serves to link the products that are consumed in the country with money from around the world.

In the case of Somalia and its diaspora, the Hawala system is the financial backbone of the country. In a country without a centralized postal system, formalized banking system or personal identification system the Hawala system has several advantages. First, individuals without a fixed address have the ability to use the system because all that is required is code or phrase from the sender to access the funds [19]. Another advantage is that the Hawala system works in places where large money transfer institutions do not serve. For example, there are no internationally recognized MTOs such as Western Union desks or Money Gram in Somalia. A third advantage is that it has a relatively low cost, the commission charged the sender is around five percent. Thus this low commission ensures the cost of transfer itself is reasonable for the senders. A fourth advantage is that the large Hawala systems is now web-based to facilitate the quick transfer of money. Once the money arrived the client is called, usually on mobile telephones which are widely available. If the amount is large a clan elder is called upon to verify the person's identity. In order to create a fast efficient system, technology has enabled this process to move at a greater speed.

The Hawala system is illustrated in the Fig. 1, the system could be summarised as a follows: The first step is that *Individual A* in Region A gives money to be sent to the *Broker A* along with a fee; the second step is that *Broker A* provides a confirmation code to *Individual A;* the third step, the *Individual A* in-turn shares the confirmation code with *Individual B;* the fourth step is that *Broker A* instructs *Broker B* to release funds to *Individual B*, the funds exchanged can sometimes be in the form of a loan between brokers; the fifth step is that *Individual B* presents the confirmation code from *Individual A* to *Broker B;* the sixth step is for *Broker B* to release funds for *Individual B*; the seventh and final step is for *Broker A* to reconcile the ledgers, primarily through a carrier system, to *Broker B*.

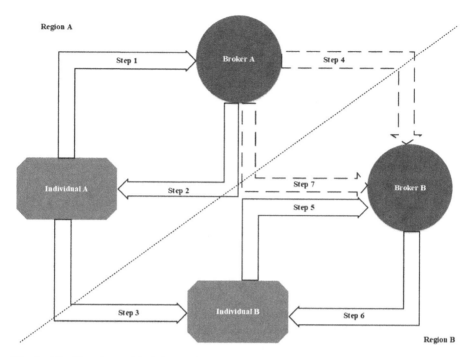

Fig. 1. The Hawala model. Adapted from: (El-Qorchi [22]; Oxfam [19]; Razavy [23]. Solid lines are interaction with individuals while broken lines are interactions between brokers. The diagonal line divides the two regions.

Adapting to new policies, regulations and to new consumer demands as they have emerged, the Hawala has survived. Recently, Information Communication Technologies (ICTs) have made the Hawala process faster and more efficient. The money transfer system has been greatly transformed by fax machines, telephones, emails and more recently, mobile phones. The World Bank (2017a) estimates that 90% of Somalis own at least one mobile phone, most (62.4%) own a basic mobile phone, some 30.8% own a smart phone and 13.1% own a feature phone. It is estimated that 73% of the Somali population over the age of 16 use mobile money services but when only people with mobile money are surveyed that number rises to 83.0%. The three main regions of the country have different mobile phone companies that dominate each of their respective regions. In South-Central, 99.5% of the local population owns a SIM card from Hormuud. In Puntland, 97.9% of the local population owns a SIM card serviced by Gollis. In the Somaliland, the 96.2% of the people own a Telesom SIM card. People in Somalia, like many in Africa, own multiple SIM cards and use networks and promotions to call each. In fact, Somalis own an average of 1.4 SIM card per person.

Within the region, 68.6% of the population use mobile money to transfer money domestically, and 24.9% have used it to send money internationally. According to the same World Bank study, 9.2% of international transfers originated from Canada, although most came form the United States (32.5%) (World Bank, 2017a). Thus, the reach of the MTO networks have been expanded and are much faster and most funds are delivered almost instantaneously. Due to the utilization of ICTs, these types of transactions can now be completed in less than 24 h [23].

In the discussion surrounding the remittance network, one group that is essential are the diaspora is essential. Although the benefits to Somalis in the country are undeniable as Hammond [34] noted:

"While one can argue that improvements in governance might increase the positive impact of remittances on the country, the value that remittances already hold for thousands of Somalis living in and around Somalia—even in the absence of peace and well-established structures of governance—is impressive" (p. 130).

The amount of money is relatively small, on average Somalis remit around $233 per month to family members in Somalia [35]. Oxfam estimated that Somalis in the United States sent the most amount of money comprising of 20% or $213 millions of funds remitted to the country annually. However, the Somalis in Germany sent, on average, more money annually, $4,383, to Somalia compared to other countries. Canadian Somalis remitted close to $49 million to Somalia or an average of $2,185 USD annually per person [19].

Since 2009, the World Bank has been tracking the cost of remittances worldwide. The World Bank Remittance Price Worldwide database makes data available in each quarter. The database was the result of the Group of 20 (G20) countries making a commitment to reduce the cost of sending remittance by five percent over five years. The database tracks 48 sending countries and 105 receiving countries [36]. For Somalia, the World Bank tracks remittance from five countries and ten Money Transfer Organisations. Among other variables, the database contains costs associated of sending 200 United States Dollars (USD), the fee charged in the local currency, the foreign exchange margin and the total cost. The average cost to send the money to Somalia from all countries tracked by the World Bank is 7.81%. The country with the lowest total cost to send $200 is the United States at 5.71%, this can be partly explained by the fact that there is no cost associated with currency exchange. Australia had the highest total cost to send money to Somalia at 11.20%. Sweden had the highest cost associated with the foreign exchange, see Table 1 [37].

Table 1. The number of firms, fees and foreign exchange margin and total cost to remit to Somalia.

Country	Amount (USD)	Firms	Fee in local currency	Foreign exchange margin (%)	Total cost (%)
Australia	200	3	16.0	4.20	11.20
Netherlands	200	3	4.23	3.53	6.55
Sweden	200	8	57.38	5.64	9.02
United Kingdom*	200	7	6.36	2.05	7.35
United States	200	5	11.60	0	5.8
Average	200	5.2	-	3.44	7.81

As the largest Somali MTO Dahabshil has agents in all five countries tracked by the World Bank, World Remit is tracked in all countries except the U.S. Dahabshil has some of the highest total cost to send money in all five countries observed, ranging from 6% in the U.S. to 16.1% in Australia. On the other hand, World Remit has some of the lowest total cost to send money in all the countries it was tracked. Specifically, World Remit has a total cost of 4.54% to send money to Somalia during the first quarter of 2018 compared to 8.05% for all the other MTOs operating in the U.K. Since 2011, the average total cost to send money to Somalia has been between 6.37% and 9.16%. The World Bank had been tracking MTOs remitting to Somalia more consistently since the first quarter of 2013, during that year, had some of the lowest total cost to send money to Somalia. One reason for the lower total cost during that year is related to the lower foreign exchange margin charged by the MTOs.

3 Hawala in the GTA

The Somali population in Canada increasingly relied on an informal transfer networks to send money from Canada to Somalia. The Hawala system in Canada and Toronto generally works as described above. However, the system in Canada had some unique features that were different from other countries. At the time of this study, there were 13 Money Transfer organizations that operated within the Greater Toronto Area. The headquarters for these companies are based around the world, however, none of the MTOs have a headquarter within Canada.

The formalized MTOs often are agents with store fronts that deal in other businesses such as retail or transportation logistics [31]. Most MTOs had less than five agents or locations across the city [38]. World Remit is an online MTO that serves parts of Somalia based in the U.K. with no physical location in the GTA. World Remit accepts bank transfer and then sends the funds electronically to either a financial institution in Somalia or Mobile Money account [39].

The MTO with the most amount of listed agents is Tawakal Express, which has the 18 across the city. However, according to the most comprehensive study about the MTO sector done by Buri M. Hamza [38] for the 'Nathanson Centre for the Study of Organized Crime and Corruption' found that Dahabshil transferred the most amount of money on a monthly basis at around 3.5 to 4 million US dollars. The other MTOs averaged between 400,000 to 800,000 US dollars per month.

When examining the process of creating a Hawala network, Hamza [38] found that the Canadian based companies operate similar to other business and are required to gain a financial transactions licence as required by financial institutions that retain money such as banks. The MTOs have to retain records of any funds of over $10,000 and must report any suspicious activities. In January 2015, the Canada Revenue Agency also required any company transferring funds electronically be reported to the tax agency [40]. Hamza [38] noted that most of the MTOs had policies that funds that are above USD $2,000 would require two forms of identification.

4 Methodology

This study employed a multiple method approach to understand the Hawala system and how the diaspora in Canada utilize it. For this paper, a survey questionnaire of Somalis who have sent money internationally in 2017 was conducted. We supplemented the survey with a short questionnaire for MTO providers within the city. The objective of this paper is gather information about how GTA Somalis utilize the MTOs, the main reasons for sending the money, the socio-economic make-up of the individuals sending money. Additionally, we aimed to examine role of the diaspora in the remittance system. By examining, evidence of how the institutions such as the monetary system, social services, education system and justice are supported by the diaspora, this study will contribute to our understanding of Somalia.

Parallel to this, we analyze the crucial role served by ICTs in the delivery of the billions of dollars into the country. More specifically, this study focuses on the communication and social networks that are utilized by the Somalis currently living abroad in order to facilitate the money transfers and foster social relationships through a unique money transfer system.

To supplement the information from the survey questionnaire, a small sample four (4) of MTO agents were interviewed to better understand the Hawala system and the process that allows it to function in Canada. These agents were selected because they are some of the largest MTO and handle a large portion of the money that is transferred to Somalia. The survey of users allows us to understand the perspective of the customers however, the agents are best positioned to enlighten on issues that affect the Hawala business. According to Crouch, McKenzie [41], this type of small-sample interviews within social science research is appropriate in understanding the social condition. Nevertheless, they argue that researchers should be aware the pitfalls of this type of data and should not be geared towards "establishing 'objective facts" (485). Within IS field, small sample research has been employed in various studies [42, 43]. The concepts of chain interviews and snowball sampling were crucial to this study's methodology. Semi-structured and conversational interviews were employed for gathering data. As a rule, this methodology is employed since "questions emerge from the immediate context and when asked in the natural course of things; there is no predetermination of question topics or wording" [44]. The interviews provided information that adds to our understanding of the Hawala process. For the survey questions and the interview questionnaire.

The survey was divided into four sections: the first section were the inclusion and exclusion questions that determined the individual's eligibility for this study. Once the participants confirmed they are over the age of 18, were ethnically Somali and had sent money internationally in the 2017, we then asked then a series of 10 questions related to the how and why they sent these remittances. Next, we asked questions about the types of technology utilized to send the funds and how they normally communicate with the family members or friends receiving those funds. The final section of the survey included demographic questions related to participant's income, education and age. It should be noted that some respondents chose not to answer certain questions and as such the frequency of some variables may not total to 143 for all questions.

Once collected, the data was then cleaned and analyzed. This study utilized descriptive and inferential statistics to gain an understanding the questions at-hand. The first step was to conduct a frequency counts, commonly called a univariate analysis, of the data. This then allowed for me to the conduct measurements of central tendency (mean, median and mode). The next level of analysis conducted was the bivariate analysis. The study also utilizes multivariate analysis.

5 Findings

The first level of analysis of the data was the demographic profile of the survey respondents. The gender make of the survey respondents was 60.6% of respondents were male, while 39.4% were female. Most of the respondents were between the ages

Table 2. Survey participants gender, age, income, and employment status (frequency and percent)

Gender	Frequency	Percent
Male	83	60.6
Female	54	39.4
Total	**137**	**100.0**
Age	Frequency	Percent
25–34 years old	33	24.1
35–44 years old	37	27.0
45–54 years old	33	24.1
55 years or older	34	24.8
Total	**137**	**100.0**
Income	Frequency	Percent
Less than $20,000	27	19.4
$20,000 to less than $30,000	34	24.5
$30,000 to less than $50,000	63	45.3
$50,000 and over	15	10.8
Total	**139**	**100.0**
Employment status	Frequency	Percent
Student	6	4.3
Housewife	13	9.4
Unemployed	12	8.6
Employed	92	66.2
Retired	13	9.4
Other	3	2.2
Total	**139**	**100.0**

of 35 to 44 (27.0%), followed by those over the age of 55 (24.8%), 25 to 34 (24.1%) and 45 to 54 (24.1%). While examining the respondents' personal income for the 2017 year, 19.4% earned personal incomes of $20,000 or less, 24.5% earned between $20,000 and $30,000, nearly half of respondents, 45.3%, earned between $30,000 and $50,000 annually and finally, 10.8% declared their personal income to be $50,000 or more. When asked about their current employment status, most of the respondents were employed (66.2%). Specifically, 35.0% were employed as a staff member, 14.0% were self-employed in professional capacity, 8.4% were self-employed as a non-retail business owner and 3.5% stated they were self-employed retail business owners. For the employment status, the next largest category of respondents were housewives at 9.4%, another 9.4% of the respondents were retired, 8.6% were currently unemployed and finally 4.3% were students. 2.2% chose 'other' category which included individuals who were on long-term disability (see Table 2).

When respondents were asked how long they have been remitting money, most people surveyed (59.2%) have been sending money for 5 years or more. 13.4% of participants have been sending money between 3 to 5 years, followed by people who have been sending money between 1 to 3 years. Whereas, people who have been sending for less than a year comprised of 9.8% of the survey participants. When we examined how long people have been sending money by their age ranges, it shows that respondents between the age of 25–34 were most likely to have sent money for less than a year (57.1%). Respondents between the ages 35 to 44 were more likely to have been remitting funds between 3 to 5 years (31.6%). The respondents between 45 and 54 years along with those 55 years and over were more likely to have been sending money more than five years at 30.0% respectively.

Most respondents sent money about once a month (55.4%), followed by people who sent every two to three months (18.7%). 59.3% of survey respondents sent $500 or less. It should be noted this question was changed at the mid-point of the survey, to gain a better understanding of amounts smaller than $500. Accordingly, of the 71 individuals who sent $500 or less, more than half of the respondents (43) selected amounts below $500 and the results showed that most people (11.4%) sent about $100 to $200. This relatively small amounts are consistent with other studies show that most people sent relatively small amounts that make a huge difference in the lives of people in the receiving countries. The other amounts sent that were more than $500 include: 11.4% for people sending $501 to $750 dollars; 10.0% for $751 to $1000, 10.7% for $1001 to $1500 and 8.6% for people who sent more than $1501.

The vast majority of Somali people in the Greater Toronto Area sent money using Somali money transfer agencies. 92.9% of the respondents used Somali Hawala services to send money. There were a small number of people who used money transfer agencies such as Western Union and Money Gram (4.3%). The survey respondents were asked to name one Hawala agency they use the most, Dahabshiil was most frequently used at 27.7%, this was followed Bakal Express at 13.9%. However other agencies were also used including Amaana Express and Amal both at 12.4% of the time. It should be noted that the part of the country the MTO operates influences the number of users. For example, people who send money to Puntland will often use Salama Express because they have a larger network in that part of the country. When people were asked about any other MTOs that they use regularly, most once again noted they use Dahabshiil (32.9%), followed by Bakal (19.6%), Amaana (14.0%), and Amal (11.9%).

An important part of the survey asked participants if they utilize technology to send money as well as which services they use. A notable number of individuals have used online or mobile banking to send money to Somalia, 38.6% of participants have used mobile or online money transfer. When the survey respondents were asked to name the service they have used, 35.1% have used Dahabshiil's eDahab service to send money. 33.3% have used EVC Plus to send money to Somalia. 12.3% have utilized Sahal to send money. 8.8% have used Zaad and only 1.8% have used the online only World Remit.

The use of technology in communication is unparalleled and as discussed earlier, people sending money from the GTA to Somalia utilize technology in nearly all aspects. We surveyed people in the GTA to see how often they communicate with family members in Somalia and what type of technologies they use when the communicate with them. First, we asked how often they communicate with family members, and most people (49.3%) stated they communicate at least once a month with their family members. Nearly a quarter (23.6%) of respondents stated they communicate with their family about once a week.

The survey respondents were asked about the types of telecommunication services they use to communicate with family members in Somalia. The question allowed for multiple responses. Most individuals use mobile phones, 49.0%, to communicate with family members. This was followed by Mobile applications such as Viber, WhatApp, and Facebook Messenger at 41.3%. 20.3% of Somalis in the GTA use internet application such as Skype, Google Talk or E-mail to communicate with family members. Finally, 12.6% of the respondents use telephone landlines to communicate with family members.

6 Mobile Money

In order to understand the role that technology plays in the remittance system we test a few hypotheses. We wanted to understand how mobile money technology is adapted. Moreover, we wanted to know the characteristics of the individual who send money using mobile money. Customer-facing technology such as mobile money has been increasingly been adapted by consumers.

The Canadian banking access closure to the Money Transfer Organizations (MTOs) has also closed access to Mobile Banking innovations that are changing remittance sector in Somalia. One MTO noted they accept online money transfers, for small amounts. They accept these payments in their personal banking accounts, its one way they try to assist customers who want to send money but cannot physically come into the office with cash. These types of customers are repeat customers and have an already established relationship with the MTO.

An example of mobile money is Zaad, which is one of the largest mobile money services in Somalia. In order to gain access to it, you need to use TeleSom mobile phone. In order to send and receive money, a potential customer needs to go a Zaad centre with some form of ID, and witness. Individuals to have a Zaad are then required to provide their Somali four names, often an individual's first name along with the names of their three fathers. The three names are often used to determine an individual's family lineage in Somalia and as away to guarantee accountability extend to the more than the individual. Moreover, the individual is also required to provide the four names of their mother. A photo and figure print of the customer is then and taken retained. For an example of the registration form. Once the Zaad account, often your TeleSom telephone number, you can use it store, send or receive the money. The money in the account are held as U.S Dollars. To withdrawal physical cash at a Zaad counter or agents on the street. The agents in the street usually have access to Somali currency with official Zaad locations providing access to U.S. dollars.

Hence, to understand the adoption of mobile money, we employ the Diffusion of Innovation (DOI), which was elucidated by Everett M. Rogers [45]. The theory posits how new ideas, innovation, "spreads via certain communication channels over time among the members of a social system" [45]. The theory can be traced to French scholar Gabriel Tarde (1903), who tried to understand the 'S' curve that emerges when examining innovation, early adaptors and opinion leaders [46]. Others have contributed to the theory, for example Elihu Katz [47] added to the notion of opinion leaders and followers along with the role of the media [48]. DOI theory is a part of change model that tries to place the people who serve as the thought leaders that eventually leads to a saturation point for the theory. However, some have argued that this theory falls short in several areas. One area is that the theory makes the assumption that the diffusion is homogenous, discounts some environmental factors such as economic constraints [49]. Although, the DOI theory has some drawbacks, we employed it for this study to understand the characteristics of the of how the mobile money is being adopted by the Somali diaspora. Tan, Teo [50] operationalized aspects of DOI theory by developing a framework that offered insight into internet banking adoption in Singapore. This framework was also tested in South Africa by Brown et al. [51] with regards to cellphone banking adaptions. The resulting framework found three major factors influenced an individual's likelihood of adapting internet banking: attitude, subjective norms and perceived behavioral control. For this study, the dependent variable was the use of mobile money while the independent variable included gender, age, length of remittance and employment status. The following three prepositions will explore the adoption of the Mobile money employing Tan and Teo's framework.

Attitude is an individual's view of mobile money contains: Relative Advantage, Compatibility, Complexity, Trialabilit and Risk.

Preposition 1: When the remitter is employed then it is more likely that they use mobile money.

Employment status seems to be related to usage of mobile money services ($p < 0.05$). When respondents were asked if they had used mobile money, 39.1% individuals answered in the affirmative. Of these 75.9% were employed and have used mobile money, while those who were unemployed who had used mobile money were 24.1%. This might suggest that employment status of Somalis makes it easier to use mobile money because they are exposed to similar technology in their work.

Subjective norms are the social influences that affect the use of mobile money to remit funds to Somalia.

Preposition 2: When an individual has remitted for a longer period of time they are more likely to use mobile or online services to remit.

A chi-square test was performed and a relationship was found between individuals who remit using mobile or online services more frequently remit and also send more money, X^2 (1, N = 138) = 4.02, p < 0.05. The convenience offered by online services might lead the senders to use mobile services rather than physically going to agent's offices.

Perceived behavioral control are the environmental conditions that allow for internet banking including: Self-efficacy and Facilitating conditions.

Preposition 3: When mobile money is used then it is likely that people will remit more.

To test this preposition, a chi-square test was conducted and we found that there is no difference in amounts sent between people who use mobile money and those who do not use it. A reason why this might be the case is that members of the diaspora are unsure about using mobile for security reasons. Another plausible reason for the lack of difference could that family members of this survey participants do not have access to mobile phones and thus can not use mobile money. They are also inclined to support the MTO agents who they might have had a long standing relationship.

Preposition 4: When the gender of the remitter is female and they use mobile money then it is likely that they will remit more.

A chi-square test was performed and a relationship was there is a difference of the genders when using mobile money and the amount remitted. Women who have been remitting longer and use mobile money are more likely to send more money, X^2 (1, N = 138) = 4.02, p < 0.05. The convenience and security offered by online services might lead the senders to use rather than physically going to agent's offices.

7 Conclusion

The aim of the paper was to understand the process behind the remittance system and the role played by the Somali diaspora in the social and economic system of Somalia. The remittance sector has served as an important segment of the Somali economy and has assisted in the stabilization of a 'failed state'. The remittances industry has served as an important link between those in the diaspora and family and friends left in the country. Since the 1990 collapse of the state in Somalia, the remittance sector has served as primary access to finance and the financial services. In fact, the remittance industry seems to work in spite of a lack of a state-regulated financial system.

Through a review of secondary sources such as Statistics Canada, UN Data, the World Bank along with a review of previous research, we established the Somali-Canadian population and the demographic profile of the community. As the number of refugees admitted into Canada increased drastically in the 1990s, and a large number chose to reside in the Greater Toronto Area (GTA). Next, we detailed the cost to send money from various countries to Somalia and along with the number of locations in the Money Transfer Organizations (MTOs) in the GTA. This type of information provides an understanding the of the reach and scale of the Hawala network. This allows us to then move to understand the users and business associated with the Somali MTOs.

In order to understand the role of both the diaspora and the remittance sector, this study employed a survey questionnaire of Somalis in the GTA along with interviewing members of Somali Money Transfer Organizations. The Somali Hawala system, although not new, has changed and adapted a unique approach within the context of Somalia. The Hawala system is fast, cheap and reliable. Even though, it has faced barriers around the world that have appeared over the years. For example, the U.S. has placed restrictions on Somali Money Transfer Organizations, in Canada the Canadian banks have closed down accounts associated with the Somali system. The British government and banking industry have attempted to curtail the Somali industry on several occasions.

The survey participants ranged in age, gender, income and education levels. The qualitative approach was utilized because it would allow the researcher to understand the process utilized by the Somali diaspora when sending funds to Somalia. This approach also allowed for us to understand the amounts sent by the diaspora, the methods they use the most and the motivations for sending the funds. The study confirmed that most Somalis, across the various demographic, socio-economic categories participate in the Hawala system.

Most survey respondents regularly send, with most sending at least once a month. A significant amount of the Somalis in the GTA send less than $500, this confirms other research that most people send smaller amounts however this small amount makes a large difference in the daily lives of people in Somalia. This study also reiterated the fact that most Somalis rely on Somali based MTOs because they are often the only remittance providers to the country. The Somali MTOs are perceived as trustworthy by members of the diaspora. Interestingly, this study also found that a Somali use the Hawala system to send money within Canada itself.

The study observed that social ties is a strong motivator as to why individuals in Canada send money to people in Somalia. The more frequently people communicate they more likely they were to remit more frequently. Another finding was people who remit more frequently tended to send more money. Although, the findings indicate that these same people remitted smaller amounts too. Confirming that the connection to people in Somalia, as witnessed by how frequently they communicate, is a strong indicator to remittances. Based on social network theory, the opposite conditions also seemed to confirm that people who have been sending money for a lesser period and were less likely to send less money. This study confirmed some aspects of social ties as a strong basis for sending money.

Another theory that we utilized for this study was Altruism theory. The survey participants confirmed that the are primarily driven by altruistic reasons why they send money to Somalia. For example, people listed that they sent money for money for family expenses. Other reasons included that assisting in buying food and educating children. When it comes to people sending money, the theory seemed to show that people send money but one part of the theory could not be replicated. An example of this was the idea that as people's income levels rose, they would send more money. My analysis did not find this to be case when it came to Somali remitters.

Next, we wanted to find out how technology is used in the remittance sector and how new innovations were being adopted. We found that a noticeable number of Somalis sending money were using online and mobile services. This seems to align with research from the World Bank that shows that people within Somalia had adopted mobile phones and banking at high rates. We found that the strongest connection to those individuals who used mobile money were more likely to be employed. Another finding that we found was that people who had remitted for longer periods of time were also more likely to use mobile service. Moreover, if the remitter is female and had been remitting for a longer period then they were likely to use mobile money. In both instances, we believe this could be to save on time that might be related with traveling to the MTO location.

The Somali individuals and businesses are aware of the security implications that arise from remitting money, especially to Somalia. This study confirms that the individuals and businesses adhere to Canadian rules and regulations when sending money. Somali individuals who remit more are often asked to provide identification. On the other hand, interviews with businesses confirmed that they ensure they track individuals who send large amounts, anything above $1000. Some view that the Hawala business will likely lose business as the Somali governments create a banking system that is stable.

Thus, the aim of this paper will be to examine role of the diaspora in the remittance system. More specially, this paper will analyze the crucial role served by ICTs in the delivery of the billions of dollars into the country. In the case of Somalia and its diaspora, the Hawala system has evolved in spite these restrictions and the lack of the formal banking system. In country without centralized postal system or personal identification system the Hawala system has several advantages. First, individuals without a fixed address have the ability to use the system because they all that is required is code or phrase from the sender to access the funds. Another advantage is that the Hawala system works in places where large money transfer institutions do not serve. For example, there are no Western Union desks or internationally recognized MTOs in Somalia. A third advantage is that it has a relatively low cost, the commission charged the sender is of around five percent. Thus this low commission ensures the cost of transfer itself is reasonable for the senders. A fourth advantage is that the large Hawala systems is now web-based to facilitate the quick transfer of money. Once the money arrived the client is called, usually, on a mobile telephone which are widely available. If the amount large a clan elder is called upon to verify the person's identity. In order to create a fast efficient system, technology has enabled this process to move at the pace of the internet.

References

1. Menkhaus, K.: Somalia and the horn of Africa. In: World Development Report 2011. The World Bank, Washington, DC (2011)
2. Byrne, M.: The failed state and failed state-building: how can a move away from the failed state discourse inform development in Somalia. Birkbeck Law Rev. **1**(1), 111–134 (2013)

3. Lindley, A.: Leaving Mogadishu: towards a sociology of conflict-related mobility. J. Refug. Stud. **23**(1), 2–22 (2010). https://doi.org/10.1093/jrs/fep043
4. Lindley, A., Haslie, A.: Unlocking protracted displacement: Somali case study. In: RSC Working Paper Series No. 79. Refugee Studies Centre, Oxford University; Norwegian Institute of International Affairs (NUPI); Internal Displacement Monitoring Centre (IDMC), Oxford, UK (2011)
5. Shay, S.: Somalia Between Jihad and Restoration. Routledge, London (2017)
6. Mohapatra, S., Ratha, D.: Migrant remittances in Africa: an overview. In: Mohapatra, S., Ratha, D. (eds.) Remittance Markets in Africa, pp. 1–70. The World Bank, Washington, DC (2011)
7. Hassan, M.A., Chalmers, C.: UK Somali Remittances Survey. Department for International Development London, UK (2008)
8. IMF: IMF to Help Somalia Rebuild Its Economy (2013). http://www.imf.org/external/pubs/ft/survey/so/2013/car062413a.htm. Accessed 1 Feb 2015
9. Orozco, M., Yansura, J.: Keeping the Lifeline Open Remittances and Markets in Somalia. Oxfam America, Washington, DC (2013)
10. United Nations: United Nations Data, New York, NY (2017)
11. Pénicaud, C., McGrath, F.: Innovative inclusion: how telesom ZAAD brought mobile money to Somaliland. In: GSMA Mobile Nanking for the Unbanked, p. 13. GSMA, London (2013)
12. Studio, D.: Always moving, always sharing mobile money practices in Somaliland. Bill & Melinda Gates Foundation, San Francisco (2015)
13. Demirgüç-Kunt, A., Klapper, L.F., Singer, D., Van Oudheusden, P.: The Global Findex Database 2014: Measuring Financial Inclusion Around the World. World Bank Policy Research Working Paper No. 7255 (2015)
14. Sayid, O., Echchabi, A.: Attitude of Somali customers towards mobile banking services: the case of Zaad and Sahal services. Econ. Insights-Trends Chall. **2**(3), 9–16 (2013)
15. Waldo, M.A.: Somalia remittances: myth and reality. In: Maimbo, S.M. (ed.) Remittances and Economic Development in Somalia: An Overview, vol. 38, pp. 19–22. The World Bank, Washington, DC (2006)
16. Guleid, H.A.R., Tirimba, O.I.: Analysis of Somaliland mobile money service on effective inflation control: case of Hargeisa Foreign exchange market in Somaliland. Int. J. Bus. Manag. Econ. Res. **6**(6), 355–370 (2015)
17. Gutale, A.: What would you do if an overseas bank cut off the financial lifeline to your family? The Guardian (2015)
18. Maimbo, S.M., Ratha, D.: Remittances: development impact and future prospects. World Bank Publications (2005)
19. Oxfam: Hanging by a thread: The ongoing threat to Somalia's remittance lifeline (2015). https://www.oxfam.org/sites/www.oxfam.org/files/file_attachments/bn-hanging-by-thread-somalia-remittances-190215-en.pdf
20. Federal Government of Somalia: Somalia Drought Impact & Needs Assessment (DINA). Federal Government of Somalia, vol. 1, p. 160. Federal Government of Somalia, Mogadishu (2018)
21. De Goede, M.: Hawala discourses and the war on terrorist finance. Environ. Plan. D Soc. Space **21**(5), 513–532 (2003)
22. El-Qorchi, M.: The Hawala System. Finance Dev. **39**(4) (2002)
23. Razavy, M.: Hawala: an underground haven for terrorists or social phenomenon? Crime Law Soc. Chang. **44**(3), 277–299 (2005). https://doi.org/10.1007/s10611-006-9019-3
24. Looney, R.: Hawala: the terrorist's informal financial mechanism. Middle East Policy **10**(1), 164–167 (2003)
25. Ladanyi, E., Kobolka, I.: The Hawala system. Interdiscip. Manag. Res. **10**, 413–420 (2014)

26. Schramm, M., Taube, M.: Evolution and institutional foundation of the Hawala financial system. Int. Rev. Financ. Anal. **12**(4), 405–420 (2003). https://doi.org/10.1016/S1057-5219 (03)00032-2
27. Maimbo, S.M., Ratha, D.: Remittances: an overview. In: Maimbo, S.M., Ratha, D. (eds.) Remittances: Development Impact and Future Prospects, pp. 1–16. World Bank Publications, Washington, DC (2005)
28. Maimbo, S.M.: The Money Exchange Dealers of Kabul: A study of the Hawala system in Afghanistan. Working Paper 13, p. 47. The World Bank, Washington, DC (2003)
29. Jost, P.M., Sandhu, H.: The Hawala alternative remittance system and its role in money laundering, p. 25. Interpol General Secretariat, Lyon (2000)
30. BBC: US ends Somali banking blacklist. British Broadcasting Corporation. BBC News, London, UK (2006)
31. Omer, A.: Feasibility study on financial services in Somalia, p. 132. UNDP, United Nations Development Programme, Online (2004)
32. Nenova, T., Harford, T.: Anarchy and invention: How does Somalia's private sector cope without government? p. 4. World Bank (2005)
33. International Monetary Fund: Regulatory Frameworks for Hawala and Other Remittance Systems. International Monetary Fund, Washington, DC (2005)
34. Hammond, L.: Obliged to give: Remittances and the maintenance of transnational networks between Somalis at home and abroad. Bildhaan Int. J. Somali Stud. **10**(1), 125–151 (2011)
35. World Bank: Somali Poverty Profile 2016: Findings from Wave 1 of the Somali High Frequency Survey. Report No: AUS19442, p. 134. World Bank, Washington, DC (2017)
36. World Bank: Remittance Prices Worldwide (2018). https://remittanceprices.worldbank.org/en/about-remittance-prices-worldwide. Accessed 15 May 2018
37. World Bank: Remittance Prices Worldwide: Q2, 2018. World Bank, Washington, DC (2018)
38. Hamza, B.M.: A report on the Somali remittance sector in Canada. Nathanson Centre for the Study of Organized Crime and Corruption, p. 53. Osgoode Hall Law School, York University, Toronto, ON (2006)
39. Mackenzie, A.: The Fintech revolution. Lond. Bus. School Rev. **26**(3), 50–53 (2015)
40. Canada Revenue Agency: Electronic Funds Transfer Reporting. Canada Revenue Agency, Ottawa (2015)
41. Crouch, M., McKenzie, H.: The logic of small samples in interview-based qualitative research. Soc. Sci. Inf. **45**(4), 483–499 (2006). https://doi.org/10.1177/0539018406069584
42. Benbasat, I., Goldstein, D.K., Mead, M.: The case research strategy in studies of information systems. MIS Q. **11**, 369–386 (1987)
43. Marshall, B., Cardon, P., Poddar, A., Fontenot, R.: Does sample size matter in qualitative research?: A review of qualitative interviews in IS research. J. Comput. Inf. Syst. **54**(1), 11–22 (2013)
44. Mikkelsen, B.: Methods for Development Work and Research: A New Guide for Practitioners. Sage, Thousand Oaks (2005)
45. Rogers, E.M.: Diffusion of Innovations, 3rd edn. The Free Press, New York (1983)
46. Valente, T.W., Rogers, E.M.: The origins and development of the diffusion of innovations paradigm as an example of scientific growth. Sci. Commun. **16**(3), 242–273 (1995)
47. Katz, E.: The two-step flow of communication: an up-to-date report on an hypothesis. Public Opin. Q. **21**(1), 61–78 (1957)
48. Kaminski, J.: Diffusion of innovation theory. Can. J. Nurs. Inform. **6**(2), 1–6 (2011)
49. Lyytinen, K., Damsgaard, J.: What's wrong with the diffusion of innovation theory? In: Ardis, M.A., Marcolin, B.L. (eds.) TDIT 2001. IFIP AICT, vol. 59, pp. 173–190. Springer, Boston, MA (2001). https://doi.org/10.1007/978-0-387-35404-0_11

50. Tan, M., Teo, T.S.: Factors influencing the adoption of Internet banking. J. AIS **1**(1es), 5 (2000)
51. Brown, I., Cajee, Z., Davies, D., Stroebel, S.: Cell phone banking: predictors of adoption in South Africa—an exploratory study. Int. J. Inf. Manag. **23**(5), 381–394 (2003)

Interactional Aesthetics of Blockchain Technology

Michael Heidt[1]([✉]), Andreas Bischof[2], and Arne Berger[2]

[1] GeDIS, University of Kassel, Pfannkuchstraße 1, 34121 Kassel, Germany
mrbheidt@gmail.com
[2] Chair Media Informatics, Chemnitz University of Technology,
Straße der Nationen 62, 09111 Chemnitz, Germany
{andreas.bischof,arne.berger}@informatik.tu-chemnitz.de

Abstract. Blockchain technology holds the potential of facilitating fundamentally novel ways for users to relate to systems of finance, governance, and identity management. At the same time, the inherent complexity of blockchain systems makes designing for and interacting with the technology profoundly challenging. Furthermore, the question of how social interactions will change under the influence of Blockchain systems remains an open one. In this paper we examine how concepts and procedures adopted from interaction aesthetics can serve as an intellectual and methodological lens to creatively and critically examine the emerging technology of the Blockchain.

Keywords: Aesthetics · Blockchain · Smart contracts ·
Critical technical practice · Interactional aesthetics

1 Introduction

Blockchain technology holds the potential of facilitating fundamentally novel ways for users to relate to systems of finance, governance, and identity management. It promises to establish innovative ways of conducting governance, to facilitate novel forms of civic engagement, to simplify interactions with smart devices, to enable new ways of interacting with digital and non-digital assets [1–5]. At the same time, the inherent complexity of blockchain systems makes designing for and interacting with the technology profoundly challenging. Already, the capabilities of blockchain systems threaten to surpass the interactional competence of its users [6,7]. Furthermore, the question of how social interactions will change under the influence of Blockchain systems remains an open one. Should blockchain technologies indeed become a defining feature of future social life, the question of how to communicate respective technological possibilities to users likewise gains in significance.

In this paper, we discuss how design considerations aimed at blockchain systems can be enriched through incorporation of elements of interactional aesthetics. We argue that interactional aesthetics holds unique possibilities in articulating novel design features, while allowing users to observe and question the

F. F.-H. Nah and K. Siau (Eds.): HCII 2019, LNCS 11588, pp. 137–147, 2019.
https://doi.org/10.1007/978-3-030-22335-9_9

technological impact of blockchain systems. This is due to the ability of aesthetic elements to implicitly communicate features of a design whose representations might not be explicitly understood by its users.

2   Blockchain Technology

A Blockchain acts as a distributed database, allowing secure transactions in the absence of trusted intermediaries [8]. Every system participant is able to verify the legitimacy of every transaction made while being able to inspect the full history of transactions conducted within the system. No actor within the network is able to forge information or disregard information once it has been approved. Crucially, blockchain systems allow for the transference of digital property in a manner ensuring that transfers are "safe and secure, everyone knows that the transfer has taken place, and nobody can challenge the legitimacy of the transfer" [9].

The class of values which can be transferred within a Blockchain backed system encompasses "birth and death certificates, marriage licenses, deeds and titles of ownership, educational degrees, financial accounts, medical procedures, insurance claims, votes, provenance of food" [10].

2.1   Smart Contracts

Furthermore, blockchain systems allow for the operation of *smart contracts* [11, 12]. Smart contracts act as software agents allowing for values to be transferred once certain criteria are met: As an example, the smart lock of a rental apartment might automatically grant access to a guest once payment is detected; a smart fridge within the apartment might automatically charge the guest for any item consumed during the stay.

Crucially, the integrity of smart-contract operation is guaranteed by the same mechanisms used for verifying transactions within the Blockchain. Hence, they cannot be hacked and their outcome is open for inspection to all parties involved. Conflicts are decided not by means of human arbitrators but by encoding conditions in the medium of formal language.

As the name implies, smart contracts are intended to partly replace contracts backed by law through those backed by algorithms: A traditional off-line contract requires participants to trust the other parties to honour the agreement made. This is not true of the smart contract, for its presence within the blockchain endows it with a self-enforcing quality. Consequently, systems built using smart contracts are described as being *trustless* [13,14].

3   Aesthetics

In its most classical form, aesthetics refers to all phenomena and faculties relating to sensory experience. As a philosophical problem it motivated studies of the beautiful and the sublime. Resultingly, aesthetical concerns do not constitute one of the classical foci of systems design and computer-science disciplines.

The dominant traditions within computer-science conceptualize of computers as abstract machines, processing lexemes that do not possess perceptual or material characteristics. Formal conceptual devices, such as the Turing machine, indeed serve to abstract from material qualities, thereby describing computing processes on the level of mathematical functions. They are independent of any material that could impact the senses. This approach to computation has been exceptionally successful, allowing for a concise formal description of computing processes while abstracting from the immense physical complexities incurred by computing system design and implementation. However, the history of computing has been closely intertwined with the concept of visualization and interaction. Interactive games seem to be a quasi-automatic by-product of any system combining display and input capabilities [15].

Furthermore, interaction implies the necessity for an, albeit rudimentary, aesthetic access to the realm of computers. Even if only setting up a computation on a mainframe computer, entering parameters, or checking the result or error code of a computing process, human perception and sensory experience, invariably is involved.

Despite this traditional focus, aesthetic perspectives have indeed gained traction within the discourses of HCI as part of a "turn to experience" [16]. Constructs such as user experiences invariably contain an aesthetic component, without necessarily referring to the critical and aesthetic positions present within the broader discourse on the matter.

During the course of this text, we will argue that conceptual elements of aesthetics can indeed serve to enrich a practice-based engagement of complex technological artefacts such as Blockchain technologies.

3.1 The Aesthetic Turn

Indeed there are authors who describe an *Aesthetic Turn* within the realm of computing. Udsen and Jørgensen describe aesthetics as a valuable extension of traditional approaches to interface design [17]. They identify four distinct aesthetic approaches: a cultural approach, a functionalist approach, an experience based approach, and a techno-futurist approach. Functionalist approaches employ aesthetics in order to analyse or optimise usability features within systems and artefacts. They are often task centric and typically aim at furthering goals such as efficiency and effectiveness. Cultural approaches treat artefacts and interfaces as aesthetic forms. They analyse them according to categories developed within philosophy, literaray and cultural studies, or the social sciences. Techno-futurist approaches adopt a visionary stance, combining philosophy with speculative practices in order to account for the coevolution of technology, social practices, and human experience. Experience based approaches base themselves on existing practices with interaction design, complementing existing HCI procedures through a focus on non-functional and phenomenological qualities.

Bardzell [18] treats critical theory and aesthetics as part of a single intellectual development aimed at complementing existing functional approaches towards interaction design.

Nake and Grabowski describe aesthetic computing as the realm of computing phenomena requiring aesthetic judgement [19].

3.2 Aesthetics and Polyperspectivity

In the classical treatment of the faculties of reason Kant describes aesthetic judgements as possessing both subjectivity and universality, as being both contingent and necessary [20]. This special status of aesthetic judgements allow them to serve as reconciliatory agent between diverse viewpoints and perspectives. Astrid Wagner discusses how Kant's conception of aesthetics is intertwined with the notions of freedom and autonomy [21]. Furthermore, it points to the necessity of accepting multiple viewpoints, due to the inherently subjective, yet non-arbitrary nature of aesthetic judgements. When adopting an aesthetic stance, we have to account for a multitude of ways of seeing the world, yet we attentively deal with the material reality enabling a shared social space of feeling and experiencing.

3.3 Interaction Aesthetics

Interaction aesthetics, conceived as the aesthetic treatment of phenomena arising from the interaction of humans with artefacts, constitutes a relatively novel focus both in the fields of science and art. Art has traditionally dealt with objects of lasting quality, less so with ephemeral and emergent qualities such as interaction.

From the mid-20th century onward, however, interactive elements have emerged as a staple within avant-garde art practices, gradually dissipating into the mainstream. Subsequently, artistic phenomena such as media-art, net.art, digital art, and paradigms such as relational aesthetics [22] served to rejuvenate the interest in aesthetic treatment of practices of interaction.

An interesting synoptic treatment of contemporary approaches to interaction aesthetics is provided by Katja Kwastek's text "Aesthetics of Interaction in Digital Art" which will act as a central point of reference for the current discussion.

Kwastek relates interaction aesthetics to three criteria:

- aesthetic distance as condition of aesthetic experience, counterbalancing the "flow" of interaction
- a specific ontological status of interactive works
- a specific mode of knowledge generation through reception of interactive artefacts.

It is especially this last criterion which provides helpful impulses for conducting practice-based research regarding the aesthetic dimensions of Blockchain technology.

4 Design Framework

We will now discuss a tentative design framework informed by the aesthetic stance detailed in the preceding sections. The goal is not to produce yet another framework as there are ample meticulously worked out propositions for the practitioner to choose from. Rather, it serves to illustrate how incorporating an aesthetic stance can inform, modify, and modulate processes of design in the context of practice-based inquiry. It thus employs both elements of condensation and forms of extension.

The framework is part of an ongoing inquiry into the conditions of practice-based research [23,24]. As such it complements earlier proposals [25,26], on whose categories it is based. Within the framework's context, additionally introduced concepts, such as digital materiality, act as lenses facilitating different perspectives on the artefact and the practices it enables. They thus aid the process of formulating knowledge claims in relationship to the artefact in question.

4.1 The Interactive Artefact

Following Kwastek's analysis, interaction artefacts are conceived as tripartite entities, comprised of the following components:

Interaction Proposition. The interaction proposition describes the auctorial intention of the interactive artefact's makers.

Material Artefact. The material components of the artefact realising the interaction proposition. This encompasses physical elements such as props, decorations, sensors, displays but also rule systems structuring, incentivising, and shaping interactions.

Interaction Processes. The processes of interaction unfolding in relationship to the artefact.

4.2 Vicarious Interaction

Furthermore, in order to account for the genuine interactional qualities of blockchain devices, their capacity to pervasively shape social interactions, it is instructive to consider the concept of *vicarious interaction.*

A key concept within the aesthetics of interaction [27], vicarious interaction occurs, when an individual not actively participates in an interactive process, yet consciously observes and processes the interactions of others (see Fig. 1). First examined within the context of educational science [28], vicarious interactions allow prospective users to learn about system behaviour even while not engaging actively with the artefact in question. Crucially, observing and learning from others' interactions allows the formation of understanding regarding the impact of the technological artefact presented. In effect, vicarious interaction allows for trust to be formed without a need for direct user-system interaction (such as seeing others making withdrawals at an ATM machine might persuade us to believe that it is safe to use).

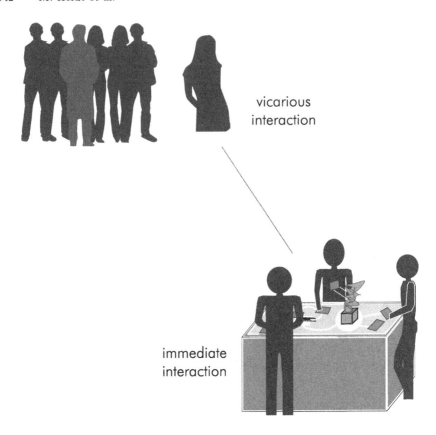

vicarious
interaction

immediate
interaction

Fig. 1. Vicarious interaction

4.3 Digital Materiality

In order to identify the unique characteristics of digital structures in relationship to interaction aesthetics, we deem it instructive to inquire into the specifics of the digital as material for artefact production. This is in line with recent trends in aesthetics "to not only view material as a technical circumstance, but also to value it as an aesthetic category" [29][1].

The reason for the popularity of the concept of materiality can also be attributed to the demise of the concept of reality [27, 139]. Talking about materiality allows for conceptualising a mutual plane of reference and interaction without having to deal with philosophically contentious concepts such as reality.

One of the most influential concepts of digital materiality was formulated by Leonardi [30,31]. Leonardi shifts emphasis away from the realm of the physical, instead focussing on questions of practical instantiation and significance. No ontological difference exists between physical and formal artefacts, they are material insofar as they make a difference, insofar as "they matter". This allows

---

[1] English translation quoted from [27].

a discussion of digital artefacts on par with other objects of study, for the only relevant question is which kind of impact a relevant artefact has on observable practice.

In order to develop an account of digital materiality conducive to a discussion of phenomena of interaction aesthetics, the aforementioned positions are related to a characterisation developed by Nake and Grabowski [32]: Material is conceptualised as that what offers resistance. Software or systems of formal rules are material since they offer resistance to our efforts to shape them. Resultingly, work is required to bend them into the shapes required for interactive artefacts. Digital materiality is involved when work is expended in order to shape digital structures.

5 Related Work

The `terra0` system builds a "self-owning" forest, able to reproduce itself through Blockchain technology [33]. Through smart contracts, the forest generates revenue by selling licenses to log trees, thereby compensating for running costs. It provides social commentary on ideas connected to Blockchain technologies in the context of an artistic project. The self-referential nature of the system (selling parts of itself) points towards the problematic of complexity while highlighting the economic implications of Blockchain technologies.

Bittercoin [34] "The World's Worst Bitcoin Miner" serves to illustrate the computational work embodied within Blockchain systems. The system consists of a mechanical calculator performing computations as dictated by Bitcoin's Blockchain protocol. Results are printed on paper. The system does not constitute a feasible approach to mining due to the incredibly slow nature of the computation. Instead it renders Blockchain's formal procedures tangible by virtue of mechanisation. It thus points both to the materiality of Blockchain technologies while facilitating critical perspectives through implicit reference to phenomena such as the enormous energy consumption of the Bitcoin system.

Di Battista et al. describe a system for visualization of flows within the Bitcoin system [35].

McGinn et al. describe visualizations of Bitcoin transaction patterns [36].

6 Observations

6.1 Trustlessness and Aesthetics

In order to account for the phenomenon of trustlessness exhibited by smart contract technology, it is instructive to frame it within the terms of sociology. Following social systems theory, trust can be conceptualised as a mechanism for reduction of social complexity: Trust allows individuals to relate to a stable set of expectations in the face of uncertainty [37].

Following this systems theoretic construal of trust allows us to put it in constructive dialogue with aesthetics: The aesthetics of a designed artefact allow users to form expectations, thereby enhancing their ability to detect affordances [38]. Hence, aesthetic qualities aid the communication of designs from designers to users, in turn reducing *design-uncertainty*.

6.2 Aesthetics of Trust

As a quality arising from and within social interaction, trust at first appears hard to visualize. It is not immediately grounded in data and possesses multiform manifestations in social life—"trust takes on many various shapes" [37, 103].

At the same time, one should not dismiss any potential mode of dialogue between conceptualisations of trust and aesthetic categories. In fact, different conceptualisations of the phenomenon of trust inform different aesthetic representations which in turn evoke different aesthetic experiences. A further complicating factor is its ubiquity [37, 5]. Since trust is an ubiquitous facet of social life, we might overlook it.

An interesting approach towards the discussed problematic is provided by Sas and Khairuddin [39], who call for "Materializing Trust in Blockchain". Their approach calls for visualization of reputation data in order to increase the social embededdness of Blockchain transactions.

Aesthetics possesses the ability to communicate aspects of a design by virtue of evoking adequate emotions. The aesthetic qualities of an artefact help to shape user expectations and thus to decrease *design uncertainty*.

If we follow the premise that trust is based on the feeling of posessing more information than is actually present [37, 36 ff.], this presents an interesting challenge for the visualization of Blockchain technologies. The problem becomes that not of providing exhaustive information or conveying a maximum amount of data, but of balancing perceptions of risk with expectation of success.

7 Conclusion

7.1 Aesthetics as Mechanism of Complexity Reduction

We argue that aesthetics is important precisely due to the highly abstract nature of Blockchain technology. Aesthetics possesses the ability to communicate aspects of a design, even if the underlying abstractions are not fully understood by system users. In line with the argumentation of Xenakis and Arnellos [38], aesthetics acts as a way of reducing *design uncertainty*. Interaction aesthetics thus parallels the social function of trust, understood as a mechanism of reducing social complexity [37,40]. Furthermore, through vicarious interaction, interactional aesthetics allow for users to observe and reflect on the technological impact of blockchain systems.

7.2 Aesthetics as Agent of Polyperspectivity

Not only does the stance of aesthetics allow for interesting impulses regarding construction of Blockchain based artefacts. Through its inherent problematisation of questions of freedom and polyperspectivity it points to the complexity of affected social systems and processes. It thus reminds us of the social problems at stake when employing potentially far reaching technological artefacts such as smart contracts.

Aesthetics provides a way for accounting for the richness of human experience, the complexity of social processes, and the challenging problem of supporting both through complicated technical structures. It thereby might provide a helpful arena for approaching the problematic of relating complicated technical systems and complex social practice.

Acknowledgements. This work was supported in part by the Andrea von Braun Foundation, Munich, under the grant "Blockchain – A Practice-Based Inquiry Into a Future Agent of Social Transformation".

References

1. Crosby, M., Pattanayak, P., Verma, S., Kalyanaraman, V.: Blockchain technology: beyond bitcoin. Appl. Innov. **2**, 6–10 (2016)
2. Pschetz, L., Tallyn, E., Gianni, R., Speed, C.: Bitbarista: exploring perceptions of data transactions in the Internet of Things. In: Proceedings of the 2017 CHI Conference on Human Factors in Computing Systems, pp. 2964–2975. ACM, February 2017
3. Speed, C., Maxwell, D., Pschetz, L.: Blockchain City: economic, social and cognitive ledgers. In: Kitchin, R., Lauriault, T., McArdle, G. (eds.) Data and the City. Regions and Cities. Routledge, August 2017
4. Dunphy, P., Petitcolas, F.A.: A first look at identity management schemes on the blockchain. IEEE Secur. Priv. **16**(4), 20–29 (2018)
5. Liu, Y., Wang, Q.: An e-voting protocol based on blockchain. IACR Cryptology ePrint Archive, Santa Barbara, CA, USA, Technical report 1043:2017 (2017)
6. Yli-Huumo, J., Ko, D., Choi, S., Park, S., Smolander, K.: Where is current research on blockchain technology?—A systematic review. PLOS ONE **11**(10), e0163477 (2016)
7. Eskandari, S., Clark, J., Barrera, D., Stobert, E.: A first look at the usability of bitcoin key management. arXiv preprint arXiv:1802.04351 (2018)
8. Nakamoto, S.: Bitcoin: a peer-to-peer electronic cash system (2008)
9. Andreessen, M.: Why bitcoin matters. New York Times, 21 2014
10. Tapscott, D., Tapscott, A.: Blockchain Revolution: How the Technology Behind Bitcoin Is Changing Money, Business, and the World. Portfolio, New York (2016)
11. Szabo, N.: Formalizing and securing relationships on public networks. First Monday **2**(9) (1997)
12. Buterin, V.: A next-generation smart contract and decentralized application platform. White paper (2014)
13. Swan, M.: Blockchain: Blueprint for a New Economy, 1st edn. O'Reilly Media, Beijing, Sebastopol (2015)
14. Dannen, C.: Introducing Ethereum and Solidity. Springer, New York (2017). https://doi.org/10.1007/978-1-4842-2535-6
15. Brand, S.: II Cybernetic Frontiers. Random House, Bookworks (1974)
16. Wright, P., Blythe, M., McCarthy, J.: User experience and the idea of design in HCI. In: Gilroy, S.W., Harrison, M.D. (eds.) DSV-IS 2005. LNCS, vol. 3941, pp. 1–14. Springer, Heidelberg (2006). https://doi.org/10.1007/11752707_1

17. Udsen, L.E., Jørgensen, A.H.: The aesthetic turn: unravelling recent aesthetic approaches to human-computer interaction. Digit. Creat. **16**(4), 205–216 (2005)
18. Bardzell, J.: Interaction criticism and aesthetics. In: Proceedings of the SIGCHI Conference on Human Factors in Computing Systems, pp. 2357–2366. ACM (2009)
19. Nake, F., Grabowski, S.: The interface as sign and as aesthetic event. In: Aesthetic Computing, pp. 53–70. MIT Press (2006)
20. Kant, I.: Kritik Der Urteilskraft. Suhrkamp Verlag (1974)
21. Wagner, A.: Kreativität und Freiheit. Kants Konzept der ästhetischen Einbildungskraft im Spiegel der Freiheitsproblematik. In: Abel, G. (ed.) Kreativität (Akten Des XX. Deutschen Kongresses Für Philosophie), Sektionsbeiträge, Bd. 1, pp. 577–588. Meiner Verlag, Hamburg (2005)
22. Bourriaud, N., Pleasance, S., Woods, F., Copeland, M.: Relational Aesthetics. Les presses du reel, Paris (2002)
23. Heidt, M., Kanellopoulos, K., Pfeiffer, L., Rosenthal, P.: Diverse ecologies – interdisciplinary development for cultural education. In: Kotzé, P., Marsden, G., Lindgaard, G., Wesson, J., Winckler, M. (eds.) INTERACT 2013. LNCS, vol. 8120, pp. 539–546. Springer, Heidelberg (2013). https://doi.org/10.1007/978-3-642-40498-6_43
24. Heidt, M.: Examining interdisciplinary prototyping in the context of cultural communication. In: Marcus, A. (ed.) DUXU 2013. LNCS, vol. 8013, pp. 54–61. Springer, Heidelberg (2013). https://doi.org/10.1007/978-3-642-39241-2_7
25. Berger, A., Heidt, M., Eibl, M.: Conduplicated symmetries: renegotiating the material basis of prototype research. In: Chakrabarti, A. (ed.) ICoRD'15 – Research into Design Across Boundaries Volume 1. SIST, vol. 34, pp. 71–78. Springer, New Delhi (2015). https://doi.org/10.1007/978-81-322-2232-3_7
26. Berger, A., Heidt, M.: Exploring prototypes in interaction design – qualitative analysis & playful design method. In: Proceedings of the International Association of Societies of Design Research Conference 2015 - Interplay, Brisbane, Australia (2015)
27. Kwastek, K.: Aesthetics of Interaction in Digital Art. MIT Press, Cambridge (2013)
28. Sutton, L.A.: The principle of vicarious interaction in computer-mediated communications. Int. J. Educ. Telecommun. **7**(3), 223–242 (2001)
29. Wagner, M.: Das Material der Kunst: Eine andere Geschichte der Moderne, 2nd edn. C.H.Beck, München (2013)
30. Leonardi, P.M.: Digital materiality? How artifacts without matter, matter. First Monday **15**(6) (2010)
31. Leonardi, P.M., Barley, S.R.: Materiality and change: challenges to building better theory about technology and organizing. Inf. Organ. **18**(3), 159–176 (2008)
32. Nake, F., Grabowski, S.: Aesthetics and algorithmics. In: Aesthetic Computing. MIT Press (2002)
33. Seidler, P., Kolling, P., Hampshire, M.: Terra0: can an augmented forest own and utilise itself? Technical report, May 2016
34. Garrett, M., Catlow, R., Skinner, S., Jones, N. (eds.): Artists Re: Thinking the Blockchain, 1st edn. Liverpool University Press, London (2018)
35. Di Battista, G., Di Donato, V., Patrignani, M., Pizzonia, M., Roselli, V., Tamassia, R.: Bitconeview: visualization of flows in the bitcoin transaction graph. In: 2015 IEEE Symposium on Visualization for Cyber Security (VizSec), pp. 1–8, October 2015
36. McGinn, D., Birch, D., Akroyd, D., Molina-Solana, M., Guo, Y., Knottenbelt, W.J.: Visualizing dynamic bitcoin transaction patterns. Big Data **4**(2), 109–119 (2016)

37. Luhmann, N.: Trust and Power. Wiley, New York (2018)
38. Xenakis, I., Arnellos, A.: The relation between interaction aesthetics and affordances. Des. Stud. **34**(1), 57–73 (2013)
39. Sas, C., Khairuddin, I.E.: Design for trust: an exploration of the challenges and opportunities of bitcoin users. In: Proceedings of the 2017 CHI Conference on Human Factors in Computing Systems, CHI 2017, pp. 6499–6510. ACM, New York (2017)
40. Sekulla, A., Tolmie, P., Randall, D., Pipek, V.: Blockchain: a shift of trust. In: CHI 2018 Workshop HCI for Blockchain, Canada, Montreal, p. 8, April 2018

Blockchain and Trust:
A Practice-Based Inquiry

Michael Heidt[1]([✉]), Arne Berger[2], and Andreas Bischof[2]

[1] GeDIS, University of Kassel, Pfannkuchstraße 1, 34121 Kassel, Germany
mrbheidt@gmail.com
[2] Chair Media Informatics, Chemnitz University of Technology,
Straße der Nationen 62, 09111 Chemnitz, Germany
{arne.berger,andreas.bischof}@informatik.tu-chemnitz.de

Abstract. Blockchain technologies, such as the distributed cryptocurrency Bitcoin, present us with a vast array of possible applications. They promise to fundamentally transform traditional systems of managing property, conducting governance, organising smart devices, and establishing online identities.

At the same time, few large scale real-world applications of the technology exist apart from Bitcoin. This makes designing Blockchain systems difficult, since there are few guidelines and frameworks available for interaction designers. Furthermore, due to the allegedly disruptive nature of these systems, user studies and observations based on current data are of limited utility. In this paper, we propose and discuss a design methodology combining practice-based research methods with elements of speculative design. In so doing we focus on one key aspect of Blockchain systems: *trust*. We thus want to show how practice-based methods can inform blockchain designs while providing an elucidative conceptualisation of the key category of trust.

Keywords: Practice-based research · Blockchain · Smart contracts · Critical technical practice

1 Introduction

Blockchain systems constitute a rapidly expanding, yet comparably less well investigated object of interaction design research [1]. A growing interest is fueled by the success of the Bitcoin cryptocurrency, the initial and still most famous instance of Blockchain technology [2]: Through an ingenious combination of distributed ledger, immutable storage, and distributed consensus algorithms, the Bitcoin system allows any participant of the system to make a secure payment without having to trust an intermediary such as a bank or broker.

1.1 Internet of Values

While revolutionary from a technological point of view, Bitcoin merely provided a novel technological model for a well established social practice, that

© Springer Nature Switzerland AG 2019
F. F.-H. Nah and K. Siau (Eds.): HCII 2019, LNCS 11588, pp. 148–158, 2019.
https://doi.org/10.1007/978-3-030-22335-9_10

of making digital payments. Due to this state of affairs, Bitcoin is sometimes categorised as a "Blockchain 1.0" technology, in contradistinction to more disruptive Blockchain 2.0 and Blockchain 3.0 technologies yet to come [3]. The latter include smart contract and smart property applications [4], distributed autonomous organizations [5], participatory budgeting [6], self-sovereign digital identity services [7], and decentralized transparent voting [8].

This emerging system of technologies and practices is described as "Internet of Values" [9] in order to point to the magnitude of expected transformations, comparable to that effected by Internet technologies [10].

If these predictions regarding the success of Blockchain technologies will indeed come to fruition remains to be seen. However, interaction designers are today faced with the challenge to design systems aimed at either contributing to these disruptive changes or operating on the assumption that these disruptions will have taken effect at the time of system deployment.

2   Methodology

In order to account for this inherent future-directedness of blockchain artefacts, we propose to combine methods of practice-based research and speculative design. This is in line with studies such as that of Elsden et al. [1] who explicitly call for combining design-led, speculative, and artistic methods in order to account for the specific set of challenges posed by Blockchain systems.

2.1   Practice-Based Research

Practice-based research is a methodology for achieving knowledge through the careful conduct of a constructive designerly or artistic process [11]. Following the principle of "Knowing through Making" [12], concepts are formed and explored through continuous engagement with constructed artefacts, paired with ongoing processes of reflection and empirical observation.

Following the argumentation of authors such as Elsden (see preceding paragraph), we see the potential of design-led thinking and artistic exploration regarding novel designs for Blockchain technology. At the same time, intelligible methodological guidelines have to be established and followed. Novel interaction patterns will not appear out of nowhere but evolve from existing relationships between users and technological artefacts.

In order to grasp the specificity of practice-based research as a method, we employ a schematic juxtaposition of research styles developed by digital media scholar Ashley Holmes (Table 1) [13]. Differentiating technology research and creative production projects, it provides a detailed set of criteria for identifying and comparing both.

2.2   Speculative Design

Speculative Design [14] and Research through Design Fictions [15–17] are methodological tools to extend the reach of design activities into the realm of the future.

Table 1. Characteristics of Technology Research and Creative-Production Projects - Reproduced from [13].

Technology research projects	Creative-production research projects
Artefact is produced	Artefact is produced
Artefact is new or improved	Artefact is of high quality and original in a cultural, social, political or/and aesthetic, *etc.*, context
Artefact is the solution to a known problem	Artefact is a response to issues, concerns, and interests
Artefact demonstrates a solution to problem	Artefact manifests these issues, concerns, and interests
The problem is recognised as such by others	These issues, concerns, and interests reflect cultural, social, political or/and aesthetic, *etc.*, preoccupations
Artefact (solution) is useful	Artefact generates apprehension
Knowledge reified in artefact can be described	Artefact is central to the process of apprehension
This knowledge is widely applicable and widely transferable	The creative-production process is self-conscious, reasoned and reflective
Knowledge reified in the artefact is more important than the artefact	Knowledge may be a by-product of the process rather than its primary objective

We argue for including speculative elements within the practice-based process in order to account for the disruptive and future oriented nature of many Blockchain systems. Including an element of speculation allows for a more adequate relationship to an anticipated, albeit not yet existing, situation of use. Speculative design specifically allows for addressing the need for widespread adoption that acts as prerequisite for many Blockchain artefacts.

3   Practice-Based Framework

The situated nature of practice-based research makes it impossible to formulate any strict procedures which could guarantee success. However, this renders detailed analysis and description of methodological elements within the research process even more valuable. The methodological approach presented here is based on previously developed design frameworks [18–20], which have been adopted in order to account for the specificity of studying Blockchain technologies.

3.1   Iterative Process

The practice-based process is structured in an iterative manner (Fig. 1). An iteration commences with description of research questions, intentions, and goals.

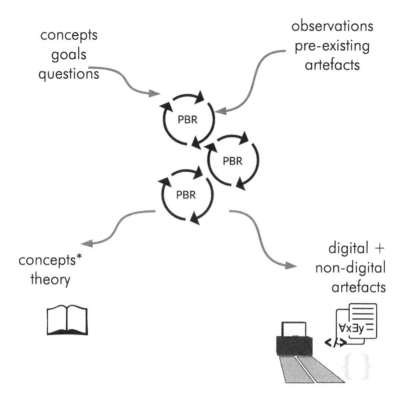

Fig. 1. Iterative practice-based process

The conceptual apparatus is irritated by artefacts generated, while interpretations formulated call for novel vehicles of expression. Resultingly, existing concepts have to be refined or rethought. Where necessary, research questions are reframed using the novel conceptual basis. The refined conceptual apparatus allows for a more nuanced articulation of research questions, in turn informing the process of further artefact construction. This succession of iterative steps drives the ensuing process, producing expanded theory over time.

Crucially, research questions themselves evolve gradually as the concepts to frame and describe them successively take shape (Fig. 2). This implies a distinction in relationship to research styles based on testing hypotheses such as hypothetico-deductive models. Testing of hypotheses usually requires a stable conceptual frame of reference: Hypotheses are commonly framed within established conceptual categories, supported by a large volume of research literature. This, in turn, is based on an abundant amount of data, all expressed within the same system of categories which is only minimally perturbed in the process of hypothesis testing.

Resultingly, practice-based research processes calling for transformations of concepts, operating across disciplinary boundaries, synthesising antagonistic forms of knowledge within processes of theory making often sit uneasily

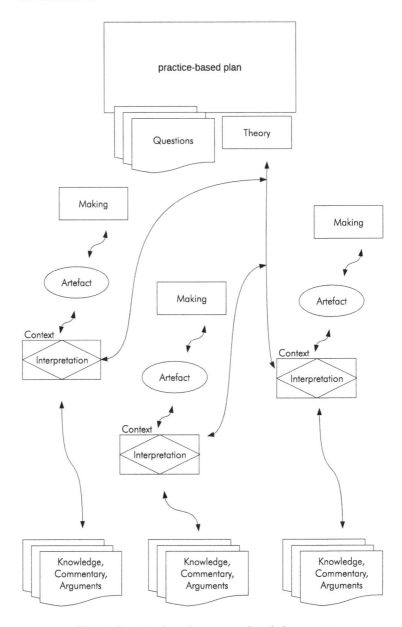

Fig. 2. Practice-based process - detailed account

with hypothetico-deductive approaches. However, practice-based processes can contain elements of hypothetico-deductive endeavours as subcomponents of the inquiry: In this case, the current practice-based conceptual apparatus is used to frame a step of hypothesis testing during which concepts remain stable. Observations made during the hypothetico-deductive step are then channeled back into the practice-based process of reflection and criticism, providing fresh questions and incentives towards its processes of theory making.

3.2 Methods

In the following, we provide a brief discussion of methods employed within the current practice-based process.

Workshops. One of the proposed ways for combination of practice-based and speculative design methods is through adequately conducted workshops. Workshop situations allow for focussed and collective forms of imagining a future state of society: Building on existing work regarding Blockchain related workshop situations [21], the concept of Blockchain computing is broached through provision of tangible computing elements. Introductory video material allows for participants to immerse themselves within the respective scenario. Subsequently, participants are presented with designed interfaces and artefacts. They are encouraged to interact with these according to the content of the presented scenario. Interactions are observed, recorded, and analysed following a mixed methods approach [22].

Workshops are unique in that they create a temporary community, able to materialise common goals, internal struggle, congeniality, bewilderment, inspiration, and strife with an intensity that is unlikely to appear outside of a closed environment. They thus provide the conditions both for practices of communal imagination and those of spirited debate.

Writing as Research Tool. Practices of writing constitute a popular vehicle of speculative research endeavours. Understood in a broad sense, as encompassing both production of narrative content and the creation of computer code, the concept of writing facilitates a synoptic perspective regarding differing disciplinary practices. At the same time, the expressive potentials of writing allow for the joint articulation of viewpoints that might otherwise remain incommensurable due to the absence of a common conceptual frame [23].

3.3 Concepts

The following sections present the conceptual apparatus of the current practice-based inquiry. As discussed, concepts both serve as the intellectual and propositional basis of research activities undertaken while in turn being produced by the research endeavour itself.

Programs and Anti-Programs. The concept of programs and anti-programs was introduced by science-and-technology-studies scholar Bruno Latour in his text *Technology is Society Made Durable* [24]. Fuchsberger et al. later adopted the concept in order to serve the purposes of HCI [25]. Programs constitute patterns of practice relating to a specific artefact. An antiprogram on the other hand constitutes a conflicting pattern, incompatible with realisation of the first.

An example might serve to elucidate the concept: In the case of a smartphone-based route planning application, a practice involving use of the app would constitute a program. It could consist of checking the app every couple of minutes or of keeping one's eyes locked to the screen, while intermittently glancing upwards as not to lose track of the real world. An antiprogram, however, could consist in putting the phone away and asking strangers for directions until the destination has been reached. As is analysed in [26] the operation of interactive artefacts depends on a successful balancing of programs and anti-programs.

Artefact and Interpretation. Within the practice-based stance adopted, artefacts become central to the proces of inquiry. Artefacts do not simply "contain" or transport knowledge. Indeed they are "mute objects" [12], in need of interpretation and intellectual engagement. Instead of being an object of study, or constituting the outcome of a development process, they thus become the condition of knowledge claims. The role of the artefact thus becomes that of the facilitator of experiences and the interpretations informed by them.

Materiality. It has to be stressed how the concept of artefact is in no way limited to the realm of the physical. Artefacts do not necessarily constitute things "you can touch". However, we do argue for conceptualising artefacts as *material* objects. Here, materiality is conceptualised, in line with Nake and Grabowski [27] as endowing objects with the capacity of resistance. Objects are not material because we can touch or sense them, but since they resist our efforts to shape them. The work needed for the imposition of form becomes the index of materiality. Ideal and imagined things are immaterial, not because they are not rooted in the physical world, but since they do not offer any resistance to the one thinking them. Analysing the materiality of a phenomenon thus entails describing its capabilities for offering resistance. Following this conceptual proposition, the materiality of the artefact stretches across physical elements such as props, decorations, sensors, and displays, into the realm of rule systems and software components.

4   Trust

A key element that emerged during practice-based engagement with Blockchain systems is the dimension of *trust*.

During the course of the practice-based inquiry we developed a conceptualisation of trust aimed at elucidating its status regarding the design space of Blockchain systems. The conceptual apparatus developed combines social systems theory, namely the approach of Niklas Luhmann [28] with conceptions of relational trust [29]. This conceptual basis is substantiated by observations specific to the field of blockchain technology.

Resultingly, the following dimensions of trust were identified, among others:

- Trust in code: Users trust the system does not contain grave programming errors which could expose them to vulnerabilities.
- Trust in data: Users trust that data entered into the system is correct and verifiable. This is of paramount importance since data directly forms the basis of decisions enforced through smart contracts.
- Trust in the vision fueling the project: Users trust that the system will gain adequate momentum to create a digital ecosystem able to sustain the platform in question.
- Systemic trust: In order to effect trust in a certain system or platform, multiple elements have to act in tandem. Whether users trust or mistrust a system or platform depends on the successful interplay of aforementioned elements.

Following the practice-based paradigm, these categories are not only the result of combined reflection and design actions but also feed back into the practice-based engagement with systems and users.

Trust thus constricts the design space for blockchain-based systems while forming the material basis for their operation: Any design has to successfully organise users' trust in a sustainable manner. Trust thus forms a precious design material that has to be skillfully crafted in order for a design to succeed.

5   Observations

Practice-Based Research and the Blockchain. Practice-based research constitutes an interesting methodological candidate for inquiring into the social dynamics effected through Blockchain technology.

Double Position of Trust in Practice-Based Research Processes. The concept of trust occurs in two positions within the project: It informs research activities, thereby contributing to an understanding of relevant social phenomena encountered. At the same time, the project contributes to a deepened understanding of trust. Ideally, applying received conceptions of trust to the problematic of the Blockchain both benefits our understanding of the emerging technology while rejuvenating our conceptions of trust as a social phenomenon.

The Work of Trust. Trust itself can be conceived as a form of work, brought about by the necessity of processing relevant information about a system's environment.

Blockchain Anti-Programs. Within the context of the current inquiry, mistrust strengthens anti-programs regarding Blockchain systems, drawing users away from respective artefacts. In contradistinction, trust strengthens programs, increasing the likelihood of user-system-interactions.

Blockchain and Complexity. The technical and formal complication of complex social phenomena emerges as one of the main challenges when introducing smart contract technology [30].

Understanding Code Based Artefacts. Building trust towards Blockchain technologies is predicated on efforts to offer users a better understanding of code-based artefacts such as smart-contracts. As a first step, we require a fuller understanding of code as a design material within design and research processes [31, 32].

Smart Contracts Act as Agents of Complexity Reduction. The feature of "trustlessness" can be described as transformation of the socially complex dynamic of trust into the technologically complicated operation of smart contracts [33].

Smart Contracts Entail a Novel Division of Labour. As pointed out by Kim and Laskowski [30], employing smart contracts entails a novel form of division of labour. This can be described as a relationship of delegation, or as complication of formerly complex trust relationships. While the work of establishing and maintaining trust is done by the machine, humans have to expend effort in order to create the material basis of system complications by virtue of formal systems, software systems, and through data provision.

6   Conclusion

The emergence of Blockchain systems creates an interesting challenge for researchers and practitioners trying to understand and shape the novel interactional dynamics the technology is promising to enable. Its implications are potentially extremely far reaching, yet few systems can be studied in a state of broad adoption. Practice-based research constitutes an auspicious mode of addressing these challenges in a principled, creative, and critical manner. Incorporating elements of speculative design allows to account for the inherent future-directedness of current Blockchain-based implementations while providing material evidence of the potential agency of the novel technology. Hopefully, knowledge generated will allow us as technology creators to sensitise the public towards the characteristics of the novel technology in an effort to jointly steer and negotiate development of emerging institutions and patterns of practice.

Acknowledgements. This work was supported in part by the Andrea von Braun Foundation, Munich, under the grant "Blockchain – A Practice-Based Inquiry Into a Future Agent of Social Transformation".

References

1. Elsden, C., Manohar, A., Briggs, J., Harding, M., Speed, C., Vines, J.: Making sense of blockchain applications: a typology for HCI. In: Proceedings of the 2018 CHI Conference on Human Factors in Computing Systems, CHI 2018, pp. 458:1–458:14. ACM, New York (2018)
2. Nakamoto, S.: Bitcoin: a peer-to-peer electronic cash system (2008)
3. Swan, M.: Blockchain: Blueprint for a New Economy, 1st edn. O'Reilly Media, Beijing, Sebastopol (2015)
4. Crosby, M., Pattanayak, P., Verma, S., Kalyanaraman, V.: Blockchain technology: beyond bitcoin. Appl. Innov. **2**, 6–10 (2016)
5. Pschetz, L., Tallyn, E., Gianni, R., Speed, C.: Bitbarista: exploring perceptions of data transactions in the Internet of Things. In: Proceedings of the 2017 CHI Conference on Human Factors in Computing Systems, pp. 2964–2975. ACM, February 2017
6. Speed, C., Maxwell, D., Pschetz, L.: Blockchain City: economic, social and cognitive ledgers. In: Kitchin, R., Lauriault, T., McArdle, G. (eds.) Data and the City. Regions and Cities. Routledge, August 2017
7. Dunphy, P., Petitcolas, F.A.: A first look at identity management schemes on the blockchain. IEEE Secur. Priv. **16**(4), 20–29 (2018)
8. Liu, Y., Wang, Q.: An e-voting protocol based on blockchain. IACR Cryptology ePrint Archive, Santa Barbara, CA, USA, Technical report 1043:2017 (2017)
9. Tapscott, D., Tapscott, A.: Blockchain Revolution: How the Technology Behind Bitcoin Is Changing Money, Business, and the World. Portfolio, New York (2016)
10. Ito, J., Narula, N., Ali, R.: The Blockchain Will Do to the Financial System What the Internet Did to Media. Harvard Business Review, March 2017
11. Scrivener, S., Chapman, P.: The practical implications of applying a theory of practice based research: a case study. Working Papers in Art and Design, vol. 3 (2004)
12. Mäkelä, M.: Knowing through making: the role of the artefact in practice-led research. Knowl. Technol. Policy **20**(3), 157–163 (2007)
13. Holmes, A.: Reconciling Experimentum and Experientia: Ontology for Reflective Practice Research in New Media (2006)
14. Dunne, A., Raby, F.: Speculative Everything: Design, Fiction, and Social Dreaming. MIT Press, Cambridge (2013)
15. Blythe, M.: Research through design fiction: narrative in real and imaginary abstracts. In: Proceedings of the SIGCHI Conference on Human Factors in Computing Systems, CHI 2014, pp. 703–712. ACM, New York (2014)
16. Bleecker, J.: Design Fiction: a short essay on design, science, fact and fiction. Near Future Laboratory 29 (2009)
17. Sterling, B.: Design fiction. Interactions **16**(3), 20–24 (2009)
18. Heidt, M., Kanellopoulos, K., Pfeiffer, L., Rosenthal, P.: Diverse ecologies – interdisciplinary development for cultural education. In: Kotzé, P., Marsden, G., Lindgaard, G., Wesson, J., Winckler, M. (eds.) INTERACT 2013. LNCS, vol. 8120, pp. 539–546. Springer, Heidelberg (2013). https://doi.org/10.1007/978-3-642-40498-6_43
19. Heidt, M.: Examining interdisciplinary prototyping in the context of cultural communication. In: Marcus, A. (ed.) DUXU 2013. LNCS, vol. 8013, pp. 54–61. Springer, Heidelberg (2013). https://doi.org/10.1007/978-3-642-39241-2_7

20. Berger, A., Heidt, M.: Exploring prototypes in interaction design - qualitative analysis & playful design method. In: Proceedings of the International Association of Societies of Design Research Conference 2015 - Interplay, Brisbane, Australia (2015)

21. Maxwell, D., Speed, C., Campbell, D.: 'Effing' the ineffable: opening up understandings of the blockchain. In: Proceedings of the 2015 British HCI Conference, British HCI 2015, pp. 208–209. ACM, New York (2015)

22. Johnson, R.B., Onwuegbuzie, A.J.: Mixed methods research: a research paradigm whose time has come. Educ. Res. **33**(7), 14–26 (2004)

23. Heidt, M., Kanellopoulos, K., Berger, A., Rosenthal, P.: Incommensurable writings - examining the status of gender difference within HCI coding practices. In: Marcus, A. (ed.) DUXU 2015. LNCS, vol. 9187, pp. 196–205. Springer, Cham (2015). https://doi.org/10.1007/978-3-319-20898-5_19

24. Latour, B.: Technology is society made durable. Sociol. Rev. **38**(S1), 103–131 (1990)

25. Fuchsberger, V., Murer, M., Tscheligi, M.: Human-computer non-interaction: the activity of non-use. In: Proceedings of the 2014 Companion Publication on Designing Interactive Systems, DIS Companion 2014, pp. 57–60. ACM, New York (2014)

26. Heidt, M., Kanellopoulos, K., Pfeiffer, L., Rosenthal, P.: HCI and the community of non-users. In: Marcus, A. (ed.) DUXU 2015. LNCS, vol. 9186, pp. 44–52. Springer, Cham (2015). https://doi.org/10.1007/978-3-319-20886-2_5

27. Nake, F., Grabowski, S.: Aesthetics and algorithmics. In: Aesthetic Computing. MIT Press, Cambridge (2002)

28. Luhmann, N.: Trust and Power. Wiley, New York (2018)

29. Trust, Relational, Assurance, Transactional: Socioeconomic Bricolage on the Blockchain: Relational Trust, Transactional Assurance: Socioeconomic Bricolage on the Blockchain. In: CHI 2018 Workshop HCI for Blockchain, Montreal, Canada, April 2018, p. 10 (2018)

30. Kim, H., Laskowski, M.: A perspective on blockchain smart contracts: reducing uncertainty and complexity in value exchange. In: 2017 26th International Conference on Computer Communication and Networks (ICCCN), pp. 1–6, July 2017

31. Heidt, M.: Reconstructing Coding Practice - Towards a Methodology for Source-Code. In: Boll, S., Maaß, S., Malaka, R. (eds.) Mensch & Computer 2013 - Workshopband, München, De Gruyter Oldenbourg, pp. 271–275 (2013)

32. Berger, A., Heidt, M., Eibl, M.: Conduplicated symmetries: renegotiating the material basis of prototype research. In: Chakrabarti, A. (ed.) ICoRD'15 – Research into Design Across Boundaries Volume 1. SIST, vol. 34, pp. 71–78. Springer, New Delhi (2015). https://doi.org/10.1007/978-81-322-2232-3_7

33. Bischof, A., Heidt, M.: Die Verkomplizierung des Komplexen. Latours Unterscheidung "komplex/kompliziert" als Perspektive auf die Genese von Kommunikations- und Medientechnologien. In: Tagungsband - Medienkommunikation Zwischen Komplexität Und Vereinfachung: Konzepte, Methoden, Praxis, Berlin (2015)

Interactive Systems in the Student-Bank Relationship: A Research on the Views of the University of Bucharest Students on the Utility and Adaptability of HCI Technologies

Valentin Mihai Leoveanu$^{(\boxtimes)}$, Mihaela Cornelia Sandu, and Adela Coman

University of Bucharest, Bucharest, Romania
{valentin.leoveanu,mihaela.sandu, adela.coman}@faa.unibuc.ro

Abstract. The analysis of how students interact with the virtual banking space through ATMs provides both banks that create and offer targeted clients customized banking services as well as HCI Banking technology designers, verifiable data about the utility and the adaptability to customer requirements of these technologies.

The present study is based on research conducted through interviews and questionnaires addressed to students from the University of Bucharest, which examines how the computer-based interface facilitates or hampers students' access to specialized services dedicated to them (bank accounts, debit or credit cards, other bank services).

The motivation for the study lies in the following considerations: students who are today's clients of a bank must be attracted and maintained as tomorrow's clients of the same bank; students are very receptive to new information technologies, understand and use them more easily than other categories of clients and can provide credible feedback on HCI; banks use the co-branding strategy (association with institutions or companies) to provide students with various types of benefits (free of charge services or discounts for shows and events).

The research is reflected in the analysis of the factors that stimulate the use of HCI technologies by students in relation to a bank and so, present study is both a quantitative and qualitative analysis of data collected by applying a questionnaire to the Romanian students of the University of Bucharest that hold an ATM cards.

The results aim to highlight the relevance of understanding the needs of student-users in the process of designing or improving both banking services and related supportive HCI technologies.

Keywords: Automated Teller Machine · Compatibility and consistency · Flexibility · Perceptual limitation · Utility and user guidance

© Springer Nature Switzerland AG 2019
F. F.-H. Nah and K. Siau (Eds.): HCII 2019, LNCS 11588, pp. 159–173, 2019.
https://doi.org/10.1007/978-3-030-22335-9_11

1 Introduction

As an important factor in recent developments in financial globalization, the development of new technologies and innovation in the IT field are currently setting a decisive imprint on the mechanisms of financial circuits in the economy, on the decision-making and action of corporate or household investors. In this regard, the analysis of Human-Computer Interaction in financial field is intended to reflect the degree of standardization of financial operations and easy access for investors and households to the use and understanding of financial instruments and procedures.

The present study is based on research conducted through interviews and questionnaires addressed to students from the University of Bucharest, which examines how the computer-based interface facilitates or hampers students' access to specialized services dedicated to them (bank accounts, debit or credit cards, other bank services).

The motivation for the study lies in the following considerations: students who are today's clients of a bank must be attracted and maintained as tomorrow's clients of the same bank; students are very receptive to new information technologies, understand and use them more easily than other categories of clients and can provide credible feedback on HCI; banks use the co-branding strategy (association with institutions or companies) to provide students with various types of benefits (free of charge services or discounts for shows, restaurants, events).

The present research is both a quantitative and qualitative analysis of data collected by applying a questionnaire to the Romanian students of the University of Bucharest that hold one or more ATM cards. The questionnaire was formulated based on some of the questions from Purdue Usability Testing Questionnaire (PUTQ) made by Lin et al. (1997) with 7 scale Likert answers, socio-demographical questions and some general questions about possessing a bank card.

The quantitative analysis is divided in two parts. At the beginning we will develop an exploratory statistical analysis in order to see general elements of sample design and ATM use. In the second part we will construct an exploratory factor analysis (EFA) to investigate elements that are not so easily measured or can not be measured directly to determine the factors that can influence the use of ATM.

2 Literature Review

The scientific literature consulted by the authors in this field includes several papers that are highlighted to be noted in the context of this study undertaken either as starting points in the analysis performed or as milestones during the research.

In the paper "A Survey on Human Computer Interaction Technology for ATM" (Zhang et al. 2013) the authors analyse the Human-Computer Interaction Technology for Automated Teller Machine, as a result of troubles in using ATM and numerous surveys on ATM's design in scientific literature regarding the shortcomings of ATMs. The research focus on the improvement of ATM based on several approaches: user-centered design for ATM, optimal menu design for ATM, solving the usability problems and specific users' needs, and secure design for ATM.

Curran and King (2008) study the ATM navigation menus for a mixture of UK banks in order to find and suggest "a 'best-of-breed' ATM menu" as being "more usable and efficient system than the existing ATMs investigated" having as target solving the problems of card reinsertion into ATM and speeding up transaction times.

A study of Camilli et al. (2011) "investigated the relation among user experience, usability and the introduction of customized functions (based on users' profiles) in a bank's ATM system interface".

The issue regarding security of using ATM was investigated by Moeckel (2011) who underline that "in contrast to earlier studies, the interplay of security and usability without a separation of factors" determine the decision makers of a bank "to understand the effects of changes in security or usability".

Another study made by a group of Brazilians' researcher and named "Automated Teller Machines' adoption: an application of the technology acceptance model" tries "to evaluate the applicability of an adapted version of the Technology Acceptance Model (TAM) to the Automated Teller Machines (ATM) adoption" (Costa et al. 2007). The authors underline the TAM model "has been broadly used to identify the antecedents to behavioral intention".

The authors El-Haddad and Almahmeed highlighted in their study that "Many advanced ATM machines offer an abundance of additional services including cash and cheque deposits, ability to pay bills at terminal, top-up pay as you go mobile phone and purchasing tickets such as train or concert tickets" (El-Haddad and Almahmeed 1992).

Calayag et al. (2018) reveal in their survey that "the study [...] aims to determine which factors have the significant effect on the interaction between humans and ATMs, and to evaluate the usability of the said ATMs and its effectiveness to users".

Particularly importance have researches on ATM users with physical or visual deficiencies, such as that of Omari and Zachary (2013) considering the mitigation of "digital exclusion of the visually impaired" by implementing assistive technologies, and also improved usability, accessibility and security of ATM regarding this segment of bank customers.

As regards the client's choice of the bank to conduct their own transactions, a study on the situation in Romania showed that "the number of ATM (automatic teller machines) booths has been found to be the most important selection criteria for bank customers from Romania" (Katircioglu et al. 2011). The study also highlighted as important factors in choosing a bank aspects like: "extensive ATM services, availability of telephone and internet banking, giving personal attention to customers, reputation and image of the banks, confidentiality of the bank for customer records, appearance of staff to be presentable and the number of branch offices around the country".

A distinct research regarding the interaction student-ATM is "The acceptance and use of Automated Teller Machines (ATMs) by undergraduate students" (Galadanci and Abdulwahab 2016) that analyse some HCI characteristics like "Performance Expectancy - the degree to which an individual believes that using the system will help him or her to attain gains in job performance; Effort Expectancy - the degree of ease associated with the use of the system; Behavioral Intention - the degree to which an individual will engage in a particular behavior" in order to validate a model for ATM systems available for students in university campus.

3 Characteristics of ATM Marketplace in Romania and Human Behavior

The ATM marketplace in Romania in the year 2018 was characterized by a 5.2% reduction over a period of 18 months as a result of the relocation of the retail business to the online environment, as evidenced by Business Review based on data centralized by the National Bank of Romania. According to the NBR, the number of ATMs decreased from 11,669 units in September 2016 to 11,058 units in March 2018 (Melenciuc 2018).

In spite of this evolution, ATM customer demand increased "from 61 million to 63 million (quarterly), while the number of active banking cards in Romania increased by 11.4% to 12.8 million" (Melenciuc 2018). The fact that cash payments are still widely used in Romania is also demonstrated by the fact that "the total value of the currency in circulation increased by 11.8% between June 2017 and June 2018 to RON 65 billion (EUR 14 billion)" (Melenciuc 2018). The decrease in the number of ATMs is explained by the need to reduce ATM network costs, but also inexplicable as a result of the reduction of some 15,000 jobs in the last ten years, as banking competition is growing to attract new customers.

The client's requirement for ATM cash transactions and hence the increase in the number of ATMs in operation is justified by the advantages offered by this type of electromechanical device such as: quick cash withdrawal, easy getting a bank card, account balance inquiry, deposit cash, transfer funds between accounts within the same bank, pay for utility bills, no less than security features, universally acceptance, time saving, overseas withdrawal and 24/7 operational.

Considering those characteristics, a speech of Yves Mersch, member of the Executive Board of the European Central Bank for Project Syndicate underline that "growth in overall demand for cash is outpacing nominal GDP growth" in European Union and "the differences among member states are pronounced: the share of cash transactions ranges from 42% in Finland to 92% in Malta. [...] the public's commitment to cash remains strong – and is becoming stronger" (Mersch 2017). As a result, it is normal to see differences between countries as well as within regions or cities of a country in terms of demand for cash transactions.

A particular impact on the use of ATMs in Romania by the population, especially by the students, has the level of financial knowledge of individuals. According to a study conduct by Provident, a financial company, on a sample of 1,265 respondents aged between 21 and 65, "more than 38% of Romanians say they are not informed about how to manage their money and only 17% of them believe they have a medium to good level of financial knowledge" (Deacu 2018). [...] "Thus, on a scale of 1 to 10, from very weak to very good, an average of almost 17% of Romanians assess their financial knowledge from medium to good. Nearly 40% say they have financial knowledge under 5, on the same scale" (Deacu 2018). Provident Financial Romania is part of the UK International Personal Finance Group (IPF) that has 2.4 million customers in 9 countries across Europe, as well as in Mexico and Australia.

Another study entitled "The Financial Behavior of Romanians", highlighted "the need for permanent information in the field of financial education, in order to better manage personal finances". Also "91% of respondents claim that it is very important to constantly update their financial knowledge for good personal budget management" (OTP Bank 2018). The study was conducted by OTP Bank Romania, through the Right to Education Foundation, from August to September 2018, by online questioning of 1,000 people over the age of 18. About half of respondents (48%) have higher education and 16% higher economics.

In this respect, the research below undertakes an analysis of the factors that stimulate the use of HCI technologies by students in relation to a bank: access 24 h a day and 7 days out of 7; multiplication of human-computer interaction techniques; ease of use of various banking products and services; providing computer assistance in entering data; financial assistance and counseling offered by the ATM in the selection and use of banking products/services; ensuring the security of data transmission and ATM transactions.

To the same extent, following this research, the bank is interested in a number of aspects that interfere with the bank-student relationship: collecting personal information about the usage habits of banking products/services; information on home and residence, information on age and income level, information on behavior in the use of banking products/services (good-payer/bad-payer), information about the client's lifestyle (inclinations for saving/accessing credit). HCI provides the bank with an efficient system for collecting student information (the average account balance, the number and type of operations he/she orders, the selection of banking products and services and the frequency of their use, with implications for innovation/abandonment of products/banking services by quantifying some parameters such as: the volume of operations, the cost and return associated with those products/services, the security conditions as well as tax issues.

4 Romanian Students Behavior on Using ATM

4.1 Methodology of Research

In this section the authors will develop a quantitative research in order to draw attention to the challenges and also to the strong and the weak points that come in the interaction of bank customers with ATM (Automated Teller Machine). In this regard, we developed first a statistical research among students from University of Bucharest, Department of Public Administration and Business. We developed a semi-structured questionnaire by using a selection of questions from Purdue Usability Testing Questionnaire (PUTQ) made by Lin et al. (1997) with 7 scale Likert answers, and by introducing socio-demographical and general questions about using an ATM in correlation with a bank card.

The survey was conducted online in the last week of the semester during the classes and it was optional, only for those students who wanted to participate by completing the questionnaire. Answering to all questions from the proposed questionnaire was mandatory so they were unable to hand over the questionnaire without answering all the questions.

The study presented in this section is divided in two parts. At the beginning there is an exploratory statistical analysis in order to see general elements of sample design and bank card use. In the second part of the study we will construct an exploratory factor analysis (EFA). Generally, EFA allows researchers to investigate elements that are not so easily measured or can not be measured directly. This type of variables are called latent variables. In order to measure them we can use observed values known as manifest variables. In our study for manifest variables we will use some question about ATM with Likert scale answers. Based on this manifest variables we will design some latent variables called also as factors and we will name those factors.

4.2   The Sample

The sample size includes a number of 208 students that agreed to participate to the study. The distribution of the respondents by socio-demographic factors is explained below. Respondents were between the ages of 19 and 35, so the average age was 21.59 years and standard deviation was 2.33 years. There were 148 (71%) female and 60 (29%) male students that participated to the study. According to the results, 99 (48%) students were from Bucharest and the other 109 (52%) were from different regions of the country. In terms of educational level, 56 (27%) students were enroled in masteral studies while others 152 (73%) were enrolled in bachelor studies (Fig. 1).

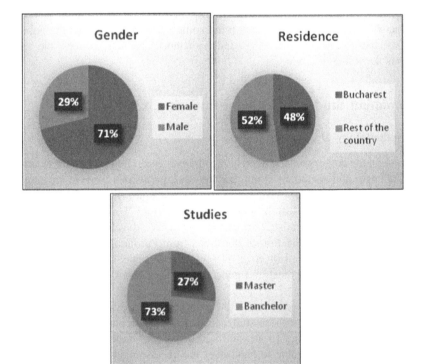

Fig. 1. Gender, residence and studies of the respondents

4.3   Exploratory Statistical Analysis for ATM

In terms of income the analysis of answers revealed that: 26 students have an income between 0 and 500 RON, 39 students - between 500 and 1,000 RON, 36 students - between 1,000 and 1,500 RON, 36 students - between 1,500 and 2,000 RON, 29 students - between 2,000 and 2,500 RON, 16 students - between 2,500 and 3,000 RON, 10 students - between 3,000 and 3,500 RON and 16 students have an income bigger than 3500 RON.

As the main sources of income for the surveyed students were featured: the wage for 113 students, the scholarship for 28 of them and the money given by parents for 78 students; two of them checked all of these answers and another two checked scholarship and parents.

Most of the students involved in the study have decided to open a bank account to receive the scholarship (60 students), full time job salary (61 students), money from the parents (45 students), part time job salary (37 students), and two students said that bank publicity made them to open a bank account.

We also asked them if they poses a mobile phone, computer or laptop and a social media account. It seems that all students involved in this study declared they have a mobile phone, 7 declared they do not own a computer or laptop and 4 that do not have a social media account.

From all respondents, 165 students said they have a debit card, 41 a credit card and 2 a shopping fidelity card. In terms of the frequency of use of the bank card, 55 students said they use it daily, 43 - once a week, 37 - every two days, 30 - once a month, 27 - three times a week and 16 - every two weeks.

The vast majority of students (105) think they have a saving-oriented behavior, 76 of them think they have a consumption-oriented behavior based on their own money, 18 of them think they are oriented towards investing and only 9 of them use credit card most of the time.

The frequency with which students use an ATM is presented below (Fig. 2): once a month (60 students), daily (44 students), once a week (44 students), three times a week (25 students), every two weeks (23 students) and every two days (12 students).

The reasons why the students use ATM are presented as follows (Fig. 3): avoid carrying to much cash in the wallet (90 students), avoid bank queues (77 students), pay for purchases at merchants (27 students) and make transactions during the bank's downtime (14 students).

The ATM is also used for bills payment (57 students from total), checking current balance of the bank account (171 student from total), extract money from the bank account (109 students from total), deposit money on the bank account (130 students from total), prepay card recharging for mobile phone (80 students from total), exchange money (8 students from total).

Further we will conduct the exploratory factor analysis using the questions from Purdue Usability Testing Questionnaire with 7 scale Likert answers. Exploratory factor analysis is a technique used to identify the correlation among variables in a dataset. It provides a factor structure and there is no need for a-priory theory. Using this statistical technique, the problematic variables can be eliminated from the study in order to reach the final result.

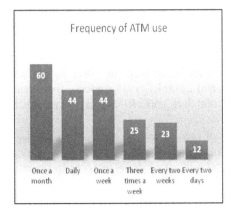

Fig. 2. Frequency in ATM usage

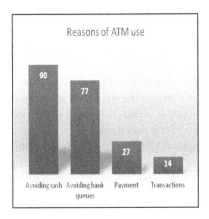

Fig. 3. Reasons for students to use ATM

4.4 Exploratory Factor Analysis (EFA) in the Case of ATM Usage

We will make this exploratory factor analysis using R Studio and some specific packages from R. The R package to conduct factor analysis is "psych". This package was developed by William Revelle in 2018 (Revelle 2018). The main reason this package was built was to make some analysis about personality, psychometric theory and experimental psychology but of course it can be used in all fields not only in psychology.

At the beginning we will check the adequacy of using factor analysis. For this we will take into account the following elements: criterion of sample size adequacy (Comrey and Lee 1992), Kaiser-Meyer-Olkin's test and Bartlett's test. Our sample has 208 respondents so criterion of sample size adequacy is satisfied. We can see below the results of those two tests.

Further we will develop Kaiser-Meyer-Olkin's test (KMO) with the purpose to determine whether there is a significant number of factors in the dataset. This test is used as a sampling adequacy criterion. Besides the indicator called KMO we will determine individual measures of sampling adequacy for each item (MSA). According to Kaiser (1974), if KMO is less than 0.5 is unacceptable, [0.5, 0.6) is miserable, [0.6, 0.7) is mediocre, [0.7, 0.8) is middling, [0.8, 0.9) is meritorious, [0.9, 1.0) is marvelous. In our case KMO = 0.835261 so we can say that there are a significant number of factors in the dataset.

The next step in checking the adequacy of using factor analysis is Bartlett's test (Snedecor and Cochran 1989) that determine if the correlation matrix is an identity matrix. Using R Studio we determined that the probability associated to the test is less than 0.05 so the null hypothesis that all off-diagonal correlations are zero is falsified. In this case we can say that is appropriate to use factor analysis in our study.

Further, we will determine the number of factors that we should use in factorial analysis. For this we consider "fa.parallel" function from R package mentioned earlier, "psych" (Revelle 2018). The result obtained said: "Parallel analysis suggests that the number of factors = 5 and the number of components = NA" and shows us that we should use maximum 5 factors. On the screen plot for parallel analysis (Fig. 4) we can observe a blue line that show eigenvalues of actual data and two red lines that show simulated and resampled data.

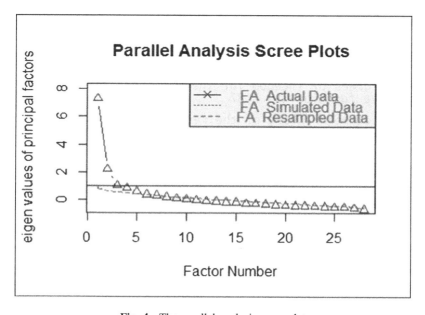

Fig. 4. The parallel analysis scree plot

We can also see on the graphic the inflection point, that point where the gap between simulated data and actual data tends to be minimum. According to this graph and the result of parallel analysis, we can choose anywhere between 2 and 5 factors. So, we choose to use 5 factors to develop the factorial analysis. The results are presented in Table 1.

Table 1. Exploratory factor analysis

```
  Factor Analysis using method = minres
  Call: fa(r = data, nfactors = 5, rotate = "oblimin",
fm = "minres")
  Standardized loadings (pattern matrix) based upon
correlation matrix

                           MR2  MR1  MR4  MR3  MR5
  SS loadings              3.43 3.26 3.10 1.86 1.73
  Proportion Var           0.12 0.12 0.11 0.07 0.06
  Cumulative Var           0.12 0.24 0.35 0.42 0.48
  Proportion Explained     0.26 0.24 0.23 0.14 0.13
  Cumulative Proportion    0.26 0.50 0.73 0.87 1.00

  With factor correlations of
        MR2  MR1  MR4  MR3  MR5
  MR2 1.00 0.20 0.39 0.15 0.32
  MR1 0.20 1.00 0.46 0.28 0.10
  MR4 0.39 0.46 1.00 0.24 0.21
  MR3 0.15 0.28 0.24 1.00 0.01
  MR5 0.32 0.10 0.21 0.01 1.00

  Mean item complexity = 1.7
  Test of the hypothesis that 5 factors are sufficient.

  The degrees of freedom for the null model are 378 and
the objective function was 13.26 with Chi Square of
2609.33
  The degrees of freedom for the model are 248 and the
objective function was 2.87

  The root mean square of the residuals (RMSR) is 0.05
The df corrected root mean square of the residuals is
0.06

  The harmonic number of observations is 208 with the
empirical chi square 327.85 with prob < 5e-04
  The total number of observations was 208 with
Likelihood Chi Square = 555.49 with prob < 1.3e-25

  Tucker Lewis Index of factoring reliability = 0.906
RMSEA index = 0.02 and the 90 % confidence intervals are
0.069 0.086
  BIC = -768.22
  Fit based upon off diagonal values = 0.97
  Measures of factor score adequacy
                                                      MR2
MR1  MR4  MR3  MR5
  Correlation of (regression) scores with factors    0.94
0.92 0.92 0.90 0.86
  Multiple R square of scores with factors           0.88
0.85 0.85 0.82 0.74
  Minimum correlation of possible factor scores      0.75
0.70 0.71 0.63 0.48
```

In Table 1 the root mean square of residuals (RMSR) is 0.05. Theory says that this value should be closer to 0. In our case we can say that it's value of 0.05 is acceptable. Root mean square error of approximation (RMSEA) is 0.02. This indicator shows good model fit if it's value is less than 0.05. The last indicator that we check is Tucker Lewis Index (TLI) which is 0.906, bigger than 0.9 as statistical rules says. Next step is to consider loadings more than 0.3 and to determine the variable that belong to each factor (Table 2).

Table 2. Factors determined using EFA

Loadings:	MR2	MR1	MR4	MR3	MR5
q19.1	0.855				
q19.2	0.628				
q19.3	0.582				
q19.4	0.645				
q19.5	0.779				
q19.6	0.493				
q19.7	0.416				
q19.8					0.334
q19.9		0.359			
q19.10		0.407			
q19.11		0.381			
q19.12			0.689		
q19.13			0.740		
q19.14			0.701		
q19.15			0.639		
q19.16			0.357		
q19.17			0.325		
q19.18		0.302			
q19.19					0.601
q19.20		0.571			
q19.21		0.543			
q19.22		0.786			
q19.23		0.601			
q19.24		0.596			
q19.25					0.567
q19.26				0.686	
q19.27				0.318	
q19.28				0.853	
	MR2	MR1	MR4	MR3	MR5
SS loadings	3.078	2.813	2.585	1.677	1.509
Proportion Var	0.110	0.100	0.092	0.060	0.054
Cumulative Var	0.110	0.210	0.303	0.363	0.416

The next step in exploratory factor analysis is to name the factors we obtained. For factor 1 we have questions from 1 to 7 that correspond to consistency and flexibility of ATM. For factor 2 we have questions that correspond to errors that can appear and how can people deal with them. For factor 3 we have questions that correspond to clarity of messages, screen luminosity and color and logical information. For factor 4 we have questions that correspond to security of the actions. For factor 5 we have questions that correspond to user guidance. So, we can name our factors as it follows: "compatibility and consistency", "flexibility", "perceptual limitation", "security" and "user guidance". Once we determined that we will work with 5 factors, we will test further the confidence that we have in this model. For this we will compute Cronbach alpha coefficient (Tavakol and Dennick 2011). If the value is bigger than 0.7 we can trust in the result obtained. In this case Cronbach alpha is 0.8988915 so the analyze that we developed up to this moment is trustable.

4.5   Results

Using exploratory factor analysis we determine 5 factors that can influence using of ATM. This factors are: "compatibility and consistency" as factor no. 1, "flexibility" as factor no. 2, "perceptual limitation" as factor no. 3, "security" as factor no. 4 and "user guidance" as factor no. 5.

5   Conclusions

Both qualitative and quantitative analysis have attempted to examine how the computer-based interface (in particular, the automatic teller machine - ATM) facilitates or hampers students' access to specialized services dedicated to them by credit institutions (bank accounts, debit or credit cards, other bank services) and also to analyze what factors stimulate the use of HCI technologies by students in relation to a bank.

Using a 7 scale Likert for questions from Purdue Usability Testing Questionnaire we tried to underline the challenges and also strong and weak point that come in the interaction of people with ATM. Even not all students have a bank account, all of them have a bank card (debit card, credit card or shopping fidelity card). The main reason students are using an ATM is avoiding keeping cash in the wallet. They also uses ATM to check the current balance of the bank account or to deposit ar extract money from the bank account. It seems that majority of students uses bank card every day and the ATM once a week.

The results presented above reflect five important factors that can influence using of ATM: "compatibility and consistency" as factor no. 1, "flexibility" as factor no. 2, "perceptual limitation" as factor no. 3, "security" as factor no. 4 and "user guidance" as factor no. 5.

The research highlighted the main strengths of ATM in terms of their use by students, such as access 24 h a day and 7 days out of 7, ease of use of various banking products and services, and ensuring the security of data transmission and computer transactions. As weak points were noted lack of providing ATM assistance in entering data and lack of financial assistance and counseling offered by the ATM in the selection and use of banking products/services.

Considering the bank's interest in presenting the main features of the student-bank relationship through ATMs, the research highlighted the following aspects: personal information about the usage habits of banking products/services, information on home and residence, information on age and income level, information on behavior in the use of banking products/services (good-payer/bad-payer), and information about the client's lifestyle (inclinations for saving/accessing credit).

5.1   Limitations

The authors of the present study recognize the limits of their research, restrictions which, as far as possible, they want to restrict them in future research. A first highlight of the study's limits is that the analysis and research results were much improved and more valuable if the sample aimed at a larger, more comprehensive number of students coming from other faculties at the University of Bucharest or even from other universities from the capital. Also, the choice of questions from the PUTQ questionnaire was limited to some questions considered more important for initial research, so future research should be based on applying all these questions to get a broader view, better outcomes. Another disadvantage of the study is the poor selection of students with disabilities who have a higher weight in the sample, which would have led to a closer reflection on the reality of the use of HCI technologies in the student-bank relationship in Romania. In this regard, future researches should consider possible ATM features like: the spread of bank computer terminals; multiplication of human-computer interaction techniques (voice, pencil etc.) and access to interactive systems for students with physical/visual disabilities. Among the shortcomings, one can also note that the students' desire for access to additional services necessary in their opinion has not been fully investigated.

These limitations of research were due, first, to the long time to be given to the questionnaire completion and, secondly, to the subjectivity, the lack of concentration or even the indifference of the students to give realistic answers to a questionnaire requiring a long time to complete. Another cause consist of possible limitary use of multiple statistical and econometric methods/tools by the researchers.

5.2   Future Research Directions

As a result of the limits of the present research, as well as of the dynamics of innovations on the HCI technologies market in banking, the authors are considering some aspects in future research.

First of all, it is necessary to consider aspects related to the elaboration and application of the questionnaire, such as the employment of the whole PUTQ questionnaire, not just a selection of questions; better articulation of general, absolutely essential questions with those regarding HCI and HCI technologies; better choice and diversification of questions regarding HCI that better target the context and current development of the ATM market in Romania; as well as taking into account the possibility of wider expression of students' opinions on ATM services by asking open answer questions.

Secondly, an action needed for future analyzes is to increase the research sample and to give more weight to students with disabilities of various types.

No less important, thirdly, is the attempt to attract Romanian banks likely interested in the results of the questionnaire and to be involved in the process of dissemination, information gathering and analysis of this questionnaire, as well as, of course, the use of such information obtained for the benefit of both banks and student clients.

Topics that cannot be overlooked could be the issues of ATM usage costs (the possibility of reducing customer use costs), of the cost of improving HCI technologies for ATMs, of the cost of implementing improved ATM networks, maintenance and security of ATM operation. Although these aspects are largely confidential and can not be in the hands of the researchers, an overall assessment of these can be made with the help of the interested banks in Romania.

5.3   Bank Implications

A wide range of studies and reports highlighted the banking industry trends for 2019 and further. Between those trends one can enroll next-gen chatbots (chatbot, short for chatterbot, "is a computer program that simulates human conversation through voice commands or text chats or both") (Investopedia 2019), blockchain technology, improved security and the rise of robots and machine learning (Quantzig 2019). Some authors (Cornell 2019) have confident predictions in the future of ATMs as "contactless ATM and payment transactions will gain traction" and also "bank branches will continue to shrink". All these predictions about the dynamics of HCI technologies and their implementation in the banking field make it necessary to consider the views of Romanian banks in future research.

References

Calayag, M.E., Regala, D.M.M., Rivera, C.J.R., Tancio, D.M.N.: A comparative study of different automated teller machine and its effectiveness based on customer's satisfaction. J. Ind. Eng. Manag. Sci. **2017**(1), 49–102 (2018). https://doi.org/10.13052/jiems2446-1822. 2017.004

Camilli, M., Dibitonto, M., Vona, A., Medaglia, C.M., Di Nocera, Fr.: User-centered design approach for interactive kiosks: evaluation and redesign of an automatic teller machine. In: Proceedings of the 9th ACM SIGCHI Italian Chapter International Conference on Computer-Human Interaction: Facing Complexity, CHItaly 2011, Alghero, Italy, 13–16 September (2011). https://doi.org/10.1145/2037296.2037319. https://www.researchgate.net/publication/221571086_User-centered_design_approach_for_interactive_kiosks_Evaluation_and_rede sign_of_an_automatic_teller_machine

Comrey, A.L., Lee, H.B.: A First Course in Factor Analysis, 2nd edn, p. 217. Erlbaum, Hillsdale (1992)

Cornell, D.: Fearless Forecast: The ATM industry in 2019 (2019). https://www.atmmarketplace. com/blogs/fearless-forecast-the-atm-industry-in-2019/. Accessed 11 Jan 2019

Costa, B., Pires, P.J., Hernandez, J.M.C.: Automated Teller Machines' adoption: an application of the Technology Acceptance Model. Revista de Administração e Inovação São Paulo 4(1), 40–56 (2007). https://doi.org/10.5585/rai.v4i1.81. https://www.researchgate.net/publication/274591498

Curran, K., King, D.: Investigating the human computer interaction problems with automated teller machine navigation menus. Interact. Technol. Smart Educ. **5**(1), 59–79 (2008). https://doi.org/10.1108/17415650810871583. https://www.researchgate.net/publication/247934150_

Investigating_the_human_computer_interaction_problems_with_automated_teller_machine_ navigation_menus

Deacu, E.: Sondaj. Aproape 4 din 10 români îşi autoevaluează cunoştinţele financiare ca fiind mediocre sau foarte slabe. Adevarul (2018). https://adevarul.ro/economie/stiri-economice/ sondaj-aproape-4-10-romani-isi-auto-evalueaza-cunostintele-financiare-fiind-mediocre-foarte-slabe-1_5bc491dadf52022f75874117/index.html

El-Haddad, A.B., Almahmeed, M.A.: ATM banking behaviour in Kuwait: a consumer survey. Int. J. Bank Mark. **10**(3), 25–32 (1992). https://doi.org/10.1108/02652329210015318. https:// www.researchgate.net/publication/235311666_ATM_Banking_Behaviour_in_Kuwait_A_ Consumer_Survey

Galadanci, B.S., Abdulwahab, L.: The acceptance and use of automated teller machine (ATMs) by undergraduate students. Dutse J. Pure Appl. Sci. **2**(1), 39–47 (2016). https://www. researchgate.net/publication/306279638_THE_ACCEPTANCE_AND_USE_OF_AUTO MATED_TELLER_MACHINES_ATMs_BY_UNDERGRADUATE_STUDENTS

Investopedia: Chatbot (2019). https://www.investopedia.com/terms/c/chatbot.asp

Kaiser, H.F.: An index of factorial simplicity. Psychometrika **39**(1), 31–36 (1974)

Katircioglu, S.T., Tumer, M., Kılınç, C.: Bank selection criteria in the banking industry: an empirical investigation from customers in Romanian cities. Afr. J. Bus. Manag. **5**(14), 5551– 5558 (2011). https://doi.org/10.5897/ajbm11.408. http://www.academicjournals.org/AJBM. ISSN 1993-8233

Lin, H.X., Choong, Y.-Y., Salvendy, G.: A proposed index of usability: a method for comparing the relative usability of different software systems. Behav. Inf. Technol. **16**(4/5), 267–278 (1997). https://garyperlman.com/quest/quest.cgi?form=PUTQ

Melenciuc, S.: The fall of the cash machine: Romanian banks cut ATM networks by 5 pct in 1.5 years, despite growing number of cards and transactions. Bus. Rev. (2018). http://business-review.eu/money/the-fall-of-the-cash-machine-romanian-banks-cut-atm-networks-by-5-pct-in-1-5-years-despite-growing-number-of-cards-and-transactions-180016. Accessed 09 Aug 2018

Mersch, Y.: Why Europe still needs cash. European Central Bank. Frankfurt/Main (2017). https://www.ecb.europa.eu/press/key/date/2017/html/ecb.sp170428.en.html

Moeckel, C.: Human-computer interaction for security research: the case of EU E-banking systems. In: Campos, P., Graham, N., Jorge, J., Nunes, N., Palanque, P., Winckler, M. (eds.) INTERACT 2011. LNCS, vol. 6949, pp. 406–409. Springer, Heidelberg (2011). https://doi. org/10.1007/978-3-642-23768-3_44

Omari, O.J., Zachary, O.B.: Investigating ATM system accessibility for people with visual impairments. IOSR J. Comput. Eng. (IOSR-JCE) **15**(5), 13–18 (2013). e-ISSN 2278–0661, p-ISSN 2278-8727. www.iosrjournals.org

OTP Bank: The Financial Behavior of Romanians. The Right to Education Foundation, Bucharest (2018). https://www.otpbank.ro/news/studiu-otp-bank-romania

Quantzig: Gear Up for The Top 5 Banking Industry Trends That are Going to Dominate in 2019 (2019). https://www.quantzig.com/blog/banking-sector-trends-2018

Revelle, W.: Package 'psych' (2018). https://personality-project.org/r/psych-manual.pdf

Snedecor, G.W., Cochran, W.G.: Statistical Methods, 8th edn. Iowa State University Press, Ames (1989)

Tavakol, M., Dennick, R.: Making sense of Cronbach's alpha. Int. J. Med. Educ. **2**, 53 (2011)

Zhang, M., Wang, F., Deng, H., Yin, J.: A survey on human computer interaction technology for ATM. Int. J. Intell. Eng. Syst. **6**(1), 20–29 (2013). https://doi.org/10.22266/ijies2013.0331.03. https://www.researchgate.net/publication/288614776_A_Survey_on_Human_Computer_ Interaction_Technology_for_ATM

Consumer Behaviour

The Role of User Emotions for Content Personalization in e-Commerce: Literature Review

Artem Bielozorov[(✉)], Marija Bezbradica, and Markus Helfert

Dublin City University, Dublin 9, Co., Dublin, Ireland
{artem.bielozorov,marija.bezbradica,
markus.helfert}@dcu.ie

Abstract. Purchasing decisions do not always come from the rational mental processes but are often being driven by emotions. This insight made researchers think of emotions as of an essential contextual variable capable of enhancing personalized services and providing more precise recommendations within e-Commerce. In this paper we explore the studies made to discover why emotions are an important research domain necessary to understand purchasing behavior of online shoppers. We also explore how user emotions can be captured and recognized by existing technologies to provide enhanced personalization. Specifically, we apply Webster and Watson (2002) literature review approach to create a sample of studies published in scientific journals and conference proceedings. We synthesize the extant studies on the role of user emotions for personalized services within e-Commerce. We also provide a comprehensive concept-matrix which aggregates the range of existing emotions recognition technologies and highlights which specific emotions these technologies are able to recognize as well as in which domains these solutions are applied. Our study extends prior reviews and provides insights into open research areas which will benefit Human-Computer Interactions (HCI) practitioners and researchers in academia and industry.

Keywords: Emotions recognition technologies · Personalization ·
Purchasing behavior · Recommender system

1 Introduction: Content Personalization as a Key Strategic Element

According to the definition given by Osterwalder and Pigneur (2002), business strategy represents an approach based on the profiles of actors, their dynamics and roles within a specific business model that determines certain operational-level steps necessary to be undertaken to implement the entire business strategy. In the context of e-Commerce, information strategy constitutes the vital part of the overall business strategy as it aims at discovering new and profitable insights to excel customer relationship and enhance customer satisfaction (Osterwalder and Pigneur 2002). The deep analysis of the customers' preferences and behaviors is among the key information strategy goals and the very success of this strategy relies on how thorough and accurate the customers' data

---

The original version of this chapter was revised: This chapter was mistakenly published as a regular chapter instead of open access. The correction to this chapter is available at https://doi.org/10.1007/978-3-030-22335-9_26

F. F.-H. Nah and K. Siau (Eds.): HCII 2019, LNCS 11588, pp. 177–193, 2019.
https://doi.org/10.1007/978-3-030-22335-9_12

are and how efficiently online vendors can react upon these data in order to provide value propositions based on the data-driven insights (Salonen and Karjaluoto 2016). This approach, however, requires fostering more customer-centric business culture and prioritizing the alignment of the company's information and analytic strategy, and business capabilities with the customers' needs (Simon et al. 2016).

To stay competitive, e-Commerce players have been developing and adopting differentiation strategies in order to attract and retain customers. A common differentiation strategic approach among online retailers is a web content personalization aimed at matching customers' needs and expectations (Tam and Ho 2006).

Various marketing studies adopt different definitions of personalization. The general concept of personalization, however, refers to the process where products and services are adjusted to match individual preferences by learning customer needs and transforming the gathered data into recommendations, offers, and promotions aimed at forming competitive advantage for the focal company by creation of idiosyncratic value (Montgomery and Smith 2009; Vesanen and Raulas 2006; Salonen and Karjaluoto 2016). In the e-Commerce context, personalization means the use of adaptive web content to convey personally relevant data to the consumer (Karat et al. 2003).

Content personalization is generally assumed to be among the most efficient information strategy approaches aimed to maximize immediate and future business opportunities for online merchants by delivering the right content to the right person at the right moment (Cao and Li 2007; Ho and Bodoff 2014; Aguirre et al. 2015). Adolphs and Winkelmann (2008) argue that content personalization is a powerful tool which can help build strong customer relationships as it allows addressing customers personally. In his research Vesanen (2007) makes a conclusion that the ability of online merchants to provide personalized services more accurately, enables their customers to enjoy a better preference match, experience, communication, reduced cognitive overload, and convenience (Ansari and Mela 2003) which eventually increases customer satisfaction and loyalty (Rust and Chung 2006).

However, as the field grows, there is a plethora of important topics around content personalization within e-Commerce field that lacks substantial clarification what creates ambiguity around this domain (Salonen and Karjaluoto 2016). One of the points, which currently remains understudied, focuses on the role of users' emotions for content personalization in the context of online shopping (Pappas et al. 2017).

Although the concept of personalized services has been known to marketers since 1987 (Surprenant and Solomon 1987), it was not largely embraced until the idea of customer-centric approach within e-Commerce attracted the attention of information systems and human-computer interaction researchers (Li and Karahanna 2015). Today web content personalization is a focus research area for many scientific fields, especially within marketing and information systems, and since web content personalization involves human-computer interaction, it is being largely investigated in relation to technological advancements and applications (Salonen and Karjaluoto 2016). Essentially, implementation of web content personalization implies extensive use of technologies, which makes such topics as recommender systems, user profiling principles, contextual data, and user emotions recognition (Adolphs and Winkelmann 2008) key research areas within multidisciplinary fields, where technological research models are supplemented with approaches from marketing and psychology studies (Salonen and Karjaluoto 2016).

The purpose of this research is to analyze the stream of studies on the role of user emotions for content personalization in e-Commerce. Specifically, the main goal of the paper is to extract the data about why emotions play an important role in online shopping and which technologies and approaches exist to detect and capture user emotions and make a comprehensive overview of these findings. We fill the research gap by synthesizing the extensive studies on the role of user emotions for personalized services within e-Commerce and provide an aggregated comprehensive concept-matrix. The proposed concept-matrix incorporates market-available emotions recognition technologies mapped against the specific emotions these technologies are able to detect and process as well as industry domains where these solutions are currently being applied.

This paper is organized as follows: Sect. 2 presents the methodology we applied in this research. Section 3 introduces the background of this paper regarding the role of user emotions in content personalization within e-Commerce field. In Sect. 4 we present a table which provides a clear snapshot of the strategic approach applied to extract user emotions as well as data acquisition methods and the list of key research contributors. Furthermore, we identify the comprehensive list of technologies which are currently available on the market and used to capture user emotions via facial expressions and voice recognition. We developed a concept matrix based on the methodology proposed by Webster and Watson (2012) to synthesize the technologies we identified with the user emotions these technologies are able to capture as well as the application fields of the selected solutions. In Sect. 5 we discuss the results, conclude the paper, and propose future research directions.

2 Methodology

The state-of-the-art review of prior relevant literature is an essential approach aimed at facilitation of further academic research through closing the gaps of areas where a plethora of studies already exists (Webster and Watson 2002). The goal of the state-of-the-art literature review is to uncover the directions where the research is needed by providing points of reflections on the present location and potential future directions of the subject matter (Salonen and Karjaluoto 2016). The current literature review is aimed at providing a comprehensive overview of the role of emotions within e-Commerce giving special attention to the significance of emotional variable in building content personalization strategies as well as to extensive theoretical background.

2.1 Literature Search

The current study is built upon the stages of the concept-centric approach defined by Webster and Watson (2002) in order to determine the most relevant sources for the literature review. The method suggests commencing the review from identifying a preliminary pool of scientific papers which will be further elaborated to extract the most relevant materials to build the review upon. The resources relevant for building the review were selected with the clear research focus after reviewing a wide variety of the respected and well-established academic and scientific materials. The primary data sources that we leveraged were peer-reviewed academic journals which fall into the set of "AIS Basket of 8", databases such as Google Scholar, PubsOnLine, EBSCOhost (Academic Search Complete), and ISI Web of Knowledge/ISI Web of Science as well as subject-specific database such as ACM Digital Library.

2.2   Keywords, Inclusion and Exclusion Criteria

The main requirement for the article to be considered for further revision was presence of the certain keywords. We were mostly focused at finding the papers which would contain the following keywords in their titles: "Personali*" (both z- and s-forms of the terms are used in the literature, so the search of the mentioned keywords we did in combination with "AND"), "Recommender system", "Customer-centric", "Customer AND user emotions", "Emotions recognition AND identification AND detection", "Behavi*" (both options "behavior" and "behaviour" can be found in the literature, so these keywords were also sought in combination with "AND") which gave us 300 papers at the end.

In order to retrieve the most relevant information, we applied the range of exclusion criteria. The first criteria concerned the review period, which included studies published between 2005 and 2018. This allowed us to elaborate on the broad range of literature, without, however, considering those studies which might have become somewhat obsolete to date. We also made a decision to focus the review solely on the concept of personalization omitting the concept of customization in order to have a clear and grounded literature review at the end. After applying the mentioned filters, we screened through the paper abstracts in order to identify how relevant the paper was to be considered for further elaboration. The scientific articles, focused on technical aspects of recommender systems or recommender algorithms were also elaborated, however, we considered them as less important for the current study. At the end of this step, we ended up with having 80 papers.

The collected papers were read with the clear research focus. At this stage, we were also applying backward referencing to examine the works cited in some of the most relevant papers as well as forward referencing to make a deep search across the papers which cited the papers we considered relevant. We finished this step with having 45 papers which we further read in details.

The remained pool was comprised of 27 papers which represented the most relevant materials as they had a clear focus on the role of user emotions in personalized services within e-Commerce. These papers became the foundation for building the current literature review. Figure 1 demonstrates the process of articles selection we applied in this review.

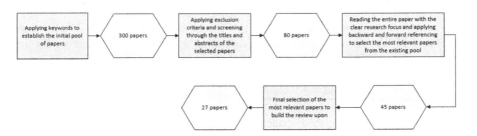

Fig. 1. Articles selection process.

3 Background

In their study Aguirre et al. (2015) claim that since personalization is all about adapting to customer preferences and needs, e-Commerce players need to be fully aware of how to collect high-quality primary data about their customers. This is made possible by deploying intelligent personalization algorithms capable of collecting and analyzing web activities to generate highly adaptive, dynamic, and personalized content for individual users (Mobasher et al. 2000). Data collection and processing involves different methods of harvesting data aimed at building customer profiles and adapting it to be used for web personalization mostly by recommender systems (Salonen and Karjaluoto 2016).

3.1 Recommender Systems as a Content Personalization Tool

Today recommender systems are widely implemented solutions and represent fully functional software systems that apply at least one "recommendation approach". This approach is specifically designed to predict the needs of online customers and recommend them the online purchase of some products based on the collected data (Bădică et al. 2011; Beel et al. 2016). According to Beel et al. (2016) a "recommendation approach" is a model which describes how to bring a recommendation concept into the practice. The mostly adopted recommendation concepts within modern recommender systems are collaborative filtering and content-based filtering which have fundamental differences in their underlying ideas (Beel et al. 2016).

- **Collaborative filtering.** Collaborative filtering was one of the first personalization technologies which became widely available within e-Commerce domain (Montgomery and Smith 2009). Collaborative filtering does not require the user's explicit profile (Koren 2010) and, in the online retail context, collaborative filtering generates recommendations by predicting the utility of particular items to a specific user based on user votes retrieved from a user database. In order to generate more specific suggestions of products or services, items or services need to be rated by many customers (Breese et al. 1998).
- **Content-based filtering.** Content-based filtering analyses the content of information sources and creates a user profile based on the customer's interests (past searches, item rating or preferences about specific goods) in terms of regularities of the items and services that have been rated highly (Pazzani 1999). Content-based filtering then relies on a user profile and recommends those items which match with the customer's needs and preferences reflected in the customer profile (Uçar and Karahoca 2015).
- **Hybrid recommender systems.** The previously introduced approaches may be combined in hybrid systems to complement and eliminate drawbacks of each other (Uçar and Karahoca 2015). For instance, collaborative filtering is based upon ratings on items made by other customers, what makes implementation of the new recommender system challenging as these data are not yet available. Leveraging of content-based filtering on top of collaborative filtering will help make a deep analysis of user profiles what will eliminate the generation of immature suggestions by collaborative filtering-based recommender system in the early stages (Tran and Cohen 2000).

All the approaches described focus on recommending items to customers based on rigidly established algorithms and operate only within a user-item matrix when new data are simply being compounded on top of the current user's profile (Lombardi et al. 2009). Costa and Macedo (2013) argue that although multiple approaches and dimensions exist which make performance of recommender systems more efficient, most of the existing recommender systems do not consider human emotions when recommending content. In his research, Polignano (2015) also concludes that traditional recommender systems mostly do not address emotions in the computational process and only recent papers have some explanation on why emotions are highly important in providing personalized services and how it is possible to recognize emotion with the help of technologies.

3.2   Emotions as a Contextual Variable in Content Personalization

Although the role of user emotions has been widely acknowledged in multiple studies, the amount of studies on the importance of emotions for content personalization within e-Commerce is relatively low. This might be explained by the lack of a commonly accepted definition of what constitutes emotions. However, scholars in e-Commerce domain have elaborated on the range of emotions and prioritized the following categories: social/personality issues (the effect of emotions on consumption judgment and reasoning), cognitive factors (cognitive and social construction in emotions), and the correlation of emotions with other consumption factors (Gaur et al. 2014).

To attain theoretical clarity a precise clarification of what is the difference between emotions and feelings is necessary. In his paper Walla (2017) makes an attempt to distinguish between emotions and feelings and provide clear definitions of both notions. According to Walla (2017) feelings represent "consciously felt bodily responses" which can appear from subcortical affective processing whereas emotions are behavioral output based on affective processing, which can help communicate but not necessarily fully reflect feelings of the person to others.

In the past decade, several context-aware recommender algorithms have been implemented and proved to be useful to enhance recommendation performance in numerous domains by additionally incorporating context information (Gorgoglione et al. 2011). The most widely adopted context factors are the time of the day, the day of the week, and location, which, according to Zheng (2016) can be relatively easy captured from the ubiquitous environment. Recommender systems have traditionally applied data-centric computational approaches for content recommendation and user modeling (Tkalčič et al. 2011). However, relatively few studies have been done about why it is important to take into consideration user emotions when designing personalized services (Zheng et al. 2013).

Research by González et al. (2007) supports that purchasing decisions are always being accompanied by emotions. This makes customer-centric companies put efforts into detecting the existing connections between users' actions and their emotions to have a better understanding of how to increase retention, loyalty, and satisfaction rates among customers through providing enhanced personalized services (González et al. 2007). In their research Zheng et al. (2013) proved that the increased precision in providing relevant suggestions by recommender systems is achieved when an emotional variable is considered. In their study Tkalčič et al. (2013) conducted a comparative analysis of the generic metadata- and affective metadata-based recommender systems. The authors designed a methodology and conducted an experiment which proved that recommender system which was capable of utilizing emotional context, demonstrated improved performance over recommender system based only on the generic metadata.

4 Results

4.1 Strategies to Identify User Emotions

According to Zheng (2016), emotional states are usually dynamic and tend to change from time to time. Therefore, the users' profiles associated with different affective reactions can be of high importance to assist recommender systems in making relevant content suggestions (Zheng 2016) what, in turn, can facilitate the decision-making process of users (Picard et al. 2004). In their study González et al. (2007) describe emotional factor as "the relevance that each user gives to differential values of items (i.e. events, services, products), which are demonstrated in the user's decision-making process by means of his or her actions". González et al. (2007) also argue that emotional factor particularly influences the rational thinking when users get any recommendations.

The important role of emotions in recommender systems has been discussed by Tkalčič et al. (2011) where the authors demonstrate how to identify emotions during the interaction with recommender system in three data acquisition stages in the consumption chain of an item: entry stage (i.e. before the activity), the consumption stage (i.e. during the activity), and exit stage (i.e. after the activity).

In Table 1 we summarize the key data about each stage and also provide the most prominent studies made to address the peculiarities of data acquisition methods within each stage. The way we compiled and synthesized the data with the help of the table gives the reader a chance to quickly capture the key points of emotions identification strategy proposed by Tkalčič et al. (2011). Furthermore, we are also presenting the list of key contributors who put significant efforts into exploring each strategic step separately to discover new and important insights.

According to Tkalčič et al. (2011), emotional states of the users can be identified by applying explicit and implicit approaches. Explicit acquisition of data about user emotions is usually carried out by applying the Self-Assessment Manikin developed by Bradley and Lang in 1994. This approach represents a non-verbal pictorial assessment technique designed as a paper-and-pencil questionnaire which is used in groups to evaluate the pleasure, arousal, and dominance associated with a person's emotional reaction in response to an object or event (Bradley and Lang 1994). The implicit detection of emotions, although being intrusive in nature, proved to be a more accurate emotions detection approach rather than an explicit one since users under surveillance are not aware of their emotions being captured what reduce the likelihood of data distortion (Tkalčič et al. 2011).

Table 1. Description of emotions identification stages, data acquisition methods, and key research contributors.

Stage	Description	Data acquisition method	Key contributors
Entry stage	When starting using the recommender system, the user is in the entry mood caused by previous activities and actions unknown to the system, which, however, have an impact on the user's decisions	• Matrix factorization approach with emotion-specific regularization enriched with contextual parameters	• Porayska-Pomsta et al. (2007) • Baltrunas (2008) • Koren (2010) • Shi et al. (2010)
Consumption stage	During the content consumption, user experiences emotional responses activated by thecontent which, however, do not induce any further actions, but rather is a passive response to the stimuli	• Explicit data can be collected through paper-and-pencil questionnaire and to be categorized according to the six universal emotions: happiness, sadness, surprise, fear, disgust, anger (Ekman and Rosenberg 1993) • Implicit emotional data could be collected through monitoring the facial or voice expressions of users with the help of specific emotions recognition tools and technologies (Polignano 2015)	• Pantic and Vinciarelli (2009) • Arapakis et al. (2009) • Soleymani et al. (2012) • Joho et al. (2011)
Exit stage	The emotions induced by the content during the exit stage will influence the user's further actions	• The implicit data on users' emotions during the exit stage can be collected by using facial or voice expressions recognition technologies as well as heart rate sensors in certain domains such as physical interactive playgrounds	• Arapakis et al. (2009) • Yannakakis et al. (2008) • Soleymani et al. (2011)

The most widely adopted emotion categories include happiness, sadness, fear, anger, disgust, and surprise. The description of these fundamental emotions was thoroughly investigated and categorized into the universal emotions model by the cross-cultural studies conducted by Ekman and Rosenberg (1993), indicating that humans perceive certain basic emotions with respect to facial expressions in the same way, regardless of their culture (Zeng et al. 2009). However, since the universal model provides a limited set of distinct emotional categories, the circumplex multidimensional VAD Model of affect was proposed by Posner et al. (2005). The proposed model describes each emotion as a dynamic concept within multidimensional space (Tkalčič et al. 2011).

The VAD Model describes emotions using 3 dimensions: Valence (V) that evaluates how positive or pleasant an emotion is, ranging from negative to positive; Arousal (A) which assesses the involvement level of the person, ranging from "nonactive", "in calm to agitated", "ready to act" and Dominance (D) that measures the level of control over the situation by the person, ranging from "submissive", "noncontrol" "dominant/in-control" (Kosti et al. 2017).

Despite the fact that most of the emotional expressions occur in a realistic interpersonal or human-computer interactions are non-basic emotions (Cowie et al. 2005) the majority of the existing technologies and approaches developed to date are mostly designed to identify the six basic human emotions (Kosti et al. 2017).

4.2 Emotions Recognition from Facial Expressions

As people use facial expressions as a natural mean of emotional communication, one of the most well-studied channels of emotional expressions is facial expressions recognition. The analysis of facial expressions is a relevant and important topic from both scientific and applied standpoints (Soleymani et al. 2012). However, in his paper, Walla (2017) states that eliciting respective responses in the observer's brain by observing someone's facial expressions might be challenging since faces do not necessarily reflect deep internal affective states of the person what might become a confounder for emotions recognition approaches.

The topic of understanding internal decision-making drivers by recognizing facial expressions, however, keeps attracting the interests of information systems and human-computer interactions researchers as well as business-oriented professionals what resulted in rapid development of multiple technology companies (Garcia-Garcia et al. 2017). We briefly present the six technologies capable of recognizing emotions from facial expressions which are available on the market today.

- **nViso.** Developed by the Swiss company, this technology can detect six basic emotional groups, described by Ekman and Rosenberg (1993) by using a proprietary deep learning algorithm. According to the data provided on the website, nViso can capture emotions of one person or a group of people in real time with the help of the webcam, which tracks muscle movements of the face (nViso 2018). nViso partnered with IBM to create an emotional intelligence cloud solution capable of analyzing facial expressions to enable financial advisors better understand their clients' financial needs (IBM 2018). Furthermore, together with ePAT Technologies, nViso actively works on a smartphone-based medical device which is able to assess pain levels in real time by analyzing facial muscle movements of patients (IBM 2018; ePAT Technologies Ltd. 2017).

- **Affectiva.** By analyzing emotions from the twenty facial zones retrieved from a database of videos and images (Affectiva 2018a), this emotion recognition software can detect seven emotions (anger, contempt, disgust, fear, happiness, sadness and surprise) as well as measure valence and arousal of the person (Affectiva 2018b). Affectiva has recently partnered with Voxpopme, which is a global emotion recognition software provider, to work on the platform to enable advanced analysis of facial expressions within video feedback (Busines Wire 2017). Furthermore, Affectiva helps clients develop analytics solutions in multiple domains, including healthcare, education, media and advertising, retail, and gaming (Affectiva 2018a).

- **EmoVu by Eyeris.** This software solution exploits the deep learning algorithms which retrieve data from large datasets about people of various ages, ethnicities, genders, etc. EmoVu can recognize such emotions as anger, disgust, fear, happiness, neutral, sadness, and surprise and can also measure the degree of arousal and valence (Eyeris 2018a). Eyeris is mostly specialized in the development of facial analytics and emotion recognition technology for the automotive sector and the most prominent Eyeris's customers include Toyota Motor Corporation and Honda Motor Co. (Eyeris 2017). Furthermore, Eyeris has recently partnered with AvatarMind, the creator of iPal® Robot, a humanoid robot which serves as a social companion, educator, and safety monitor for children and elderly (Eyeris 2018b).

- **Kairos.** This technology provides data about persons' six emotions, level of attention, and sentiment based on the analyzed videos or images. Furthermore, the services provided by Kairos include age, ethnicity, and gender identification as well as group faces recognition and detection (Kairos 2018b). The emotion recognition software, provided by Kairos was implemented by companies such as The Interpublic Group of Companies, Legendary Entertainment, PepsiCo, etc. operating in multiple domains including advertising and media, retail, and banking and insurance (Kairos 2018a).

- **Microsoft Cognitive Services.** The Cognitive Services Pack provided by Microsoft can identify the face and emotional expressions of people after processing pictures and videos. This software identifies six basic emotional groups described by Ekman and Rosenberg (1993) as well as contempt and neutrality (Microsoft Microsoft 2018a). Microsoft provides its Cognitive Services to the businesses involved in manufacturing, healthcare, media and telecommunications, education, banking and insurance, retail, etc. The featured clients are ABB Group, Daimler AG, Allergan, Telefonica, etc. (Microsoft 2018b).

- **FaceReader by Noldus.** This automatic recognition software can analyze up to 500 facial points to recognize such emotions as neutral, contempt, boredom, interest, and confusion. Furthermore, FaceReader also calculates gaze direction, head orientation, and person characteristics (Noldus 2018a). The Noldus's clients mostly involved in healthcare, retail, and education services and include such companies as Pfizer, GlaxoSmithKline, Carnegie Mellon University, University of Maryland, Johnson & Johnson, etc. (Noldus 2018b).

4.3   Emotions Recognition from Speech

Human speech is another essential channel for gathering emotional data since accurate and real-time understanding of human-speech can significantly facilitate human-computer interactions (Tao et al. 2018) and therefore improve the work of personalized services and technologies within online shopping. In the last few years, emotions recognition from speech has become of particular scientific interest which resulted in multiple studies conducted by scientists (El Ayadi et al. 2011) which in turn became a solid ground for rapid technological development. We make a brief overview of five technologies which utilize speech to elicit emotions and are available on the market.

- **Vokaturi.** The Amsterdam-based company developed a solution, which can measure whether people are happy, sad, afraid, angry, or have a neutral state of mind directly from their voice. Vokaturi has been validated with the multiple existing emotion databases and works in a language-independent manner (Vokaturi 2018). Vokaturi has recently established a partnership with Affectiva with the purpose of joining efforts to work on the emotion-sensing product into the autonomous vehicles sector (Affectiva 2018).
- **Good Vibrations Company B.V.** This solution can recognize the emotions of the person by processing recorded voice. Good Vibrations measures acoustic properties of the user's voice and performs a real-time analysis of the user's emotions to recognize stress, pleasure, and arousal (Good Vibrations Company B.V. 2018). According to the official website of Good Vibrations Company B.V., the areas where the developed solution has the greatest potential include healthcare, advertising, gaming, sports, business, robotics, safety, and matching (Good Vibrations Company B.V. 2018).
- **audEERING.** This Munich-based tech company developed intelligent audio analysis algorithms to help organizations integrate audio analysis technology into their products. The embedded automated paralinguistic speech analysis allows detecting a multitude of attributes from the human voice, such as emotions and affective states (valence, arousal, dominance), age, alertness, or personality (audEERING 2018a). audEERING'c clients represent multiple domains such as manufacturing, telecommunications, education, retail and include BMW, Daimler, T-Mobile, Deutsche Welle, Huawei, etc. (audEERING 2018b).
- **Beyond Verbal.** The solution, provided by this Israel-based company, is capable of extracting multiple acoustic features from a speaker's voice in real time and providing insights into the emotional, health, and wellbeing condition of the user. By utilizing voice-driven emotions analytics, the technology can recognize anger, sadness, neutral, and happiness as well as can measure valence, arousal, and temper in the voice of the speaker. Beyond Verbal's clients mostly represent companies from retail, and media and marketing sectors and include such companies as Amdoc, FRONTLINE Selling, and Department26 (Beyond Verbal 2018).
- **Nemesysco.** The company provides advanced voice analysis technologies for emotion detection, personality, and risk assessment. The technology is based on the proprietary signal-processing algorithms which can extract over 150 acoustic parameters from voice and classify the collected properties into major emotional groups including anger, happiness, satisfaction, and arousal. The key domains currently covered by Nemesysco are retail, banking and insurance, and security. Among the key customers we featured Nestle, Allianz, and Europ Assistance (Nemesysco 2018).

Table 2 aggregates the technologies described and maps them against emotional dimensions of human beings we have described in the Sect. 4.1. Furthermore, the concept-matrix also demonstrates in which domains the listed technologies are

Table 2. Emotions recognition technologies, targeted emotions, and technologies application fields.

Emotions & Application fields	Facial expressions recognition technologies						Speech expressions recognition technologies				
	nViso	Affectiva	EmoVu	Kairos	MS Cognitive Services	FaceReader	Vokaturi	Good Vibrations	audEERING	Beyond Verbal	Nemesysco
Emotions											
Anger	✓	✓	✓	✓	✓		✓			✓	✓
Disgust	✓	✓	✓	✓	✓						
Fear	✓	✓	✓	✓	✓		✓	✓			✓
Happiness	✓	✓	✓	✓	✓		✓	✓		✓	
Sadness	✓	✓	✓	✓	✓		✓			✓	
Surprise	✓	✓	✓	✓	✓						
Neutral	✓	✓	✓		✓	✓	✓			✓	
Contempt		✓			✓	✓					
Boredom						✓					
Interest						✓					
Confusion						✓					
Satisfaction						✓					✓
Valence		✓	✓					✓	✓	✓	
Arousal		✓	✓						✓	✓	✓
Dominance									✓		
Application fields											
Banking & Insurance	✓			✓	✓						✓
Healthcare	✓	✓			✓	✓		✓			
Education		✓			✓	✓		✓	✓		
Gaming		✓						✓			
Security & Safety			✓					✓			✓
Robotics			✓					✓			
Manufacturing					✓		✓				
Media & Telecommunications	✓	✓			✓			✓	✓		
Retail & Marketing	✓	✓			✓	✓			✓	✓	✓

currently in use. The data provided in this table are retrieved from the official websites and contains only information which has been officially published by the software vendors.

5 Discussion

People's emotions play an essential role in many aspects of life, especially in decision-making processes. When it comes to user-centric approaches in e-Commerce, enriching the capabilities of recommender systems with the emotions recognition functionality is a vital technical and strategic decision which can amplify generation of useful and relevant content suggestions. There is an obvious shift towards embracement of emotional variable into personalized services, however, technical capabilities of recommender systems available today are still quite limited in terms of emotions recognition and utilization for content personalization.

Multiple studies prove that technologies and recommender systems capable of recognizing and interpreting emotions in the same way as other human beings have tremendous potential in human-computer interaction, human-assistive technologies, and e-Commerce. According to Walla (2017), however, the scientific community currently does not have a unified definition of what is an emotion as some of the scholars understand emotions as neural activities, others describe them as felt affective phenomena, and some scientists see emotions as facial expressions. Furthermore, in his paper Walla (2017) argues that affective processing does not always result in observable and measurable emotions. This might have serious implications for marketing and IS experts since emotions to be elicited and measured might not fully reflect the underlying affective processing. This, in turn, might mislead the interpretation of outcomes and result in irrelevant products and services that nobody wants or needs (Walla 2017).

According to Kreibig (2010), collecting reliable and valid data on autonomic responding in emotions has long been and remains a challenge within emotions research. To gain a deeper understanding of the functional role of emotions, future researchers need to thoroughly investigate and verify the particular type of emotions elicited (Kreibig 2010). This needs to be done in order to get a deeper understanding of how emotions, as well as their variations, reflect a specific state of affective processing of a particular individual. A comprehensive approach aimed at retrieving user emotions by deep analysis of affective processing may be created to facilitate understanding of users' tasks and goals, internal decision drivers, contextual properties and characteristics. This scientific method can be of great significance for providing insights into how to make personalized services within e-Commerce more precise, effective, and efficient.

The deep knowledge of the correlation between user emotions utilization and development of content personalization systems would lead to significant improvement in creation of specific personalization features and technologies. Furthermore, a better understanding of impact of emotional variable on decision-making during online shopping would facilitate designing of recommender systems architectures to enable online merchants to provide a better customer experience. A deep understanding of how user emotions impact and shape decision-making process could give rise to a new generation of personalization technologies providing value both to the users and the organizations.

In the future, we will provide a systematic study, which would consider a higher number of studies, including the most recent state-of-the art research in order to provide even more valuable insights into how user emotions are being captured and processed by emerging technologies. As a further step, our next research will go deeper into the concept of context-aware recommender systems and affective computing to identify which scientific methods and approaches are being created to advance development of personalization-focused technologies.

Acknowledgments. The present work was conducted within the training network project PERFORM funded by the European Union's Horizon 2020 research and innovation program under the Marie Skłodowska-Curie grant agreement No. 76539. This study reflects only the authors' view, the EU Research Executive Agency is not responsible for any use that may be made of the information it contains.

This work was supported, in part, by Science Foundation Ireland grant 13/RC/2094 and co-funded under the European Regional Development Fund through the Southern & Eastern Regional Operational Programme to Lero - the Irish Software Research Centre (www.lero.ie).

References

Adolphs, C., Winkelmann, A.: Personalisation in E-Commerce - a state of the art review (2000–2008). J. Electron. Commer. Res. **11**(4), 326–341 (2008)

Affectiva: About Us (2018a). https://www.affectiva.com/who/about-us/

Affectiva: Determining Accuracy (2018b). https://developer.affectiva.com/determining-accuracy/

Affectiva (2018). http://go.affectiva.com/auto

Aguirre, E., Mahr, D., Grewal, D., de Ruyter, K., Wetzels, M.: Unraveling the personalization paradox: the effect of information collection and trust-building strategies on online advertisement effectiveness. J. Retail. **91**(1), 34–49 (2015)

Ansari, A., Mela, C.F.: E-Customization. J. Mark. Res. **40**(2), 131–145 (2003)

Arapakis, I., Konstas, I., Jose, J.M.: Using facial expressions and peripheral physiological signals as implicit indicators of topical relevance categories and subject descriptors. In: Proceedings of the 17th ACM International Conference on Multimedia, Beijing, China, pp. 461–470 (2009)

audEERING (2018a). https://www.audeering.com/technology/customized-audio-analysis/

audEERING (2018b). https://www.audeering.com/references/

Bădică, C., Budimac, Z., Burkhard, H.D., Ivanović, M.: Software agents: languages, tools, platforms. Comput. Sci. Inf. Syst. **8**(2), 255–296 (2011)

Baltrunas, L.: Exploiting contextual information in recommender systems. In: Proceedings of the 2008 ACM Conference on Recommender Systems, Lausanne, Switzerland, pp. 295–298 (2008)

Beyond Verbal (2018). http://www.beyondverbal.com/going-emotional/

Beel, J., Gipp, B., Langer, S., Breitinger, C.: Research-paper recommender systems: a literature survey. Int. J. Digit. Libr. **17**(4), 305–338 (2016)

Bradley, M.M., Lang, P.J.: Measuring emotion: the self-assessment manikin and the semantic differential. J. Behav. Ther. Exp. Psychiatry **25**(1), 49–59 (1994)

Breese, J.S., Heckerman, D., Kadie, C.: Empirical analysis of predictive algorithms for collaborative filtering. In: Proceedings of the Fourteenth Conference on Uncertainty in Artificial Intelligence, Madison, Wisconsin, pp. 43–52 (1998)

Business Wire: Voxpopme Partners with Affectiva to Enhance Emotional Analysis of Video (2017). https://www.businesswire.com/news/home/20170109005950/en/Voxpopme-Partners-Affectiva-Enhance-Emotional-Analysis-Video

Cao, Y., Li, Y.: An intelligent fuzzy-based recommendation system for consumer electronic products. Expert Syst. Appl. **33**(1), 230–240 (2007)

Cowie, R., Douglas-Cowie, E., Cox, C.: Beyond emotion archetypes: databases for emotion modelling using neural networks. Neural Netw. **18**(4), 371–388 (2005)

Ekman, P., Rosenberg, E.: Facial expression and emotion. Am. Psychol. **48**(4), 384–392 (1993)

El Ayadi, M., Kamel, M.S., Karray, F.: Survey on speech emotion recognition: features, classification schemes, and databases. Pattern Recognit. **44**(3), 572–587 (2011)

ePAT Technologies Ltd. (2017). https://www.painchek.com/wp-content/uploads/2018/01/1684087.pdf

Eyeris (2018a). http://emovu.com/docs/html/getting_started.htm

Eyeris (2018b). http://www.eyeris.ai/pressrelease/eyeris-partners-ipal-robot-enable-face-face-interaction/

Garcia-Garcia, J.M., Penichet, V.M.R., Lozano, M.D.: Emotion detection. In: Proceedings of the XVIII International Conference on Human Computer Interaction, Cancun, Mexico, pp. 1–8 (2017)

Gaur, S.S., Herjanto, H., Makkar, M.: Review of emotions research in marketing, 2002–2013. J. Retail. Consum. Serv. **21**(6), 917–923 (2014)

González, G., de la Rosa, J.L., Montaner, M.: Embedding emotional context in recommender systems. In: 23rd International Conference on Data Engineering, Istanbul, Turkey, pp. 50–53 (2007)

Gorgoglione, M., Panniello, U., Tuzhilin, A.: The effect of context-aware recommendations on customer purchasing behavior and trust. In: Proceedings of the Fifth ACM Conference on Recommender Systems, Chicago, Illinois, USA, pp. 85–92 (2011)

Good Vibrations (2018). http://www.good-vibrations.nl/#concept

Good Vibrations Company B.V. (2018). http://www.good-vibrations.nl/api

Ho, S.Y., Bodoff, D.: The effects of web personalization on user attitude and behavior: an integration of the elaboration likelihood Model and Consumer Search Theory. MIS Q. **38**(2), 497–520 (2014)

IBM (2018). https://www.ibm.com/case-studies/nviso

Joho, H., Staiano, J., Sebe, N., Jose, J.M.: Looking at the viewer: analysing facial activity to detect personal highlights of multimedia contents. Multimed. Tools Appl. **51**(2), 505–523 (2011)

Kairos: What is Kairos? (2018). https://www.kairos.com/features

Kairos (2018a). https://www.kairos.com/customers

Karat, C., Blom, J., Karat, J.: Designing personalized user experiences for eCommerce: theory, methods, and research. In: CHI 2003 Extended Abstracts on Human-Computer Interactions, pp. 1040–1041 (2003)

Koren, Y.: Factor in the neighbors. ACM Trans. Knowl. Discov. Data **4**(1), 1–24 (2010)

Kosti, R., Alvarez, J.M., Recasens, A., Lapedriza, A.: Emotion recognition in context. In: Conference on Computer Vision and Pattern Recognition, Honolulu, HI, USA, pp. 1667–1675 (2017)

Kreibig, S.D.: Autonomic nervous system activity in emotion: a review. Biol. Psychol. **84**(3), 394–421 (2010)

Li, S.S., Karahanna, E.: Online recommendation systems in a B2C E-commerce context: a review and future directions. J. Assoc. Inf. Syst. **16**(2), 72–107 (2015)

Lombardi, S., Anand, S.S., Gorgoglione, M.: Context and customer behaviour in recommendation. In: Workshop on Context-Aware Recommender Systems, New York, NY, USA (2009)

Microsoft (2018a). https://azure.microsoft.com/en-us/services/cognitive-services/emotion/

Microsoft (2018b). http://customers.microsoft.com/en-us/search?sq=%22MicrosoftCognitive Services%22&ff=&p=2&so=story_publish_datedesc

Mobasher, B., Cooley, R., Srivastava, J.: Web usage mining can help improve the scalability, accuracy, and flexibility of recommender systems. Commun. ACM **43**(8), 142–151 (2000)

Montgomery, A.L., Smith, M.D.: Prospects for personalization on the internet. J. Interact. Mark. **23**(2), 130–137 (2009)

Nemesysco (2018). http://nemesysco.com/speech-analysis-technology

Noldus (2018a). https://www.noldus.com/human-behavior-research/products/facereader?gclid= Cj0KCQiAoo7gBRDuARIsANeJKUYgnTMQtuD7NhBOcga-Uaf_DUEKBlM6YGVHs3XJ k6-whaf7PcGhjGAaAm-sEALw_wcB

Noldus (2018b). https://www.noldus.com/EthoVision-XT/client-list

nViso: Advancing Human Potential (2018). https://www.nviso-insights.com/en

Osterwalder, A., Pigneur, Y.: An eBusiness model ontology for modeling eBusiness. In: 15th Bled Electronic Commerce Conference, Bled, Slovenia, pp. 75–91 (2002)

Pantic, M., Vinciarelli, A.: Implicit human-centered tagging. IEEE Signal Process. Mag. **26**(6), 173–180 (2009)

Costa, H., Macedo, L.: Emotion-based recommender system for overcoming the problem of information overload. In: Corchado, Juan M., Bajo, J., Kozlak, J., Pawlewski, P., Molina, Jose M., Julian, V., Silveira, R.A., Unland, R., Giroux, S. (eds.) PAAMS 2013. CCIS, vol. 365, pp. 178–189. Springer, Heidelberg (2013). https://doi.org/10.1007/978-3-642-38061-7_18

Pappas, I.O., Kourouthanassis, P.E., Giannakos, M.N., Chrissikopoulos, V.: Sense and sensibility in personalized e-commerce: how emotions rebalance the purchase intentions of persuaded customers. Psychol. Mark. **34**(10), 972–986 (2017)

Pazzani, M.J.: A framework for collaborative, content-based and demographic filtering. Artif. Intell. Rev. **13**(5), 393–408 (1999)

Picard, R.W., et al.: Affective learning - a manifesto. BT Technol. J. **22**(4), 253–268 (2004)

Polignano, M.: A framework for emotion-aware Recommender systems supporting decision making. In: Proceedings of the 6th Symposium on Future Directions in Information Access, Thessaloniki, Greece, pp. 12–15 (2015)

Porayska-Pomsta, K., Mavrikis, M., Pain, H.: Diagnosing and acting on student affect: the tutor's perspective. User Model. User-Adapt. Interact. **18**(1–2), 125–173 (2007)

Posner, J., Russell, J.A., Peterson, B.: The circumplex model of affect: an integrative approach to affective neuroscience, cognitive development, and psychopathology. Dev. Psychopathol. **17**(3), 715–734 (2005)

Rust, R.T., Chung, T.S.: Marketing models of service and relationships. Mark. Sci. **25**(6), 560–580 (2006)

Salonen, V., Karjaluoto, H.: Web personalization: the state of the art and future avenues for research and practice. Telemat. Inform. **33**(4), 1088–1104 (2016)

Shi, Y., Larson, M., Hanjalic, A.: Mining mood-specific movie similarity with matrix factorization for context-aware recommendation. In: Proceedings of the Workshop on Context-Aware Movie Recommendation, Barcelona, Spain, pp. 34–40 (2010)

Simon, M., Van Den Driest, F., Wilms, T.O.M.: Driving customer-centric growth: a practical roadmap. J. Advert. Res. **56**(2), 159–168 (2016)

Soleymani, M., Koelstra, S., Patras, I., Pun, T.: Continuous emotion detection in response to music videos. Face Gesture **2011**, 803–808 (2011)

Soleymani, M., Lichtenauer, J., Pun, T., Pantic, M.: A multimodal database for affect recognition and implicit tagging. IEEE Trans. Affect. Comput. **3**(1), 42–55 (2012)

Surprenant, C.F., Solomon, M.R.: Predictability and personalization in the service encounter. J. Mark. **51**(2), 86–96 (1987)

Tam, Y.K., Ho, S.Y.: Understanding the impact of web personalization on user information processing and decision outcomes. MIS Q. **30**(4), 865–890 (2006)

Tao, F., Liu, G., Zhao, Q.: An ensemble framework of voice-based emotion recognition system for films and TV programs. In: Proceedings of the First Asian Conference on Affective Computing and Intelligent Interaction, Beijing, China, pp. 363–364 (2018)

Tkalčič, M., Košir, A., Tasič, J.: Affective recommender systems: the role of emotions in recommender systems. CEUR Work. Proc. **811**(i), 9–13 (2011)

Tkalčič, M., Odić, A., KoTkalšičir, A., Tasič, J.: Affective labeling in a content-based recommender system for images. IEEE Trans. Multimed. **15**(2), 391–400 (2013)

Tran, T., Cohen, R.: Hybrid recommender systems for electronic commerce. AAAI Technical report (2000)

Uçar, T., Karahoca, A.: Personalizing trip recommendations: a framework proposal. Glob. J. Comput. Sci. **05**(51), 30–35 (2015)

Vesanen, J., Raulas, M.: Building bridges for personalization: a process model for marketing. J. Interact. Mark. **20**(1), 5–20 (2006)

Vesanen, J.: What is personalization? A conceptual framework. Eur. J. Mark. **41**(5/6), 409–418 (2007)

Vokaturi (2018). https://vokaturi.com/

Walla, P.: Affective processing guides behavior and emotions communicate feelings: towards a guideline for the NeuroIS community. Lect. Notes Inf. Syst. Organ. **25**, 141–150 (2017)

Webster, J., Watson, R.T.: Analyzing the past to prepare for the future: writing a literature review. MIS Q. **26**(2), 13–23 (2002)

Yannakakis, G.N., Hallam, J., Lund, H.H.: Entertainment capture through heart rate activity in physical interactive playgrounds. User Model. User-Adapt. Interact. **18**(1–2), 207–243 (2008)

Zeng, Z., Pantic, M., Roisman, G.I., Huang, T.S.: A survey of affect recognition methods: audio, visual, and spontaneous expressions. IEEE Trans. Pattern Anal. Mach. Intell. **31**(1), 39–58 (2009)

Zheng, Y.: Adapt to emotional reactions in context-aware personalization. In: CEUR Workshop Proceedings, vol. 1680, pp. 1–8, September 2016

Zheng, Y., Burke, R., Mobasher, B.: The role of emotions in context-aware recommendation. In: CEUR Workshop Proceedings, vol. 1050, pp. 21–28 (2013)

Ad Click Prediction: Learning from Cognitive Style

Tingting Cha, Shaohua Lian, and Chenghong Zhang[✉]

School of Management, Fudan University, Shanghai, China
{13110690009,shlian16,chzhang}@fudan.edu.cn

Abstract. In the past two decades, online advertising increased rapidly. It is now an integral part of the web experience. In this study, we divide webpages into two types: image-based and text-based webpages. We also differentiate user cognitive style as verbalizers and visualizers. Then we investigate how user's visual preference and the webpage type jointly influence the click-through rates of online flash ads. Our empirical results indicate that visual preference can significantly increase the click probability of flash ads. In addition, flash ads on text-based webpages are more likely to draw the attention of those users who prefer visual materials than on image-based webpages. Our findings contribute to the literature of online advertising by explaining how cognitive style and page context jointed affect ad click probability and providing guidelines for advertisers to target users more precisely.

Keywords: Cognitive style · Webpage type · Exposure frequency · Online flash ad

1 Introduction

In recent years, even though online advertising revenues have grown dramatically, click-through rates (CTR) for online advertising continue to decrease, raising hard questions regarding its effectiveness of targeting users [1]. Online users tend to pay more attention to the payload of the page and it is difficult for an ad to draw users' attention [2]. Improving advertising effectiveness is imperative for both advertising practitioners and academics [3].

Advertisers need to match online ads to relevant consumers. For example, advertisers try to match ad contents to user characteristics or webpage contents. Regarding the webpage content, it could include plain text, hyperlinks, graphics, audio, and video. In this study, if the main content of a webpage is images, e.g., pictures of a car on a dealer's website, it is an image-based page. If the main content is text, as typical in news portals, it is a text-based page.

Cognitive style theory suggests that users with different cognitive style have significant differences in inspecting learning materials [4]. Some people tend to spend more time inspecting visual materials such as picture or video. They are known as visualizers. Others tend to spend more time inspecting texts, known as verbalizers. This study uses visual (verbal) preference to refer to an individual's preference for processing visual (verbal) information. Nevertheless, cognitive style may affect users'

© Springer Nature Switzerland AG 2019
F. F.-H. Nah and K. Siau (Eds.): HCII 2019, LNCS 11588, pp. 194–205, 2019.
https://doi.org/10.1007/978-3-030-22335-9_13

allocation of cognitive resource when browsing an image-based or text-based page. It could also affect their responses to online ads which could be displayed in a visual or verbal webpage.

In this study, we use clickstream data provided by a China's digital advertising agency to explore how ad exposure frequency, cognitive style, and webpage type jointly affect the click-through rates of image-based online flash ads. The key research question is whether visualizers and verbalizers differ in their ad click behaviors in different webpage contexts.

Our results show that ad exposure frequency has a positive effect on the ad click probability in both image-based and text-based pages. Visual preference has a positive effect on the click-through rate of online flash ads. For interaction effect, flash ads on text-based webpages are more likely to draw visualizers' attention than those on image-based webpages.

The remainder of this paper is organized as follows: Sect. 2 reviews the literature related to online advertising and cognitive style theory. Rooted in previous literature, we propose our hypotheses in Sect. 3. Section 4 reports data collection and variable measurement. Section 5 reports model development and estimation results. Finally, in Sect. 6, we provide a discussion, managerial implication, limitations, and directions for future research.

2   Theoretical Background

2.1   Online Advertising System

An instance of online advertising comprises of three dimensions: the ad, the user, and the medium context. In this system, advertisers place their ads on a webpage to attract the attention of online users. Online users tend to regard the ad as an integral component of the page [2]. Therefore, the effectiveness of online advertising depends on not only the ad itself but also user characteristics and medium context.

The first dimension of advertising effectiveness is the properties of an ad, such as ad content, display format, and exposure frequency [3]. Numerous research and practice have examined the effects of different ad properties on its effectiveness. For example, Lee et al. [5] analyzed the effects of display format and ad repetition on user attention. They found that static banner ads are better in attracting and holding users' attention in the very beginning. However, the gaze duration to static ads rapidly decreased with repetition, while the gaze duration to animated ads decreases relatively slowly.

The second dimension of ad effectiveness is user characteristics. User characteristics usually comprise of demographics and behavioral information, which has been demonstrated to affect click-through rates of online ads [6]. Through integrating ad properties and user characteristics, advertisers can deliver their ads to specific user groups based on demographic information or behavioral features. For example, if a user has filled in car-related online forms or browsed car-related webpages, car ads could be delivered to the user when she surfs online.

The third dimension of online advertising is to deliver an ad in the right page context. A user's browsing behavior always occurs in a medium context. Therefore, medium features play a significant role in advertising effectiveness. Some studies have analyzed the effects of medium properties on ad effectiveness. Hsieh and Chen [2] examined how the information types of webpages influence the viewer's attention on banner advertising. Their study found that viewer's attention is stronger for image-based and video-based webpage than for text-based or text–picture mixed webpage. Other studies have attempted to enhance ad effectiveness by matching ads to relevant websites [7]. The underlying assumption is that ads that match the content of the page are relevant to the need of the user.

2.2 Cognitive Style Theory

The term 'cognitive style', which was first used by Allport [8], has been defined as a person's typical or habitual mode of problem-solving, thinking, perceiving, and remembering. Cognitive styles are often defined with bipolar dimensions, among which the verbalizer-visualizer style is one of the most fundamental dimensions [4]. The rationale of the verbalizer-visualizer cognitive style stems from the Dual Coding Theory (DCT), which states that verbal and nonverbal mental systems are specialized for processing linguistic and imagery information, respectively [9]. According to DCT, the verbalizer-visualizer style indicates whether an individual is inclined to mentally represent information in a verbal or visual form.

A wide range of studies on learning behavior has suggested that the verbalizer-visualizer cognitive style and the presentation of information interact to affect learning performance [10, 11]. A basic tenet is that individuals can achieve a better performance when they have the opportunity to receive their preferred presentation of information [12]. That is, verbalizers learn best from the text, while visualizers are better off with visual presentations. Although the DCT indicates that most individuals are capable of switching between verbal and nonverbal mental systems, they seem to find a particular mode easier to comprehend and to heavily rely on that information processing mode [13].

In recent years, eye-tracking technology has been increasingly used as a method to identify users' preference for verbal or visual presentation instead of traditional questionnaires [14]. Tsianos et al. [15] have used eye-tracking to identify users' actual behavior in adaptive e-learning systems. Their findings reveal that visualizers concentrate on visual content, verbalizers on text, while intermediates are placed in-between. Koć-Januchta et al. [16] have investigated the gaze behavior of college students and found that visualizers spend significantly more time inspecting pictures than verbalizers, while verbalizers spend more time inspecting texts. These results further verify that there are significant differences in the cognitive preference of different types of users.

3   Hypothesis Development

Most previous research on online advertising has focused on one or two advertising dimensions to improve ad effectiveness. In this paper, we integrate ad properties, user, and media into a unified framework and investigate how ad exposure frequency, user cognitive style, and webpage content type jointly and interactively influence the click-through rates of online flash ads.

3.1   Ad Exposure Frequency

For any online ad, exposure frequency is the fundamental factor that influences the persuasiveness of communications [17]. Previous studies examining the effects of repetition on message recall (the memory of the stimulus, i.e., brand name, advertising content) have found a positive effect of advertising repetition on consumers' recall [18, 19]. Repeating advertising to consumers boosts content learning and eventually results in action, such as a click or a sale [20]. Some studies have found that increased exposures to advertising are positively related to repeat purchase probabilities [21]. Thus, we expect that repeated ad exposures will generally increase the click-through rates of online ads.

In this study, we define two types of webpage: image-based webpage and text-based webpage. The former refers to webpages that dominantly contain pictures, and the latter refers to webpages that dominantly contain text. For each user, we count the ad exposure frequency on the two types of webpages separately. Without considering the impact of other factors, exposure frequency should have a positive effect on the click-through rates of online advertising, regardless of the page type. Thus, we hypothesize:

> *H1: The ad exposure frequency on image-based webpages has a positive effect on the click-through rate of an online flash ad.*
> *H2: The ad exposure frequency on text-based webpages has a positive effect on the click-through rate of an online flash ad.*

3.2   The Match Between Cognitive Style and Ad Format

The cognitive style theory indicates that the cognitive style could be a critical factor affecting users' attention to stimuli in different formats. However, until recently, cognitive style is rarely utilized by advertisers. Although advertisers have developed various methods to optimize an ad for users, they have not found a way to personalize their ad based on users' cognitive style [1].

Chiou et al. [22] compared the effectiveness of traditional textual brochures with image-based virtual advertising which provides panoramic views, animation, and interactive photos for both visualizers and verbalizers. They found that traditional brochures are more effective for verbalizers, whereas virtual advertising is more effective for visualizers. Urban et al. [23] have dynamically changed banner ads based on the inferred cognitive style of users, including impulsive-analytic, impulsive-holistic, deliberative-analytic, and deliberative-holistic dimensions. Their experimental results show that ads matched to cognitive styles increase click-through rates, brand consideration, and purchase likelihood.

We believe visualizers and verbalizers can be inferred based users' browsing history, and matching online ads to inferred cognitive style would boost click-through rate. All online ads in our dataset are flash images. We use the percentage of image-based webpages a user has browsed in comparison to the total number of pages he has browsed to gauge her visual preference. Based on the literature, because image ad matches the cognitive style of visualizers, visualizers are more likely to click online flash ads. Thus, we hypothesize:

H3: A user's visual preference is positively associated with the click-through rate of an online flash ad.

3.3 The Match Among Ad, User, and Media

A webpage, either image-based or text-based, demands user attention cognition. Online ads, as a component of webpages, compete with other webpage elements for users' attention. When clicking an online ad, a user's attention shifts from the webpage content to the ad. Previous research has found that a user shifts her attention to an information object which is more efficient to process, and shifts away her attention from an unwanted or irrelevant object [24].

For visualizers, when they are browsing image-based webpages, we expect that a flash ad is less likely to distract their attention away from the webpage content. This is because an image-based webpage already has more relevant and easy-to-process images for visualizers. An ad is neither a more relevant object nor an easier-to-process object to process. Consequently, visualizers are unwilling to shift their attention to ads.

In contrast, when visualizers are browsing text-based webpages, an image-based flash ad is more likely to distract their attention away from the webpage text. This is because the text in such webpages is cognitively more costly for visualizers. A flash ad, even if it is less relevant to the user, is more likely to attract users' attention.

Based on the above reasoning, flash ads on text-based webpages are more likely to draw visualizers' attention than those on image-based webpages. Consequently, the effect of the exposure frequency on the click-through rate will be attenuated by visual preference on image-based webpages but be strengthened on text-based webpages.

H4: The effect of ad exposure frequency on the click-through rates of online flash ads on image-based webpages will be negatively moderated by visual preference.
H5: The effect of ad exposure frequency on the click-through rates of online flash ads on text-based webpages will be positively moderated by visual preference.

4   Research Methodology

4.1   Data Collection

We use secondary data provided by a China's digital advertising agency to test our hypotheses. From August 18, 2014 to December 31, 2014, the agency launched 42 online advertising campaigns that involved 11 car brands and five media websites. Each campaign displayed ads of a specific car brand on a specific media website. We randomly selected one advertising campaign, which was conducted from October 1, 2014 to October 31, 2014. The selected campaign delivered the ads of a Japanese car on Bitauto.com. We obtained users' browsing history on all five websites covered by the agency from August 18, 2014 to October 31, 2014. Eventually, we had 215,477 users.

4.2   Variable Measurement

Dependent Variables. In our dataset, each ad exposure was tagged to indicate whether the ad was clicked. We use *Click* to represent the status of ad click. If a user has clicked ads at least once, we set *Click* to one. Meanwhile, we used browsing history before the user's first ad click to calculate independent and control variables. Otherwise, we set *Click* to zero and used the full browsing history of the user to calculate independent variables.

Independent Variables. First, we created two variables to represent the ad exposure frequency to each user for the selected campaign. *ExpVisual* represents the ad exposure frequency in image-based webpages before user's first click, and *ExpVerbal* represents the ad exposure frequency in text-based webpages before user's first click. The classification of image-based and text-based pages in the automobile portal websites is straightforward. While most pages are text-based, each model of car has a few image-based pages which display various pictures of the model. These image pages have a clear URL pattern. Since there was a large number of zero values for the two variables (i.e., some users had ad exposure only on text-based pages or image-based pages), we created two dummy variables *DumVisual* and *DumVerbal* to indicate whether a user has browsed ads in image-based webpages or text-based webpages respectively. Second, we defined a variable *RatioVisual* to denote a user's ratio of browsing image-based webpages over all pages the user browsed. It gauges users' visual preference or their degree of being a visualizer. After removing duplicate URLs, we used browsing history of all campaigns in our dataset to calculate *RatioVisual*.

Control variables. To control user heterogeneity, we also coded additional variables according to users' browsing history. First, we included ad-related control variables. *ExpDay* represents the number of days when users have been exposed to the ad of the selected campaign. *AdAccept* represents a user's ratio of clicking ads across all ad exposures of all campaigns. This variable gauges users' propensity to click online ads. Second, we controlled the user preference for different cars. The advertised car in the selected campaign is a medium-sized and medium-priced car[1]. Thus, we used *RatioSize* to represent user's ratio of browsing medium-sized cars across all websites. We used *RatioPrice* to represent user's ratio of browsing medium-priced car models. Third, we also controlled user's preference to auto-related websites. *NumSite* represents the

---

[1] Bitauto.com tags the cars with prices between 180,000 RMB and 250,000 RMB as medium-priced ones.

Table 1. Definitions and basic descriptive statistics of variables

Variable	Definition	Mean	S.D.	Min	Max
Click	A binary variable indicating whether a user clicked on an ad in the selected campaign	0.005	–	0	1
ExpVisual	Ad exposure frequency in image-based webpages in the selected campaign	3.877	10.368	0	595
ExpVerbal	Ad exposure frequency in text-based webpages in the selected campaign	1.238	2.323	0	129
DumVisual	A dummy variable indicating whether a user browsed ads in image-based webpages in the selected campaign	0.615	–	0	1
DumVerbal	A dummy variable indicating whether a user browsed ads in text-based webpages in the selected campaign	0.536	–	0	1
RatioVisual	The ratio of browsing image-based webpages in all campaigns of our dataset	0.424	0.365	0	1
ExpDay	The number of days when users have been exposed to the ad in the selected campaign	1.645	1.423	1	29
AdAccept	The ratio of clicking ads in all campaigns	0.002	0.018	0	1
RatioSize	The ratio of browsing medium-size car webpages in all campaigns	0.265	0.197	0.001	1
RatioPrice	The ratio of browsing medium-priced car webpages in all campaigns	0.034	0.101	0	0.952
NumSite	The number of auto websites that a user has visited in all campaigns	1.653	0.809	1	5
RatioBitauto	The ratio of browsing Bitauto.com webpages in all campaigns	0.801	0.289	0.002	1
UrlAll	The number of unique webpages that a user has visited in all campaigns	19.252	24.740	1	896
UrlDaily	The daily average number of webpages that a user has visited in all campaigns	1.845	1.018	0.500	228.667
NumCity	The number of cities where a user's IP address has ever appeared in all campaigns	1.360	0.879	1	74

number of websites that a user has visited in all campaigns. *RatioBitauto* represents the ratio of browsing Bitauto.com in all campaigns. Next, we defined two variables to measure user activeness. *UrlAll* represents the number of unique webpages that a user has visited. *UrlDaily* represents the daily average number of unique webpages that a user has visited, which equals *UrlAll* divided by *ExpDay*. Finally, considering that users' geographic mobility may also affect automobile ad clicks, we create a variable *NumCity* to represent the number of cities where a user's IP address has ever appeared. Table 1 illustrates the definition and the basic descriptive statistics of all variables.

5 Empirical Analysis

5.1 Model Development

We used a logit model to analyze users' ad click behavior. We model users' ad click probability as a function of exposure frequency, cognitive style, page type, and other control variables. We assume that users' latent utility determines their ad click behaviors. For a user i, we use $Click_i$ to denote the user's binary response and U_i to denote the user's latent utility.

$$Click_i = \begin{cases} 1, \; if \; U_i > 0 \\ 0, \; if \; U_i \leq 0 \end{cases} \; where \; U_i = v_i + \varepsilon_i \tag{1}$$

The main part of U_i is represented by v_i, which is a linear function of the independent and control variables. The second part ε_i is the stochastic component, which contains non-systematic or random factors affecting U_i. When users are exposed to an ad on the webpage, they click on the ad only if their latent utility U_i is greater than zero.

By applying a logit model, we aim to measure the effects of cognitive style and ad exposures on click-through rates of online ads. We also aim to examine the interactions between cognitive style and exposure frequency on different types of webpage. The utility function of our model is as follows:

$$\begin{aligned} U_i = {} & \beta_0 + \beta_1 ExpVisual_i + \beta_2 DumVisual_i + \beta_3 ExpVerbal_i + \beta_4 DumVerbal_i \\ & + \beta_5 RatioVisual_i + \beta_6 ExpDay_i + \beta_7 AdAccept_i + \beta_8 RatioSize_i + \beta_9 Ratio\,Price_i \\ & + \beta_{10} NumSite_i + \beta_{11} RatioBitauto_i + \beta_{12} UrlAll_i + \beta_{13} UrlDaily_i + \beta_{14} NumCity_i \\ & + \beta_{15} RatioVisual_i * ExpVisual_i + \beta_{16} RatioVisual_i * ExpVerbal_i + \varepsilon_i \end{aligned}$$

$$\tag{2}$$

5.2 Estimation Results

For comparison, we first converted *ExpVisual*, *ExpVerbal*, *UrlAll*, *UrlDaily*, and *NumCity* to its natural logarithm values. Then, we standardized all variables except for binary ones.

We present the estimation results in Table 2. Model 1 is the main effect model without consideration of the interaction between cognitive style and exposure frequency. In this model, the coefficient of *ExpVisual* is significantly positive. Thus, the exposure frequency on image-based webpages has a significantly positive effect on the ad click probability. This finding supports H1. Similarly, the result of Model 1 also

Table 2. Estimation results

	Model 1	Model 2	Model 3
ExpVisual	0.316***	0.429***	0.406***
	(0.042)	(0.045)	(0.046)
DumVisual	1.093***	0.650***	0.480*
	(0.155)	(0.183)	(0.189)
ExpVerbal	0.420***	0.314***	0.466***
	(0.104)	(0.107)	(0.117)
DumVerbal	−0.664***	−0.620***	−0.882***
	(0.155)	(0.155)	(0.178)
RatioVisual	1.166***	1.498***	1.717***
	(0.178)	(0.191)	(0.198)
ExpDay	−0.752***	−0.736***	−0.732***
	(0.046)	(0.046)	(0.046)
AdAccept	3.579***	3.585***	3.523***
	(0.602)	(0.589)	(0.605)
RatioSize	4.928***	5.125***	5.126***
	(0.235)	(0.243)	(0.241)
RatioPrice	2.385***	2.489***	2.510***
	(0.566)	(0.567)	(0.562)
NumSite	0.072	0.061	0.067
	(0.056)	(0.056)	(0.056)
RatioBitauto	1.683***	1.685***	1.723***
	(0.243)	(0.243)	(0.242)
UrlAll	1.747***	1.773***	1.767***
	(0.082)	(0.082)	(0.081)
UrlDaily	−1.527***	−1.479***	−1.469***
	(0.144)	(0.145)	(0.145)
NumCity	0.032	0.034	0.035
	(0.070)	(0.070)	(0.070)
RatioVisual*ExpVisual		−0.495***	−0.464***
		(0.194)	(0.108)
RatioVisual*ExpVerbal			0.822***
			(0.218)
Constant	−6.631***	−6.305***	−5.967***
	(0.181)	(0.194)	(0.222)
N	215,477	215,477	215,477
Log Likelihood	−5607.89	−5598.77	−5591.36
Pseudo R2	0.1364	0.1378	0.1390

Standard errors in parentheses: * $p < 0.05$, ** $p < 0.01$, *** $p < 0.001$

shows that the exposure frequency on text-based webpages has a significantly positive effect on the ad click probability, which supports H2. Besides, the coefficient of *DumVisual* is significantly positive while *DumVerbal* is significantly negative, which indicates that users are more likely to click online flash ads on image-based webpages. This is because processing image-based webpage requires less mental resource so that more attention is available for ads on the webpage. As for cognitive style, the coefficient of *RatioVisual* is significantly positive. That is, a visualizer has a higher probability of clicking online flash ads. This finding supports H3.

Next, we included the interaction of cognitive style and ad exposure frequency on image-based webpages in Model 2. The model shows that the coefficient of the interaction between *RatioVisual* and *ExpVisual* is significantly negative. Then, we continued to include the interaction of cognitive style and ad exposure frequency on text-based webpages in Model 3. The coefficient of the interaction between *RationVisual* and *ExpVerbal* is significantly positive. The two findings indicate that those users who prefer visual materials are more inclined to click flash ads on text-based webpages than on image-based webpages. More specifically, the effect of ad exposure frequency on image-based webpages on the click-through rates of online flash ads is attenuated by visual preference. However, the effect is strengthened visual preference on text-based webpages. The results support H4 and H5.

6 Discussion and Conclusions

This paper empirically investigates how cognitive style affects users' response to flash ads displayed in different webpage types. We divide webpages into two types: image-based webpages and text-based webpages. Then, we examine the effects of exposure frequency on these two types of webpages and cognitive style on users' ad click behavior. Besides, we also explore whether and how cognitive style moderates exposure frequency on ad click behavior. Our results indicate that exposure frequency has a positive main effect on ad click behavior. Cognitive style also has a significant impact on users' response to flash ads. Users with a higher visual preference are more likely to click flash ads. For the interaction effect between exposure frequency and cognitive style, we find that the effect of exposure frequency on flash ad click in image-based webpages is attenuated by visual preference. Conversely, the effect of exposure frequency on ad click in text-based webpages is strengthened by visual preference. The findings of our study offer several implications for research and practice, which are discussed as follows.

6.1 Theoretical Implications

First, this study contributes to the literature of online advertising by utilizing cognitive style theory to predict ad click probability, which has not been investigated before. Cognitive style theory has been widely applied to learning behaviors. Our findings suggest that cognitive style plays a significant role in affecting users' response to online ads. This perspective provides a valuable complement for existing target methods such as context matching, demographic matching, and behavioral matching.

Second, this study integrates advertising characteristics, user characteristics, and media context into a unified framework from the cognitive style perspective. We investigate the interaction effects between cognitive style and exposure frequency on different types of webpage. Our findings provide new insights regarding the interplay among various components in online advertising system. This may provide incremental lift beyond previous target patterns that only consider the match between any two parts.

6.2 Managerial Implications

The findings in our study also provide valuable guidelines for advertisers to target users more precisely. First, since cognitive style has a significant impact on ad click behavior, advertisers can reach customers based on their cognitive style in addition to their interest profile. Advertisers can infer cognitive style of online users by their browsing history and then selectively expose ads to users with corresponding cognitive style. For example, picture or video ads should be delivered to users who prefer browsing image-based webpages while text ads should be delivered to users who prefer browsing text-based webpages.

Second, besides the match between ad format and cognitive style, advertisers should also consider the impact of media context. For example, in terms of delivering flash ads to users with visual preference, exposures on text-based webpages may result in higher click-through rates than on image-based webpages.

6.3 Limitation and Future Directions

There are some limitations to this study. First, because of the limitation of secondary data, we can only approximately measure users' cognitive style by the ratio of browsing image-based webpages. Future study should verify our results by more accurate measurement of cognitive style, such as survey or eye-tracking technology. Second, we only consider the effects of exposure frequency and two types of webpage structures on ad click. Future study could extend our results by including more ad-related factors and media context. Finally, there is still some confusion about how cognitive style interacts with media context. Figuring out the mechanism with a more informative dataset could further elucidate the pivotal effect of cognitive style in online advertising system and enhance the understanding of this field.

Acknowledgments. This work was supported by the National Natural Science Foundation of China (grant #71531006, #11571081, and #71471044), the Program for Professor of Special Appointment (Eastern Scholar) at Shanghai Institutions of Higher Learning, and the Scientific Research Project of Shanghai Science and Technology Committee (grant #17DZ1101002).

References

1. Liberali, G.: Morphing advertising to improve online campaign success. RSM Discov. Knowl. **20**, 12–14 (2014)
2. Hsieh, Y.C., Chen, K.H.: How different information types affect viewer's attention on internet advertising. Comput. Hum. Behav. **27**, 935–945 (2011)

3. Li, K., Huang, G., Bente, G.: The impacts of banner format and animation speed on banner effectiveness: evidence from eye movements. Comput. Hum. Behav. **54**, 522–530 (2016)
4. Riding, R., Cheema, I.: Cognitive styles—an overview and integration. Educ. Psychol. **11**, 193–215 (1991)
5. Lee, J., Ahn, J.H., Park, B.: The effect of repetition in Internet banner ads and the moderating role of animation. Comput. Hum. Behav. **46**, 202–209 (2015)
6. Joshi, A., Bagherjeiran, A., Ratnaparkhi, A.: User demographic and behavioral targeting for content match advertising. In: Proceedings of the Fifth International Workshop on Data Mining and Audience Intelligence for Advertising (ADKDD 2011), pp. 53–60 (2011)
7. Moore, R.S., Stammerjohan, C.A., Coulter, R.A.: Banner advertiser-web site context congruity and color effects on attention and attitudes. J. Advert. **34**, 71–84 (2005)
8. Allport, G.W.: Personality: a psychological interpretation (1937)
9. Paivio, A.: Imagery and Verbal Processes. Psychology Press, Hove (2013)
10. Riding, R., Douglas, G.: The effect of cognitive style and mode of presentation on learning performance. Br. J. Educ. Psychol. **63**, 297–307 (1993)
11. Frias-Martinez, E., Chen, S.Y., Liu, X.: Investigation of behavior and perception of digital library users: a cognitive style perspective. Int. J. Inf. Manage. **28**, 355–365 (2008)
12. Plass, J.L., Chun, D.M., Mayer, R.E., Leutner, D.: Supporting visual and verbal learning preferences in a second-language multimedia learning environment. J. Educ. Psychol. **90**, 25–36 (1998)
13. Ernest, C.H., Paivio, A.: Imagery and verbal associative latencies as a function of imagery ability. Can. J. Psychol. Can. Psychol. **25**, 83 (1971)
14. Mehigan, T.J., Barry, M., Kehoe, A., Pitt, I.: Using eye tracking technology to identify visual and verbal learners. In: 2011 IEEE International Conference on Multimedia and Expo (ICME), pp. 1–6 (2011)
15. Tsianos, N., Germanakos, P., Lekkas, Z., Mourlas, C., Samaras, G.: Eye-tracking users' behavior in relation to cognitive style within an e-learning environment. In: Ninth IEEE International Conference on Advanced Learning Technologies, ICALT 2009, pp. 329–333 (2009)
16. Koć-Januchta, M., Höffler, T., Thoma, G.B., Prechtl, H., Leutner, D.: Visualizers versus verbalizers: effects of cognitive style on learning with texts and pictures – an eye-tracking study. Comput. Hum. Behav. **68**, 170–179 (2017)
17. Cacioppo, J.T., Petty, R.E.: Persuasiveness of communications is affected by exposure frequency and message quality: a theoretical and empirical analysis of persisting attitude change. Curr. issues Res. Advert. **3**, 97–122 (1980)
18. Anand, P., Sternthal, B.: Ease of message processing as a moderator of repetition effects in advertising. J. Mark. Res. **27**, 345–353 (1990)
19. Burke, R.R., Srull, T.K.: Competitive interference and consumer memory for advertising. J. Consum. Res. **15**, 55–68 (1988)
20. Broussard, G.: How advertising frequency can work to build online advertising effectiveness. Int. J. Mark. Res. **42**, 439–458 (2000)
21. Schmidt, S., Eisend, M.: Advertising repetition: a meta-analysis on effective frequency in advertising. J. Advert. **44**, 415–428 (2015)
22. Chiou, W.B., Wan, C.S., Lee, H.Y.: Virtual experience vs. brochures in the advertisement of scenic spots: how cognitive preferences and order effects influence advertising effects on consumers. Tour. Manag. **29**, 146–150 (2008)
23. Urban, G.L., Liberali, G., MacDonald, E., Bordley, R., Hauser, J.R.: Morphing banner advertising. Mark. Sci. **33**, 27–46 (2013)
24. Johnson, A., Proctor, R.W.: Attention: Theory and Practice. Sage, Thousand Oaks (2004)

Presenting Your Products in Virtual Reality: Do not Underestimate Cybersickness

Kai Israel[1], Christopher Zerres[1(✉)], Dieter K. Tscheulin[2],
Lea Buchweitz[1], and Oliver Korn[1]

[1] University of Applied Sciences Offenburg,
Badstrasse 24, 77652 Offenburg, Germany
christopher.zerres@hs-offenburg.de
[2] University of Freiburg, Platz der Alten Synagoge, 79085 Freiburg, Germany

Abstract. For e-commerce retailers it is crucial to present their products both informatively and attractively. Virtual reality (VR) systems represent a new marketing tool that supports customers in their decision-making process and offers an extraordinary product experience. Despite these advantages, the use of this technology for e-commerce retailers is also associated with risks, namely cybersickness. The aim of the study is to investigate the occurrence of cyber-sickness in the context of the customer's *perceived enjoyment* and the *perceived challenge* of a VR product presentation. Based on a conceptual research framework, a laboratory study with 533 participants was conducted to determine the influence of these factors on the occurrence of cybersickness. The results demonstrate that the *perceived challenge* has a substantially stronger impact on the occurrence of *cybersickness*, which can only be partially reduced by *perceived enjoyment*. When realizing VR applications in general and VR product presentations in particular, e-commerce retailers should therefore first minimize possible challenges instead of focusing primarily on entertainment aspects of such applications.

Keywords: Cybersickness · Virtual reality · Product presentation ·
User experience

1 Introduction

In the last few years, virtual reality (VR) has become a very important instrument for companies to present their products in e-commerce. VR provides unique visualization possibilities and gives users the feeling of being in a different place. Especially in industries where products are difficult to evaluate by consumers prior to purchase, VR can support consumers during their decision-making process [1]. For example, large hotel chains such as Marriot and Hilton are already presenting hotels with VR. As with games, product presentations in VR provide an enjoyable user experience that awakens curiosity and challenges the potential guest [2]. Current study results show that modern VR applications for product presentation are suitable for both apparel retailing [3] and the tourism industry [4], and that they support customers in product assessment. Furthermore, it has been shown that consumers would purchase a virtual reality system if

© Springer Nature Switzerland AG 2019
F. F.-H. Nah and K. Siau (Eds.): HCII 2019, LNCS 11588, pp. 206–224, 2019.
https://doi.org/10.1007/978-3-030-22335-9_14

more useful applications were available on the market [5]. Despite the great advantages of this new technology, cybersickness is a serious problem for e-commerce retailers. The contribution of this paper is threefold: based on a literature review, we will develop a conceptual research framework that describes the relationships between the identified factors influencing cybersickness (1). A large-scale empirical laboratory study with 533 participants was conducted to determine the effects on cybersickness (2). Furthermore, we will provide practical recommendations for e-commerce retailers to avoid cyber-sickness in VR product presentations (3).

2   Related Work

Immersive VR technology is continuously improving and spreading. Large application areas include the game industry ("The Lost Future: VR Shooter", [6]), education ("Chemistry VR Cardboard", [7]), medicine ("Stanford Health Anatomy Tours", [8]), as well as business [9] and tourism applications ("VR Cities", [10]). However, a shared negative side effect is common in most usage types: cybersickness. This denotes a form of motion sickness suffered frequently by users exposed to virtual environments. Compared to normal motion sickness, cybersickness arises when a subject feels motion, due to changing visual stimuli, while actually staying stationary [11].

Cybersickness manifests in various forms, such as headaches, blurred vision, salivation, eye strain, dizziness or even vomiting [12]. However, symptoms and their level of severity differ considerably between individuals.

2.1   Cybersickness Causes

In literature [13, 14], three main theories on the cause of cybersickness can be found: (1) the theory of sensory conflict, (2) the theory of postural instability and (3) the poison theory.

The sensory conflict theory states that motion sickness results from discrepancies in the information provided by different sensory modalities. Each time we move, the brain computes the difference of the outgoing motor signals and the incoming sensory input. If the signals do not match, a "sensory conflict" occurs [15]. For instance, if a person sits on a chair while wearing a head-mounted display using smartphone based virtual reality (SBVR) and moves around in the hotel resort, the eye signals that the person is moving, whereas the motor-sensory information of the body is stating 'no movement'. Hence, the motor-signal of the body (rest) is different from the sensory input of the eye (movement). According to the sensory conflict theory, these discrepancies in infor-mation cause cybersickness.

The theory of postural instability was developed by Riccio and Stoffregen [16]. They assumed a fundamental link between perception and action. Since postural control is essential to every kind of behavior, motion sickness is conceived as a result of prolonged postural instability. Depending on the ability to control one's own body and on the passive stability of the body in the absence of restraints, postural instability occurs. This means that if users are not familiar with moving in virtual environments, they may feel unable to maintain postural control. This lack of control causes temporal postural instability and therefore, cybersickness until the user has adapted.

The poison theory looks at cybersickness from an evolutionary point of view. As early as 1977, Treisman [17] claimed motion sickness to be a result of difficulties in programming eye or head movements. These difficulties arise when consistent and unpredictable disturbances between the spatial frameworks of vestibular, visual or proprioceptive inputs occur. The brain's automated reply when encountering such "hallucinated" disturbances is acting against poison ingestion. In this view, cybersickness is based on a maladaptive process, which originally helped the body to get rid of toxic substances.

Besides the three main theories on the causes of cybersickness, there are other factors discussed in the literature. Not surprisingly, technological issues can favor cybersickness, such as flicker, time lag or positions outside the design of eye point. Additionally, not every VR device and virtual environment holds the same risk of triggering cybersickness [18].

Considering the perception of the virtual environment itself, susceptibility to cybersickness may also vary if the position of the user in the imagery is not at the design eyepoint. Every virtual scene has a viewing region in which the user perceives the imagery best. The optimal viewing position is called the "design eyepoint". As the user moves away from this center, the perception of imagery becomes more and more distorted until the imagery is totally imperceptible. Perceiving those distorted visual keys may induce symptoms of cybersickness [19].

Military research suggests that watching other people interacting with the virtual environment is more likely to trigger cybersickness than controlling the input by oneself [19]. Probably, movements and interaction results can be more easily anticipated when interacting directly with a virtual environment [19, 20]. This is even more relevant when interactions might be unexpected, e.g. in flight simulators with advisors and trainee pilots [19].

In order to reduce as much as possible the risk of cybersickness due to such technical factors, the application used in the study locates the user right in the design of the eye point. Since only one user interacts with the application, unanticipated interactions are eliminated.

3   Research Framework and Hypotheses Development

VR is receiving increasing attention and thus more effort is being put into the development of new gadgets and applications [21–24]. The main aim of these is to offer new and more realistic experiences and interactions in a virtual world. To become a successful and widely used technology (like for example smartphones), the acceptance of users is essential. Not only for VR, but for any other kind of information technology (IT) several criteria need to be satisfied to gain user acceptance. The "Technology Acceptance Model" (TAM) combines these factors and predicts the individual adoption and usage of ITs [25]. This study examines the effects of SBVRs on the user's well-being and its research hypotheses are derived from the criteria for user acceptance of TAM 3 [26]. In TAM 3 several additional determinants were developed, which refer to perceptions based on the general beliefs of an individual regarding computers and their usage [27]. The relevant factors of the TAM 3 examined in this study are described in the following sections.

3.1 Perceived Challenge

The construct of *perceived challenge* is based on a combination of various different factors, all posing possible risks to maintaining an enjoyable virtual product experience for a user. For instance, a feeling of anxiety or a lack of confidence in one's own capabilities of using VR systems can prevent a user from having a pleasant virtual product experience [28].

Other reasons for not having an enjoyable virtual product experience may be excessive effort to clearly perceive the VR imagery due to visual limitations, or high cognitive effort to understand a task in general. Additionally, unfamiliarity with the functionalities of VR technology is another common reason, as well as task-specific factors such as time constraints or bad visibility conditions. As the theory of postural instability states, if users are not familiar with moving in virtual environments, they may feel unable to maintain postural control, which triggers *cybersickness*. Therefore, the research hypothesis to be verified is as follows:

H_1:   *The challenge perceived by the user while using a VR product presentation has a positive influence on the occurrence of cybersickness*

In addition, we suggest that the *perceived challenge* influences not only the occurrence of *cybersickness*, but also the *perceived enjoyment* of a VR product presentation. If the *perceived challenge* is caused by physical factors, such as blurred imagery due to visual limitations, unintuitive control or complex functionalities, this is an unpleasant experience for the user. We therefore assume that tasks giving users the feeling of being overstrained will have a negative impact on their *perceived enjoyment*. In view of this, the hypothesis to be examined is as follows:

H_2:   *The challenge perceived by the user while using a VR product presentation has a negative influence on the perceived enjoyment of such an application*

3.2 VR Anxiety

VR anxiety describes the apprehension or even a sort of fear which arises when facing the possibility of using a VR System. As previous research has shown, this apprehension regarding computer systems may arise from unknown developments and their underlying processes, or a lack of detailed introduction to a new technology or bad early experiences with it [26]. Since SBVRs is a very new marketing tool for virtual product presentation, most customers know little about the development and underlying processes of this new technology. Rather, an SBVR looks very futuristic for the customer in comparison to traditional digital devices (e.g. laptop, desktop, tablet) and is thus reminiscent of science fiction. Therefore, we assume that if a general apprehension in using such futuristic systems exists, these feelings are also transferred to technologies using virtual environments. Accordingly, we assume in this study that if users are afraid of using a SBVR, they could perceive the actual use of a SBVR as demanding. Consequently, the research hypothesis to be verified is as follows:

H_3:   *The users VR anxiety about using a VR product presentation has a positive influence on the challenge perceived by the user while using such an application*

3.3   VR Self-efficacy

VR self-efficacy refers to the control belief of an individual during the usage of a VR system [27]. The belief that one does or does not have control over a system depends on personal judgment of one's own capabilities in interacting with it. Users who are not confident about successfully performing a given task using VR technologies perceive the task as very challenging or complex. If users believe they are able to perform a specific task using a specific computer system, their self-efficacy is strong, and they will not have the feeling of being confronted with a challenging problem. Therefore, the research hypothesis to be verified is as follows:

H_4:   *The users VR self-efficacy regarding using a VR product presentation has a negative influence on the challenge perceived by the user while using such an application*

3.4   Perceived Enjoyment

The construct of *perceived enjoyment* describes the intrinsic motivation of an individual to use a system independent of any performance benefits, just because the use of the system generates enjoyment [29]. Within the scope of this study, the construct of *perceived enjoyment* quantifies whether and to what extent the VR product presentation provides the user with enjoyment or pleasure. It thus reflects the hedonistic perspective of the system experience [30].

The unique visualization options in SBVRs open up a completely new form of product presentation (e.g., hotels, automobiles). Due to the immersive experience, users feel that they actually are in another world. In this artificially created world, users can independently explore the virtual environment in a natural way, to get an impression of the offered product. For instance, the detailed and realistic presentation of a travel accommodation creates a unique, immersive and interactive product experience, whereby the feelings of fun and pleasure for the customer may be stimulated. As previous research shows, vivid three-dimensional product presentations and the possibility of direct interactions with the product are important factors that increase the *perceived enjoyment* of the potential customer [31–33].

In addition, several studies have revealed that *perceived enjoyment* has a negative effect on the occurrence of simulator sickness [34, 35]. As the researchers argue, users suppress symptoms of simulator sickness when they enjoy the virtual environment.

Consequently, users are more willing to experience a degree of these negative symptoms if the virtual experience is related to pleasure, enjoyment and fun. The users' perception is thus outweighed by the feeling of enjoyment, which reduces the occurrence of *cybersickness*. In view of this, the hypothesis to be examined is as follows:

H_5:   *The perceived enjoyment by the user while using a VR product presentation has a negative influence on the occurrence of cybersickness*

3.5   Curiosity

Curiosity is defined as *"a desire to know, to see, or to experience that motivates exploratory behavior directed towards the acquisition of new information"* [36, p. 793]. *Curiosity* thus represents the intrinsic expectation of the user that the acquisition of additional information is a joy [36]. Furthermore, *curiosity* is one of the central factor, which is frequently used in behavioral research to explain the intrinsically motivated usage of technology [37, 38].

As previous research shows [36, 39–41], the intrinsically motivated *curiosity* is responsible for the development of *perceived enjoyment*. Rouibah argues in his study on the use of instant messaging services, that the *perceived enjoyment* of direct online-based communication is not the result of the conversation itself, but rather the intrinsic motivation of learning something new about the communication partner [39].

This intrinsic desire to discover, to see or to experience something new could be stimulated by the immersive experience of an SBVR. With the innovative visualization and interaction possibilities of this technology, the virtual world becomes an impressive interactive experience, which continuously stimulates the user's *curiosity*. In the current study, *curiosity* is created by both well prepared contents and technology that triggers the 'wow' effect. The panoramic images of the hotel resort show the most beautiful views of the complex and convey a relaxing, quiet, clean and modern atmosphere. On the technological side, curiosity is created by offering several locations in the hotel complex that can be visited by the user. These movement possibilities make the users curious to explore the available locations in the hotel further. Thus, the acquisition of new knowledge becomes an entertaining experience for the users. Accordingly, the hypothesis to be verified is as follows:

H_6:   *The curiosity aroused in the user through a VR product presentation has a positive influence on the user's perceived enjoyment of such an application*

3.6   Telepresence

Telepresence describes the subjective perception of users as to what extent the physical reality is wholly or partly substituted by the VR [42–44]. Thus, the *telepresence* reflects the perceived feeling of users of being more in the VR than in the physical reality [44, 45]. The more immersive the design of a VR product presentation, the more users feel isolated from the physical world [46]. By this decoupling the immersion of users is further strengthened, until they feel they totally belong to the virtual world. As previous research has revealed, this immersive feeling of being there could enhance *perceived enjoyment*. In the context of virtual changing rooms the findings indicate that while using a virtual changing room, users escape into a fictional world, which gives them pleasure and thus increases the *perceived enjoyment* [47].

Such fictional worlds can be created with SBVR. By using 360-degree panoramic images, an extraordinary user experience is created in which users immerse themselves in an unknown world. In addition, the natural interaction with the virtual world increases the degree of immersion. This gives users the intense feeling of being there. Wherever users turn their heads, they can see another aspect of the virtual product, which provides a strong feeling of immersion and can increase the *perceived enjoyment* of the virtual product presentation. The research hypothesis to be verified is as follows (Fig. 1):

H_7:   *The feeling of telepresence provided to the user by a VR product presentation has a positive influence on the user's perceived enjoyment of such an application*

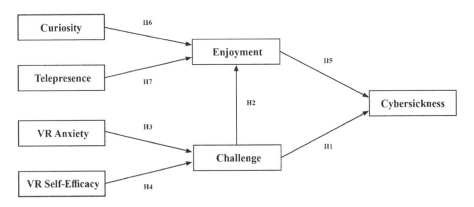

Fig. 1. Conceptual research framework.

4   Study

4.1   Study Participants

In total, 569 questionnaires were collected. After the elimination of 36 questionnaires, which were incomplete, a total of 533 questionnaires were used for the analysis. Table 1 indicates that of the 533 participants 44.8% were female. Over 94% of the respondents were familiar with the term 'virtual reality' and around 50% of them already used VR. A large group of our study participants, almost 60%, were students between 20 and 29 years old. About 25% of the participants were between 30 and 49 years old and working as employees (33.2%).

Table 1. Characteristics of respondents (n = 533).

Characteristics		Frequency	Percentage (%)
Gender	Female	239	44.8
	Male	294	55.2
Age	Under 20	21	3.9
	20–29	321	60.2
	30–39	89	16.7
	40–49	41	7.7
	50–59	33	6.2
	60+	28	5.3
Profession	Student	324	60.8
	Employee	177	33.2
	Pensioner	17	3.2
	Others	15	2.8
Smartphone owner	Yes	525	98.5
	No	8	1.5
Familiar with term "virtual reality"	Yes	503	94.4
	No	30	5.6
Virtual reality used	Yes	273	51.2
	No	260	48.8

For the analysis of the proposed model, we used structural equation modeling. Especially in the context of new technologies like VR and for modeling latent variables the Partial Least Squares (PLS) approach is well suited [48]. In addition, PLS has proven to be suitable for modeling structural equations, exploring the structure of existing theories, and identifying the dominant constructs of a model. [49]. Therefore, the model estimation was performed with SmartPLS 3.2.6 [50].

4.2   Task: VR Product Presentation

Since SBVRs are a new technology we could not assume that all the study participants were familiar with the technology and thus able to evaluate it. Therefore, it was necessary to provide a VR product presentation to familiarize them with the technology. The self-developed application contains 43 professional 360-degree panorama photographs of a hotel in Greece. It allows users to virtually explore the hotel by navigating via hotspots to certain points of interest such as the wellness area, the beach and the lobby. In addition, an extra menu was implemented that could be displayed if the user looks downwards, for a certain amount of time. From a technical point of view, the application consists of the above described photographs which were exported using the 3D visualization software Unity and the Oculus Rift Application Programming Interface for the Samsung Galaxy S7 (Fig. 2).

Fig. 2. Screenshot from VR product presentation.

4.3 Operationalization

The constructs of the research model were operationalized on the basis of established items that were adapted to our study design. While standards such as age, gender, travel habits and prior experience with VR are incorporated, we also examine the effects of VR exposure on users. The questionnaire consists of 28 statements, covering the following factors: *perceived challenge, curiosity, perceived enjoyment, cybersickness, telepresence, VR anxiety* and *VR self-efficacy*.

The participants rate each statement on a Likert-scale, where seven signals 'I strongly agree' and one means 'I strongly disagree'. The construct *perceived challenge* (four items) is based on the scale of Novak et al. [51]. Three items from Agarwal and Karahanna were adapted to measure *curiosity* [37]. The construct of *perceived enjoyment* comprises six items, derived from Childers et al. [52]. Four items from the scale of Kennedy et al. were used for the operationalization of the *cybersickness* construct [53]. The construct of *telepresence* was operationalized using three items from Klein [42]. Four items from Venkatesh and Bala were adapted for the measurement of the construct *VR anxiety* [26]. Also, the construct *VR self-efficacy* based on the scale of Venkatesh was queried by four items [27].

4.4 Data Collection and Design of the Study

In preparation for the recruitment of the study participants, we developed a website containing important information on the study. This also helped us to coordinate the appointments. The recruitment was carried out in two steps. Firstly, a personalized invitation was sent by e-mail to all students to draw attention to the study. In total, about 4,000 students were approached. In addition, we personally contacted companies and organizations by telephone. In consequence, 235 employees agreed to participate in the research. The study was conducted from November 2016 to February 2017 in a laboratory where all subjects could move freely. During the study, 569 users participated: 334 students and 235 non-students.

Step 1. Introductory video. **Step 2.** First questionnaire.

Step 3. VR demonstration video and product presentation. **Step 4.** Second questionnaire.

Fig. 3. Design of the study.

The study was conducted in four major steps (Fig. 3): we started the research by showing the participants a self-produced introductory video that explained the aim of the study. In a second step an initial short questionnaire was handed to the participants asking for their travel habits and some sociodemographic information such as gender, age and occupation. It was also important in this step to ask them about their experience with VR before they actually used the VR device. At the beginning of the third phase, the subjects were given the VR glasses to watch a demonstration video. After the demonstration, an audio playback started, in which the scenario was described: the participants had to imagine that they were planning a two-week all-inclusive trip and they had the chance to get an impression of a hotel by using a VR product presentation. To make sure that the participants actively used the application we gave them a small task. The task was to find out what color the chairs at the beach were. The participants had 10 min to explore the VR product presentation. Finally, a second questionnaire was given to the participants that aimed to assess the VR product presentation of the hotel. To ensure anonymity, both questionnaires were put into a sealed envelope on completion.

5   Results

5.1   Assessment of the Measurement Model

The assessment of the measurement model included the evaluation of the internal consistency reliability, convergence validity, and discriminant validity [49]. For internal consistency, typically the Cronbach's alpha coefficient (α) is calculated. Following Nunnally's recommendation of a minimum value of 0.7 all factors fulfilled this requirement [54]. In addition, an assessment of the composite reliability (ρc) and the Dijkstra-Henseler's coefficient (ρA) was performed [55]. Again, all values were above the required minimum values for the respective criteria. Therefore, the internal consistency was given.

Table 2. Validity and reliability of the constructs.

Construct and items	Loading	α	ρA	ρc	AVE
Criteria	> 0.7	> 0.7	> 0.7	> 0.7	> 0.5
Challenge (CHAL)		0.736	0.781	0.826	0.544
Using the virtual reality application ...					
was a challenge for me	0.702				
was exhausting for me	0.771				
was demanding for me	0.814				
challenges me to perform the best of my ability	0.653				
Curiosity (CURI)		0.858	0.871	0.914	0.780
The virtual tour ...					
excites my curiosity	0.914				
arouses my imagination	0.801				
makes me curious	0.930				
Enjoyment (ENJ)		0.908	0.921	0.929	0.688
Using the virtual reality application ...					
is fun	0.867				
is enjoyable	0.899				
is pleasant	0.905				
is entertaining	0.771				
is boring[a]	0.738				
is exciting	0.780				
Cybersickness (CSICK)		0.852	0.880	0.899	0.691
While I was using the virtual reality application, ...					
I had a queasy feeling in my stomach	0.784				
I got nauseous	0.820				
I got vertigo	0.828				
I had an uncomfortable feeling	0.890				

(continued)

Table 2. (*continued*)

Construct and items	Loading	α	ρA	ρc	AVE
Telepresence (TELE)		0.810	0.822	0.888	0.727
While I was using the virtual reality application, I felt as if I were in another world	0.768				
Through the virtual simulation I had the feeling of really experiencing the situation	0.884				
When I navigated through the virtual world, I felt I was in a different place	0.899				
VR anxiety (VRANX)		0.906	0.911	0.934	0.781
If I imagine having to use virtual reality glasses,...					
it scares me	0.876				
it makes me nervous	0.827				
it makes me uncomfortable	0.934				
it makes me uneasy	0.895				
VR self-efficacy (VRSE)		0.864	0.876	0.908	0.711
I would dare to use virtual reality glasses...					
if I had only the manual for reference	0.761				
if I had seen someone else using it before trying it myself	0.892				
if someone showed me how to do it first	0.882				
if I had enough time to become familiar with virtual reality glasses	0.832				

[a] Reverse coded.

In a second step, the convergence validity of the measurement model was examined by the outer factor loadings and the average variance extracted. The outer factor loadings of the assigned indicators should exceed 0.7 [49]. Almost all items fulfilled this requirement, which is visualized in detail in Table 2. Only one item of the construct challenge had a lower outer loading. In this regard, we investigated whether the elimination of this indicator leads to an increase in composite reliability. This was not the case, so the indicator was maintained as it increased internal consistency and contributes to content validity [49]. After the examination of the outer loadings the average variance (AVE) was determined. As shown in Table 3, the minimum requirement of 0.5 was met by all factors [48]. Consequently, convergence validity was confirmed by both outer factor loadings and the average variance.

To assess discriminant validity the Fornell-Larcker criterion was used [56]. According to the Fornell-Larcker criterion the average variance of a construct must be

Table 3. Squared-inter-correlations between constructs (AVE shown in bold on diagonal) and HTMT.$_{85}$ criterion (gray).

	CHAL	CURI	ENJ	CSICK	TELE	VRANX	VRSE
CHAL	**0.544**	0.185	0.265	0.452	0.136	0.410	0.078
CURI	0.030	**0.780**	0.782	0.229	0.570	0.209	0.237
ENJ	0.064	0.484	**0.688**	0.275	0.557	0.295	0.218
CSICK	0.176	0.040	0.066	**0.691**	0.085	0.275	0.036
TELE	0.006	0.225	0.228	0.004	**0.727**	0.111	0.128
VRANX	0.116	0.035	0.077	0.061	0.008	**0.781**	0.141
VRSE	0.004	0.042	0.038	0.000	0.011	0.014	**0.711**

higher than the squared inter-correlations between the constructs. From Table 3 we can observe that the criterion was met by all constructs. We also used the heterotrait-monotrait (HTMT) ratio of correlations to verify discriminant validity. Taking the more conservative value HTMT.$_{85}$ the results in Table 3 show that the discriminant validity of the measurement model was also confirmed by the HTMT method since all results are below the threshold value of 0.85 [57].

5.2 Assessment of the Structural Model

Several measures are suggested to assess the structural model. In a first step we used the coefficient of determination (R^2) [49]. According to Cohen the proportion of the explained variance is considered as small from 0.02, as medium from 0.13, and as large from 0.26 [58]. Figure 4 shows that all endogenous variables had medium and large values. Besides the coefficient of determination, the predictive relevance (Q^2) of the structural model was assessed with the Stone-Geisser test [59, 60]. The Stone-Geisser makes it possible to determine whether the established model is suitable for the reconstruction of empirical data ($Q^2 > 0$) [61]. The Stone-Geisser criterion was met by all endogenous variables (Fig. 4). Finally, the structural model was assessed by using the standardized root mean square residual (SRMR) value. The model fit can be

Table 4. Results of hypothesis testing.

	Relationships	Path coefficient	CI (Bias Corrected)	t-Value	p-Value	Supported
H1	CHAL → CSICK	0.402***	[0.282, 0.471]	7.844	0.000	Yes
H2	CHAL → ENJ	−0.138***	[−0.214, −0.068]	3.695	0.000	Yes
H3	VRANX → CHAL	0.338***	[0.237, 0.442]	6.239	0.000	Yes
H4	VRSE → CHAL	−0.021	[−0.081, 0.120]	0.478	0.633	No
H5	ENJ → CSICK	−0.161***	[−0.270, −0.070]	3.204	0.000	Yes
H6	CURI → ENJ	0.582***	[0.481, 0.669]	12.102	0.000	Yes
H7	TELE → ENJ	0.191***	[0.120, 0.269]	5.075	0.000	Yes

Note: *** p < 0.001.

confirmed if values are below 0.08 [48, 49]. For our model the SRMR had a value of 0.06, so the requirements were fulfilled.

In order to examine the research hypotheses a analysis of the path coefficients was conducted. However, the significance of the respective paths is verified by using the bootstrapping method (5,000 subgroups). The results showed that six of the seven proposed relationships were highly significant. (Table 4). The factors *curiosity* and *telepresence* both had a positive influence on the *perceived enjoyment* with an SBVR ($\beta = 0.582^{***}$; $\beta = 0.191^{***}$). *Perceived enjoyment* was on the other hand negatively influenced by the factor *perceived challenge* ($\beta = -0.138^{***}$). The results also showed that *perceived enjoyment* significantly reduced *cybersickness* ($\beta = -0.161^{***}$), while *perceived challenges* increased *cybersickness* ($\beta = 0.402^{***}$). Additionally, we found a significant effect of *VR anxiety* on the *perceived challenge* associated with using the SBVR ($\beta = 0.338^{***}$). Only the proposed relationship between *VR self-efficacy* and *perceived challenge* ($\beta = -0.021$) could not be confirmed.

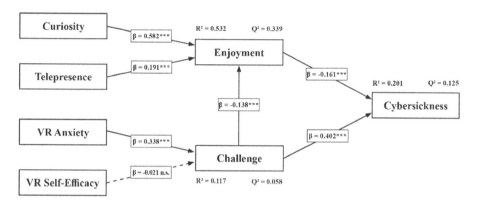

Fig. 4. PLS results of the structural model.

6 Discussion and Recommendations for VR Product Presentations

Cybersickness can be a large obstacle to a successful application of VR product presentations. If users start feeling sick while navigating in a virtual world, their excitement obviously decreases, and it is likely that the customers' satisfaction with an innovative product experience decreases likewise. According to the results of this study, retailers need to design VR product presentations with low user requirements. The main reason for this is that demanding VR product presentations significantly increase the occurrence of *cybersickness* ($\beta = 0.402^{***}$). Furthermore, a high level of *perceived challenge* significantly decreases the *perceived enjoyment* of a virtual world ($\beta = -0.138^{***}$). These two impacts make *perceived challenge* the most important factor that needs to be regulated in order to create a VR product presentation with a low risk of triggering *cybersickness*.

The *perceived challenge* of a VR product presentation describes the level of difficulty when dealing with it. There are several factors that enhance the *perceived challenge*, such as an unintuitive control, complex functionalities, or anxiety. Customers who are not technophiles might have concerns about using new technology: they do not know how the systems work and are reluctant to use them. In particular, for innovative technology, such as VR, a fear of the unknown virtual world quickly arises. This *VR anxiety*, results in a significant increase of the *perceived challenge* of VR product presentations (ß = 0.338***).

On the other hand, the findings suggest that *VR self-efficacy* has no impact on the *perceived challenge*. Apparently, even a poor evaluation of a user's own capabilities does not increase the *perceived challenge* of a VR product presentation. This is an advantage for retailers offering VR product presentations in non-technical areas: even unexperienced customers can enjoy the full benefits of an exciting, interactive product experience.

However, the *perceived challenge* of a VR product presentation does not only increase the occurrence of *cybersickness* – it also affects the *perceived enjoyment* of the application (ß = –0.138***), which itself has the potential to reduce *cybersickness*. A high level of *perceived challenge* obviously decreases the *perceived enjoyment*. The feeling of being challenged too much, or even being overstrained, enhances frustration and clearly reduces fun. If customers get the feeling of not being able to manage the requirements of a VR product presentation, they will stop using it. This impact of *perceived challenge* on *perceived enjoyment* further strengthens the design recommendation for retailers to focus on a low-level challenging virtual product presentation.

Furthermore, increased *perceived enjoyment* reduces the occurrence of *cybersickness* (ß = –0.161***). The more enjoyable a VR product presentation is, the fewer symptoms of cybersickness occur. A reason for this might be that if the interaction with the virtual world is fun, users pay less attention to distracting details. The focus lies on the content, the acquisition of information and the interaction with the environment, which pushes technical inaccuracies into the background. In order to create an exciting "wow" effect for customers, *curiosity* (ß = 0.582***) and *telepresence* (ß = 0.191***) are crucial factors.

A VR product presentation, which creates *curiosity* about the product and makes the consumers feel present in the virtual world, enhances the subjective *perceived enjoyment* most effectively (ß = 0.582***). For some customers, innovative technology itself is the basic motivation to test the application. The crucial aspect for retailers is then to pick up on this curiosity and stimulate it further. The VR product presentation needs to present the product in an interesting way. For example, a virtual customization in real-time (e.g. by changing the color of a product or adding optional functionalities), or the possibility to explore details of the product, might encourage customer *curiosity*. If the intrinsic wish of acquiring as much information about a product as possible (*curiosity*) is successfully created, the customer feels entertained while using the VR product presentation and enjoys the innovative experience.

The *perceived enjoyment* can be enhanced even further if an immersive *(telepresence)* virtual environment is offered (ß = 0.191***). The more immersion users feel in a virtual world, the more fascinated they are and the more enjoyable and interesting the experience becomes. If interactions with the virtual product feel real, customers create positive memories, which typically will support a purchase decision.

7 Conclusion

In the current study, we created a conceptual research framework which describes the relationships between the factors influencing cybersickness. The relationships of the different factors were evaluated in a study with 533 participants. At first, all participants watched a self-produced introductory video that explained the aim of the study. In a second step a short questionnaire was used to collect the participants' travel habits, sociodemographic information and their experience with VR. After completing the first questionnaire the subjects were given 10 min to explore the virtual tour in a hotel resort using 43 professional 360-degree panoramic images. Finally, a second questionnaire assessed the VR product presentation.

As a result, it turned out that six out of the seven relationships in question had significant positive and negative effects on each other. *Perceived challenge* was the most important factor to cope with: a highly challenging application increases *cybersickness* and reduces *perceived enjoyment. Perceived challenge* can be enhanced by *VR anxiety* but is not affected by *VR self-efficacy. Curiosity* and *telepresence* both support *perceived enjoyment* significantly, which itself significantly reduces the occurrence of *cybersickness.*

We conclude that the findings generally support the positive effect of a virtual product presentation on consumers. This unfamiliar experience poses challenges, which can reduce the fun of using the VR product presentation and increases the occurrence of cybersickness.

Using the results of this study, some basic recommendations for developing a successful VR application can be deduced. VR developers in general and e-commerce retailers in particular should pay special attention to the two influencing factors of *perceived challenge* and *perceived enjoyment.* It is crucial to keep the recommended order of: first reduce *perceived challenge* in the VR application and then enhance *perceived enjoyment.* Since *perceived challenge* has effects on *cybersickness* and *perceived enjoyment,* it is also important to reduce the risk of *cybersickness* as much as possible and then make use of the additional, beneficial impact of *perceived enjoyment.* If these recommendations are taken into account carefully, the VR product presentation for marketing purposes can be beneficial for retailers and consumers alike. Whereas consumers enjoy a new and exciting product experience, retailers earn the benefits of this innovation via positive purchase decisions.

7.1 Limitations and Future Research

In the present study, a conceptual research model was developed in which important factors were identified that both increase and decrease the occurrence of *cybersickness.* Although this study provides important academic and practical insights into the occurrence of *cybersickness,* the findings are subject to several limitations that may be investigated in future research.

While our study had a large sample size, one limitation is that all participants had a similar cultural background. Future research results conducted with participants from other cultures may therefore differ from the results of this study. In particular, cultural differences in technology affinity may have an influence on the occurrence of cybersickness and should therefore be investigated in further studies.

Furthermore, the sample included a large proportion of participants under the age of 30. Through a more homogeneous distribution of the study participants among the different age groups, age-specific differences could be identified in future studies, which would contribute to a more general understanding of the occurrence of cybersickness in VR applications.

Due to the central role of the *perceived challenge* for the occurrence of *cybersickness*, this factor should be further specified in future studies. In this respect, it would be interesting to investigate to what extent technology-related features of SBVRs (e.g. display resolution, usability, wearing comfort) influence the *perceived challenge* for users.

References

1. Guttentag, D.A.: Virtual reality. Applications and implications for tourism. Tour. Manag. **31**(5), 637–651 (2010)
2. Malone, T.W.: Heuristics for designing enjoyable user interfaces. In: Nichols, J.A., Schneider, M.L. (eds.) Proceedings of the 1982 Conference on Human Factors in Computing Systems, pp. 63–68. ACM Press, New York (1982)
3. Lau, K.W., Lee, P.Y.: Shopping in virtual reality: a study on consumers' shopping experience in a stereoscopic virtual reality. Virtual Reality (2018, in press)
4. Disztinger, P., Schlögl, S., Groth, A.: Technology acceptance of virtual reality for travel planning. In: Schegg, R., Stangl, B. (eds.) Information and Communication Technologies in Tourism 2017, pp. 255–268. Springer, Cham (2017). https://doi.org/10.1007/978-3-319-51168-9_19
5. Manis, K.T., Choi, D.: The virtual reality hardware acceptance model (VR-HAM): extending and individuating the technology acceptance model (TAM) for virtual reality hardware. J. Bus. Res. (2018, in press)
6. DiVi Inc: The lost future: VR shooter. https://www.icaros.com. Accessed 16 Jan 2019
7. ARLOOPA Inc. Augmented and virtual reality apps: chemistry VR – cardboard. https://play.google.com/store/apps/details?id=com.arloopa.chemistryvr. Accessed 16 Jan 2019
8. Fusion Tech Inc: Stanford health anatomy tours. https://appadvice.com/app/stanford-health-care-anatomy-tours-with-vr/1101932135. Accessed 16 Jan 2019
9. Sotheby's international realty: 3D tours and virtual reality on sothebysrealty.com. https://www.sothebysrealty.com/eng/virtual-reality. Accessed 16 Jan 2019
10. Smart2IT B.V.: VR cities. https://play.google.com/store/apps/details?id=com.Smart2it.VR.Smart2VR.VRCities. Accessed 16 Jan 2019
11. Arns, L.L., Cerney, M.M.: The relationship between age and incidence of cybersickness among immersive environment users. In: IEEE Proceedings. VR 2005. Virtual Reality, 2005, pp. 267–268. IEEE (2005)
12. Stanney, K.: Realizing the full potential of virtual reality: human factors issues that could stand in the way. In: Proceedings Virtual Reality Annual International Symposium 1995, pp. 28–34. IEEE Computer Society Press (1995)
13. LaViola, J.J.: A discussion of cybersickness in virtual environments. ACM SIGCHI Bull. **32**(1), 47–56 (2000)
14. Mousavi, M., Jen, Y.H., Musa, S.N.B.: A review on cybersickness and usability in virtual environments. Adv. Eng. Forum **10**, 34–39 (2013)

15. Reason, J.T.: Motion sickness adaptation: a neural mismatch model. J. R. Soc. Med. **71**(11), 819–829 (1978)

16. Riccio, G.E., Stoffregen, T.A.: An ecological theory of motion sickness and postural instability. Ecol. Psychol. **3**(3), 195–240 (1991)

17. Treisman, M.: Motion sickness: an evolutionary hypothesis. Science **197**(4302), 493–495 (1977)

18. Shafer, D.M., Carbonara, C.P., Korpi, M.F.: Modern virtual reality technology: cybersickness, sense of presence, and gender. Media Psychol. Rev. **11**(2) (2017)

19. Pausch, R., Crea, T., Conway, M.: A literature survey for virtual environments: military flight simulator visual systems and simulator sickness. Presence Teleoperators Virtual Environ. **1**(3), 344–363 (1992)

20. Jinjakam, C., Hamamoto, K.: Simulator sickness in immersive virtual environment. In: The 5th 2012 Biomedical Engineering International Conference, pp. 1–4. IEEE (2012)

21. Manus VR: The pinnacle of virtual reality controllers. https://manus-vr.com. Accessed 16 Jan 16 Jan 2019

22. Birdly®: The ultimate cream of flying. https://www.somniacs.co/. Accessed 16 Jan 2019

23. Teslasuit: full body haptic suit. https://teslasuit.io. Accessed 16 Jan 2019

24. Taclim: The VR haptic feedback system for human limbs that further immerses you in VR worlds. https://taclim.cerevo.com. Accessed 16 Jan 2019

25. Davis, F.D.: Perceived usefulness, perceived ease of use, and user acceptance of information technology. MIS Q. **13**(3), 319–340 (1989)

26. Venkatesh, V., Bala, H.: Technology acceptance model 3 and a research agenda on interventions. Decis. Sci. **39**(2), 273–315 (2008)

27. Venkatesh, V.: Determinants of perceived ease of use: integrating control, intrinsic motivation, and emotion into the technology acceptance model. Inf. Syst. Res. **11**(4), 342–365 (2000)

28. Ghani, J.A., Deshpande, S.P.: Task characteristics and the experience of optimal flow in human-computer interaction. J. Psychol. **128**(4), 381–391 (1994)

29. Davis, F.D., Bagozzi, R.P., Warshaw, P.R.: Extrinsic and intrinsic motivation to use computers in the workplace. J. Appl. Soc. Psychol. **22**(14), 1111–1132 (1992)

30. Hirschman, E.C., Holbrook, M.B.: Hedonic consumption: emerging concepts, methods and propositions. J. Market. **46**(3), 92 (1982)

31. Kim, J., Fiore, A.M., Lee, H.-H.: Influences of online store perception, shopping enjoyment, and shopping involvement on consumer patronage behavior towards an online retailer. J. Retail. Consum. Serv. **14**(2), 95–107 (2007)

32. Ozkara, B.Y., Ozmen, M., Kim, J.W.: Examining the effect of flow experience on online purchase: a novel approach to the flow theory based on hedonic and utilitarian value. J. Retail. Consum. Serv. **37**, 119–131 (2017)

33. Scarpi, D.: Work and fun on the internet the effects of utilitarianism and hedonism online. J. Interact. Market. **26**(1), 53–67 (2012)

34. Nichols, S., Haldane, C., Wilson, J.R.: Measurement of presence and its consequences in virtual environments. Int. J. Hum. Comput. Stud. **52**(3), 471–491 (2000)

35. Lin, J.J.-W., Duh, H.B.L., Parker, D.E., Abi-Rached, H., Furness, T.A.: Effects of field of view on presence, enjoyment, memory, and simulator sickness in a virtual environment. In: Proceedings IEEE Virtual Reality 2002, pp. 164–171. IEEE Computer Society (2002)

36. Litman, J.: Curiosity and the pleasures of learning: wanting and liking new information. Cogn. Emot. **19**(6), 793–814 (2005)

37. Agarwal, R., Karahanna, E.: Time flies when you're having fun: cognitive absorption and beliefs about information technology usage. MIS Q. **24**(4), 665–694 (2000)

38. Moon, J.-W., Kim, Y.-G.: Extending the TAM for a world-wide-web context. Inf. Manag. **38**(4), 217–230 (2001)

39. Rouibah, K.: Social usage of instant messaging by individuals outside the workplace in Kuwait: a structural equation model. Inf. Technol. People **21**(4), 34–68 (2008)

40. Kashdan, T.B., Rose, P., Fincham, F.D.: Curiosity and exploration: facilitating positive subjective experiences and personal growth opportunities. J. Pers. Assess. **82**(3), 291–305 (2004)

41. Loewenstein, G.: The psychology of curiosity: a review and reinterpretation. Psychol. Bull. **116**(1), 75–98 (1994)

42. Klein, L.R.: Creating virtual product experiences: the role of telepresence. J. Interact. Market. **17**(1), 41–55 (2003)

43. Nowak, K.L., Biocca, F.: The effect of the agency and anthropomorphism on users' sense of telepresence, copresence, and social presence in virtual environments. Presence Teleoperators Virtual Environ. **12**(5), 481–494 (2003)

44. Steuer, J.: Defining virtual reality. Dimensions determining telepresence. J. Commun. **42**(4), 73–93 (1992)

45. Sanchez-Vives, M.V., Slater, M.: From presence to consciousness through virtual reality. Nat. Rev. Neurosci. **6**, 332–339 (2005)

46. Lombard, M., Snyder-Duch, J.: Interactive advertising and presence. J. Interact. Advertising **1**(2), 56–65 (2001)

47. Song, K., Fiore, A.M., Park, J.: Telepresence and fantasy in online apparel shopping experience. J. Fashion Market. Manag. Int. J. **11**(4), 553–570 (2007)

48. Henseler, J., Hubona, G., Ray, P.A.: Using PLS path modeling in new technology research: updated guidelines. Ind. Manag. Data Syst. **116**(1), 2–20 (2016)

49. Hair, J.F., Hult, T.M., Ringle, C.M., Sarstedt, M.: A primer on partial least squares structural equation modeling (PLS-SEM). SAGE Publications, Inc., Thousand Oaks (2017)

50. Ringle, C.M., Wende, S., Becker, J.-M.: SmartPLS 3. http://www.smartpls.com. Accessed 16 Jan 2019

51. Novak, T.P., Hoffman, D.L., Yung, Y.-F.: Measuring the customer experience in online environments: a structural modeling approach. Market. Sci. **19**(1), 22–42 (2000)

52. Childers, T.L., Carr, C.L., Peck, J., Carson, S.: Hedonic and utilitarian motivations for online retail shopping behavior. J. Retail. **77**(4), 511–535 (2001)

53. Kennedy, R.S., Lane, N.E., Berbaum, K.S., Lilienthal, M.G.: Simulator sickness questionnaire: an enhanced method for quantifying simulator sickness. Int. J. Aviat. Psychol. **3**(3), 203–220 (1993)

54. Nunnally, J.C.: Psychometric Theory. McGraw-Hill, New York (1978)

55. Dijkstra, T.K., Henseler, J.: Consistent partial least squares path modeling. MIS Q. **39**(2), 297–316 (2015)

56. Fornell, C., Larcker, D.F.: Evaluating structural equation models with unobservable variables and measurement error. J. Mark. Res. **18**(1), 39–50 (1981)

57. Henseler, J., Ringle, C.M., Sarstedt, M.: A new criterion for assessing discriminant validity in variance-based structural equation modeling. J. Acad. Mark. Sci. **43**(1), 115–135 (2015)

58. Cohen, J.: Statistical Power Analysis for the Behavioral Sciences. Elsevier Science, Burlington (2013)

59. Geisser, S.: A predictive approach to the random effect model. Biometrika **61**(1), 101–107 (1974)

60. Stone, M.: Cross-validatory choice and assessment of statistical predictions. J. Roy. Stat. Soc. Ser. B (Methodol.) **36**(2), 111–147 (1974)

61. Marcoulides, G.A.: Modern Methods for Business Research. Psychology Press, New York (2013)

Transforming User Experience of Nutrition Facts Label - An Exploratory Service Innovation Study

Prateek Jain[✉] and Soussan Djamasbi

Worcester Polytechnic Institute, Worcester, USA
{pjain,djamasbi}@wpi.edu

Abstract. Nutrition facts label is an important tool for consumers to get information regarding servings, calories and nutrients in a packaged food product. Previous research shows that nutrition labels are generally confusing and difficult to use. Nutrition information in the label can be transformed into dynamic feedback to make nutrition facts labels easy to use and helpful in making healthy decisions. In this research, we created a decision support system using a smartphone application that scans the label using OCR, then apply the FDA's 5-20 rule to determine if a particular nutrient is in healthy amount and visualizes this feedback in either an augmented reality or a static popup format using color-coded thumbs up and thumbs down signs. Our results show that the app significantly helped consumers in making healthy decisions and improved the overall experience of using nutrition facts labels. While our results did not show a significant difference between the impact of augmented reality and static popup feedback on user behavior, they indicated a slightly more favorable reaction toward feedback that used augmented reality.

Keywords: Nutrition facts label · Augmented reality · Decision making · Percent daily value

1 Introduction

Eating habits play an important role in health and wellness. Research shows that not only the types of nutrients that we eat but also their quantity (amount consumed) has an impact on our health. Therefore, it is important for people to know type and quantity of nutrients in their food so that they can make healthy food choices. This is particularly important for people with dietary restrictions and/or those with chronic illnesses [10]. When it comes to packaged food items, making healthy decisions would be extremely difficult if not impossible without nutrition fact labels.

Nutrition facts labels typically list all the nutrients and their respective amounts in a tabular form. These labels, which convey nutrition information in form of numbers, are only effective if consumers know how to use them [21]. These labels provide information; they do not provide guidance or advice [11]. The numeric format of nutrition labels requires simple calculations to interpret the provided information. While such calculations are not inherently difficult for interpreting a single nutrient, they become relatively more complex when multiple nutrients are track at once (e.g., sugar, fat,

© Springer Nature Switzerland AG 2019
F. F.-H. Nah and K. Siau (Eds.): HCII 2019, LNCS 11588, pp. 225–237, 2019.
https://doi.org/10.1007/978-3-030-22335-9_15

protein, sodium, etc.) [16]. In United States, nutrition facts label typically include 'percent daily value' to convey information regarding the amount of nutrients in one serving. Unfortunately, consumers often do not know how to interpret percent daily values, i.e., how to use them to make healthy decisions [12].

In this research, we created a decision support system to make it easier for people to make healthy decisions. To achieve this goal, we developed a mobile application for smartphone that can scan nutrition information from labels and convert it into an easy to understand personalized feedback. We believe that such an easy to understand personalized feedback will help consumers to make healthier decisions.

We developed this decision support system in two steps. In the first step we used the optical character recognition (OCR) technology to scan the nutrition information. We then converted this information into an easy to process feedback. In the second step we worked on visualizing the feedback using two different prototypes: one porotype showed the advice in augmented reality (AR) and the other showed it in a static pop-up format. We used the 5-20 rule recommended by the FDA to create feedback signifying whether the value of a particular nutrient was in a "good" or "bad" range [29].

2   Theoretical Background

Different countries have different government agencies to regulate food packaging and provide guidelines for listing ingredients and nutrition information on packaged food products. The objective of these guidelines is to make the general public aware of nutrients in the food and recommend the healthy quantity for each nutrient. In the United States, ingredients and nutrition information on packaged food products are regulated by the Food and Drug Administration (FDA). In this research we focused on nutrition facts labels, more specifically the macronutrient information on packaged food items available in the United States. Therefore, we used FDA's regulations, US Department of Health and Human Services and U.S. Department of Agriculture guidelines, e.g., Dietary Guidelines for Americans [28] throughout this research.

2.1   Nutrition Facts Label

Multiple studies on nutrition facts labels found a positive relation between the use of nutrition facts labels and diet and health. For example, increased use of nutrition facts labels improved healthier dietary pattern [9, 13, 15, 20]. Studies show a strong relationship between health beliefs and nutrition label usage or intention to use labels [9, 21]. They also show that consumers with health conditions and special dietary requirements are more likely to use nutrition facts labels [18–20]. Additionally, research indicates that nutrition label knowledge has a positive impact on consumer's ability to distinguish between nutritional value of different food products [17].

While providing useful information, generally nutrition facts labels tend to be hard to read and understand; they can be confusing [11, 12, 14, 16]. Factors such as age, level of education and income can further affect understanding of nutrition labels and hence negatively affect their usefulness in guiding consumers' decisions [16]. Additionally, eye tracking studies reveal that provided information on nutrition labels is not processed equally or fully. Components near the top of a nutrition label grab considerably more attention than components at the bottom [14, 23], in other words, consumers tend to read only the top lines on the label. The placement of the nutrition facts labels on a package can also contribute to their usefulness as it can affect consumers' ability to locate the provided information [14].

One way to make nutrition facts labels more useful is by providing percent daily values for nutrients. Percent daily values are calculated based on the type of nutrients and their recommended amount. While percent daily values can provide useful information, they are not always present for every nutrient on nutrition facts labels. Moreover, percent daily values are typically calculated based on a 2000 calorie intake threshold. If consumers are not familiar with the 2000 calorie intake guideline or follow a different one, the percent values on the label can be confusing. For example, research shows that consumers with dietary restrictions, such as those with medical conditions, tend to find percent daily values hard to understand [10].

Another important factor about nutrition facts labels is that updating them on food packages is not a quick process. For example, while in May 2016 the FDA announced new guidelines for providing nutrition facts, consumers may have to wait for a few years before they see updates on every food product because the compliance dates for manufacturers was set to a much later date, e.g., January 2020 and January 2021. The updated guidelines in May 2016 seem to have made little difference in engaging consumers to pay attention to provided information. For example, an eye tracking study comparing the old and new labels, found no difference in terms of attention given to different components of the new nutrition labels nor did it reveal any difference in consumers' decisions for making healthier food purchases [22].

2.2 Augmented Reality (AR) Feedback in Food and Nutrition

Various attempts were made in the past to improve the delivery of nutrition or ingredient information on the label with the help of augmented reality for making them easier to understand and more helpful in making decisions. Augmented reality tends to elicit more engagement from user and tend to enhance their perception of reality thereby create positive experiences for them [24, 25]. The review of prior AR research in food and nutrition shows that AR technology has been successfully used to teach individuals with intellectual disabilities to identify food allergens [1]. Using an AR app participants were able to identify potential food allergens successfully and many participants learned to use the app right away. In another study, researchers proposed the development of an application that can scan unpackaged food items and display their nutrition information using color coded gauges [2]. They argued that users can better manage their diet with such an easy to understand feedback. Another group of researchers proposed an augmented reality application that could scan unpackaged grocery items and display feedback in the form of ranking bars based on a user's dietary profile [3]. Ahn et al. developed an AR grocery shopping application that recommends healthy products and highlights products to avoid on a grocery store aisle based on user preferences [4]. Their results showed that their app significantly reduced the amount of time to select healthy products and helped users to avoid unhealthy products.

Prior research in augmented reality in other contexts shows that not all AR applications provide significant positive experiences [26, 27]. For example, in a recent study the AR app providing social media reviews (textual information) for a product, received relatively low ease of use ratings [27].

2.3   Optical Character Recognition (OCR)

To get the nutrition data from packaged food products, there are two methods available. The first method is using or maintaining a product database, which can be accessed by scanning barcode of the product. The second method utilizes OCR to capture information directly from nutrition facts labels (e.g., using the phone camera). Various algorithms have been developed that make OCR useful in extracting information from nutrition facts labels. For example, Kulyukin et al. developed an algorithm that can correct the OCR output on mobile phones in real time [5]. They also developed an algorithm for extracting text chunks from nutrition facts labels [6]. Additionally, other algorithms have been developed to detect text skew angles [7] and localization of skewed nutrition facts labels [8].

3   Improve User Experience of Nutrition Facts

Given the difficulty of users to understand nutrition labels, in this study we propose and develop an app to help users process nutrition facts based on their dietary restrictions and/or preferences. Our proposed app scans nutrition facts labels using OCR to extract nutrition information. Our app applies FDA's 5-20 rule on the percent daily value of nutrients and displays the results as thumbs up or thumbs down if the amount is healthy or unhealthy, respectively. Prior research suggests the use of traffic light style color coding on labels to make them more understandable [11]. Hence, we used green to color code the thumbs up feedback and red to color code the thumps down feedback in our app.

We provided this feedback using two different formats. Research shows that AR can enhance the way we engage with the world around us [24]. However, previous research also suggests that AR interfaces in some situations may be harder to use than static interfaces such as pop ups [27]. Therefore, we created two different interfaces for the feedback generated by the app to see which one is more effective in communicating information to users. In augmented reality interface, feedback was augmented next to the nutrition name on the label while it was being scanned by the smart phone. In static popup interface, a static screen popped up on smartphone screen with nutrient names and feedback after the label was scanned by the smart phone.

We argue that regardless of the feedback interface, the app will make it easier for the consumers to make healthy decisions as compared to using just the label. This in turn is likely to improve overall experience of using nutrition labels. We also examine which of the two feedback format (AR vs. pop up) can provide a better user experience.

4   Methodology

In this experiment we focused on three nutrients: saturated fat, sugar and protein. Foods containing fats and sugars are highly preferred [30] and consuming them in high amounts have adverse effects on health [31, 32]. High protein is generally desirable particularly for weight management [33, 34]. We created two anonymous food products (Product A and B). For each of the two food products we created a set of four nutrition fact labels. The nutrition labels in this set were designed to represent products with different nutrition values. For example, in one of the nutrition labels all three nutrients were in healthy amount, in another one of the three nutrients was in an unhealthy amount, in another two of the nutrients were in an unhealthy amount, and in another all three nutrients were in an unhealthy amount (Fig. 1).

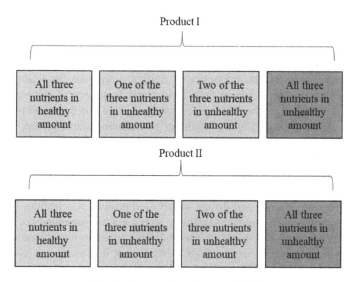

Fig. 1. Types of products and labels

We recruited twenty-two participants for the study. All participants were students from a university in Northeast US. All participants completed the task of choosing a product (product I or II) among a set of four alternatives twice, hence, they looked at 8 labels in total (4 for each product). Participants completed these two tasks one time by looking at the labels without using the app that was developed in our study (Task A) and one time by using the app (Task B). We assigned the order of the two tasks in a Latin Square fashion. For the portion of the experiment where participants used the app (Task B), we used Latin Square to randomly assign the participants into two groups. One group used the app with the AR interface (Task B1), while the other group used the app with the static popup interface (Task B2). Therefore, we used a with-in subject design for comparing user reaction to traditional way of looking at nutrition labels and using the apps, and a between subject study design to compare reactions to AR and static pop-up interfaces (Fig. 2).

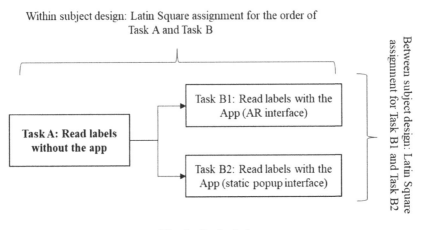

Fig. 2. Study design

Before the task, participants answered a few pre-task questions regarding frequency of using nutrition facts labels, frequency of finding nutritional facts labels helpful, difficulty in understanding nutrition facts labels, and frequency of trouble in understanding labels. Participants then were given a scenario that asked them to imagine that they recently decided to start eating healthier by reducing saturated fat, sugar, and increasing protein intake while staying within a two-thousand calories daily limit. In each task, they saw a set of four generic boxes in front of them with nutrition facts labels displaying their ingredients. They were told that these products contained the same type of food from four different undisclosed brands. Participants were required to look at the labels one by one and decide which food product was healthy for them to consume. They were again reminded that they were on a low saturated fat, low sugar, high protein diet, and wish to limit their total calorie intake to two-thousand per day. Once they made a selection, they received another set of four products. As mentioned earlier, one of the two sets of products was viewed via an app that was designed in our study. In that portion of the experiment we provided an android smartphone with the app for participant to view the labels. Participants were instructed to think out loud while performing the task.

Once participants completed a task, they were asked to assess their decision-making process in terms of difficulty in making decisions, confidence in the decisions, ease of use, helpfulness of label and app, and overall experience. We also asked participants whether they would be willing to use the app in future. Participants rated overall experience by giving stars (out of 5), all other factors were assessed on 7-point scale. Demographic information (e.g., age and gender) was also collected at this part of the experiment. Finally, we conducted an interview asking open ended questions regarding factors considered while making decisions, the overall experience of using label and app, knowledge and use of the percent daily value, use of other nutrition related apps, and suggestions for our app.

5   Results

Ten males and 12 females participated in our study. Age range of participants varied from 22 years to 47 years, with average age of 27.1 years. During pre-task survey participants reported that while buying a food product they typically look at the nutrition facts 'half of the time', with mean rating of 3.2 out of 5. They found nutrition labels helpful 'most of the time', with mean rating of 3.7 out of 5. They indicated that it was 'slightly easy' for them to understand nutrition facts labels for any food product, with mean rating of 4.6 out of 7 and they indicated that 'sometimes' they had trouble understanding the label, with mean rating of 2.2 out of 5. Ratings for pre-task questions are summarized in the Figs. 3 and 4. Percentages may not total 100 due to rounding.

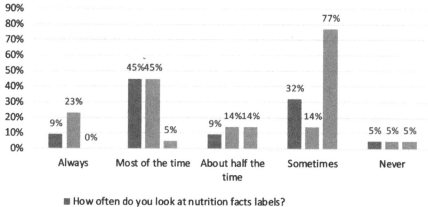

Fig. 3.   Result of frequency related pre-task questions

The results showed that 91% of participants made healthiest selection using the app compared to only 45% participants without the app. Participants found that decision making was significantly easier with the app (p = 0.000) and were significantly more confident in decisions that were made with the app (p = 0.001). In both treatments participants found that the provided information, via labels or through app feedback, was helpful in making decisions. However, participants found the information provided though the app was significantly easier to use (p = 0.004). Similarly, participants reported that the overall experience of using labels was significantly better when they used the app (0.002) (Table 1).

Next, we compared user reactions to AR and pop up interfaces. The results did not show significant differences between the two interfaces. Out of 5, mean overall rating for using the app with AR interface was 4.3 compared to 4.2 for using the app with static popup app. Participants reported that both interfaces were easy to use, with mean ratings of 5.9 out of 7 for both. The results showed favorable ratings for adopting the

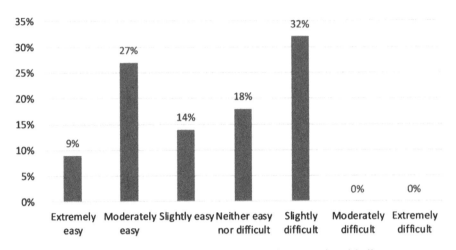

Fig. 4. Result of difficulty related pre-task question

Table 1. Results of t-test comparing user reactions with and without the app

	Mean (Label)	Mean (App)	df	t-stat	p-value
How difficult it was to make the decision?	3.9	6.5	21	6.66	0.000
How confident are you in your decision?	5.5	6.5	21	3.80	0.001
The provided information (via label or app) was helpful in making the decision	5.8	6.3	21	1.47	0.157
The app was easy to use	4.7	5.9	21	3.25	0.004
Please rate your overall experience (out of 5 stars)	3.3	4.2	21	3.47	0.002

app. Participants' rating for willingness to use the app with AR interface was 6 out of 7, a slightly lower (5.4) for the app with pop up. These results are shown in Table 2.

Table 2. Results of t-tests comparing AR and static interfaces

	Mean (AR)	Mean (Static)	df	t-stat	p-value
The app was easy to use	5.9	5.9	20	0	1
Please rate your overall experience (out of 5 stars)	4.3	4.2	20	0.34	0.737
I will use this app in future	6	5.4	18	1.41	0.177

The interviews at the end of the experimental session revealed that only 41% of participants looked at percent daily values on nutrition facts labels when they purchase products. Out of those only 22% knew what percent daily values signified; 22% used it incorrectly and 56% used percent daily values as a way to compare food products without knowing what these values signified (Fig. 5).

Knowledge and Use of Percent Daily Value

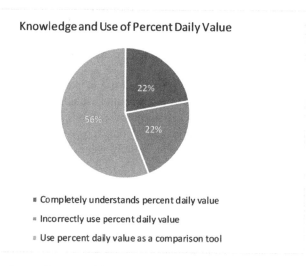

■ Completely understands percent daily value

■ Incorrectly use percent daily value

■ Use percent daily value as a comparison tool

Fig. 5. Knowledge and use of percent daily value (of participants who look at percent daily value)

The interviews also revealed that the color coding and thumbs up and thumbs down images were the deciding cues for participants to select healthy products. Participants reported that their experience with nutrition facts label without using the app was confusing, time consuming, and required a great deal of cognitive effort (calculations and comparisons). While most participants (91%) found the app easy to use and helpful a few (9%) preferred using the labels without the app. Some participants (9%) indicated that more detailed feedback (other than color-coded thumps) would be helpful in conveying information.

6   Discussion

Our results show evidence that the app had significant advantage over using just the label. The results showed that 91% of participants made healthiest selection using the app while only 45% of participants were able to do the same without the app. Participants reported confusion and complexity in using the labels during the task. These findings are consistent with the previous research that nutrition facts labels are hard to understand and confusing in general [11, 12, 14, 16].

With significantly higher ratings for the app in regard to ease of decision making, confidence in decision, and ease of use along with 95% of participants being able to make healthiest choice, it is reasonable to argue that the app had a significant positive impact on decision making. Our app also received significantly higher overall experience rating compared to just using the label.

The results did not show significant differences in ease of use and overall experience between the two feedback interfaces. The average scores for these measures were relatively high and very close for both interfaces. While participants exhibited willingness to use both interfaces in future, they rated their willingness to use the AR interface slightly higher than their willingness to use the popup interface. Although this difference was not significant, they indicate the possibility that augmented reality may be a more enticing adoption factor. Future research is needed to explore these possibilities.

Our results regarding the perception and use of percent daily value are also consistent with previous research showing low understanding of these important values [12]. Only 22% of participants in our study had a correct understanding of percent daily values. This highlights the importance of our app, which provides feedback using FDA's 5-20 rule that is based on percent daily values.

7   Limitations and Future Research

As in any experimental study, our research is limited to its setting and tasks. Our results show that our app has a potential to change the behavior of consumers in the long term towards making healthy decisions. However, more research is needed to extend the generalizability of our results and to verify the behavioral impact that our app can have to help consumers make healthy decisions.

Some participants pointed out that the app feedback was not detailed enough. Adding more information to the feedback and testing its effectiveness provides a direction for future research. While we found significant differences in decision making and overall experience in decision making with and without the app, we did not find significant differences between the two feedback interfaces. Repeating the experiment with a larger sample size is likely to provide more insights about the impact of these two feedback interfaces on consumer behavior regarding nutrition information and decision making.

In this study, our app provided feedback based on a two-thousand calorie diet. Future studies using personalized dietary plans are needed to increase confidence in generalizability of our results. Moreover, the app was developed only for Android smartphones. More platform compatibility is required in the future for maximum consumer reach.

8   Conclusion

As one revision of official nutrition label design could take a considerable amount of time to be completely implemented, our approach of transforming the nutrition facts label in real-time with the help of augmented reality provides an effective and efficient way to keep consumers informed. No matter what the physical form of the label is, we can modify and personalize that information using the most updated government health guidelines. The use of OCR technology in our app creates a seamless experience and eliminates the dependency on a food product database. Consumers can use the app on any nutritional facts label of any product.

Our app can help consumers to make healthy decisions. Consumers seem to have little knowledge about various components of the nutrition facts labels, especially percent daily value. Research indicates that for regular consumers nutrition facts labels are confusing, complex and difficult to use. Our app scans information from nutrition labels, applies calculations based on FDA's recommendations, and visualizes the results in an intuitive way to help consumers make healthier decisions.

References

1. McMahon, D.D., Cihak, D.F., Gibbons, M.M., Fussell, L., Mathison, S.: Using a mobile app to teach individuals with intellectual disabilities to identify potential food allergens. J. Spec. Educ. Technol. **28**(3), 21–32 (2013)
2. Bayu, M.Z., Arshad, H., Ali, N.M.: Nutritional information visualization using mobile augmented reality technology. Procedia Technol. **11**, 396–402 (2013)
3. Waltner, G., et al.: MANGO - mobile augmented reality with functional eating guidance and food awareness. In: Murino, V., Puppo, E., Sona, D., Cristani, M., Sansone, C. (eds.) ICIAP 2015. LNCS, vol. 9281, pp. 425–432. Springer, Cham (2015). https://doi.org/10.1007/978-3-319-23222-5_52
4. Ahn, J., Williamson, J., Gartrell, M., Han, R., Lv, Q., Mishra, S.: Supporting healthy grocery shopping via mobile augmented reality. ACM Trans. Multimedia Comput. Commun. Appl. (TOMM) **12**(1s), 16 (2015)
5. Kulyukin, V., Vanka, A., Wang, H.: Skip trie matching: a greedy algorithm for real-time OCR error correction on smartphones. Int. J. Digit. Inf. Wirel. Commun. (IJDIWC) **3**(3), 261–270 (2013)
6. Kulyukin, V., Kutiyanawala, A., Zaman, T., Clyde, S.: Vision-based localization and text chunking of nutrition fact tables on android smartphones. In: Proceedings of International Conference on Image Processing, Computer Vision, and Pattern Recognition (IPCV 2013), pp. 314–320 (2013)
7. Zaman, T., Kulyukin, V.: Text skew angle detection in vision-based scanning of nutrition labels. In: Proceedings of the International Conference on Image Processing, Computer Vision, and Pattern Recognition (IPCV), p. 139. The Steering Committee of the World Congress in Computer Science, Computer Engineering and Applied Computing (WorldComp) (2015)
8. Kulyukin, V., Blay, C.: An algorithm for mobile vision-based localization of skewed nutrition labels that maximizes specificity. In: Emerging Trends in Image Processing, Computer Vision and Pattern Recognition, pp. 277–293 (2015)
9. Neuhouser, M.L., Kristal, A.R., Patterson, R.E.: Use of food nutrition labels is associated with lower fat intake. J. Am. Diet. Assoc. **99**(1), 45–53 (1999)
10. Rothman, R.L., et al.: Patient understanding of food labels: the role of literacy and numeracy. Am. J. Prev. Med. **31**(5), 391–398 (2006)
11. Temple, N.J., Fraser, J.: Food labels: a critical assessment. Nutrition **30**(3), 257–260 (2014)
12. Levy, L., Patterson, R.E., Kristal, A.R., Li, S.S.: How well do consumers understand percentage daily value on food labels? Am. J. Health Promot. **14**(3), 157–160 (2000)

13. Ollberding, N.J., Wolf, R.L., Contento, I.: Food label use and its relation to dietary intake among US adults. J. Am. Diet. Assoc. **111**(5), S47–S51 (2011)
14. Graham, D.J., Orquin, J.L., Visschers, V.H.: Eye tracking and nutrition label use: a review of the literature and recommendations for label enhancement. Food Policy **37**(4), 378–382 (2012)
15. Kreuter, M.W., Brennan, L.K., Scharff, D.P., Lukwago, S.N.: Do nutrition label readers eat healthier diets? Behavioral correlates of adults' use of food labels. Am. J. Prev. Med. **13**(4), 277–283 (1997)
16. Cowburn, G., Stockley, L.: Consumer understanding and use of nutrition labelling: a systematic review. Public Health Nutr. **8**(1), 21–28 (2005)
17. Li, F., Miniard, P.W., Barone, M.J.: The facilitating influence of consumer knowledge on the effectiveness of daily value reference information. J. Acad. Mark. Sci. **28**(3), 425–436 (2000)
18. Nayga Jr., R.M., Lipinski, D., Savur, N.: Consumers' use of nutritional labels while food shopping and at home. J. Consum. Aff. **32**(1), 106–120 (1998)
19. Nayga Jr., R.M.: Nutrition knowledge, gender, and food label use. J. Consum. Aff. **34**(1), 97–112 (2000)
20. Campos, S., Doxey, J., Hammond, D.: Nutrition labels on pre-packaged foods: a systematic review. Public Health Nutr. **14**(8), 1496–1506 (2011)
21. Taylor, C.L., Wilkening, V.L.: How the nutrition food label was developed, Part 1: the Nutrition Facts panel. J. Am. Diet. Assoc. **108**(3), 437–442 (2008)
22. Graham, D.J., Roberto, C.A.: Evaluating the impact of US Food and Drug Administration–proposed nutrition facts label changes on young adults' visual attention and purchase intentions. Health Educ. Behav. **43**(4), 389–398 (2016)
23. Graham, D.J., Jeffery, R.W.: Location, location, location: eye-tracking evidence that consumers preferentially view prominently positioned nutrition information. J. Am. Diet. Assoc. **111**(11), 1704–1711 (2011)
24. Azuma, R.T.: A survey of augmented reality. Presence Teleoperators Virtual Environ. **6**(4), 355–385 (1997)
25. Olsson, T., Salo, M.: Online user survey on current mobile augmented reality applications. In: 2011 10th IEEE International Symposium on Mixed and Augmented Reality (ISMAR), pp. 75–84. IEEE(2011)
26. Akçayır, M., Akçayır, G.: Advantages and challenges associated with augmented reality for education: a systematic review of the literature. Educ. Res. Rev. **20**, 1–11 (2017)
27. Jain, P., Hall-Phillips, A., Djamasbi, S.: Effect of social media product reviews on buying decision when presented in augmented reality. In: Nah, F.F.-H., Xiao, B.S. (eds.) HCIBGO 2018. LNCS, vol. 10923, pp. 313–326. Springer, Cham (2018). https://doi.org/10.1007/978-3-319-91716-0_24
28. US Department of Health and Human Services and U.S. Department of Agriculture. 2015–2020 Dietary Guidelines for Americans, 8th edn., December 2015. https://health.gov/dietaryguidelines/2015/guidelines/
29. Center for Food Safety and Applied Nutrition: Labeling & Nutrition - How to Understand and Use the Nutrition Facts Label (n.d.). https://www.fda.gov/food/labelingnutrition/ucm274593.htm
30. Levine, A.S., Kotz, C.M., Gosnell, B.A.: Sugars and fats: the neurobiology of preference. J. Nutr. **133**(3), 831S–834S (2003)
31. Tran, D.M., Westbrook, R.F.: Rats fed a diet rich in fats and sugars are impaired in the use of spatial geometry. Psychol. Sci. **26**(12), 1947–1957 (2015)
32. Drewnowski, A.: The real contribution of added sugars and fats to obesity. Epidemiol. Rev. **29**(1), 160–171 (2007)

33. Johnston, C.S., Tjonn, S.L., Swan, P.D.: High-protein, low-fat diets are effective for weight loss and favorably alter biomarkers in healthy adults. J. Nutr. **134**(3), 586–591 (2004)
34. Westerterp-Plantenga, M.S., Lejeune, M.P.G.M., Nijs, I., Van Ooijen, M., Kovacs, E.M.R.: High protein intake sustains weight maintenance after body weight loss in humans. Int. J. Obes. **28**(1), 57 (2004)

Exploring Relationships Between e-Tailing Website Quality and Purchase Intention

Hibah Khalil[1](✉), Karthikeyan Umapathy[1](✉), Lakshmi C. Goel[2], and Sandeep Reddivari[1]

[1] School of Computing, University of North Florida,
Jacksonville, FL 32224, USA
Hibah.khalil0@gmail.com,
{k.umapathy,n00959246}@unf.edu
[2] Department of Management, University of North Florida,
Jacksonville, FL 32224, USA
l.goel@unf.edu

Abstract. Attracting and retaining customers in an online environment is crucial to remain a successful retail business. Although purchase intentions have been recognized as a major factor affected by the website quality, few studies have examined how initial purchase intention affects the continued purchase intention. We want to further investigate the relationship between website quality (system, information, and service) and purchase intention categories with perceived risk as the moderator. We developed a questionnaire and three different websites for a fictional office furniture retail business to aid our investigation. The questionnaire was distributed to university students in a large U.S metropolitan city. We received 256 valid responses. Our empirical results confirmed that information and service quality of the e-tail website positively impact initial purchase intentions, and consequently continued purchase intention. Of the three website quality variables measured, the perceived risk seems to have an adverse effect only on the relationship between system quality and purchase intentions. Based on our findings, e-tailing websites should consider focusing more on website quality factors such as responsiveness, utility, reliability, availability, and the content of the website as well as the service provided such as customization, users feedback and rating, and good tracking of user complaints.

Keywords: Website quality · Purchase intention · Perceived risk · Multiple regression analysis · Survey method

1 Introduction

The widespread access to the Internet has allowed businesses to present information, sell products, and provide relevant services through websites. Many researchers argue that websites are an imperative channel for communication and online shopping [1]. However, businesses struggle to retain customers due to low switching cost and lack of face-to-face communication [2]. Therefore, attracting and retaining customers in an online environment is crucial for remaining a successful business.

© Springer Nature Switzerland AG 2019
F. F.-H. Nah and K. Siau (Eds.): HCII 2019, LNCS 11588, pp. 238–256, 2019.
https://doi.org/10.1007/978-3-030-22335-9_16

Studies have shown that a high-quality website increases the likelihood of retaining customers, as it is known to affect the customer's perceived risk [1, 3]. Therefore, having a high perceived risk effect negatively on purchase frequency, and increases the likelihood of negative customers reviews. Website reviews can impact a customer's choice as well [3]. Thus, website quality should be improved to avoid negative reviews and dissatisfaction [4]. Even though studies have indicated that customers are more hesitant to purchase from online channels due to the various kinds of risks presented by the online environment, the majority of customers utilize websites to get information regarding products and services [5].

This study proposes that perceived risk is a moderator between website quality and purchase intentions. Existing literature has identified the key variables of website quality and purchase intentions [1, 6, 7]. Still, the interrelationships among the above with the moderator - perceived risk have not been explored. It is important to mention that purchase intentions can be subdivided into initial purchase intention and continued purchase intention [8]. Both initial and continued purchase intentions are affected by website quality, which can be categorically divided into perceived system quality, perceived information quality, and perceived service quality [8]. The moderator of perceived risk would clarify the relationship among website quality categories and initial/continued purchase intentions. Consequently, the objective of this study is to empirically investigate the moderating effect of perceived risk on the relationship between website quality and initial/continued purchase intentions, and how initial purchase intention impacts continued purchase intention.

2   Background

2.1   Website Quality

Website quality is characterized by a website's ability to allow users to fulfill their goals and willingness of users to revisit the site [9]. It affects the credibility and reliability of a business, which in turn is directly associated with customers' intention to make an online purchase [7]. Various measurements for website quality have been recognized by other researches including information quality, ease-of-use, usability, aesthetics, trust, and emotional appeal [10]. Lin [6] proposed that website design and interactivity as variables of system quality; informative content and security variables as information quality; and responsiveness, trust, and empathy as service quality variables. Similar to Lin [6], Hsu et al. [11] used three features—information, system, and service quality—to measure website quality. The claim that the website quality should be measured as a multi-dimensional construct is consistent with the findings of users' expectations [4], and satisfaction of online customers [12]. Given the consistency in the literature, we have adopted website quality as a multi-dimensional construct comprising information quality, system quality, and service quality.

System Quality. In the Internet environment, system quality is associated with ease of use, which is a characteristic of system design [13]. Kirakowski et al. [14] defined perceived system quality as the extent to which the user thinks the website is easy, reliable, accessible, and adaptable as well as the interface interaction is consistent.

Therefore, poor system characteristics such as lack of responsiveness, usefulness, and suitability discourage the customer from using an e-commerce website, which in turn leads to declines in sales and demand. In addition, security is another critical issue in the system quality, since many sensitive transactions are conducted over the Internet [12].

Information Quality. Rai et al. [15] illustrated information quality as a degree of perceived value of the output provided from the website; which means that the information on the website has to be accurate, relevant, personalized, well-formatted, and easy to understand to encourage initial purchase intention and to have the user return to the site on a regular basis. Because the information quality of e-commerce websites has an extensive effect on the purchase intention, Ahn et al. [16] indicated that to provide an enjoyable shopping experience for customers and help them make ideal purchasing decisions, it is important that the website provides quality information.

Service Quality. Palmer [17] describes service quality as the extent to which a website is reactive, cooperative, and efficient. Service quality includes overall customer assessments and judgments about the service provided through the website [17]. Zeithaml [18] clarified that to increase the purchase intention rate, establish online loyalty, and guarantee that buyers get satisfying results from e-commerce websites, retailers must move their focus from the aspect of exchanges and transactions to the aspect of service. Website quality is a key component in electronic business because customer's perception of website positively impacts their intentions to use and purchase from the website [19]. The real challenge for the e-business is how to convert the website visitors into buyers when they view the website for the first time [20].

2.2 Purchase Intentions

Purchase intention is defined as customers' intention to buy a product in the future [21]. Purchase intention has been widely studied as it can be used to predict real purchase behavior [21]. There are two kinds of purchase intentions when it comes to e-commerce websites: initial purchase intention and continued purchase intention. These two categories are intimately correlated to the customer conversion and retention rates of e-commerce websites [22]. Customer conversion is characterized as an ability of the website to convert prospective customers into buyers, while customer retention refers to the extent to which the website can engage buyers in purchasing again [23, 24]. Thus, e-businesses need strategic focus and innovative techniques concerning website quality to optimally use their limited resources to increase and expand customer conversion and retention rates.

2.3 Perceived Risk

Perceived risk refers to the degree to which a customer thinks there is potential for unpredictable outcomes resulting from the transaction [5]. The presence of perceived risks is likely to discourage customers from making a purchase regardless of the quality of the website [25]. An uncertain customer is less likely to make an initial purchase or a subsequent purchase. A customer, for instance, may shift loyalty if there is a negative review of the e-commerce website.

3   Related Works

Several researchers have shown website quality affects the customers' purchase intention behavior [4, 7, 26]. Kuan, Bock, and Vathanophas [8] studied the relationship between three website quality categories and two purchase intention categories; and found that system quality has a significant relationship with initial purchase intention whereas service quality has a significant relationship with continued purchase intention. Hsu, Chang and Chen [11] used stimulus, organism, and response framework to identify five quality factors (information quality, system quality, e-service quality, customer perceived flow, and perceived playfulness) that may influence purchase intentions. Their findings indicated that only e-service quality had direct influence. Chang et al. [27] explored the influence of website quality and perceived trust and then on the customer purchase intention with website brand and perceived value as moderators. Their results indicated that the website brand increased hotel purchases and orders, when there was a strong connection among website quality and perceived trust for the users. Their study also showed that relationship among perceived trust and purchase intention is moderated by high perceived service value.

Chang and Chen [2] analyzed the impact of customer interface quality, satisfaction, and switching costs. Their analysis of survey responses indicated that professional communication and interaction positively affected customer feelings. Moreover, their study also revealed interaction, convenience, speed, and personalized interface are critical to attracting traffic and switching costs. Further, their analysis established that switching costs were one of the main factors influencing e-loyalty. Kim and Lennon [1] used web-based surveys to analyze the effect of reputation on consumer purchase intention. They found the reputation and the website quality had a positive impact on consumers' emotion and a negative impact on perceived risk. Masoud [28] analyzed the effects of perceived risks on an online shopping setting in Jordan using focus group interviews with online shoppers. Their findings show that dimensions of perceived risks such as financial risks, products risks, delivery risks, information security risks, and time risks, directly influenced online shopping.

Hsieh and Tsao [5] studied the effects of website (system, information, and service) quality on perceived risk and then on online loyalty. Their results show that both system and information quality did not have as much of a negative effect on perceived risk as service quality had. Also, they found that perceived risk had a negative impact on e-loyalty and that the negative impact would be stronger on customer-to-customer relationships rather than on business-to-customer relationships. Gregg and Walczak [3] investigated the relationship between perceived website quality, trust, and price premiums at various online auctions. The analysis of survey responses indicated that the trust derived from the website quality affects the intention to transact and the price premium significantly. He et al., [29] analyzed the impact of usability features on consumer preferences and repurchase intention on e-commerce. Empirical data from this study showed that e-commerce personalization features enhanced the credibility of the website and increased price tolerance. Bai et al. [7] analyzed the direct effects of information content on satisfaction and purchase intention on website visitors in China. The results indicated that the website quality positively affects customer satisfaction, which leads to purchase intention.

Based on the existing literature, we can note that there are significant gaps in the research carried out to find the relationships between website quality and purchase intentions. Literature has ample evidence for a positive relationship between website quality and purchase intentions in the context of online shopping. However, there is a need to find the impact of website quality on purchase intentions with perceived risk as a moderator, and to measure the influence of the initial purchase intention on continued purchase intention on an e-retailing website.

4   Research Model and Hypothesis Development

Existing research studies posits that if online shoppers perceive high-website quality variables, then they are more likely to initiate the purchase process, which in turn contributes to continued purchase intention. We argue to extend further research efforts on website quality to study the moderating effect of perceived risk on the relationship among website quality and purchase intention variables. Figure 1 shows the research model and hypothesized relationships.

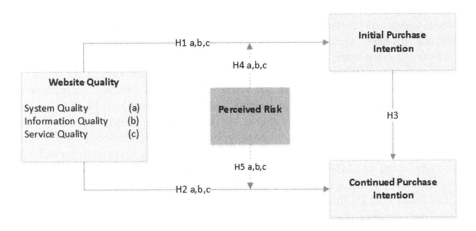

Fig. 1. Research model.

4.1   Relationships Between Website Quality and Purchase Intentions

As mentioned earlier, website quality encompasses system, information, and service quality. System quality is critical to an e-tailing website as the online shoppers would be reluctant to purchase if they experience challenges using the system [1, 8]. Customers rely on the information presented on the website to make their purchasing decisions and complete the transaction. Thus, perceived information quality is known to affect customer's purchase intention [6, 8, 15]. Due to the lack of face-to-face interaction, service quality is vital to the success of an e-retailer [16]. [8, 11, 27] have found the website quality categorized into system, information, and service quality has a significant impact on the purchase intention construct which is further categorized into initial and continued purchase intentions. Basing on the above arguments, we hypothesize the following:

H1a, b, c: System (a) | information (b) | service (c) quality has a significant positive influence on initial purchase intention on e-tailing websites.

H2a, b, c: System (a) | information (b) | service (c) quality has a significant positive influence on continued purchase intention on e-tailing websites

4.2   The Relationship Between Initial Purchase Intention and Continued Purchase Intention

Gaining customer loyalty is a process that begins with an initial purchase [30]. The initial purchase may be intended or probabilistic. A customer, for example, may purchase an item online because it is needed urgently. Such a purchase is probabilistic. However, a customer may make the initial purchase because the website and the goods on sale have been promoted and packaged to fit his/her needs. Such a purchase is intended. Therefore, the biggest challenge is to ensure that both intended and probabilistic customers come back for their next purchase. Once the organization ensures that the customer makes a continued purchase, loyalty may be achieved [27]. [8] has shown that initial purchase intention is formed based on the features offered by the website. However, none have studied the relationship between initial and continued purchase intention. Given that loyalty towards a website must be achieved over a period of time, it is essential to study the relationship between the first purchase and the continued purchase intentions. Therefore, we hypothesize the following:

H3:   Initial purchase intention has a significant positive influence on continued purchase intention

4.3   The Moderating Role of Perceived Risk on the Relationship Between Website Quality and Purchase Intention Variables

A website that reflects high website quality is likely to attract users to make the initial and continued purchases. An organization can create a website of high quality by establishing processes, procedures, responsibilities, and other activities that ensure that the customer receives value when a purchase is made. Although the quality of a website encourages a customer to make a purchase, the possibility of any risk may discourage a customer from making the purchase [25]. Customers are also likely to give little consideration to the quality of the website when they perceive transaction on the website to be risky [7]. In the arena of online shopping, customers are not very knowledgeable of the quality of products or services provided by the website, and because of these customers are looking for informational cues that let them recognize a good quality product from another of lesser quality. Thus, perceived risks scare customers away. Bad website reviews and other risks may increase the alertness of a customer, hence reducing their interest in buying on the website. It is hypothesized that perceived higher risk is likely to negatively influence the relationship between website quality (system, information, and service) and purchase intention (both initial and continued). We, therefore, hypothesize the following:

H4a, b, c: The relationship between system (a) | information (b) | service (c) quality and initial purchase intention is weaker when customers perceive higher risk levels.

H5a, b, c: The relationship between system (a) | information (b) | service (c) quality and continued purchase intention is weaker when customers perceive higher risk levels

5   Research Methodology

5.1   Survey Development

Based on the research model constructs and previous literature, a survey instrument was created to test the factors of website quality, purchase intentions, and perceived risk. The survey was developed using a seven-point Likert scale for each of the model components ranging from (1) Strongly Disagree to (7) Strongly Agree. The survey questions for each variable have been used in prior research; however, some were modified to suit the context of this research. The sources of the survey constructs are provided in Table 1.

Table 1. Construct sources and number of items used.

Construct name	No. of items	Measurement sources
Website quality		
System quality	4	[6, 11]
Information quality	4	[11]
Service quality	4	[4, 6, 11]
Perceived risk	3	[1]
Purchase intention		
Initial purchase intention	4	[1]
Continued purchase intention	4	[31]

5.2   Experimental Website

Participants of graduate and undergraduate students were asked to browse an experimental office furniture website of a fictional e-retailer to purchase a desk. The survey was designed as one-factorial experiment manipulating three levels of website quality: high, medium, and low following the condition types established by [32] to study online shopping features. Each group of participants was assigned randomly to one quality level of the website. Specifically, each participant in each group was exposed to a single level of the website to increase the reliability of the responses. Based on the research model, each level of the website was created based on the factors of system, service, and information quality. The three varying quality websites were created based on the characteristics of each level of the website quality as described in Table 2. All the website samples presented the same content regarding the office furniture purchase but differed only in terms of the level of website quality. Figure 2 provides sample screenshots of the three levels of the website.

Table 2. Levels of website quality.

Factors of website quality	Levels of website quality		
	Low	Medium	High
Information Quality (Sources: from [4, 15])	Minimal information is provided about the product such as name and a picture	In addition to low-level information, brief product description is provided, including overview description, and product dimensions Also, negative reviews provided in the product reviews	In addition to medium level information, the high level of information quality contains comprehensive description of the product specification, and feature descriptions Furthermore, positive reviews provided in the product reviews
Service quality (Source: [17])	Few services provided such as FAQ page, and Tag product. No product reviews Few 404 error on some product pages	In addition to low level of service quality, the number of services provided include: • View reviews from other users • Contact Us page • No 404 error pages	In addition to medium level service, the high level of service quality contains the following: • Slide of product pictures • Writing reviews/feedback for the product and rating it • Product Customization • Share product (Facebook, Twitter) • Add to Wish list • Add to Compare
System quality (Source: [1])	Few system quality features are provided such as consistency of the interface elements, such as logos and icons	In addition to low system quality, the website uses consistent layout in all pages	In addition to the medium level, the website contains overall well-organized user interface including consistent placement of interface elements and site features

A. High Quality Website   B. Medium Quality Website

C. Low Quality Website

Fig. 2. Office furniture website screenshots.

5.3 Task and Data Collection Procedure

The survey was conducted online, and the participants could access it from any computer with Internet connection. The study was conducted in a medium-sized university in the southeast United States. We requested instructors in the university to post the experimental website link in their Course Management System. After the links were posted, willing volunteers clicked on the survey participation link, which led them to a consent page explaining the purpose of the study as well as the associated tasks for participants. The participants who agreed to take part in the study were directed to one of the three office furniture websites. Participants were requested to navigate the website and to purchase their favorite desk. Once the item had been selected and the decision had been made, the participant proceeded to check out. When the participant selected a desk by clicking on "add to cart" the task was considered complete, and the survey questionnaire was presented to the participant. The survey questionnaire was developed using Qualtrics software [33]. The researchers obtained the university Institutional Review Board permissions to conduct the study.

To ensure that all the items of the survey, as well as task instructions, were well written and understandable, a pretest was conducted prior to sending out the final survey to the actual sample of the study. A group of 30 people reviewed the survey items and instructions to report any ambiguities or difficulties in terms of responding to certain items. Following the pre-test, survey items and instructions were modified based on the feedback received from the reviewers.

6 Data Analysis and Results

6.1 Sample Population and Demographic Profile

A total of 262 responses were received. Of the responses received, 256 were usable survey responses that were analyzed. Statistical analyses were conducted using Statistical Package for Social Science (SPSS) software package. The demographic profile of the respondents is presented in Table 3.

To ensure that the rating of the website quality level was completed at the proper time (once the participant had experience with the website), the manipulation question was only visible to the participants after they reviewed the website. This question was phrased as follows: "After reviewing the Office Shoppe website, how would you rate

Table 3. Demographic information and level of websites usage.

Demographic variable	Sub-items	Frequency	Percent
Gender	Male	149	58.2
	Female	107	41.8
Age	18–25	133	52
	26–35	81	31.6
	36–45	38	14.8
	45+	4	1.6
Times of shopping online	Once a week or more	84	32.8
	2–3 times a month	75	29.3
	Once a month	50	19.5
	Every few months	34	13.3
	Rarely/Never	13	5.1
Rate of the website	Very Good	46	18
	Good	98	38.3
	Above average	11	4.3
	Average	61	23.8
	Below average	30	11.7
	Poor	9	3.5
	Very poor	1	0.4
Responses received	High-quality website	89	34.8
	Medium-quality website	47	18.4
	Low-quality website	120	46.9

the level of the website quality?" Seven options were provided on a scale ranging from "very good" to "very poor" as shown in Table 3. This study assumes that the average of participant responses to the high-quality website sample would be rated and categorized as either "very good", "good", or "above average"; the average of the medium-quality website would be rated and categorized as "average", or "below average"; and the average of the low-quality website would be rated and categorized as "poor" or "very poor". However, the high-quality website sample (n = 89) was rated on average as "good" and the medium (n = 47) and low-quality website samples (n = 120) on average were reviewed as "below average" websites. Therefore, it can be concluded that the expectations regarding the high website quality and medium website quality manipulations were met more than the low-quality website.

6.2   *t*-Tests

We conducted *t*-tests to determine whether there is a significant difference between responses received for high-quality, medium-quality, and low-quality websites for each independent variable. Results indicate that there were significant differences for all four questions relevant to system quality, information quality, and service quality. Average means for each website quality independent variables and website levels are shown in Table 4. We also conducted one-way ANOVA for examining whether there are significant differences between the means of the moderator, perceived risk, and dependent variables, purchase intentions, among the three samples of the website. Results are shown in Table 5 which indicates there were statistical differences between the means of the three samples of the website (p-value < .05). Thus, we conclude that users have different perceptions of the website quality attributes, perceived risk, and purchase intentions. Therefore, we decided to use the entire sample (n = 256) for testing the hypotheses.

Table 4. *t*-tests for independent variables.

Independent variables	Average of means for websites			Sig. (2-tailed)
	High	Medium	Low	
System quality	5.983	4.644	5.184	0.000
Information quality	5.744	4.697	4.087	0.000
Service quality	5.983	4.628	4.01	0.000

Table 5. One-way ANOVA for moderator and dependent variables.

Variables		Average of means for websites			F	Sig. (2-tailed)
		High	Medium	Low		
Moderator	Perceived Risk	3.232	4.794	4.403	25.072	0.000
Dependent Variables	Initial Purchase Intention	4.629	3.787	3.725	10.424	0.000
	Continued Purchase Intention	4.5	3.585	3.558	10.101	0.000

6.3   Reliability Analysis

We performed principal component analysis (PCA) with Varimax rotations on the 12 items for website quality independent variables to assess the internal consistency among survey items. Cronbach's alpha coefficient values are used to measure the reliability of the survey instrument with 0.7 as the minimum acceptable value [34]. Cronbach's alpha was calculated to confirm the reliability of the moderator and dependent variables as well. Table 6 shows the results of PCA with Varimax for independent variables and Table 7 shows Cronbach's alpha values for the moderator and dependent variables. For all items, the Cronbach's value was greater than 0.8, thus indicating good internal consistency.

Factor analysis was performed to determine how well website quality items are related to one another and form factors. As a rule of thumb, a measurement item loads highly if its loading coefficient is above 0.6 and does not load highly if the coefficient is below 0.4 [34]. From Table 6, it can be noted that all factors load highly greater than 0.6 and all coefficient alpha greater than 0.7, these results imply that all three website quality constructs comply with the requirement of high internal consistency. All factors illustrate good internal consistency and factor analysis results, thereby, demonstrating the construct validity.

Table 6. PCA with Varimax for independent variables.

Independent variables	Scale items	Factor loadings	Cronbach α	Explained variance
System quality	SQ1	0.861	0.844	81.35%
	SQ2	0.906		
	SQ3	0.906		
	SQ4	0.932		
Information quality	IQ1	0.907	0.801	82.78%
	IQ2	0.929		
	IQ3	0.875		
	IQ4	0.927		
Service quality	SVQ1	0.825	0.833	79.45%
	SVQ2	0.926		
	SVQ3	0.895		
	SVQ4	0.916		

Table 7. Cronbach estimates for moderator and dependent variables.

	Variables	# Items	Cronbach α
Moderator	Perceived risk	3	0.879
Dependent variables	Initial Purchase Intention	4	0.932
	Continued Purchase Intention	4	0.941

6.4   Testing Hypotheses: Multiple Regression Analysis

Hypotheses H1 through H5 was evaluated using multiple regression analysis. In this study, multiple regression determined the relative importance and significance of the relationships between website quality, purchase intentions, and perceived risk as a moderator. Multicollinearity among independent variables was detected by examining the Variance Inflation Factor (VIF) in all three samples. A VIF value of above 10 was used as a cut-off threshold, showing multicollinearity problems among independent variables in multiple regression models. The VIF values among all independent variables measuring website quality are shown in Table 8. Since all the VIF values among multiple independent variables within an acceptable range, there is no multicollinearity issue in this study.

Table 8. Collinearity statistics.

Construct	System quality	Information quality	Service quality
Variance Inflation Factor (VIF)	2.792	3.782	3.763

To test H1a, b, c, and H2 a, b, c, multiple regression analysis was used. The three factors of website quality were used as independent variables or predictors, and initial purchase intention was a dependent variable for H1 while continued purchase intention was a dependent variable for H2. Regards to H1, the results show that there are significant positive relationships between two factors of website quality (information quality (Beta = .210, p > .05) and service quality (Beta = . 486, p < . 001)) and initial purchase intention (F = 56.625, Adj. R2 = .396, p < .001). Therefore, H1b and H1c are supported (See Fig. 2 and Table 9). Results for H2 shows significant positive relationships between website quality factors (information quality (Beta = .250, p < .05) and service quality (Beta = .496, p < .001)) and continued purchase intention (F = 54.424, Adj. R2 = .386, p < .001). Therefore, H2b and H2c are supported (See Fig. 2 and Table 9).

To test H3, linear regression was used. Initial purchase intention was used as an independent variable or predictor, while continued purchase intention was used as the dependent variable. The result shows there is a significant positive relationship between the above factors. Specifically, initial purchase intention is positively related to continued purchase intention (F = 788.605, Adj. R2 = 0.755, Beta = .929, p < .001). Therefore, H3 is supported (See Fig. 2 and Table 10).

For examining H4a, b, c, and H5a, b, c, multiple regression analysis was used. The three factors of website quality including system quality, information quality, and service quality were used as independent variables or predictors, and initial purchase intention was a dependent variable for H4 while continued purchase intention was the dependent variable for H5, whereas the perceived risk was a moderator between the above relationships. As hypotheses proposed a negative moderating effect of perceived risk on the relationship between website quality factors and initial purchase intention. The results show that a significant relationship was found only among system quality, initial purchase intention, and the moderator of perceived risk (F = 7.137, Adj.

$R2 = .067$, $p < .001$). To be specific, perceived risk negatively moderated the effect of system quality and initial purchase intention (Beta = $-.027$, $p < 001$). However, in terms of service quality, a positive relationship was found; the relationship between service quality and initial purchase intention were stronger when perceived risk was high, to be specific, (Beta = $.022$, $p < .05$). That is, perceived risk positively moderated the effect of service quality on initial purchase intention, contrary to H4c. Therefore, only H4a is supported (See Fig. 2 and Table 11). Results for H5 is similar to H4, a significant relationship was found only between system quality, continued purchase intention (Beta = $-.028$, $p < 000$), and the moderator of perceived risk (F = 6.089, Adj. $R2 = .056$, $p < .01$). Unpredictably, regarding service quality, a positive relationship was found; the relationship between service quality and continued purchase intention were stronger when perceived risk was high. That is, perceived risk positively moderated the effect of service quality on continued purchase intention, contrary to hypothesis 5c. Analysis for information quality did not reveal any statistically significant results for H4b as well as H5b. Therefore, only H5a is supported (See Fig. 2 and Table 11) (Fig. 3).

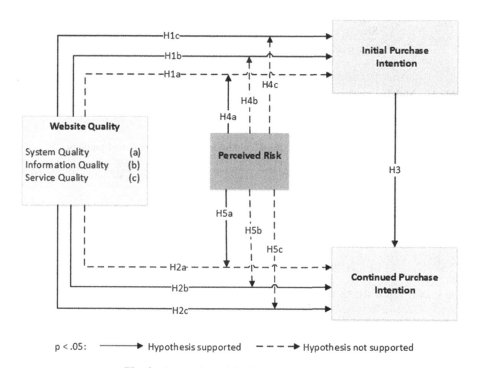

Fig. 3. Research model with hypotheses results.

Table 9. Multiple regression between website quality and purchase intentions.

Predictor	Outcome	
	Initial purchase intention	Continued purchase intention
System quality	n/s	n/s
Information quality	0.210*	0.250*
Service quality	0.486***	0.496**
F	56.625	54.424
Adj. R^2	0.396	0.386
Sig.	0.000	.000

***p < .001, **p < .01, *p < .05, n/s: not significant

Table 10. Linear regression between initial and continued purchase intentions.

Predictor	Outcome
	Continued purchase intention
Initial Purchase Intention	0.929***
F	788.605
Adj. R^2	0.755
Sig.	.000

***p < .001

Table 11. Multiple regression between website quality and perceived risk on purchase intentions.

Predictor	Outcome	
	Initial purchase intention	Continued purchase intention
System Quality * Perceived Risk	−.027***	−.028***
Information Quality * Perceived Risk	n/s	n/s
Service Quality * Perceived Risk	.022	0.020*
F	7.137	6.089
Adj. R^2	0.067	0.182
Sig.	.000	.001

***p < .001, **p < .01, *p < .05, n/s: not significant

7 Discussion and Conclusion

In this paper, we argue that the quality of a website is a vital aspect in influencing consumers purchase intentions which can be used to determine and influence their perceived risk. This study assumed that the system quality of a website positively influences initial and continued purchase intentions (H1a, H2a). Conversely, this hypothesis was not supported because the obtained results did not demonstrate statistical significance. This study did, however, support the hypothesis that system quality negatively influences the purchase intentions through moderator—perceived risk (H4a, H5a). System design that meets the aspects of utility, suitability, reliability, and availability will influence the customers initial and continued purchase intentions.

A good display of the content in the interface of the website enhances the security perception of the customers, which positively influences their purchase intentions. This study provided support for the hypotheses that information on a website positively influences initial and continued purchase intentions (H1b, H2b). Therefore, to maintain a competitive advantage and raise customer purchase intention, e-tailing websites must continuously improve the information quality of their site to attract new customers and retain existing ones. We also assumed that the perceived risk of the website would negatively influence the purchase intentions of the customer (H4b, H5b). However, these hypotheses were not supported, as the relationship among the above factors were statistically insignificant.

The quality of service influences the perceived value, which the customer receives during the purchasing process [27]. In compliance with the results of this study, the relationship between website service quality and purchase intentions (initial and continued) was statistically significant. Thus, this study results supported the relationships between the website service quality and purchase intentions (initial and continued) (H1c, H2c). Additionally, we hypothesized that service quality of a website negatively influences initial and continued purchase intentions of the customer if the user perceives high risk (H4c, H5c). However, our study findings did not find support for this negative relationship. These findings differ from those of some previous studies [5], which suggested that perceived risk and website service quality may negatively interact with each other in driving purchase intentions. Maybe the moderating effect of perceived risk on the service quality and purchase intentions link is affected by market competition and structure. That is, a dissatisfied customer with the perceived risk of service provided unlikely to perceive risk when there are only a few alternative providers. Therefore, the perceived risk might positively moderate the effect of service quality on purchase decisions.

This study supported the hypothesis that initial purchase influenced by safety and guarantee from website quality which stimulates on the continued purchase intention (H3), which implied that gaining customer satisfaction in the initial purchase could improve customer intention to return and vice-versa. Therefore, factors such as safety and guarantee measures that the website has in place will contribute immensely in increasing user retention level.

There are several limitations in this study that needs to be brought to the forefront. First, website quality is a multi-faceted construct. However, this study involved only three dimensions in measuring the website quality. There are other various website quality factors (such as usability, security, reliability, performance, portability, accessibility, and conformance to web standards) that may bring different results. Future studies should consider including some of the other website quality attributes that were not included in this study. Second, this study adopted perceived risk as the only moderator. Further studies need to be conducted to examine the effects of variables such as switching costs, reputation, payment methods, and after sale risks. Third, this study used purchase intentions as a proxy for actual customer purchasing behavior.

While information systems researchers predominantly agree that purchase intention is a valid proxy for actual purchase, consumer behavior researchers argue for studies on the actual purchase behaviors. Finally, even though there is racial and ethnic diversity in this sample study, the sampling of only college students does not yield a representative sample of all of the general population of online shoppers. In addition, since this study only considered an office furniture purchase, it is not possible to generalize analytical outcomes to other e-commerce websites. Further research can be conducted to examine a variety of online retailers, products, and services. Furthermore, this study was investigated using a traditional website; future researchers may want to consider broadening this perspective and employing a mobile platform that can be launched from a participant's phone or tablet.

In conclusion, our study examined the influence of website quality factors and the moderator of perceived risk on purchase intentions (initial and continued). Our empirical results confirmed that website quality positively affected initial intention, and consequently continued purchase intention. While building and boosting customer retention in the e-business sectors is difficult; it requires lots of effort to distinguish themselves from their competitors through the website quality features. Therefore, based on our findings, e-tailers should consider focusing more on website quality factors as a marketing strategy, mainly improving responsiveness, utility, reliability, availability, and the content of the website as well as the service provided such as customization, users feedback and rating, and appropriately addressing user complaints.

References

1. Kim, J., Lennon, S.J.: Effects of reputation and website quality on online consumers' emotion, perceived risk and purchase intention. J. Res. Interact. Market. 7(1), 33–56 (2013)
2. Chang, H.H., Chen, S.W.: The impact of customer interface quality, satisfaction and switching costs on e-loyalty: internet experience as a moderator. Comput. Hum. Behav. 24(6), 2927–2944 (2008)
3. Gregg, D.G., Walczak, S.: The relationship between website quality, trust and price premiums at online auctions. Electron. Commerce Res. 10(1), 1–25 (2010)
4. Liang, C., Chen, H.-J.: A study of the impacts of website quality on customer relationship performance. Total Qual. Manag. Bus. Excellence 20(9), 971–988 (2009)
5. Hsieh, M., Tsao, W.-C.: Reducing perceived online shopping risk to enhance loyalty: a website quality perspective. J. Risk Res. 17(2), 241–261 (2014)
6. Lin, H.: The impact of website quality dimensions on customer satisfaction in the B2C e-commerce context. Total Qual. Manag. Bus. Excellence 18(4), 363–378 (2007)
7. Bai, B., Law, R., Wen, I.: The impact of website quality on customer satisfaction and purchase intentions: evidence from Chinese online visitors. Int. J. Hospitality Manag. 27(3), 391–402 (2008)
8. Kuan, H., Bock, G.-W., Vathanophas, V.: Comparing the effects of website quality on customer initial purchase and continued purchase at e-commerce websites. Behav. Inf. Technol. 27(1), 3–16 (2008)
9. Loiacono, E.T., Watson, R.T., Goodhue, D.L.: WebQual: an instrument for consumer evaluation of web sites. Int. J. Electron. Commerce 11(3), 51–87 (2007)

10. Barnes, S.J., Vidgen, R.: An evaluation of cyber-bookshops: the WebQual method. Int. J. Electron. Commerce **6**(1), 11–30 (2001)
11. Hsu, C., Chang, K.-C., Chen, M.-C.: The impact of website quality on customer satisfaction and purchase intention: perceived playfulness and perceived flow as mediators. IseB **10**(4), 549–570 (2012)
12. DeLone, W.H., McLean, E.R.: Measuring e-commerce success: applying the DeLone & McLean Information Systems Success Model. Int. J. Electron. Commerce **9**(1), 31–47 (2004)
13. Harper, B.D., Slaughter L., Norman K.L.: Questionnaire administration via the WWW: a validation and reliability study for a user satisfaction questionnaire. In: Proceedings on World Conference on the WWW, Internet & Intranet (WebNet), pp. 808–810 (1997)
14. Kirakowski, J., Claridge, N., Whitehand, R.: Human centered measures of success in web site design. In: Proceedings on Conference on Human Factors and the Web, pp. 40–44 (1998)
15. Rai, A., Lang, S.S., Welker, R.B.: Assessing the validity of IS success models: an empirical test and theoretical analysis. Inf. Syst. Res. **13**(1), 50–69 (2002)
16. Ahn, D.H., Kim, J.K., Choi, I.Y., et al.: A personalised recommendation procedure based on dimensionality reduction and web mining. Int. J. Internet Enterp. Manag. (IJIEM) **2**(3), 280–298 (2004)
17. Palmer, J.W.: Web site usability, design, and performance metrics. Inf. Syst. Res. **13**(2), 151–167 (2002)
18. Zeithaml, V.A.: Service excellence in electronic channels. Managing Serv. Qual. **12**(3), 135–139 (2002)
19. Chen, W.S., Chang, H.H.: The impact of online store environment cues on purchase intention: trust and perceived risk as a mediator. Online Inf. Rev. **32**(6), 818–841 (2008)
20. Srinivasan, S.S., Anderson, R., Ponnavolu, K.: Customer loyalty in e-commerce: an exploration of its antecedents and consequences. J. Retail. **78**(1), 41–50 (2002)
21. Hsu, H.Y., Tsou, H.-T.: Understanding customer experiences in online blog environments. Int. J. Inf. Manag. **31**(6), 510–523 (2011)
22. Gefen, D., Karahanna, E., Straub, D.W.: Inexperience and experience with online stores: the importance of TAM and trust. IEEE Trans. Eng. Manage. **50**(3), 307–321 (2003)
23. Ittner, C.D., Larcker, D.F.: Are nonfinancial measures leading indicators of financial performance? An analysis of customer satisfaction. J. Account. Res. **36**, 1–35 (1998)
24. Reichheld, F.F., Schefter, P.: E-loyalty: your secret weapon on the web. Harvard Bus. Rev. **78**(4), 105–113 (2000)
25. McKnight, H.D., Choudhury, V., Kacmar, C.: The impact of initial consumer trust on intentions to transact with a web site: a trust building model. J. Strateg. Inf. Syst. **11**(3), 297–323 (2002)
26. Park, D., Lee, J., Han, I.: The effect of on-line consumer reviews on consumer purchasing intention: the moderating role of involvement. Int. J. Electron. Commerce **11**(4), 125–148 (2007)
27. Chang, K., Kuo, N.-T., Hsu, C.-L., et al.: The impact of website quality and perceived trust on customer purchase intention in the hotel sector: website brand and perceived value as moderator. Int. J. Innov. Manag. Technol. **5**(4), 255–260 (2014)
28. Masoud, E.Y.: The effect of perceived risk on online shopping in Jordan. Eur. J. Bus. Manag. **5**(6), 76–87 (2013)
29. He, Y., Chan, L.K., Tse, S.-K.: From consumer satisfaction to repurchase intention: the role of price tolerance in a competitive service market. Total Qual. Manag. Bus. Excellence **19**(9), 949–961 (2008)

30. Jiang, P., Rosenbloom, B.: Customer intention to return online: price perception, attribute-level performance, and satisfaction unfolding over time. Eur. J. Mark. **39**(1), 150–174 (2005)
31. Shen, J.: Social comparison, social presence, and enjoyment in the acceptance of social shopping websites. J. Electron. Commerce Res. **13**(3), 198–212 (2012)
32. Cyr, D., Hassanein, K., Head, M., et al.: The role of social presence in establishing loyalty in e-Service environments. Interact. Comput. **19**(1), 43–56 (2007)
33. Qualtrics. https://www.qualtrics.com/. Accessed 9 Jan 2019
34. Hair, J.F., Money, A.H., Samouel, P., et al.: The Essentials of Business Research Methods, 3rd edn. Routledge, New York (2015)

Adding 'Social' to Commerce to Influence Purchasing Behaviour

Zainab Mehdi Hussain Khan[(⊠)] and Norman Shaw[(⊠)]

Ryerson University, Toronto, ON M5B 2K3, Canada
{zainab.m.khan,norman.shaw}@ryerson.ca

Abstract. As social media technologies become more embedded within the online shopping interface, the phenomenon of social commerce arises. This research examines the role of social commerce in influencing consumer purchase intention. Specifically, factors investigated are social presence, consumer's security perceptions, perceived internet privacy risk, trust and willingness to provide personal information to transact. The study found that security perception, trust and willingness to provide personal information to transact have a significant influence on consumer purchase intention.

Keywords: Social commerce · Purchase intention · Trust · Social presence · Security perception

1 Introduction

In recent years, online shopping has become a dominant form of online commercial activity, with statistics predicting global e-commerce sales to reach $4.5 trillion by 2021 [1]. One reason for this rapid growth may be attributed to the increasing integration of social media technologies within the online shopping interface, resulting in a more socially oriented form of online shopping appropriately termed social commerce [2]. Social commerce has been regarded as a subset of e-commerce, characterized by use of social technologies that allow for user-generated content [2]. Because of the growing popularity of social commerce, it is becoming the focus of several research studies [3, 4]. One area of research that warrants attention is how consumers' purchasing behavior are influenced in the social commerce context.

This study draws on the stimulus-organism-response (SOR) framework [5] as the theoretical foundation to trace the antecedents and mediators that influence a consumer's purchasing intention in the social commerce context. The stimuli are the social presence and security perceptions that an individual is privy to when he/she makes the initial contact with the social commerce platform. The organism refers to the internal process that occurs after this initial contact, which, in the case of social commerce, is the formation of a trusting belief. The response is the decision to purchase on-line.

Many studies have been conducted in the past to examine the effect of social commerce on businesses and consumers' intention to make purchases through social commerce platforms. The motivation of this study is to focus on social commerce as a medium used to buy products in the context of e-commerce for Canadian consumers.

F. F.-H. Nah and K. Siau (Eds.): HCII 2019, LNCS 11588, pp. 257–273, 2019.
https://doi.org/10.1007/978-3-030-22335-9_17

The purpose of this study is to provide a deeper understanding of the role that social media play when consumers are making online purchases. There has been very little research on this topic and this study aims to fill this gap. We are posing the following research question:

What factors influence the intention to purchase when consumers are engaged in social commerce.

2 Literature View

2.1 Social Commerce

Online shopping (E-commerce) refers to buying and selling of products over the internet [6]. Social commerce is a sub-set that uses social technologies that allow user-generated content [2]. However, the difference between social commerce and e-commerce has been met with confusion and much debate and the term social commerce itself has seen multiple definitions [3, 4]. Research identifies two broad views in terms of its conceptualization [3, 4] the first view of social commerce consists only of social networking sites (like Facebook, Twitter, Instagram). In the second view, social commerce is much broader and includes any website that uses social media technologies to facilitate online transactions. In this view, traditional e-commerce sites like Amazon and eBay can be considered social commerce because of their use of social media technologies [7]. The development of Web 2.0 technologies, which has enabled social media such as blogs, online communities, forums and social networks, has changed the framework of the web [8], by allowing user interaction and sharing.

With the help of social commerce, vendors can reach different markets by incorporating the social interactions of consumers [9]. Web-based associations give an option to organizations to build effective connection with their customers [10]. These will create positive value for consumers and will help vendors refine their marketing strategies [11].

In contrast to shopping in physical stores, online interaction does not give a consumer the chance of having direct human contact [12], and has lead to an automated, unknown and neutral relationship between vendor and consumer [13]. However, with the wide-spread use of social media technologies, and its incorporation in the social commerce medium, this neutral relationship is shifting, and there is a more dynamic relationship between the consumer and vendor.

The intention of this literature review is to examine some factors that influence the purchasing behaviour of consumers on social commerce platform.

2.2 Social Presence (SP)

Social presence is an important notion in social media and social commerce infrastructure. Social presence is known as interacting and socializing inside a website. To be specific, social presence is "the extent to which a medium allows users to experience others as psychologically present" [14, p. 2]. The notion of social presence is found in the social presence theory that clarifies the capability of a communication method to transfer social signs [15]. A media is considered likeable if it allows human dealings, friendliness, and reactivity [14]. Customer reviews and recommendations provide electronic vendors a way to have a personalized relationship with the customers, that is the underlying framework of social presence [16]. Good features of social commerce websites strengthen the perception of social presence, such as images and recommendations, etc. Naylor et al. [17] showed that the Like feature of Facebook helps to strengthen the customers brand opinion and purchase intentions. Gefen and Straub [12] suggest that pictures and text can convey personal presence in the same manner as do personal photographs or letters. Hassanein and Head [14] showed emotive text and pictures of humans as resulting in higher perceptions of social presence within websites.

Since human interaction is viewed as a precondition of trust [18] the buyer's web interactions should also contribute to the building of trust online. A website with high social presence conveys more information and social cues and is perceived to be more transparent [19], which may lead to feelings of trust.

Hypothesis 1: Social Presence has a positive influence on Trust when consumers are intending to purchase online.

2.3 Security Perception (SEP)

Security is a very important consideration in online shopping and has been cited as one of the main concerns consumers require in their decision to pursue online purchases [20–25]. Security perception can be defined as the extent to which a person trusts that the online vendor or website is secure. Transfer of important information like credit card details is considered of significant value.

Because of the many risks involved with security over the internet, online vendors are taking measures to safeguard the data of their customers. Common online security concerns involve the security of credit cards, third-party services, and online privacy [26] and [27]. It is mentioned by Furnell [28] that showing policy statements and presenting a third-party seal like Verisign in the website are important factors to make consumers feel safe to perform a transaction. Because of the many risks involved with security over the internet, online vendors are taking measures to safeguard the data of their customers. These mechanisms help vendors gain the trust of their customers resulting in positive intentions to purchase.

If customer feels a sense of security with the safety procedure put in place, then it will likely impact their perceptions of trust, which ultimately affect their intention to purchase. Thus, it leads to the following hypothesis:

Hypothesis 2: Security Perception has a positive influence on Trust when consumers are intending to purchase online.

2.4 Perceived Internet Privacy Risk (PIPR)

An individual's perceived internet privacy refers to their beliefs about whether or not there is a risk of disclosure of their private information which they input over the Internet. [29]. These risks show the degree to which individuals believe they might lose their privacy. Privacy has been studied by researchers in a wide range of disciplines

[30] although research on internet privacy has only surfaced in the last few years. Privacy risk could include leakage or misuse of personal information [31, 32]. Privacy concerns influence the readiness of providing personal information to transact on the Internet. A lot of consumers are reluctant to shop online due to privacy and personal information submission concerns [33]. To overcome this fear of consumers, online business is taking steps to safeguard user's private information. However, if individuals feel that there are not enough online safeguards to ensure privacy of their personal information, this can have a negative impact on their development of trusting beliefs in the vendor. This leads to the following hypothesis:

Hypothesis 3: Perceived Internet Privacy Risk has a negative influence on Trust when consumers are intending to purchase online.

2.5 Willingness to Provide Personal Information to Transact (WPPIT)

An individual's willingness to provide personal information to transact describes one's "willingness to provide personal information required to complete transactions on the Internet" [29, p. 219]. This construct differs from an individual's perceived internet privacy risk (PIPR) which refers to "Concerns about opportunistic behavior related to the personal information submitted over the Internet by the respondent" [29, p. 219]. One's willingness to provide personal information to transact suggests the extent to which an individual is likely to trust another party enough to provide them with personal information that can result in a transaction over the internet. In this sense, trust may play an important role in developing such a willingness. Culnan and Armstrong [34] found aid for the idea that users would be more willing to provide information if they knew who will have access to it and how it will be used. This leads to the following two hypotheses:

Hypothesis 4: Willingness to Provide Personal Information to Transact has a positive influence on Trust when consumers are intending to purchase online.

Hypothesis 5: Willingness to Provide Personal Information to Transact has a positive influence on consumer purchase intention.

2.6 Trust (T)

Trust is a construct in e-commerce [35, 36] and social commerce [38–41]. Hart and Saunders [42] have defined trust as the confidence that another party will behave as expected, combined with expectations of the other party's good will. Zucker [43] has defined trust as a set of shared social expectations that are essential for and determine social behavior, enabling individuals to respond to each other without the explicit specification of contractual details. As several definitions of trust have been proposed [44], we adopt the view that trust is about the consumer's belief that sellers will keeps their promises based on user generated feedback posted on the social networking sites (SNSs) (e.g. Facebook, WhatsApp, Yahoo) page regarding the quality of business offerings. Several factors influence customers intention to purchase from e-vendors, among these factors trust is found to positively influence customer retention [20, 45, 46]. If customers have less trust in an online business, they will be less inclined to engage in transactions on the web [47–49].

Online trust has multiple dimensions and is a major factor in an online purchase. Researchers have indicated that trust plays a role as mediator between website design details and intention to purchase [50, 51]. Given the context of social commerce, uncertainty is usually higher due to the high level of user-generated content and the lack of face-to-face interactions [41]. With the help of social commerce and the development of Web 2.0, trust can be increased, thereby reducing customers' fear of online purchase. Web 2.0 has different applications like ratings, recommendations and review, which can be a helpful solution to increase trust. The greater the trust in the online vendor, the greater the purchase intention.

Hypothesis 6: Trust has a positive, significant influence on purchase intention.

2.7   Purchase Intention (PI)

Purchase intentions in social commerce contexts refer to the customers' intentions to engage in online purchases from e-vendors on social networking sites (SNSs) like (Facebook, WhatsApp, Yahoo). Intentions are the determinants of behaviour and defined as "the strength of one's intentions to perform a specific behaviour" ([52, p. 288]. Purchase intention is the result of various factors that influence the online shopping customer. Jarvenpaa et al. [53] have discussed that a customer will buy more from the online marketplace if the business is capable to win the trust of the customer.

3   Theoretical Foundation and Research Model

3.1   Stimulus Organism Response (SOR)

The study of purchase intention, which has a direct link to consumer behaviour, has grown over the last two decades, from the traditional store shopping to the present internet-based ones. Despite the changes, the fundamental aspects have remained, and researchers have adapted the SOR model to study different industrial sectors and business types. Based on the literature review, a conceptual model was developed on the stimulus-organism-response framework to guide this research. Since [5] suggested that environmental stimuli (S) lead to an emotional reaction (O) that evokes behavioral responses (R), the model has been applied in various retail settings to explain the consumer decision making process [54, 55]. As online retailing has grown [56], researchers have begun to focus on various aspects of this new medium using the S-O-R framework [57]. Past researchers have used Stimulus Organism Response (S-O-R), to examine the direct and indirect effects of retail environmental characteristics on impulse buying behavior [58].

In the context of this study, the stimuli include the various elements in the social commerce platform that indicate the presence of others (social presence) [14, 36, 59–61] as well as the elements that induce perceptions of security [38, 39] and those that help indicate perceptions of privacy risk and willingness to provide personal information to transact [38, 40]. The organism in the context of this study is the trusting belief in the online vendor. Morgan and Hunt [62] disclosed that trust is an important factor in the success of the social organization. This can be extrapolated to social commerce, to suggest that trust forms an important component of success in the viability of the social commerce platform. Research suggests that trust plays a central role in influencing consumer decisions through both e-commerce [35–37] and social commerce [61, 63–65]. The response in this study refers to the outcomes that individuals will receive once they experience stimuli in the social commerce platform: their emotional state of forming trusting beliefs is aroused and, the response is their purchase intention (Fig. 1).

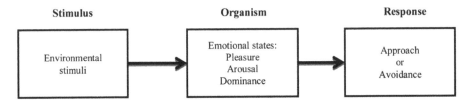

Fig. 1. S-O-R framework. Source: Mehrabian and Russell (1974).

3.2   Research Model

The research model is shown in Fig. 2.

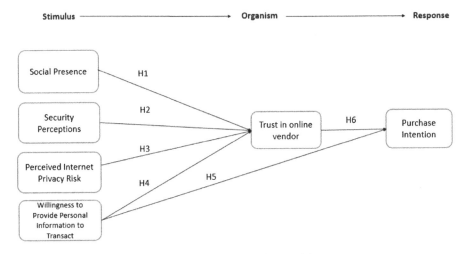

Fig. 2. Proposed research model.

4   Methodology

4.1   Survey

The methodology is deductive. A questionnaire was used to collect data to validate the research model using a specialized software tool [66]. A seven-point Likert scale was used to measure each item, and all scales were adapted from the extant literature to ensure content validity.

Participants were asked about their opinions and judgements concerning the following five variables: social presence, security perception, perceived internet privacy risk, willingness to provide personal information to transact and trust.

The survey was user-friendly and, with the help of the Qualtrics software, some built-in attention filters were added to the survey, where participants had to answer a question with a very specific answer. The questionnaire was distributed through the Student Research Pool (SRP) to a convenient sample of undergraduate students at Ryerson University in Toronto, Canada.

4.2 Analysis

Partial Least Squares has been chosen as the statistical tool because of its ability to simultaneously evaluate both the measurement and structural model, allowing for rigorous analysis [67]. The specific tool was SmartPLS [68]. PLS has the advantage that it can model latent constructs that do not conform to the conditions of normality, and it can handle small to medium sample sizes [69]. It has recently been enhanced to include moderator analysis and heterotrait-monotrait (HTMT) ratio of correlations for discriminant analysis [68].

Initial analysis consisted of obtaining the maximum, minimum mean, median, and standard deviation for the research variables of social presence, security perception, perceived internet privacy risk, willingness to provide personal information to transact, perceived usefulness, trust and purchase intention. Cronbach's alpha (reliability coefficient) was used to measure the internal consistency and reliability of the dataset obtained from the questionnaires [42]. The Fornell-Larcker table and heterotrait-monotrait (HTMT) ratio of correlations were used to Lastly, we calculated the path coefficients and their significance.carry out discriminant validity.

5 Results

5.1 Descriptive Statistics

594 completed questionnaires were returned. After eliminating unfilled, partially filled and those which failed the attention filters, 245 valid responses were included in the analysis, which is a completion rate of 41.3%. The survey participants were 30% (n = 73) male and 70% (n = 172) female. See Table 1.

Table 1. Descriptive statistics of sample.

Gender	Number (n)	Percent (%)
Male:	73	30%
Female:	172	70%
Total:	245	100

5.2 Measurement Model

The measurement model, or outer model, represents the relationship between constructs and their corresponding indicator variables [70]. The values in Table 2 are measuring each indicator's impact on the allocated variable construct [70]. The correlation coefficients were greater than 0.724 [71] for the majority of the indicators. See Table 2. However, we dropped Social Presence (SP) from the model because of its non-converging indicators.

Table 2. Outer Loadings.

Indicators	Perceived internet privacy risk	Purchase intention	Security perception	Trust	Willingness to provide personal information to transact
PIPR-1	0.866				
PIPR-2	0.836				
PIPR-3	0.943				
PI-1		0.899			
PI-2		0.74			
PI-3		0.812			
SEP-1			0.869		
SEP-2			0.819		
SEP-3			0.871		
T-1				0.832	
T-2				0.921	
T-3				0.83	
WPPIT-1					0.886
WPPIT-2					0.724
WPPIT-3					0.897

The reliability and validity of the constructs were tested by calculating Cronbach's alpha, composite reliability and average variance extracted. Cronbach's alpha was greater than 0.7 [72], where Cronbach's alpha 0.724 or higher is considered acceptable in most research studies and is considered to be reliable [73]. The composite reliability was greater than 0.7, for composite reliability, where a value greater than 0.70 is considered adequate in exploratory research [70]. The average variance extracted was greater than 0.5 [68]). See Table 3.

The Heterotrait - Monotrait Ratio (HTMT) criterion is a new approach to assess discriminant validity and is considered superior to the other approaches such as Fornell-Larcker criterion and (partial) cross-loadings [70]. The HTMT should be less than 1 [70]. See Table 4. All values are less than 1, which supports the discriminant validity among the constructs. The PLS algorithm was run to calculate the Fornell-Larcker criterion from the cross loadings to assess the discriminant validity. Based on the Fornell-Larcker criterion, the AVE square root of every construct should be more than the highest correlation construct with any other in the model [74]. See Table 5.

Table 3. Construct reliability and validity.

Latent Variables	Cronbach's Alpha	Composite Reliability	Average Variance Extracted (AVE)
Perceived Internet Privacy Risk (PIPR)	0.87	0.913	0.779
Purchase Intention (PI)	0.785	0.859	0.672
Security perception (SEP)	0.818	0.889	0.728
Trust (T)	0.828	0.896	0.743
Willingness to provide personal Information to transact (WPPIT)	0.791	0.876	0.704

Table 4. Heterotrait - Monotrait Ratio (HTMT) value.

Latent variables	Perceived internet privacy risk	Purchase intention	Security perception	Trust	Willingness to provide personal information to transact
Perceived Internet Privacy Risk					
Purchase Intention	0.133				
Security perception	0.134	0.472			
Trust	0.057	0.407	0.431		
Willingness to provide personal Information to transact	0.12	0.389	0.525	0.598	

Table 5. Fornell-Larcker Scores.

Latent variables	Perceived internet privacy risk	Purchase intention	Security perception	Trust	Willingness to provide personal information to transact
Perceived internet privacy risk	0.883				
Purchase intention	−0.095	0.82			
Security perception	−0.116	0.38	0.853		
Trust	0.042	0.355	0.369	0.862	
Willingness to provide personal information to transact	0.081	0.349	0.431	0.493	0.839

5.3   Structural Model

The coefficient of determination, denoted as R^2, is the most commonly used measurement to evaluate the strength of the relationships in the structural model [70]. The R^2 value ranges between 0 and 1, and it represents how closely the model with the independent variables explains the variation of the dependent variable. The higher levels indicate that more of the variance is due to the independent variables [70]. In our research model, "purchase intention" has a $R^2 = 0.165$, which is not in the moderate range from 0.5 to 0.75 [75]. However, according to [76] suggested R^2 values for endogenous latent variables are assessed as follows: 0.26 (substantial), 0.13 (moderate), 0.02 (weak). Joseph et al. [71] addressed the difficulty of providing rules of thumb for acceptable R^2 as it is reliant upon the model complexity and the research discipline. While R^2 values of 0.20 are deemed as high in disciplines such as consumer behavior, R^2 values of 0.75 would be perceived as high in success driver studies (e.g., in studies that aim at explaining customer satisfaction or loyalty).

Significance was determined by running the bootstrapping calculations with 5000 samples and no sign change. Four paths were significant. Table 6 shows security perception to trust is significantly and positively correlated. t-values greater than 1.96 represent a significance with probability of 95% that the hypothesis is true.

Table 6. Summary of results

Number	Hypothesis	Path coefficient	T statistics	P values	Supported
H1	Social Presence - > Trust	Not tested because Social Presence was dropped due to indicators not converging			Dropped
H2	Security Perception - > Trust	0.065	3.037	0.002 **	✓
H3	Perceived Internet Privacy Risk - > Trust	0.086	0.379	0.704	X
H4	Willingness to Provide Personal Information to Transact - > Trust	0.059	6.847	0 ***	✓
H5	Willingness to Provide Personal Information to Transact - > Purchase Intention	0.076	3.014	0.003 **	✓
H6	Trust - > Purchase Intention	0.103	2.349	0.019 *	✓

*** $p < 0.001$; ** $p < 0.01$: $p < 0.05$

6 Discussion

This study investigated the influence of social presence, trust, security perception, perceived internet privacy risk and willingness to provide personal information on consumers' intention to purchase via a social commerce platform. The data illustrates which of the five elements have influence on consumers purchase intention. Four hypotheses are supported, while one hypothesis was rejected at the significance level of $p < 0.05$ (indicated by $t > 1.96$) (Table 6).

Dropped - Hypothesis 1: Social Presence has a positive influence on Trust when consumers are intending to purchase online.

As online purchasing does not give consumer's the opportunity to interact face to face with the vendor, it is important for the social commerce websites to strengthen the perception of social presence, by incorporating good features such as images and recommendations, etc. Naylor et al. [17] showed that the Like feature of Facebook helps to strengthen brand opinion and purchase intentions. Unfortunately, when empirically testing the model, it was determined that social presence was not measured well as its indicators did not converge even though they were based on the extant literature [36, 37]. We therefore eliminated social presence from the model. One reason for the non-converging indicators of social presence may be because the data was collected via an online questionnaire which lacks realism, and the sample of students were not able to visualize the possible personal relationship with the website defined in the questionnaire. Future research should further investigate the indicators so that social presence can be measured with valid scales.

Supported - Hypothesis 2: Security Perception has a positive influence on Trust when consumers are intending to purchase online.

Because many users feel that the Internet is not a safe environment for online shopping, online websites must put in place security measures to protect customers' data. Transfer of important information like credit card details is considered of significant value [77]. As previously noted, Furnell [28] mentioned that a third-party seal like Verisign on the website is an important factor in the perception of security from the consumer's viewpoint. When customers feel a sense of security with the safety procedures put in place by the online vendor, they will be more inclined to make a purchase.

Not Supported - Hypothesis 3: Perceived Internet Privacy Risk has a negative influence on Trust when consumers are intending to purchase online.

Privacy risk over the internet could include leakage or misuse of personal information, such as insider revelation or forbidden access [31]. Despite the many risks involved with disclosing personal information over the internet, online vendors are taking measures to safeguard the data of their consumers. However, this hypothesis was not supported. This may be because in the context of this study the sample of university students do not consider privacy risk over the internet to be an issue. They are already sharing personal information via social media and, from the results of this study, are not concerned about the risk to their privacy.

Supported - Hypothesis 4: Willingness to Provide Personal Information to Transact has a positive influence on Trust when consumers are intending to purchase online.

Supported - Hypothesis 5: Willingness to Provide Personal Information to Transact has a positive influence on consumer purchase intention.

Some individuals have a greater propensity to share personal information. They may not care about their data being shared or they may believe that the websites provide sufficient security. Our results show that individuals who are willing to share are more ready to place their trust in the website and they are more ready to purchase online. Again, this may be a reflection of the sample of students, who tend to pay less attention to privacy concerns.

Supported - Hypothesis 6: Trust has a positive, significant influence on purchase intention.

Trust is an important element in the context of online purchasing. If customers have trust in an online business, they will engage in transactions on the web [47–49]. The greater the trust in the online vendor the greater the purchase intention. Our results show that security perception, willingness to provide personal information to transact and trust has a positive influence on purchase intention.

6.1 Theoretical Contributions

This research study has proposed and empirically validated a research model that evaluates the factors that influence an individual's intention to purchase in the context of social commerce. This study draws on the stimulus-organism-response (SOR) framework [5] as a theoretical guide to map the antecedents involved in influencing a consumer's purchasing intention. SOR posits that stimuli (stimulus) in an individual's environment can work through various internal processes within the individual (organism) to elicit an outward reaction (response). This research sought to examine whether social presence and security elements in the social commerce platform (stimulus) can impact a consumer's trust in the platform (organism) and how this in turn impacts his/her intent to engage in a purchase through that platform (response).

The final research model indicates that security elements inherent within the social commerce platform do indeed impact consumers' trust in the platform and their privacy perceptions, and that these go on to impact a consumer's purchasing intention.

There are multiple theoretical contributions of this study. The first contribution is that the SOR model has been applied to the newer context of social commerce to map the factors impacting a consumer's purchasing intention. As social commerce is a new mode of online shopping, research in this area is only just emerging. As such, this study bridges this gap in the literature by identifying security elements as important aspects of the social commerce interface that work through trust and privacy perceptions to influence a consumer's intent to purchase through the medium. Although purchase intentions of consumers have been studied within the broader e-commerce context [37], we examine this within the social commerce context.

6.2   Implications for Practice

This study makes important practical contributions. Vendors should make their online business platform sociably attractive through rich content. Good features of social commerce websites strengthen the perception of social presence, such as images and recommendations, etc. Vendors should also include security elements to improve sales within the social commerce context. Security elements provide a sense of safety when transacting online, and, as suggested by this study, they can lead to greater trust in the platform as well as decrease perceptions of privacy risk.

Trust is an important construct that besides encouraging one's initial purchase intention, can also lead to recurring and repeat purchases [39]. Thus, if a platform can encourage and build trust, it can lead not only to initial purchase intention, but may facilitate future purchases. Furthermore, privacy is an important topic today, with attention given to the importance of protecting privacy online [78]. If a social commerce platform, through highlighting security elements within its interface, can enhance privacy perceptions, this in turn can translate to more confident consumers that are willing to engage in transactions through the platform.

6.3   Limitations and Future Research

This study utilized a convenience sample of undergraduate university students obtained through the Student Research Pool (SRP) at Ryerson University. This is a limitation because this sample does not represent the general population. Furthermore, this subset is more likely to consist of proficient internet users who may be more trusting and less likely to be concerned about loss of privacy. As such, for this specialized subset of the population, even limited security perceptions may bolster a stronger trusting intention in the platform, and stronger perceptions of privacy, leading to more of a willingness to provide information and then to purchase online. Future studies may find it useful to test this model against a more generalized population. Convenience samples have, however, been utilized in numerous research studies, and although this is a limitation, it is still an acceptable method of sampling [79]. Another limitation is that this study used a questionnaire, and questionnaires are sometimes lacking in realism, especially when examining a consumer's intent to purchase. Assessing an individual's purchase intention through a questionnaire may not necessarily reflect whether the individual is in fact likely to engage in the actual transaction. Future studies may attempt to incorporate an experimental procedure, or a natural experiment developed in a manner that incorporates mundane realism.

Finally, this study utilized a more positivist approach in addressing its research questions. The study's findings could be further strengthened by including a qualitative component to aid in triangulation of the results. The qualitative component could be in the form of open-ended questions aimed at better understanding the perceptions of the participants regarding underlying factors motivating their purchase intention through the social commerce medium.

Future research can further examine this model in different countries. For example, what factors influence purchase intention on social commerce platforms amongst Chinese consumers vs. Canadians, or Pakistani consumers vs. Canadians. Furthermore, understanding personality traits and their influence on purchase intention in social commerce may also provide valuable insight. This study looked at purchase intention in social commerce; it may also be interesting to see how these same factors influence impulse purchasing within the social commerce context.

Further research can be conducted to critically review and investigate the construct of social presence as it was dropped due to its non-convergent indicators.

7 Conclusion

This research study provides a deeper understanding of consumer purchase behaviour in the online social commerce context. As social commerce is a newer mode of online shopping, with researchers regarding it as a subset of e-commerce, research in this area is only just emerging. Because of the rapid uptake of social commerce usage by consumers, there is a pressing need for scholarly contributions to this developing field. This study provides one such contribution, by tracing the factors involved in influencing a consumer's purchase intent through this medium. This research highlights that security elements inherent in the platform (those that allow a consumer to feel secure about his/her transaction) can lead to trust formation and the development of privacy perceptions, and that these in turn can influence a consumer's willingness to provide personal information regarding a transaction, ultimately influencing his/her purchase intention. By developing this research model, which is grounded in the stimulus-organism-response framework, this study provides a novel theoretical contribution. It also provides a practical contribution by allowing vendors to understand the elements of the social commerce interface that motivate a consumer's purchase behaviour through their platform.

References

1. Global Ecommerce: Statistics and International Growth Trends [Infographic] (n.d.). https://www.shopify.com/enterprise/global-ecommerce-statistics. Accessed 23 Apr 2018
2. Hajli, N., Lin, X., Featherman, M., Wang, Y.: Social word of mouth: how trust develops in the market. Int. J. Mark. Res. 56(5), 673–689 (2014)
3. Zhang, K.Z., Benyoucef, M.: Consumer behavior in social commerce: A literature review. Decis. Support Syst. 86, 95–108 (2016)
4. Hajli, M.N.: The role of social support on relationship quality and social commerce. Technol. Forecast. Soc. Change 87, 17–27 (2014)
5. Mehrabian, A., Russell, J.A.: The basic emotional impact of environments. Percept. Mot. Skills 38(1), 283–301 (1974)
6. Nazir, S., Tayyab, A., Sajid, A., ur Rashid, H., Javed, I.: How online shopping is affecting consumers buying behavior in Pakistan? Int. J. Comput. Sci. Issues (IJCSI) 9(3), 486 (2012)
7. Munawar, M., Hassanein, K., Head, M.: Understanding the Role of Herd Behaviour and Homophily in Social Commerce (2017)
8. Lai, L.S., Turban, E.: Groups formation and operations in the Web 2.0 environment and social networks. Group Decis. Negot. 17(5), 387–402 (2008)

9. Hargadon, A.B., Bechky, B.A.: When collections of creatives become creative collectives: a field study of problem solving at work. Organ. Sci. **17**(4), 484–500 (2006)
10. Ridings, C.M., Gefen, D.: Virtual community attraction: why people hang out online. J. Comput.-Mediated Commun. **10**(1), JCMC10110 (2004)
11. Liang, T.-P., Turban, E.: Introduction to the special issue social commerce: a research framework for social commerce. Int. J. Electron. Commer. **16**(2), 5–14 (2011)
12. Gefen, D., Straub, D.: Managing user trust in B2C e-services. E-Service **2**(2), 7–24 (2003)
13. Wang, Y.D., Emurian, H.H.: An overview of online trust: concepts, elements, and implications. Comput. Hum. Behav. **21**(1), 105–125 (2005)
14. Hassanein, K., Head, M.: The impact of infusing social presence in the web interface: an investigation across product types. Int. J. Electron. Commer. **10**(2), 31–55 (2005)
15. Short, J., Williams, E., Christie, B.: The social psychology of telecommunications (1976)
16. Piller, F.T., Walcher, D.: Toolkits for idea competitions: a novel method to integrate users in new product development. R&d Manag. **36**(3), 307–318 (2006)
17. Naylor, R.W., Lamberton, C.P., West, P.M.: Beyond the "like" button: The impact of mere virtual presence on brand evaluations and purchase intentions in social media settings. J. Market. **76**(6), 105–120 (2012)
18. Blau, P.M.: Exchange and Power in Social Life. Wiley, New York (1964)
19. Kim, J., Lennon, S.J.: Effects of reputation and website quality on online consumers' emotion, perceived risk and purchase intention: Based on the stimulus-organism-response model. J. Res. Interact. Market. **7**(1), 33–56 (2013)
20. Flavián, C., Guinalíu, M.: Consumer trust, perceived security and privacy policy: three basic elements of loyalty to a web site. Ind. Manag. Data Syst. **106**(5), 601–620 (2006)
21. Hsin Chang, H., Wen Chen, S.: The impact of online store environment cues on purchase intention: trust and perceived risk as a mediator. Online Inf. Rev. **32**(6), 818–841 (2008)
22. Tariq, A.N., Eddaoudi, B.: Assessing the effect of trust and security factors on consumers' willingness for online shopping among the urban Moroccans. Int. J. Bus. Manag. Sci. **2**(1), 17 (2009)
23. Belanger, F., Hiller, J.S., Smith, W.J.: Trustworthiness in electronic commerce: the role of privacy, security, and site attributes. J. Strateg. Inf. Syst. **11**(3–4), 245–270 (2002)
24. Park, C.-H., Kim, Y.-G.: A framework of dynamic CRM: linking marketing with information strategy. Bus. Process Manag. J. **9**(5), 652–671 (2003)
25. Delafrooz, N., Paim, L.H., Khatibi, A.: Understanding consumers internet purchase intention in Malaysia. Afr. J. Bus. Manage. **5**(7), 2837–2846 (2011)
26. Pavlou, P.A., Gefen, D.: Building effective online marketplaces with institution-based trust. Inf. Syst. Res. **15**(1), 37–59 (2004)
27. Furnell, S.: E-commerce security: a question of trust. Comput. Fraud Secur. **2004**(10), 10–14 (2004)
28. Dinev, T., Hart, P., Mullen, M.R.: Internet privacy concerns and beliefs about government surveillance–An empirical investigation. J. Strateg. Inf. Syst. **17**(3), 214–233 (2008)
29. Margulis, S.T.: Privacy as a social issue and behavioral concept. J. Soc. Issues **59**(2), 243–261 (2003)
30. Berkowitz, J., O'Brien, J.: How accurate are value-at-risk models at commercial banks? J. Finance **57**(3), 1093–1111 (2002)
31. Rindfleisch, T.C.: Privacy, information technology, and health care. Commun. ACM **40**(8), 92–100 (1997)
32. Policy, U. C. for C.: The UCLA Internet Report, Surveying the Digital Future. UCLA Center for Communication Policy (2003)
33. Culnan, M.J., Armstrong, P.K.: Information privacy concerns, procedural fairness, and impersonal trust: an empirical investigation. Organ. Sci. **10**(1), 104–115 (1999)

34. Hart, P., Saunders, C.: Power and trust: critical factors in the adoption and use of electronic data interchange. Organ. Sci. **8**(1), 23–42 (1997)

35. McKnight, D.H., Choudhury, V., Kacmar, C.: Developing and validating trust measures for e-commerce: an integrative typology. Inf. Syst. Res. **13**(3), 334–359 (2002)

36. Gefen, D., Straub, D.W.: Consumer trust in B2C e-Commerce and the importance of social presence: experiments in e-Products and e-services. Omega **32**(6), 407–424 (2004)

37. Gefen, D.: E-commerce: the role of familiarity and trust. Omega **28**(6), 725–737 (2000)

38. Hajli, N., Lin, X.: Exploring the security of information sharing on social networking sites: the role of perceived control of information. J. Bus. Ethics **133**(1), 111–123 (2016)

39. Fang, Y., Qureshi, I., Sun, H., McCole, P., Ramsey, E., Lim, K.H.: Trust, satisfaction, and online repurchase intention: the moderating role of perceived effectiveness of e-commerce institutional mechanisms. Mis Q. 38(2) (2014)

40. Dinev, T., Hart, P.: An extended privacy calculus model for e-commerce transactions. Inf. Syst. Res. **17**(1), 61–80 (2006)

41. Featherman, M.S., Hajli, N.: Self-service technologies and e-services risks in social commerce era. J. Bus. Ethics **139**(2), 251–269 (2016)

42. Saunders, M.N.K., Lewis, P., Thornhill, A.: Res. Meth. Bus. Stud., 6th edn. Prentice Hall, Harlow (2013)

43. Zucker, L.G.: Production of trust: Institutional sources of economic structure, 1840–1920. Res. Organ. Behav. **8** (1986)

44. McKnight, D.H., Chervany, N.L.: What trust means in e-commerce customer relationships: an interdisciplinary conceptual typology. Int. J. Electron. Commer. **6**(2), 35–59 (2001)

45. Gefen, D.: Reflections on the dimensions of trust and trustworthiness among online consumers. ACM SIGMIS Database: DATABASE Adv. Inf. Syst. **33**(3), 38–53 (2002)

46. Qureshi, I., Fang, Y., Ramsey, E., McCole, P., Ibbotson, P., Compeau, D.: Understanding online customer repurchasing intention and the mediating role of trust–an empirical investigation in two developed countries. Eur. J. Inf. Syst. **18**(3), 205–222 (2009)

47. Hoffman, D.L., Novak, T.P., Peralta, M.: Building consumer trust online. Commun. ACM **42**(4), 80–85 (1999)

48. Lee, M.K., Turban, E.: A trust model for consumer internet shopping. Int. J. Electron. Commer. **6**(1), 75–91 (2001)

49. Pavlou, P.A.: Consumer acceptance of electronic commerce: integrating trust and risk with the technology acceptance model. Int. J. Electron. Commer. **7**(3), 101–134 (2003)

50. Bart, Y., Shankar, V., Sultan, F., Urban, G.L.: Are the drivers and role of online trust the same for all web sites and consumers? A large-scale exploratory empirical study. J. Market. **69**(4), 133–152 (2005)

51. Dash, S.B., Saji, K.B.: Role of effective website-design in online shopping: a large scale empirical study in the Indian context. In: NASMEI International conference on 'Marketing in the new global order' Dec, pp. 18–20 (2006)

52. Fishbein, M., Ajzen, I.: Belief, attitude, intention and behavior: an introduction to theory and research (1975)

53. Jarvenpaa, S.L., Tractinsky, N., Saarinen, L.: Consumer trust in an Internet store: a cross-cultural validation. J. Comput.-Mediated Commun. **5**(2), JCMC526 (1999)

54. Chebat, J.-C., Michon, R.: Impact of ambient odors on mall shoppers' emotions, cognition, and spending: a test of competitive causal theories. J. Bus. Res. **56**(7), 529–539 (2003)

55. Richard, M.-O., Chebat, J.-C., Yang, Z., Putrevu, S.: A proposed model of online consumer behavior: assessing the role of gender. J. Bus. Res. **63**(9–10), 926–934 (2010)

56. Mulpuru, S., Hult, P., Evans, P.F., Sehgal, V., McGowan, B.: US online retail forecast, 2009 to 2014. Forrester Res. (5) (2010)

57. Peng, C., Kim, Y.G.: Application of the stimuli-organism-response (SOR) framework to online shopping behavior. J. Internet Commer. **13**(3–4), 159–176 (2014)
58. Chang, H.-J., Eckman, M., Yan, R.-N.: Application of the Stimulus-Organism-Response model to the retail environment: the role of hedonic motivation in impulse buying behavior. Int. Rev. Retail, Distrib. Consum. Res. **21**(3), 233–249 (2011)
59. Cyr, D., Hassanein, K., Head, M., Ivanov, A.: The role of social presence in establishing loyalty in e-service environments. Interact. Comput. **19**(1), 43–56 (2007)
60. Hess, T.J., Fuller, M., Campbell, D.E.: Designing interfaces with social presence: Using vividness and extraversion to create social recommendation agents. J. Assoc. Inf. Syst. **10** (12), 1 (2009)
61. Lu, B., Fan, W., Zhou, M.: Social presence, trust, and social commerce purchase intention: an empirical research. Comput. Hum. Behav. **56**, 225–237 (2016)
62. Morgan, R.M., Hunt, S.D.: The commitment-trust theory of relationship marketing. J. Market. **58**, 20–38 (1994)
63. Kim, S., Park, H.: Effects of various characteristics of social commerce (s-commerce) on consumers' trust and trust performance. Int. J. Inf. Manage. **33**(2), 318–332 (2013)
64. Shin, D.-H.: User experience in social commerce: in friends we trust. Behav. Inf. Technol. **32**(1), 52–67 (2013)
65. Hajli, N.: Social commerce constructs and consumer's intention to buy. Int. J. Inf. Manage. **35**(2), 183–191 (2015)
66. Qualtrics. (2018). n.t. https://www.qualtrics.com/
67. Gefen, D., Straub, D., Boudreau, M.-C.: Structural equation modeling and regression: guidelines for research practice. Commun. Assoc. Inf. Syst. **4**(1), 7 (2000)
68. Henseler, J., Ringle, C.M., Sarstedt, M.: A new criterion for assessing discriminant validity in variance-based structural equation modeling. J. Acad. Mark. Sci. **43**(1), 115–135 (2015)
69. Chin, W.W., Marcolin, B.L., Newsted, P.R.: A partial least squares latent variable modeling approach for measuring interaction effects: results from a Monte Carlo simulation study and an electronic-mail emotion/adoption study. Inf. Syst. Res. **14**(2), 189–217 (2003)
70. Hair Jr., J.F., Hult, G.T.M., Ringle, C., Sarstedt, M.: A Primer on Partial Least Squares Structural Equation Modeling (PLS-SEM). Sage Publications (2016)
71. Hair, J.F., Ringle, C.M., Sarstedt, M.: Partial least squares structural equation modeling: rigorous applications, better results and higher acceptance (2013)
72. Cronbach, L.J., Meehl, P.E.: Construct validity in psychological tests. Psychol. Bull. **52**(4), 281 (1955)
73. Santos, J.R.A.: Cronbach's alpha: a tool for assessing the reliability of scales. J. Extension **37**(2), 1–5 (1999)
74. Fornell, C., Larcker, D.F.: Structural equation models with unobservable variables and measurement error: algebra and statistics. J. Market. Res. 382–388 (1981)
75. Hair, J.F., Ringle, C.M., Sarstedt, M.: PLS-SEM: Indeed a silver bullet. J. Market. Theory Pract. **19**(2), 139–152 (2011)
76. Cohen, J.: A power primer. Psychol. Bull. **112**(1), 155 (1992)
77. Salisbury, W.D., Pearson, R.A., Pearson, A.W., Miller, D.W.: Perceived security and World Wide Web purchase intention. Ind. Manag. Data Syst. **101**(4), 165–177 (2001)
78. Kokolakis, S.: Privacy attitudes and privacy behaviour: a review of current research on the privacy paradox phenomenon. Comput. Secur. **64**, 122–134 (2017)
79. Etikan, I., Musa, S.A., Alkassim, R.S.: Comparison of convenience sampling and purposive sampling. Am. J. Theor. Appl. Stat. **5**(1), 1–4 (2016)

The Effect of Internet Celebrity's Endorsement on Consumer Purchase Intention

Yi-Cheng Ku[✉], Yie-Fang Kao, and MingJiao Qin

Fu Jen Catholic University, New Taipei City 24205, Taiwan
ycku@mail.fju.edu.tw

Abstract. This study investigated the interactive endorsement effect of internet celebrities on the brand attitude, attitude toward advertising and purchase intention. A total of 466 valid questionnaires were collected to test the research model. The research results show that the source credibility and the sense of virtual community are positively related to the brand attitude and attitude toward advertising, which in turn affect the purchase intention. However, the effect of the content quality is not significant. In addition, the moderating effect of the degree of consumer expertise and involvement are not significant. According to the result of this study, the characters of an Internet celebrity is a paramount factor to an endorsement campaign.

Keywords: Internet celebrity · Endorsement · ELM model

1 Introduction

With the development of information technology, Internet has taken people's daily life beyond physical limitations. Internet allows them to have a quick access to information, learn whenever and wherever they want, interact with others, and share experiences online. This new phenomenon where people gain information from online social groups coined a new business model, known as Internet celebrity economy. It is a business chain that includes several elements, from Internet celebrities, social media platforms, e-commerce websites to advertising agencies. Internet celebrities conduct marketing campaign via social media and influence their fans' shopping decisions. Internet celebrities, known as "Wang Hong" in Chinese society, have become famous on social or live streaming media. Characteristics of Internet celebrities include a high number of followers, and the abilities to advance their Internet traffic to real cash. Most Internet celebrities show their brilliance, professional skills, or unique personality via social media to attract audiences' eyeballs and keep customers sticky. Throughout this innovative business chain, Internet celebrities are responsible for keeping the platform's network traffic busy and achieve their commercial goals via social media (Xu 2017).

One can categorize Internet celebrities in three different types, product sellers, content creators, and public figure. The first one finds its origin on Taobao, a leading online shopping site in China. Product sellers are good at maintaining a good interaction with followers and guiding them to online stores from a live streaming event. Content creators work on different channels to deliver visual contents, such as articles

F. F.-H. Nah and K. Siau (Eds.): HCII 2019, LNCS 11588, pp. 274–287, 2019.
https://doi.org/10.1007/978-3-030-22335-9_18

or video clips, to their followers. They make money from their fans by stealth advertising because Chinese audience does not favor display advertising. Also, one also sees certain controversial public figures enjoying their popularity on the Internet.

Zhang Dayi and Papi Jiang are two famous Internet celebrities in China. Zhang Dayi sells clothes and cosmetics on Taobao. She makes a considerable amount of revenues by posting pictures of herself wearing the clothes she sells. Since she is her own shop's only model, some of her followers became her loyal customers. Her annual income was reported as RMB300 million (US$46 m) in 2016 (Tsoi 2016). On the other hand, Papi Jiang, a fashionista, creates original content to attract fans. She posts satirical video clips on social media, such as Weibo and YouTube. In those video clips, Papi Jiang talks about her daily life, show business, hot issues and relationships in a sarcastic manner. She secured a joint investment of RMB12 million (around US$1.84 million). This piece of news surprised the audience and demonstrated that Internet celebrities have the abilities to advance their Internet traffic to real cash.

While China's Internet celebrity industry started developing rapidly in 2014, some western Internet celebrities have become key opinion leaders (KOL) in America and Europe. Youtube is an important Internet celebrity incubator. Content creators can earn money from advertisements found on their video clips and from YouTube Premium subscribers watching their content. Many famous YouTubers, such as PewDiePie, Germán Garmendia, and Jenna Marbles, have racked up millions of subscribers over the years through a direct relationship with their fans. Following Facebook and You-tube, Instagram (also known as IG) enhances the trend of Internet celebrity. Instagram provides photo and video-sharing social networking service and supports Internet celebrities to attract followers rapidly. For example, Selena Gomez, an actress, and singer, has more than 140 million followers, while Cristiano Ronaldo, one of the world's leading soccer players, has more than 150 million in January 2019[1]. Some Internet celebrities successfully established their brands on IG, and sell products effectively. Hence, with the developing of social media and mobile devices, social media stars are becoming more influential in the celebrity marketing. Furthermore, Platforms, MCN (multi-channel network) and Internet celebrity are working together to improve the efficiency and enlarge the size of Internet celebrity economy.

While the phenomenon of Internet celebrities continues to grow, what matters to business owners the most though, is whether Internet celebrity economy is taking effect? Past studies on celebrity endorsement mostly focused on experts or celebrities in the entertainment industry via conventional platforms, such as television, newspapers or magazines. Research from Amos et al. (2008) shows that the endorser's characters, such as his/her professional knowledge or physical attractiveness and so on, help achieve a better advertising result. As using Internet celebrities for product endorse-ments only started a few years ago, there have been very few analyses of the effect of interactive Internet celebrity's endorsement via social media platforms such as live-streaming, Facebook or Weibo. The few pieces of research on Internet celebrities focus mainly on how they manage their audience. Cocker and Cronin (2017) point out that Internet celebrities get their audiences' attention by sharing their daily activities, ideas

---

[1] https://www.statista.com/statistics/421169/most-followers-instagram/ (Retrieved Feb. 1, 2019).

or shopping experiences online, and interact with their followers. Marwick and Boyd (2011) think that Internet celebrities take contexts and their audiences into account, and maintain a process of managing impressions by presenting tailor-made performances. However, rare studies that explore how Internet celebrities influence consumers and their purchase intention.

The purpose of this study is to investigate the effect of the Internet celebrity's endorsement. As this newly-emerged advertising method has not been verified and campaign field not explored, whether the result will be the same as those from the past studies seems unknown at the moment. Against the backdrop as mentioned above, this study proposes three main objectives:

1. Explore the influence of the endorser's characters on the endorsement effect.
2. Analyze the influence of the consumer's characteristics on the endorsement effect of Internet celebrities.
3. Explore whether the interactive atmosphere created by Internet celebrities for the endorsed products influence the endorsement effect.

This paper consists of five sections. The first explains the motivation and objectives of the study. The second describes the theoretical foundation and the development of hypotheses. The third explains the design of the empirical study and the survey method by using questionnaires. The fourth tells the results of the analysis. The fifth are the conclusion and suggestions for future studies.

2   Theoretical Foundation and Hypotheses Development

2.1   Celebrity Endorsement in Social Media Marketing

Internet celebrities are individuals with a pronounced characters and charisma. Through multiple ways of presenting themselves, they disseminate messages quickly and gain attention from a large number of users. Their followers are netizens and fans of a certain type. Internet celebrities exercise a high capacity in disseminating information and influencing people in a specific domain or group. The author considers that Internet celebrities have the following pronounced characteristics: 1. They draw support from Internet platforms to become famous. 2. Each has a distinctive personality with features based on his/her physical appearance, expertise, such as creative writing, or knowledge in a particular area, such as fitness or beauty. 3. They continuously and routinely create content online. 4. They build a strong bonding with their fans and possess a strong interactive ability. 5. They have a large number of fans and fans tagging. 6. They exercise a high capacity in disseminating information and influencing people.

To generate revenues, Internet celebrities will become the endorser for a company or a particular product. An endorser is any public figure, such as an actor, an actress, an athlete, an entertainer or a political figure, who uses his/her popularity or personal achievement to recommend a product or a service to the public through any kind of format for a company or an organization (McCracken, 1989). As Internet celebrities have many fans, they have the advantage of becoming an endorser to promote a product or a service. Freiden (1984) categorizes endorsers as four types, the celebrity, the expert, CEO, and the typical consumer. According to an empirical study by Friedman and Friedman (1979), when a product involves in high financial, performance, and physical risks, using an expert will reach a better endorsement effect. When a product involves high psychological and social risks, using a celebrity will achieve a better endorsement effect. There is no evident difference between using a celebrity or an expert as an endorser when it comes to general consumption goods. From the statements above, one learns that different types of endorsers create different kinds of endorsement effect. Wang (2005) points out further that the appropriate use of endorsers will enhance the consumer's behavioral intention. It is evident that professional opinions provided by experts intensify the attitude toward an endorsed product. However, for a product that requires user's experience, viewers of the advertisement are prone to develop a sense of trust and better behavioral intention because they can identify themselves with typical consumers.

Different types of endorsers may have different endorsement effects. With the newly emerged Internet celebrity economy, their way of endorsing a product may influence the endorsement effect differently. However, in today's society, the roles of different types of endorsers tend to overlap, so their boundaries become vaguer and vaguer. As far as how Internet celebrities advance Internet traffic to real cash in China, there are several ways. 1. Product selling. Internet celebrities use Weibo windows to display products to their fans and direct them to e-commerce platforms, such as Taobao. 2. Marketing endorsement. Internet celebrities advertise for major brands on social platforms, such as Weibo or WeChat by placing advertising messages cleverly via different forms, such as in a blog article or a video clip. By doing so, they earn endorsement fees from sponsors. 3. Being a content producer. They make money by selling their content IP (intellectual property). An example is Zhang Jiajia. She initially became famous by telling bedtime stories on Weibo. Those stories later became a book under the title "I Belonged to You," which was later adapted to a script and then a film. Thus, Zhang also became a scriptwriter and a director. 4. Receiving tips from fans. Through interacting with fans on live streaming platforms, such as Douyu, Huajiao, Panda or Miaopai, Internet celebrities receive virtual gifts as tips from fans. 5. Becoming entertainers and participating in productions of online dramas, TV series or movies.

Through observations on various Internet celebrities' modes of endorsement, this study concluded that they are as the following. 1. Via social platforms such as online live streaming, Weibo or Facebook. 2. Independent creations of content, including online live streaming, video clips, images, and texts, to present products. 3. Stimulating fans' interests for the endorsed product by interacting with them. 4. Encouraging fans to forward so the content can go viral. 5. Redirecting to online stores by displaying a shopping link, or to a physical store. Table 1 summarizes comparisons of different endorsement methods between an Internet celebrity and a non-Internet celebrity.

2.2   Research Hypotheses

The process of Internet celebrities' endorsement is via interaction with netizens (or fans) on social media or other online platforms. Since digital media's content is presented as multi-media, the content by an Internet celebrity's endorsement can be

Table 1. A comparison chart of endorsement methods between an Internet celebrity and a non-Internet celebrity.

Endorser	Internet celebrities	Non-internet celebrities
Platform	Online social platforms, such as live streaming, Weibo or Facebook	All the media other than an online social platform, such as television, newspapers, and magazines etc.
Presentation methods	Different forms, such as images with texts, video clips, audio clips, and live streaming, appear alternately. Most of them are original or convey a sense of originality	Mainly by publishing the sponsor's advertising copies
Virtual social interaction	By interacting actively with fans and responding to their messages on a social platform, this creates an effect of collective interaction through a minimal one. By observing the interaction of a few and interactions among fans, a social group is established	Via fan convention or all kinds of off-line activities, very little online interaction is involved
Experience effects	Internet celebrities share their experiences of using the products and the product effects with their fans. By seeing their favorite Internet celebrities' product experiences, fans start having this sense of longingness and go through an experience of replacing the subject (the Internet celebrity) by themselves	Mainly by publishing messages concerning products
Trendy degree	Being at the frontline of Internet hotspots, and following closely social hotspots, topics, gossips, and news	Mainly focus on the sponsor's designated advertising strategy without taking the initiative to follow social hotspots
Methods of dissemination	By encouraging users on social media platforms to click, comment or share. The most common ways are by providing incentives, such as presents or cash, to encourage fans to follow, leave a comment or share so the messages can go viral	Mainly by television, newspapers, magazines or outdoor advertisements
Objectives of dissemination	Mainly to direct potential customers to online stores, usually by displaying a shopping link	Mainly to advertise the product and the brand

considered as a message, Internet celebrities themselves as message transmitters, and the party that interacts with them as message receivers. One can infer how the message of endorsement influences the message receiver's attitude, and furthermore his/her purchase intention by applying the Elaboration Likelihood Model (ELM; Petty and Cacioppo 1981). According to ELM, during the process of attitude change or formation, the message is more persuasive when the receiver holds a higher value toward its source. When the message's source credibility is low, consumers will have doubts about the message (Eagly and Chaiken 1993; Zhang and Buda 1999). When an endorser has higher credibility, the message receiver has a more positive understanding of messages in the advertisement, and attitudes toward the advertisement and brand.

While a message receiver deliberates the content, it is possible that receiver will go through in-depth thinking, analyze and evaluate the message content. This is called the central route. On the contrary, it will be called a peripheral route when a message receiver makes his/her judgment based simply on a positive or negative element of the message without in-depth analysis. Via which path a message receiver deliberates a message depends on his/her ability and motivation. When message receiver has better expertise or a higher motivation deciphering the content of a message, the central route will be taken. Otherwise, the message is deliberated via a peripheral route (Petty and Cacioppo 1981). As a result, the author proposes the following hypophyses:

H1: The message's source credibility will positively affect the consumer's brand attitude.

H1a: The consumer's expertise level moderates the association between source credibility and brand attitude.

H1b: The consumer's degree of product involvement moderates the association between source credibility and brand attitude.

H2: The message's source credibility will positively affect the consumer's attitude toward advertising.

H2a: The consumer's expertise level moderates the association between source credibility and attitude toward advertising.

H2b: The consumer's degree of product involvement moderates the association between source credibility and attitude toward advertising.

H3: The content quality will positively affect the consumer's brand attitude.

H3a: The consumer's expertise level moderates the association between content quality and brand attitude.

H3b: The consumer's degree of product involvement moderates the association between content quality and brand attitude.

H4: The content quality will positively influence the consumer's attitude toward advertising.

H4a: The consumer's expertise level moderates the association between content quality and attitude toward advertising.

H4b: The consumer's degree of product involvement moderates the association between content quality and attitude toward advertising.

Social media created an online virtual community in which social awareness is present, similar to the one found in a community's behaviors and process (Blanchard and Markus 2004; Forster 2004). To put this a more concrete way, this sense of virtual community (SOVC) is defined as feelings, identity, a sense of belongings or association, and attachment and association to a group of which members share the same interest or goal (Koh and Kim 2003), which involve four aspects, its members, influence, fulfillment of needs and emotional connection. Past studies that explored SOVC reveal a new discovery in the purchase intentions of live streaming room users. The identity, emotional connection and influence of the members during live streaming are all associated positively with the users' purchase intention. As a result, users are more willing to purchase virtual gifts on real-time media. This is because members have a sense of belongings, and consider themselves as part of the live streaming room. This recognition propels them to contribute, and take part in their "community" (Kim et al. 2004). Kim et al. (2009) also discovered that a higher SOVC might increase the members' purchase intention. As a result, we argue that a virtual community helps enhance its members' attitudes toward the brand and the advertising, and therefore has an influence on the purchase intention, and proposes the following hypotheses:

H5:   SOVC will positively affect the brand attitude.
H6:   SOVC will positively affect the attitude toward advertising.

According to Bauer (1960), consumers select products based on the brand's popularity or reputation. These two elements also serve as an assurance to reduce risks of the product they purchase. In consumers' decision-making behaviors, the purchase intention has a significant influence on the purchasing policy. The factors that lead consumers to be willing to purchase a product depend on consumers' belief, attitude, quality assessment and perceived value toward the product or the brand. Zeithaml (1988) proposes using the perceived value as a way to measure the purchase intention and uses maybe buying, desire to buy and considering to pay as variables for the item variables. Purchase intention arises from consumers' evaluation of the product or brand attitude, as well as action triggers that serve as extrinsic factors, such as advertising message.

Chaudhuri (1999) points out that the brand attitude will influence the decision maker's purchasing behavior. It may affect his/her loyalty to the brand. A positive brand attitude will lead the consumer to trust the brand even more and to think that there is a lower possibility of uncertainty when purchasing the product, thereby, increase the consumer's purchase intention. Good brand and attitude toward advertising make it easy to resonate in consumers and persuade them. Consumers, therefore, will have interests in the product and purchase it. As a result, this study proposes:

H7:   Brand attitude will positively affect the purchase intention.
H8:   Attitude toward advertising will positively affect the purchase intention.

Based on the process of a message communication and the consumer's experience in the virtual community, this study establishes a research framework (as shown in Fig. 1) from the influence created during the Internet celebrities' endorsement process, the content of the endorsement, and the SOVC created while interacting with fans, to how the process influences brand attitude and attitude toward advertising, and furthermore the consumer's purchase intention.

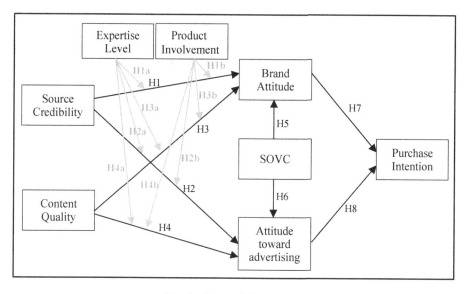

Fig. 1. Research framework

3   Research Method

3.1   Developing a Questionnaire

A questionnaire was developed for the survey used in this study. It is divided into four sections. The first section is a photo of the endorser to examine to what extent is the endorser familiar to the consumer, and his/her popularity among the fans. The second section is the demonstration of an actual case where an Internet celebrity endorsed for a product. The demonstration is presented via a video clip in which a simulated situation of the respondent experiences the whole process of a commercial clip on Weibo. The third section is to examine every question of the study's constructs. The fourth section is relevant questions of variables demographic statistics.

To control the effects of product types, we chose two types of products for the survey. One product is clothing (a consumer product), and the other is gaming (an entertainment product). In terms of selection of Internet celebrities, an e-commerce type and a gaming type were chosen respectively. The former mainly advertises and endorses her brand, and the latter for different game companies and other advertisements. Thus, there are two types of Internet celebrities and products respectively. Besides, the author also used a control group by adding a movie star as an endorser. The combination became four different kinds, an Internet celebrity and a movie star with a clothing product, and an Internet celebrity and a movie star with a gaming product respectively. By having four different combinations, one could avoid potential influence on the statistic results as a single endorser, or a single product would have.

In the construct measurement, this study used the three dimensions of an endorser's source credibility proposed by Ohanian (1991). They are attractiveness, expertise, and source credibility. 15 items are developed based on the message's source credibility, i.e. each dimension consists of five items. The quality of the content consists of five items (Zhang 1996). The consumer's expertise level is measured by three items (Sussman and Siegal 2003). The degree of the consumer's involvement is a revised version based on a measure designed by Laurent and Kapferer (1985), and five items were created for the study. In the construct for SOVC, we adapted the questions proposed by McMillan and Chavis (1986), Blanchard (2007) and Hsieh et al. (2018) to design items, including members, emotional connection, influence and fulfillment of needs. There are four second-order constructs, and each construct has three items for the evaluation. Furthermore, there are five, four and three items for measurements corresponding to brand attitude, attitude toward advertising, and purchase intention respectively. All items are based on Likert's five-point scale.

The survey was conducted online. The fill-in process is as the following. When a respondent opens the questionnaire, the respondent will first see a photo of an Internet celebrity endorser. The respondent gives a truthful answer as to whether he/she recognizes or knows about the endorser. Four questions were added and still used the Likert's five-point scale. The questions include:

1. I think the person in the photo is (endorser's name).
2. I think (endorser's name) is a famous Internet celebrity.
3. I am a fan of (endorser's name).
4. I usually visit the social media's account (Weibo or live streaming) of (endorser's name) to learn about her latest development.

After answering the above questions, a video clip will be shown to the respondent, who will see a simulated situation of he/she watches a presentation of an endorsement campaign, from an advertising copy, images or animation, netizens' comments to the content of discussions. After viewing the video clip, the respondent will carry on answering items in each construct and of variables concerning demographic statistics.

3.2 Survey Administration

As the development of Internet celebrities in China is phenomenal, and the scale of Internet celebrity economy considerable, this study chose China as the research scope to collect samples, and Internet celebrities on Sina Weibo as the objects of the study. There are three reasons for choosing Internet celebrities on Sina Weibo. Firstly, Sina Weibo had 392 million active users as of Feb 2017. It has vast and wide-range users. Secondly, most of Internet celebrities in China choose to set up a Sina Weibo account and run a social group from there. Thirdly, Sina Weibo works closely with major mobile phone makers and top mobile phone apps to build a complete ecosystem for its platform. As its sales campaigns and online content become more and more complementary to each other, Sina Weibo provides a robust platform for the development of Internet celebrity economy. An online questionnaire was used to collect data. The pilot run's sampling period was between March 15 and 24, 2018. 60 copies of valid pilot-run questionnaires were collected. After verifying the reliability and validity of all constructs, the result indicated that the items in the model constructed in this study proved to have good reliability and validity. A formal survey could be conducted.

This study used online questionnaires for data collection. The distribution period was between April 15 and May 20, 2018. 512 respondents were collected at the end of the survey. 466 copies were valid after removing questionnaires with foolproof questions being answered or careless responses. The valid answer rate is 91%. The gender ratio of valid samples is 36.3% male and 63.7% female. The main age distribution is between 26 to 30 years old (47%), and then 21 to 25 years old (37%). In terms of occupation, office workers are the majority (55.4%), and full-time students (37.1%) come in second. Most of the respondents (42.5%) spend daily an average of one to three hours online. When asked how frequently they took the initiative to follow an Internet celebrity, most of them (46.1%) answered they rarely followed.

4 Research Results

To test the study's framework and different hypotheses, this study used PLS method for analysis, and used the Multi-Group Analysis (MGA) from SmartPLS 3.0 to analyze the discriminant effect of endorsements by an Internet celebrity and a movie star.

4.1 Reliability and Validity

Firstly, a test was conducted on the reliability and validity of each item's construct. Reliability was tested by Cronbach's Alpha value and composite reliability, of which each construct is above 0.86, demonstrating each measuring item is consistent and stable. Validity was tested by the average variance extracted (AVE), and each construct is above 0.5. While applying factor loading to verify the construct validity of each sub-item, each construct reached the threshold of 0.65 (Hair et al. 2006). Also, the discriminant validity analysis was examined. Based on the suggestions by Hair et al. (2006), the discriminant validity of each construct in this survey is defined as the following, the correlation of two different constructs should be smaller than the square root of each construct's AVE, as the values presented diagonally in the Table 2. As shown in Table 2, the square roots of the AVE are all greater than all other cross-correlations. This proves that each construct has a certain degree of discriminant validity (Hair et al. 2006).

4.2 Result of PLS Analysis

We tested the Hypotheses H1 to H8 with the overall sample. The PLS results of the structural model show that the path coefficient of the influence of the endorser's source credibility on brand attitude and attitude toward advertising are significant ($\beta = 0.26$, $p < 0.001$; $\beta = 0.287$, $p < 0.001$). Therefore hypotheses H1 and H2 are supported. However, the path coefficient of the moderating effect of the consumer's expertise level and degree of product involvement did not reach the significance level. Therefore H1a, H1b, H2a and H2b are not supported. The path coefficient of the influence of the content quality on the brand attitude did not reach the significance level, but showed an effect of the marginal support ($\beta = 0.153$, $p < 0.1$). Therefore H3 is marginally

Table 2. Discriminant validity and correlation matrix

	Source Credibility	Content Quality	SOVC	Brand Attitude	Attitude toward Advertising	Purchase Intention
Source Credibility	0.730					
Content Quality	0.680	0.907				
SOVC	0.664	0.734	0.843			
Brand Attitude	0.669	0.657	0.707	0.906		
Attitude toward Advertising	0.612	0.655	0.664	0.780	0.917	
Purchase Intention	0.607	0.664	0.701	0.768	0.774	0.940

Note: Diagonal elements are the square root of AVE.

supported. The path coefficient of the influence of the content quality on the attitude toward advertising is not significant ($\beta = 0.126$, $p > 0.05$). Hence, H4 is not supported.

Moreover, the path coefficient of the moderating effect of the consumer's expertise level and degree of product involvement did not reach the significance level. Therefore, H3a, H3b, H4a and H4b are not supported. The path coefficients of the influence of the SOVC on the brand attitude and attitude toward advertising are significant ($\beta = 0.368$, $p < 0.001$; $\beta = 0.288$, $p < 0.001$). Therefore H5 and H6 are supported. The path coefficient of the influence of the brand attitude and attitude toward advertising on the purchase intention reached the significance level ($\beta = 0.619$, $p < 0.001$; $\beta = 0.216$, $p < 0.001$). Therefore, H7 and H8 are supported.

This study compared the effects of endorsements between an Internet celebrity and a movie star. The result shows that from examining (without moderating effect) the outcome of the structural model of a movie star's endorsement, the path coefficient for the influence as an endorser's source credibility on the attitude toward advertising did not reach significant level (different from an Internet celebrity's endorsement), but reached the marginal support one ($\beta = 0.186$, $p < 0.1$). Furthermore, the path coefficients for the influence of the content quality on both brand attitude and attitude toward advertising both reached significant levels ($\beta = 0.19$, $p < 0.05$; $\beta = 0.373$, $p < 0.001$), which is different from the outcome of the Internet celebrity's endorsement. However, the moderating effects of the consumer's expertise level and degree of product involvement are not significant. No significant difference was observed between endorsements by Internet celebrities and movie stars in other areas.

5 Conclusion

This study aims at exploring the influence of an Internet celebrity's endorsement on the consumer's purchase intention by focusing on three areas for investigation. They include the Internet celebrities' characters (i.e. source credibility), the published content (i.e. its quality) of the endorsed products, and the overall atmosphere created (i.e. SOVC) by the Internet celebrities. Based on the study's framework, the endorser's credibility and SOVC are both positively associated with the consumer's brand attitude and attitude toward advertising and increases their purchase intention. However, the influence of the content quality on the brand attitude and attitude toward advertising did not reach the significant level. We argue that in the context of Internet celebrities' endorsement, consumers are prone to be attracted by the Internet celebrities' characters and immerse themselves in the influence of SOVC without paying too much attention to the content of the endorsed product published by the endorser. Instead, a peripheral route is taken upon receipt of the product's information. The inference and association made by the consumer are simple without deliberating about the content.

Also, the moderating effects of the consumer's expertise level and degree of product involvement are not significant. One potential reason is that this is because the mean of these two factors based on the chosen product categories, clothing and gaming, is not high, and even toward a lower end. Furthermore, these two product categories do not require a high purchase or usage cost. Consumers for these two categories do not have enough motivation and the ability to learn about the products. As a result, there is no significant influence on brand attitude and attitude toward advertising.

The difference between a product endorsement by movie stars and by Internet celebrities is that the former's source credibility on the influence of attitude toward advertising did not reach a significance level. We infer that when the image of a movie star is positive, it will lead the consumer to associate it with the brand image. Therefore, the brand image is enhanced positively without much influence on the consumer's attitude toward advertising. For the endorsement by movie stars, the influence of the content quality on brand attitude and attitude toward advertising both reached a significance level, but the same situation was not observed in the endorsement by Internet celebrities. We infer that most of the information published in a movie star's endorsement campaign is advertising copies by the product sponsor. When a movie star has a relatively positive image, the more outstanding an advertising copy (i.e. a higher content quality) is, the more significant influence there will be on brand attitude and attitude toward advertising because consumers equate the image of the movie star to the one of the sponsors. In the context of an Internet celebrity's endorsement campaign, consumers pay more attention to the Internet celebrity him/herself.

According to the result of this study, the characters of an Internet celebrity is a paramount factor to an endorsement campaign. This is because source credibility enhances significant brand attitude and attitude toward advertising, and therefore the purchase intention. Thus, in a business process, Internet celebrities need to continually maintain and improve their attractiveness, expertise, and source credibility, as well as add a personal flavor to attract the consumer's attention. They also have to pay attention to their own life because many times consumers judge whether an endorser is trustworthy or not based on some of his/her everyday behaviors. At the same time, SOVC plays a vital role. In the process of the interaction between the consumer and Internet celebrities, a new social circle is formed, and a feeling of belonging to the same community emerged. Internet celebrities are therefore encouraged to develop their communities, and exert their formidable abilities to interact and to run social groups to interact with fans and share experiences. All of these create a sense of membership, influence, emotional connection and fulfillment of needs among fans in a social group. When a member considers him/herself as part of a community, a belief is formed to want to contribute and grow with it. This will help with the brand attitude and attitude toward advertising for the product endorsed, and will even promote a purchase intention so that the member shares the same thoughts as other members and share the same shopping experiences.

While there is no salience effect on the content quality in an Internet celebrity's endorsement campaign, the effect is evident in a movie star's one. Nowadays as the role of an endorser is getting vaguer and vaguer, a movie star can also be an Internet celebrity or vice versa. Paying attention to the content quality of an endorsed product still merits great attention. Furthermore, as there is no significant difference between a product endorsed by an Internet celebrity or by a movie star, sponsors with budget concerns are advised to choose the former as the costs may be lower and conveys distinctive characters. If the Internet celebrity's personality happens to be identical to the brand image, targeted marketing's purpose will be fulfilled.

In terms of future studies, this study explored the influence of an Internet celebrity's endorsement on the consumer's purchase intention. However only China was selected as the research area. Studies in the future may choose multiple locations. Different cultural backgrounds may lead to different research results. Moreover, this study only chose one platform, Weibo, and investigated how Internet celebrities endorsed a product on it. Studies in the future can extend the research spectrum to other platforms, such as live streaming, explore the characteristics of endorsement campaigns by an Internet celebrity on such platform, or compare the differences of endorsement campaigns on various platforms.

Acknowledgements. This work was supported in part by the Ministry of Science and Technology of the Republic of China under the grant MOST 103-2410-H-030-087-MY3.

References

Hsieh, P.S., Ou, J., Xu, J.: Will you "tip" celebrated streamers? Sense of virtual community and the moderating role of subjective happiness. Paper presented at the 51st Hawaii International Conference on System Sciences, Hawaii, USA (2018)

Amos, C., Holmes, G., Strutton, D.: Exploring the relationship between celebrity endorser effects and advertising effectiveness: a quantitative synthesis of effect size. Int. J. Advertising 27(2), 209–234 (2008)

Bauer, R.A.: Consumer behavior as risk taking. Paper presented at the 43rd National Conference of the American Marketing Association, Chicago, Illinois (1960)

Blanchard, A.L.: Developing a sense of virtual community measure. CyberPsychology Behav. 10(6), 827–830 (2007)

Blanchard, A.L., Markus, M.L.: The experienced "sense" of a virtual community: characteristics and processes. ACM SIGMIS Database 35(1), 64–79 (2004)

Chaudhuri, A.: Does brand loyalty mediate brand equity outcomes? J. Market. Theory Pract. 7(2), 136–146 (1999)

Cocker, H.L., Cronin, J.: Charismatic authority and the YouTuber: unpacking the new cults of personality. Market. Theory 17(4), 455–472 (2017)

Eagly, A.H., Chaiken, S.: The Psychology of Attitudes. Harcourt Brace Jovanovich College Publishers, New York (1993)

Forster, P.M.: Psychological sense of community in groups on the internet. Behav. Change **21**(2), 141–146 (2004)

Freiden, J.B.: Advertising spokesperson effects - An examination of endorser type and gender on 2 audiences. J. Advertising Res. **24**(5), 33–41 (1984)

Friedman, H.H., Friedman, L.: Endorser effectiveness by product type. J. Advertising Res. **19**(5), 63–71 (1979)

Hair, J.F., Anderson, R., Tatham, R., Black, W.: Multivariate Data Analysis, 6th edn. Pearson Prentice Hall, Upper Saddle River (2006)

Kim, W.G., Lee, C., Hiemstra, S.J.: Effects of an online virtual community on customer loyalty and travel product purchases. Tour. Manag. **25**(3), 343–355 (2004)

Koh, J., Kim, Y.G.: Sense of virtual community: a conceptual framework and empirical validation. Int. J. Electron. Commer. **8**(2), 75–94 (2003)

Laurent, G., Kapferer, J.N.: Measuring consumer involvement profiles. J. Mark. Res. **22**(1), 41–53 (1985)

Marwick, A.E., Boyd, D.: I tweet honestly, I tweet passionately: Twitter users, context collapse, and the imagined audience. New Media Soc. **13**(1), 114–133 (2011)

McCracken, G.: Who is the celebrity endorser? Cultural foundations of the endorsement process. J. Consum. Res. **16**(3), 310–321 (1989)

McMillan, D.W., Chavis, D.M.: Sense of community: a definition and theory. J. Community Psychol. **14**(1), 6–23 (1986)

Ohanian, R.: The impact of celebrity spokespersons' perceived image on consumers' intention to purchase. J. Advertising Res. **31**(1), 46–54 (1991)

Petty, R.E., Cacioppo, J.T.: Attitudes and Persuasion: Classic and Contemporary Approaches. WC Brown Co., Dubuque (1981)

Sussman, S.W., Siegal, W.S.: Informational influence in organizations: an integrated approach to knowledge adoption. Inf. Syst. Res. **14**(1), 47–65 (2003)

Tsoi, G.: Wang Hong: China's online stars making real cash, 1 August 2016. http://www.bbc.com/news/world-asia-china-36802769. Accessed 1 Feb 2019

Wang, A.: The effects of expert and consumer endorsements on audience response. J. Advertising Res. **45**(4), 402–412 (2005)

Xu, K.: What is "Internet Celebrity Economy" in China, Target China, 28 April 2017. http://targetchina.com.au/article/internet-celebrity/. Accessed 1 Feb 2019

Zeithaml, V.A.: Consumer perceptions of price, quality, and value: a means-end model and synthesis of evidence. J. Mark. **52**(3), 2–22 (1988)

Zhang, Y.: Responses to humorous advertising: the moderating effect of need for cognition. J. Advertising **25**(1), 15–32 (1996)

Zhang, Y., Buda, R.: Moderating effects of need for cognition on responses to positively versus negatively framed advertising messages. J. Advertising **28**(2), 1–15 (1999)

Kim, S.H., Yang, K.H., Kim, J.K.: Finding critical success factors for virtual community marketing. Serv. Bus. **3**(2), 149–171 (2009)

Moderating Effect of Country of Origin to the Evaluation of Cellphones

Chih-Chin Liang[(✉)]

National Formosa University,
No. 64, Wenhua RD., Huwei Township, Yunlin County 632, Taiwan
lgcwow@gmail.com

Abstract. Smartphone technology gives customers many choices. Some extrinsic and intrinsic cues of the product, as well as internal factors from the consumers, affect these choices. This study investigated country of origin (COO), an extrinsic cue that affects consumer product evaluation (PE) on smartphones in Taiwan. This study proposed a model named Product-Evaluation Model (PEM) extending the scopes from literature to evaluate the relationship of COO, consumer ethnocentrism (CE), product knowledge (PK), and PE through analyzing 600 smartphone users surveyed in Taiwan. Analytical results display that country of origin and product knowledge have impacts on consumer evaluation whereas consumer ethnocentrism does not have. Additionally, PK has the moderating effect on the relationship between PE and COO, and COO has the moderating effect on the relationship between PK and PE.

Keywords: Country of origin · Consumer ethnocentrism ·
Product knowledge · Product evaluation

1 Introduction

Smartphones have gradually become popular in the global market (Jiménez and San Martín 2010). In America, smartphone users in 2018 are 230 million (Statista 2019). Smartphones enable the use of various applications other than making calls and sending messages. Nowadays, many brands of smartphones are in the market at different prices. Consumers have difficulty determining which smartphone is the most suitable for personal use because they have too much information regarding smartphones. One important information having a significant influence on product evaluation (PE) is a country of origin (COO) (Hsieh 2004). Roth and Romeo (1992) defined COO as the stereotypes of the country that manufacturers a product. Such a perception can make the consumer a good or bad evaluation of the product based on customer perceptions to the manufacturing country. For example, consumers perceive that medicine from Japan is of high quality. People trust in a good because it is made by the country expertizing on producing the goods (Creusen et al. 2013). Through COO, people can judge the product is good or not through the manufacturing country subjectively.

However, it is different from the literature that subjective perceptions of a product are affected not only by COO, but also by psychological factors. For example, consumer ethnocentrism (CE) can be defined as a belief held by consumers on the

© Springer Nature Switzerland AG 2019
F. F.-H. Nah and K. Siau (Eds.): HCII 2019, LNCS 11588, pp. 288–297, 2019.
https://doi.org/10.1007/978-3-030-22335-9_19

appropriateness with the domestic products and indeed morality purchasing the domestic products (Maehle and Supphellen 2011; Keillor et al. 2001; Shimp and Sharma 1987). This definition also shows clearly that ethnocentric consumers are more likely to use domestic products because they think that using the foreign product is harmful to the domestic economy (Maehle and Supphellen 2011; Keillor et al. 2001). Thus, they exhibit CE when their country can manufacture the same products. Many corporations in Taiwan produce smartphones. This study investigated whether Taiwan consumers are ethnocentric and whether their ethnocentrism differs by age, gender, and education level.

This study also investigated the effects of product knowledge (PK) on consumer evaluation (Healy et al. 2007; Cordell 1997). Hong and Wyer (1989) find the factors affected product evaluation. The analytical results showed that country of origin is a heuristic basis for judgment on a product. A consumer potentially finds their intention through recalling the product knowledge. PK will be defined as the information stored in memory, such as information about brands, products, attributes, evaluations, decision heuristics and usage situations (Aichner 2014; Aichner et al. 2017; Marks and Olson 1981). Thus, consumers use their knowledge to evaluate the quality of a product before buying the product. If the consumers have more knowledge, they will be more proactive in their option and can find the best product. Especially, with many functions of a smartphone, we cannot know how to use it if we have not used before. Therefore, choosing the most appropriate smartphone can be very difficult for consumers. Therefore, this study examined whether consumer PK affects consumer PE.

In conclusion, we hypothesized that COO, CE, and PK affect consumer PE. However, each factor has a different effect on customer selection because COO and PK have the positive relationship on consumer PE, but CE generates the negative relationship on consumer PE on a foreign product while getting the positive relationship with the domestic product. Restated, COO generates a negative relationship on CE and PK. Additionally, this study fills a gap in the literature on the moderating effect of COO and provides practical rules of thumb to find the moderating effect. The moderating effects of COO on the relationship between PK and PE were identified by partial least squares structural equation modeling (PLS) (Henseler and Fassott 2010; Henseler et al. 2016).

The remainder of this paper is organized as follows. Section 2 reviews the literature. Section 3 outlines the research method. Section 4 summarizes the analytical results. Finally, Sect. 5 draws conclusions and makes recommendations regarding future research.

2 Literature Review

2.1 Country of Origin (COO)

Product evaluation (*PE*) is the consumer beliefs about the product, which can be affected in consumer perception (Durvasula et al. 1997; Ozer 1999). It can be imaged that is the belief in the specific product. Based on their beliefs, consumers decide which product is the best choice (Mukherjee and Hoyer 2001).

Country of Origin *(COO)* of the product is the area where the product is designed and assembled. Not all consumers consider *COO* when they purchase a product. Some studies define *COO* as an element of a brand that leads consumers to associate the firm with its original domicile, even when the product under evaluation is manufactured in a different country (Aichner 2014; Aichner et al. 2017; Ahmed and d'Astous 1996). *Country of Origin* is a complex dimension, it is the combination of many factors. *COO* of the product is the area where the product is designed and assembled. *Country of Origin* has three dimensions: cognitive, affective and co-native dimensions. Many researchers also define *COO* as a country manufactures of assembly. For example, Sony is a Japanese brand, but it has some products assembled outside Japan, such as Singapore, hence, there is a sentence outside the box which is "assembled in Singapore", If they are *Sony products* assembled in Japan, the sentence is "made in Japan" (MohdYasin et al. 2007).

If the manufacturers in a country have a good image, *COO* is an advantage when exporting their products to other countries. However, in some countries, which have worse images, *COO* is a barrier to exporting their products (Ma et al. 2014). According to Wang and Lam (1983), *COO* is an intangible barrier to entry into new markets if consumers have negative perceptions about the importing country. Based on this, we have the hypothesis 1 regarding the effect of *COO* on consumer evaluation (MohdYasin et al. 2007).

Hypothesis H1: COO positively affects the selection of a smartphone by a consumer.

Especial, *COO* positively affects consumer *PE*.

Hypothesis H1.1: COO positively affects consumer PE on a smartphone.

One of the oldest and most persistent concerns in international marketing is how *COO* affects consumer preferences for a product (Koschate-Fischer et al. 2012). The *COO* is associated with diverse marketing factors that affect consumer's behavior, including trust and familiarity (Michaelis et al. 2008). This means the more customers have a positive relationship with one country, the more they are satisfied with this country and affected to choose the product of this country. The origin of a product has an effect on the consumers' opinion of this product, thus *COO* may be seen as one of a good proxy to evaluate the product (Jiménez and San Martín 2010).

The *COO* affects consumer *PE,* which then affects *PK.* Lee and Lee (2009) point out that the effect of *COO* on consumer *PE* is affected by *PK.* That is, consumers with high *PK* are unlikely to consider *COO* cues in their *PE,* and consumers with low *PK* are likely to consider *COO* cues in their *PE.* Thus, knowledgeable consumers are unlikely to use the *COO* information for the *PE. COO* has the effects on consumer *PE* if they have low subjective knowledge; if they have high subjective knowledge, the consumer will make a decision based on massage strength (Moon 2004). Therefore, COO should affect subjective product knowledge. In sum, COO should have the moderating effect on the relationship between PK and PE.

We have the hypothesis 1.2 regarding the influence of *COO* on PK as following.

Hypothesis H1.2: COO is negatively associated with consumer PK.
Hypothesis H2: COO has the moderating effect on the relationship between PK and PE.

2.2   Consumer Ethnocentrism (*CE*)

This study of consumer behavior not only focused on external factors that have an influence on consumer *PE*, but also on internal factors that have an influence on consumer *PE*, especially in psychology and sociology. In some cases, before buying any merchandise, consumers usually notice the *COO* of the product and they will have some emotion with these products. Their emotions may be good or bad, and sometimes they just think that buying foreign products is harmful to the domestic economy. In this way, several marketers concentrate on *CE* concept. Thus, we can see that *COO* has a positive effect on *CE* with a cellphone (Hsieh 2004; Maehle and Supphellen 2011).

Hypothesis 1.3: Country of origin positively affects CE with a cellphone.

Consumer ethnocentrism is defined as "the beliefs held by consumers about the appropriateness, indeed morality of purchasing a foreign-made product and the loyalty of consumers to the products manufactured in their home country" (Keillor et al. 2001; Shimp and Sharma 1987). According to this definition, ethnocentric consumers have positive emotions about domestic products and have negative emotions about foreign products. Because in their mind, buying foreign products that are not loyalty and harmful for the domestic economy, they will have the negative perception when they have the judgment about this product (Hsieh 2004; Shimp and Sharma 1987). Consumer ethnocentrism also causes negative emotions about foreign products. It leads to the consumers really care about the place where the products were produced, and the higher ethnocentrism consumers will care more about the *COO* of this product than less ethnocentrism (Zafer et al. 2010). Therefore, CE should the moderating effect on the relationship between COO and PE. Thus, we have hypothesis 3 talk about the influence of *consumer ethnocentrism* on the consumer evaluation.

Hypothesis H3: CE positively affects consumer PE with a cellphone.
Hypothesis H4: CE has the moderating effect on the relationship between COO and PE.

2.3   Product Knowledge (*PK*)

Another internal factor that affects consumer *PE* as *CE*, is *PK*. However, it is different. Consumer ethnocentrism results from feelings about foreign countries, but *PK* based on an understanding of consumer about this product. *PK* has defined that is all of everything which the consumer knows about this product or based on their memories about this product (Rubio and Yagüe 2009), it can be called the consumers' awareness about this product (Creusen et al. 2013; Lin and Chen 2006; Johnson et al. 2016).

Based on the definition of *product knowledge*, Buck (1985) divides it into three categories:

- Subjective knowledge is what and how much consumers know about a product.
- Objective knowledge is the accurate information stored in the long-term memory of consumers.
- Experience-based knowledge is an individual previous product usage or experience of an indicator of objective knowledge.

Through the definition and classification of *product knowledge*; in this study, the author would like to research the influences of subjective *product knowledge* on the information search behavior, consumers' *product evaluation*, processing of advertising messages.

Based on that, hypothesis 5 concerning the effect of *PK* on *CE* is proposed:

Hypothesis H5: PK has a positive impact on consumer PE.

3   Research Method

Based on the above literature, this study focused on people using smartphones. One objective was to identify factors that affect consumer *PE*, especial with *COO, CE,* and *PK* and the relationship between *COO, CE,* and *PK*. This study proposed a Product-Evaluation Model (PEM) based on the models proposed by Hong and Wyer (1989) and added consumer ethnocentrism to help the understand of evaluating the product before purchase. Causal relationships among the factors were also analyzed by using SmartPLS version 3. The component-based PLS (partial least squares structural equation modeling) (PLS-SEM) method is non-parametric. That is, PLS-SEM makes no restrictive assumptions about the data distributions (Dijkstra and Henseler 2015). Additionally, PLS-SEM is feasible to verify a new model. In this study, the new proposed model can be evaluated through PLS-SEM (Liang and Shiau 2018). In summary, the discussion about the effect of *COO, CE,* and *PK* on consumer *PE* and some suggestion for the smartphone will be shown. Figure 1 shows the model of possible causal relationships.

Because almost everyone has a cell phone, the authors want to survey qualified volume of users. The authors select participants from phone book through fair dicing. The authors choice the page of a phonebook through the random function of Microsoft Excel ranging from 1 to 682. The authors will select the sequence number on the page randomly using Microsoft Excel ranging from 1 to 150. All 4000 samples were selected, but only 631 is accessible as the participants. The questionnaire was dispatched to the participants through email or social media (i.e. Facebook Messenger). All of the 631 smartphone users who answered the questionnaire were Taiwanese. All of the participants are using smartphones. After being checked and classified, 600 samples met the criteria for inclusion in the analysis.

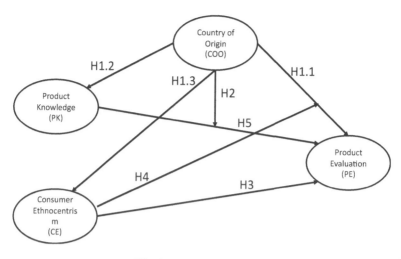

Fig. 1. Relationship model

4 Analytical Results

Most respondents in this survey were young who were interested in information technology products and who used smartphones heavily. Table 1 presents and discuss the results of the profile analysis. Valid questionnaires were received from 280 males and 320 females (46.6% and 53.33% of total participants, respectively). The largest age group was 18 to 25 years old, (73.5%), and the second largest age group was 26 to 35 years old (15.83%). The group aged 36 to 45 years old had 45 respondents (7.5%). Just 3.167% of people joining the survey who are in the age between 46 and 55 years old and there are not any over-56-years-old participants answering the questionnaire.

In tests of multicollinearity, the variance inflation factor (VIF) values calculated for all of the constructs were well below the acceptable threshold of 5.0 (Neter *et al.* 1990). In this study, the VIF values ranged from 1.18 to 2.65. Discrepancies between the empirical and the model-implied correlation matrix can be quantified with either the geodesic discrepancy d_G or the unweighted least squares discrepancy d_{ULS} (Dijkstra and Henseler 2015). Both measurement model misspecification and structural model misspecification can be detected by testing model fit (Chen 2008; Dijkstra and Henseler, 2015). The proposed path model and the model fit were evaluated by PLS bootstrapping algorithm. Cronbach α value for each construct was well above the recommended threshold of 0.70 (Hair *et al.* 2006) and ranged from 0.70 (COO) to 0.86 (PE). Composite reliability ranged from 0.80 (CE) to 0.91 (PE). For each construct, the average variance extracted (AVE) exceeded 0.50 (Chin 1998; Fornell and Larcker 1981) and ranged from 0.57 (CE) to 0.78 (PE), which met the requirement for convergent validity. The fit of the estimated model was tested with SRMR, the unweighted least squares discrepancy d_{ULS}, and the geodesic discrepancy d_G. These values should be smaller than 95% bootstrap quantile for an acceptable model fit (HI95 of SRMR, HI95 of d_{ULS}, and HI95 of d_G) (Dijkstra and Henseler 2015). The SRMR was 0.07, which is smaller than 0.08 and smaller than HI95, which indicated an acceptable model fit (Dijkstra and Henseler 2015). The value for d_{ULS} was 0.52, and the value for d_G was 0.21 which were smaller than HI95 (d_{ULS} is 0.56 and d_G is 0.34). Most paths had an acceptable effect size (f^2 is larger than 0.15) (Ringle et al. 2015). The exceptions were *PK* to *PE* (0.08). Although the impact was statistically significant, the effect size was small. The discriminant validity of the constructs was evaluated using the approaches recommended by Fornell-Larcker method (1981) and Heterotrait-monotrait (HTMT). The HTMT should be significantly smaller than 0.85 (Henseler et al. 2015).

PK and *PE* had a significant and direct positive relationship (0.236) (p < 0.05). Thus, hypothesis 5 is supported. Additionally, *COO* had a significant and direct positive relationship to consumer *PE* (0.132) (p < 0.05). Thus, hypothesis 1.1 is supported. That is, when consumers do not understand how to use a smartphone, they use the information regarding the *COO* to help them to get a better choice. The *COO* also has the direct and negative relationship between *COO* and *CE* are statistically significant (-0.544) (p < 0.05). Thus, hypothesis 1.2 is supported. This means that the consumer really cares about the *COO* information. If the smartphone is produced in their country, they tend to have a positive perception of the smartphone. If the smartphone is produced in a foreign country, they tend to have a negative perception of the smartphone. Besides, the *CE* has no impact on the consumer *PE*, but the *COO* has an impact on the consumer *PE*. Finally, the direct and positive relationship between *COO* and *PK* are statistics significant negatively (-0.555) (p < 0.05). Hence, hypothesis 1.3 is supported. The impact of *CE* and *PE* was investigated. The direct and positive relationship between *CE* and *PE* are statistically significant (0.511) (p < 0.05). Thus, hypothesis 3 is supported. Table 7 shows the summary of causal relationships. Hypothesis H2 was supported, which is consistent with Moon (2004). Figure 2 shows the simple slope analysis of COO. The analytical results show that COO have a significant moderating effect on the positive effect of PK on PE. That is, participants were most concerned about the country of the origin of a cell phone, which reduced the impact of the knowledge to evaluate the cellphone. Finally, Hypothesis H4 was supported, which is consistent with Zafer et al. (2010). Figure 3 shows the simple slope analysis of CE. The analytical results show that CE has a significant moderating effect on the positive effect of COO on PE. That is, participants, concerned more on consumer ethnocentrism, which positively affected their knowledge to their evaluation of the cellphone. However, participants who are not highly concerned about consumer ethnocentrism, the participants with low knowledge of phone will reduce their positive evaluation to a cellphone.

5 Conclusion

Scientific and technological developments have diversified IT products in appearance, color and so on. The consumers find it more difficult to decide or evaluate the quality of the products, especially for smartphones. Thus, finding the best smartphone is difficult for customers. Smartphone purchases are also affected by many factors, including country of origin (Hsieh 2004), product knowledge (Healy et al. 2007; Cordell 1997), and even the consumer ethnocentrism (Maehle and Supphelen 2011; Keillor et al. 2001). Therefore, this study investigates factors that affect smartphone purchases by consumers.

The first factor is the extrinsic cues, which examine whether it effect on the consumer *PE* or not. When discussing the effects of extrinsic cues on consumer *PE*, we need to check *COO* whether *COO* has an influence on consumer *PE* or not. Previous studies indicate that *COO* is one of the extrinsic cues making the effect on the consumer *PE*. However, the *COO* may include more than one country; sometimes, this product is designed in one country, manufactured in another country and assembled in other country and after that made the brand in one country. Hence, consumers who do not understand a product may still buy it because of its famous brand or *COO*; and after the process of using, the quality was not as good as they expect. It makes the consumers disappointed with this product and would not buy from this brand in the future. Smartphones now have so many functions that few people clearly understand its functions, so most of them buy it. Due to the *COO*, it will make them trust it more or will be disappointed. Besides, the influence on consumer *PE*, *COO* also has a negative impact on consumer *CE* and consumer *PK*. Thus, we can conclude that if a company want to promote smartphone in Taiwan, the relationship between *COO, CE, and PK* must be handled carefully.

The second factor that affects consumer PE is CE. This study found that CE does not have an influence on consumer PE. It implies that CE should be ignored from the effect of customer PE in purchasing a smartphone. In Taiwan, the Taiwan brand, hTC, hurt consumers several times due to the cheating in manufacturing smartphone. The company sold a smartphone to Taiwanese at a more expensive price with low-quality equipment, but not for the exporting products to Korea, Japan, and the USA.

The last factor investigated in this study is *PK*. The *PK* is the knowledge which the consumers know and understand about a product. It reveals what the consumers know and keeps in mind of the product information. This study showed that consumer perception and memory of product information are positively associated with consumer *PE*.

References

Ahmed, S.A., d'Astous, A.: Country-of-origin and brand effects: a multi-dimensional and multi-attribute study. J. Int. Consum. Mark. 9(2), 93–115 (1996)

Aichner, T.: Country-of-origin marketing: a list of typical strategies with examples. J. Brand. Manag. 21(1), 81–93 (2014)

Aichner, T., Forza, C., Trentin, A.: The country-of-origin lie: impact of foreign branding on customers' willingness to buy and willingness to pay when the product's actual origin is disclosed. Int. Rev. Retail. Distrib. Consum. Res. 27(1), 43–60 (2017)

Chen, C.F.: Investigating structural relationships between service quality, perceived value, satisfaction, and behavioral intentions for air passengers: evidence from Taiwan. Transp. Res. Part A Policy Pract. 42(4), 709–717 (2008)

Chin, W.W.: The partial least squares approach for structural equation modeling. In: Marcoulides, G.A. (ed.) Modern Methods for Business Research, pp. 295–336. Lawrence Erlbaum Associates, Mahwah (1998)

Geusen, M., Hultink, E.J., Eling, K.: Choice of consumer research methods in the front end of new product development. Int. J. Mark. Res. **55**(1), 81–104 (2013)

Cordell, V.V.: Consumer knowledge measures as predictors in product evaluation. Psychol. Mark. **14**(3), 241–260 (1997)

Dijkstra, T.K., Henseler, J.: Consistent partial least squares path modeling. MIS Q. Manag. Inf. Syst. Q. **39**(2), 297–316 (2015)

Durvasula, S., Andrews, J.C., Netemeyer, R.G.: A cross-cultural comparison of consumer ethnocentrism in the United States and Russia. J. Int. Consum. Mark. **9**(4), 73–93 (1997)

Fornell, C., Larcker, D.F.: Evaluating structural equation models with unobservable variables and measurement error. J. Mark. Res. **18**(1), 39–50 (1981)

Healy, M.J., Beverland, M.B., Oppewal, H., Sands, S.: Understanding retail experiences-the case for ethnography. Int. J. Mark. Res. **49**(6), 751–778 (2007)

Hair, J.F., Black, W.C., Babin, B.J., Anderson, R.E., Tatham, R.L.: Multivariate Data Analysis, 6th edn. Prentice Hall, Upper Saddle River (2006)

Henseler, J., Fassott, G.: Testing moderating effects in PLS path models: an illustration of available procedures. In: Esposito Vinzi, V., Chin, W., Henseler, J., Wang, H. (eds.) Handbook of Partial Least Squares. Springer Handbooks of Computational Statistics, pp. 713–735. Springer, Heidelberg (2010). https://doi.org/10.1007/978-3-540-32827-8_31

Henseler, J., Ringle, C.M., Sarstedt, M.: A new criterion for assessing discriminant validity in variance-based structural equation modeling. J. Acad. Mark. Sci. **43**(1), 115–135 (2015)

Henseler, J., Ringle, C.M., Sarstedt, M.: Testing measurement invariance of composites using partial least squares. Int. Mark. Rev. **33**(3), 405–431 (2016)

Hong, S.T., Wyer, R.S.: Effects of country-of-origin and product-attribute information on product evaluation: an information processing perspective. J. Consum. Res. **16**(2), 175–187 (1989)

Hsieh, M.H.: An investigation of country-of-origin effect using correspondence analysis: a cross-national context. Int. J. Mark. Res. **46**(3), 267–296 (2004)

Jiménez, N.H., San Martín, S.: The role of country-of-origin, ethnocentrism and animosity in promoting consumer trust. The moderating role of familiarity. Int. Bus. Rev. **19**(1), 34–45 (2010)

Johnson, Z.S., Tian, Y., Lee, S.: Country-of-origin fit: when does a discrepancy between brand origin and country of manufacture reduce consumers' product evaluations? J. Brand. Manag. **23**(4), 403–418 (2016)

Keillor, B., Owens, D., Pettijohn, C.: A cross-cultural/cross-national study of influencing factors and socially desirable response biases. Int. J. Mark. Res. **43**(1), 63–84 (2001)

Koschate-Fischer, N., Diamantopoulos, A., Oldenkotte, K.: Are consumers really willing to pay more for a favorable country image? A study of country-of-origin effects on willingness to pay. J. Int. Mark. **20**(1), 19–41 (2012)

Lin, L.Y., Chen, C.S.: The influence of the country-of-origin image, product knowledge and product involvement on consumer purchase decisions: an empirical study of insurance and catering services in Taiwan. J. Consum. Mark. **23**(5), 248–265 (2006)

Ma, B., Zhang, L., Wang, G., Li, F.: The impact of a product-harm crisis on customer perceived value. Int. J. Mark. Res. **56**(3), 341–366 (2014)

Marks, L.J., Olson, J.C.: Toward a cognitive structure conceptualization of product familiarity. Adv. Consum. Res. **8**(1), 145–150 (1981)

Maehle, N., Supphellen, M.: In search of the sources of brand personality. Int. J. Mark. Res. **53**(1), 95–114 (2011)

Michaelis, M., Woisetschläger, D.M., Backhaus, C., Ahlert, D.: The effects of country of origin and corporate reputation on initial trust: an experimental evaluation of the perception of Polish consumers. Int. Mark. Rev. **25**(4), 404–422 (2008)

Mukherjee, A., Hoyer, W.D.: The effect of novel attributes on product evaluation. J. Consum. Res. **28**(3), 462–472 (2001)

MohdYasin, N., Nasser Noor, M., Mohamad, O.: Does image of country-of-origin matter to brand equity? J. Prod. Brand. Manag. **16**(1), 38–48 (2007)

Moon, B.J.: Effects of consumer ethnocentrism and product knowledge on consumers' utilization of country-of-origin information. Adv. Consum. Res. **31**(1), 667–673 (2004)

Neter, J., Wasserman, W., Kutner, M.H.: Applied Linear Statistical Models, 3rd edn. Irwin, Boston (1990)

Ozer, M.: A survey of new product evaluation models. J. Prod. Innov. Manag. **16**(1), 77–94 (1999)

Roth, M.S., Romeo, J.B.: Matching product category and country image perceptions: a framework for managing country-of-origin effects. J. Int. Bus. Stud. **23**(3), 477–497 (1992)

Rubio, N., Yagüe, M.J.: The determinants of store brand market share-a temporal and cross-sectional analysis. Int. J. Mark. Res. **51**(4), 1–15 (2009)

Liang, C.C., Shiau, W.L.: Moderating effect of privacy concerns and subjective norms between satisfaction and repurchase of airline e-ticket through airline-ticket vendor. Asia Pac. J. Tour. Res. (2018). https://doi.org/10.1080/10941665.2018.1528290

Shimp, T.A., Sharma, S.: Consumer ethnocentrism: construction and validation of the CETSCALE. J. Mark. Res. **24**, 280–289 (1987)

Ringle, C.M., da Silva, D., Bido, D.D.S.: Structural equation modeling with the SmartPLS (2015)

Statista: Smartphone sales in the United States from 2005 to 2019 (2019). https://www.statista.com/statistics/191985/sales-of-smartphones-in-the-us-since-2005/

ZaferErdogan, B., Uzkurt, C.: Effects of ethnocentric tendency on consumers' perception of product attitudes for foreign and domestic products. Cross Cult. Manag. Int. J. **17**(4), 393–406 (2010)

How Does Social Tie Influence the User Information Sharing Behavior in Social Commerce Sites

Libo Liu[1(✉)], Yani Shi[2], Xuemei Tian[1], and Jiaqi Yan[3]

[1] Department of Business Technology and Entrepreneurship,
Faculty of Business and Law, Swinburne University of Technology,
Melbourne, Australia
liboliu@swin.edu.au
[2] School of Economics and Management, Southeast University, Nanjing, China
[3] Nanjing University, Nanjing, China
jiaqiyan@nju.edu.cn

Abstract. Social commerce is an extension of e-commerce in which social media is integrated with e-commerce transactions and activities to promote user contributions. Users often learn from others through a social learning process before making decisions related an information contribution or purchase on social commerce sites. Despite the extensive literature on social learning, there is a research gap regarding the impact of various sources on user information sharing behaviors. A majority of the previous studies examined the impact of social learning information from the perspective of friends or other sources (e.g., opinion leaders or friends) without considering their relative impact among different sources. We will conduct a field study and analyze a large-scale data collected from a social commerce site. We expect that friend-network information (i.e., friends' purchase behavior and friends' sharing behavior) and opinion leader-network information (i.e., opinion leaders' purchase behavior and opinion leaders' sharing behavior) have similar effect on user information sharing behavior. Follower-network information has a greatest influence on user information sharing behavior relative to the friend-network information and opinion leader-network information. In addition, the number of followers has a non-linear relationship with user information sharing behavior. This study has important implications for both theory and practice.

Keywords: Social learning · Followers · Opinion leader-network · Friend-network · Social commerce · Information sharing behavior

1 Introduction

1.1 A Subsection Sample

Social commerce is "a subset of e-commerce that involves using social media to assist in e-commerce transactions and activities" (p. 6) [16]. Empowered by ubiquitously accessible and scalable social networks, social commerce enables users to seek product information, share and recommend their favorite products, create product collections, and interact with other shoppers [24]. Stephen and Toubia [21] mentioned that "social

© Springer Nature Switzerland AG 2019
F. F.-H. Nah and K. Siau (Eds.): HCII 2019, LNCS 11588, pp. 298–305, 2019.
https://doi.org/10.1007/978-3-030-22335-9_20

commerce networks between sellers can play an important economic, value-creating role" (p. 226). That is, they increase the buyers' bargaining power and sellers' profit margin by lowering marketing costs.

In recent years, social commerce is gaining popularity; thus, its adoption rates have significantly increased over the past five years [18]. For example, Pinterest had 175 million monthly active users as of April 2017[1], making it one of the fastest-growing social commerce sites. In 2016, Meilishuo, the leading female-fashion social commerce in China, merged with the second biggest site in China—Mogujie—to create a combined business net worth of RMB 3 billion[2]. Due to the low entry barrier, social commerce sites face intense competition; thus, their survival in this hyper-competitive business environment is highly uncertain [10]. More importantly, without user contributions in terms of product ratings and recommendations or user interactions with other users, social commerce sites are no different than ordinary e-commerce sites and therefore can easily become obsolete as many other e-commerce sites. Given that social commerce sites survival largely depends on user contributions, in this study, we examine how interface design of social commerce sites can stimulate user contribution.

A common belief in the social commerce context is the idea of information cascade, in which individuals are easily influenced by the decisions of others. An individual will observe the referrals or actions others close to him or her, and follow the referrals or behavior of the preceding individuals. This belief sets forth social media marketing strategies to advantage of people's social relationship [22]. Prior research has shown consistent evidence that people tend to mimic others' choices. To this end, a sizable body of research in information systems (IS) and marketing have emerged over the last decade, attempting to identify and examine which type of preceding user is more influential in shaping subsequent user decisions and choices in an online social communities [e.g., 4, 8, 9, 13, 20, 26].

Social commerce has incorporated social networking functions. A user can subscribe to other users' shared posts by following them. This creates a directed social network in which the number of outbound links from a user to others (e.g., opinion leaders) indicates the user's immersion in the community and attention paid to others' shared content [21]. The number of inbound links (i.e., followers) from others to the user indicates their popularity on social commerce site and the amount of others' attention paid to their shared posts [21]. Other type of users (e.g., friends) have a mutually exclusive social connection between two users and thus their interactions are typically bi-directional [6]. In this paper, we explore the information cascade in the context of social comment and, in particular, investigate the relative influence of opinion leaders, friends, and followers on user information sharing behavior.

Prior literature provided mixed findings concerning the impacts of user-generated product information from different sources on subsequent user information sharing

---

[1] 175 million people discovering new possibilities on Pinterest. Retrieved from https://business.pinterest.com/en/blog/175-million-people-discovering-new-possibilities-on-pinterestKahneman, D. 1973. *Attention and effort*: Citeseer.

[2] Chinese fashion site mogujie acquires meilishuo In $3 billion deal. Retrieved from https://www.forbes.com/sites/ywang/2016/01/10/chinese-fashion-site-mogujie-acquires-meilishuo-in-3-billion-deal/-6b6d2c4b457d.

behavior [6, 25]. Collectively, all of these papers examined the impact of user-generated product information from the perspectives of friends, opinion leaders, and followers without further consideration for their relative impact. To fill this theoretical gap, we intend to answer which source of information has the strongest impact on users' information sharing behavior. We empirically test the relative impacts of information shared by opinion leaders as well as friends and followers, and single out which one is most influential in stimulating user information sharing decision. Furthermore, we will test a non-liner model for follower relationship and investigates the non-linear relationship between the number of followers and user information sharing behavior in social commerce sites.

In this study, data will be crawled from a popular social commerce site in Asia that provides an online platform for users to share with others regarding their personal experience related to a specific product or service. We expected that information sharing behavior of friends and opinion leaders induced subsequent users to share information in social commerce site. In addition, the number of followers has the strongest effect on user information sharing behavior relative to that of friend-network information and opinion leader-network information. This study will provide action-able guidance for marketing practitioners to better manage and utilize user-generated product information and thus increase the information sharing behavior in social commerce sites.

2 Literature Review and Hypotheses Development

2.1 Literature Review on Social Learning

Previous studies have confirmed the significant impact of friends on individuals' behaviors. For example, Feng, Wang and Zhang [6] found that online friends rather than informants exerted greater conformity pressure, motivating consumers to generate similar product ratings. In the movie industry context, Lee, Hosanagar and Tan [13] also documented a more robust conformity phenomenon in friend relationships; that is, relative to prior ratings by strangers, friends' ratings always induced herding regardless of movie popularity. Recently, using a quasi-experimental design, Wang, Zhang and Hann [26] showed that rating similarity between friends was significantly higher after the friend relationship was established, indicating that users' earlier ratings could exert social influence on their friends' later rating even beyond the taste similarity among them (i.e., the homophily effect).

Existing evidence has also showed that opinion leaders could disproportionately influence subsequent users' decision in multiple ways. As a result of the knowledge capital possessed by opinion leaders, Iyengar, Van den Bulte and Valente [9] found that better connected adopters (i.e., opinion leaders) exerted more influence on new product diffusion than less connected ones even after controlling for marketing effort and arbitrary system wide changes. Similarly, van Eck, Jager and Leeflang [23] demonstrated that opinion leaders were less susceptible to norms and more innovative, which subsequently facilitated the adoption process of new products.

Most of those papers examined the impact of user-generated product information from the perspectives of friends, opinion leaders, and followers without further consideration for their relative impact. To fill this theoretical gap, we intend to answer which source of information has the strongest impact on users' information sharing behavior.

2.2 Social Learning and User Sharing Behavior

The *social learning process* refers to a user updates his or her belief of a behavior via signals (e.g., observations of use and observations of purchase) on information that was received from others [12]. We focus on social learning that operates through signals from observations of purchase (i.e., purchase behavior) and observations of sharing (i.e., sharing experience). In particular, we examine three types of relationship between users in social commerce sites, including ones with opinion leaders (i.e., following relationship), friends (i.e., friendship), and followers (i.e., being followed relationship). The first type, *opinion leader-network*, refers to a group who are normally interconnected and have a higher status, education, and social standing and therefore exert a disproportionate amount of influence on social networks [7, 14, 15, 26]. A user's relationship with an opinion leader is typically described as "one-way" information-based, in which the user initiates a follow connection to the opinion leader to access the updates of the opinion leader's activities [6]. The second type of users, *friend-network,* by contrast, are a mutually exclusive social connection between two users where their interactions are typically bi-directional [6]. The third type of users, *follower-network* are the users with inbound links (i.e., followers) from others to the user indicates their popularity on a social commerce site and the amount of others' attention paid to their shared posts [21].

A great of attention has been paid to the social learning theory introduced by Banerjee [2]. Social learning theory poses that individuals learn by observing the behaviors of others [3]. According to this theory, observational learning information contains the discrete signals expressed by the actions of other users but not the reasons behind their actions. When people observe the actions of all previous users, this publicly observed information outweighs their own private information in shaping their beliefs. As a result, people follow their predecessors' actions and become engaged in a type of herd behavior [2]. Therefore, we hypothesize:

H1. Opinion leaders-network information (i.e., friends' sharing behavior and friends' purchase behavior) has significant influence on user sharing behavior.
H2. Friends-network information (i.e., friends' sharing behavior and friends' purchase behavior) has significant influence on user sharing behavior.
H3. Followers-network information (i.e., number of followers) will exert significant influence on user sharing behavior.

2.3   Friend-Network Versus Opinion Leader-Network Versus Follower-Network

Network and the embedded relationships are critical determinants of how people communicate and form belief [27]. In social commerce sites, when users generate updates (e.g., purchase a new product), those updates will be display to their friends and followers, but not to the opinion leaders. To this end, a user's performance will be visible or be known only to friends and followers, but not to opinion leaders. Given that visibility of performance is a determinant of social learning, following the information by a friend provides a user with an opportunity to manage his or her public image and signal his or her desire for establishing social intimacy to others.

In comparison, following the information by an opinion leader will not be visible at all; hence, this is not conductive in maintaining social bonds with the opinion leader [27]. Acemoglu et al. [1] studied a theoretical observational learning model over a general social network. The findings showed that people observe only subsets of their predecessors. Conventional wisdom suggests that the consumer is more likely to emulate his/her friends. Individuals tend to follow their friends in decision such as which movie to watch and which political candidates to vote for [17, 19].

In social commerce sites, friendship is a closer relationship compared to opinion leader relationship and follower relationship, individual know their friends and trust them more. Zhang, Liu and Chen [27] examined observational learning in the social network of friends versus strangers. They found that information cascades are more likely to occur in friend networks than in stranger networks. Feng, Wang and Zhang [6] found that online friends rather than informants exerted greater conformity pressure, motivating consumers to generate similar product ratings. In the domain of movie industry, Lee, Hosanagar and Tan [13] also documented a more robust conformity phenomenon in friend relationships; that is, relative to prior ratings by strangers, friends' ratings always induced herding regardless of movie popularity.

Using a quasi-experimental design, Wang, Zhang and Hann [25] showed that rating similarity between friends was significantly higher after the friend relationship was established, indicating that users' earlier ratings could exert social influence on their friends' later rating even beyond the taste similarity among them (i.e., the homophily effect). Conversely, existing evidence has also implied that opinion leaders could disproportionately influence subsequent users' decision via multiple ways. As a result of the knowledge capital possessed by opinion leaders, Iyengar, Van den Bulte and Valente [9] found that the better connected adopters (i.e., opinion leaders) exerted more influence on new product diffusion than do less connected ones even after controlling for marketing effort and arbitrary system wide changes. Similarly, van Eck, Jager and Leeflang [23] demonstrated that opinion leaders were less susceptible to norms and more innovative, which subsequently facilitated the adoption process of new products. Therefore, we hypothesize,

H4. Friends-network information will exert the strongest influence on user sharing behavior than will opinion leaders-network information and followers-network information.

3   Methodology

3.1   Data Collection

The data for this study will be crawled from a social commerce site in Asia, which provides a platform for users to share their experience, and to interact with other users. We will randomly select users from 42 groups.

Users in the social commerce site can post the experience that they have had with the use of any product, provide a rating (from 1 to 7) on the product, and share the products that they have purchased by adding products to their "buy" lists. Users can also choose to "follow" other users whose posts or ratings are useful in the social commerce site. The following relationship does not need mutual consent, nor has to be reciprocal. The number of followings a user has indicates his/her immersion in the social commerce site. The number of followers a user has indicates his/her popularity. Furthermore, the social commerce site enables users to observe following users' behaviors (i.e., purchase behavior and rating behavior).

In this study, we aim to explore how a user's sharing behavior is influenced by other users' sharing and purchase (i.e., including friends and opinion leaders) as well as number of followers. Based on users ID, we crawled the network data for each user. Specifically, we collected the "following" (i.e., opinion leaders), "friends" and "followers" of users' lists and built an egocentric network for each user. Then we formed friends-based behavior (i.e., friends' sharing and friends' purchase) and opinion leaders-based behavior (i.e., opinion leaders' sharing and opinion leaders' purchase).

3.2   Operationalization of Constructs

The constructs included in the research model are operationalized as follows:

Opinion leaders' sharing is operationalized as the total number of experience (on products) provided by user' followings (exclude reciprocal following relationship).
Friends' sharing is operationalized as the total number of experiences provided by individuals who are reciprocal followed by a user, or the user's friends.
Opinion leaders' purchase is operationalized as the total number of products in the buy-lists of a user's followings in the social commerce site.
Friends' purchase is operationalized as the total number of products in the buy-lists of a user's friends in the social commerce site.
Followers is operationalized as the total number of users followed the focal user.
User sharing behavior is operationalized as the number of experience a user shared in social commerce site.

4   Conclusion

This paper addresses the influence of social learning on users sharing behavior, and whether this differs in networks of friends, opinion leaders, or followers. We will use a field study to test the research model. We expect that observing opinion leaders and friends' actions encourage user share more information. This study contributes to the existing literature by offering important and interesting insights to research and practice.

References

1. Acemoglu, D., Dahleh, M.A., Lobel, I., Ozdaglar, A.: Bayesian learning in social networks. Rev. Econ. Stud. **78**(4), 1201–1236 (2011)
2. Banerjee, A.V.: A simple model of herd behavior. Q. J. Econ. **107**, 797–817 (1992)
3. Çelen, B., Kariv, S.: Distinguishing informational cascades from herd behavior in the laboratory. Am. Econ. Rev. **94**(3), 484–498 (2004)
4. Dewan, S., Ho, Y.-J.I., Ramaprasad, J.: Popularity or proximity: characterizing the nature of social influence in an online music community. Inf. Syst. Res. **28**(1), 117–136 (2017)
5. Fang, E., Palmatier, R.W., Steenkamp, J.-B.E.: Effect of service transition strategies on firm value. J. Mark. **72**(5), 1–14 (2008)
6. Feng, Y.K., Wang, C.A., Zhang, M.: The impacts of informant and friend relationships on online opinion sharing (2013)
7. Flynn, L.R., Goldsmith, R.E., Eastman, J.K.: Opinion leaders and opinion seekers: two new measurement scales. J. Acad. Mark. Sci. **24**(2), 137–147 (1996)
8. Herrando, C., Jiménez-Martínez, J., Martín-De Hoyos, M.J.: Passion at first sight: how to engage users in social commerce contexts. Electron. Commer. Res. **17**(4), 701–720 (2017)
9. Iyengar, R., Van den Bulte, C., Valente, T.W.: Opinion leadership and social contagion in new product diffusion. Mark. Sci. **30**(2), 195–212 (2011)
10. Kassim, E.S., Othman, A.K., Zamzuri, N.H.: Strategies for sustainable social commerce: the roles of customer focus, innovative business model. Leg. Trust. Inf. J. **19**, 2907–2912 (2016)
11. Kohtamäki, M., Partanen, J., Parida, V., Wincent, J.: Non-linear relationship between industrial service offering and sales growth: the moderating role of network capabilities. Ind. Mark. Manag. **42**(8), 1374–1385 (2013)
12. Lee, J.Y., Bell, D.R.: Neighborhood social capital and social learning for experience attributes of products. Mark. Sci. **32**(6), 960–976 (2013)
13. Lee, J.Y., Hosanagar, K., Tan, Y.: Do I follow my friends or the Crowd? Information cascades in online movie ratings. Mark. Sci. **61**(9), 2241–2258 (2015)
14. Li, F., Du, T.C.: Who is talking? An ontology-based opinion leader identification framework for word-of-mouth marketing in online social blogs. Decis. Support Syst. **51**(1), 190–197 (2011)
15. Li, Q., Liang, N., Li, E.Y.: Does friendship quality matter in social commerce? An experimental study of its effect on purchase intention. Electron. Commer. Res. **18**(4), 693–717 (2018)
16. Liang, T.-P., Turban, E.: Introduction to the special issue social commerce: a research framework for social commerce. Int. J. Electron. Commer. **16**(2), 5–14 (2011)
17. Moretti, E.: Social learning and peer effects in consumption: Evidence from movie sales. Rev. Econ. Stud. **78**(1), 356–393 (2011)
18. Olbrich, R., Holsing, C.: Modeling consumer purchasing behavior in social shopping communities with clickstream data. Int. J. Electron. Commer. **16**(2), 15–40 (2011)
19. Sinha, R.R., Swearingen, K. Comparing recommendations made by online systems and friends. In: DELOS Workshop: Personalisation and Recommender Systems in Digital Libraries (2001)

20. Sotiriadis, M.D., Van Zyl, C.: Electronic word-of-mouth and online reviews in tourism services: the use of twitter by tourists. Electron. Commer. Res. **13**(1), 103–124 (2013)
21. Stephen, A.T., Toubia, O.: Deriving value from social commerce networks. J. Mark. Res. **47**(2), 215–228 (2010)
22. Trusov, M., Bucklin, R.E., Pauwels, K.: Effects of word-of-mouth versus traditional marketing: findings from an internet social networking site. J. Mark. **73**(5), 90–102 (2009)
23. van Eck, P.S., Jager, W., Leeflang, P.S.H.: Opinion leaders' role in innovation diffusion: a simulation study. J. Prod. Innov. Manag. **28**(2), 187–203 (2011)
24. Wang, C., Zhang, P.: The evolution of social commerce: the people, management, technology, and information dimensions. CAIS **31**, 5 (2012)
25. Wang, C., Zhang, X., Hann, I.-H.: Socially nudged: a quasi-experimental study of friends' social influence in online product ratings. Inf. Syst. Res. **29**, 641–655 (2018)
26. Wang, C.A., Zhang, X.M., Hann, I.-H.: Social bias in online product ratings: A quasi-experimental analysis. In: The Workshop on Information Systems Economics, St. Louis, 2010 (2010)
27. Zhang, J., Liu, Y., Chen, Y.: Social learning in networks of friends versus strangers. Mark. Sci. **34**(4), 573–589 (2015)

Avoiding Mistakes in Medical High-Tech Treatments and E-Commerce Applications – a Salutary UX-Research Innovation

Christina Miclau[1]([✉]), Oliver Gast[2], Julius Hertel[3], Anja Wittmann[3], Achim Hornecker[3], and Andrea Mueller[2]

[1] Hochschule Offenburg, University of Applied Sciences,
Badstrasse 24, 77652 Offenburg, Germany
`christina.miclau@hs-offenburg.de`
[2] User Interface Design GmbH, Wilhelm-Bleyle-Straße 10-12,
71636 Ludwigsburg, Germany
[3] Dr. Hornecker Software-Entwicklung und IT-Dienstleistungen,
Leo-Wohleb-Strasse 6, 79098 Freiburg im Breisgau, Germany

Abstract. Medical devices accompany our everyday life and come across in situations of worse condition, in significant moments concerning the health or during routine checkups. To ensure flawless operations and error-free results it is essential to test applications and devices. High risks for patient's health come with operating errors [33] so that the presented research project, called Professional UX, identifies signals and irritations caused by the interaction with a certain device by analyzing mimic, voice and eye tracking data during user experience tests. Besides, this paper will provide information on typical errors of interactive applications which are based on an empirical lab-based survey and the evaluated results achieved. The pictured proceeding of user experience tests and the following analysis can also be applied to other fields and serves as a support for the optimization of products and systems.

Keywords: Medical technology · User experience · Operation errors · High risk systems

1 Introduction: UX-Challenges for Medical High-Tech Treatments and E-Commerce

The user experience (UX) of graphical user interfaces is becoming an increasingly important prerequisite for the acceptance of software in the age of digitalization. In many areas, easily and intuitively comprehensible user interfaces are also a qualification for the use of software systems, for example in the field of medical devices or in automotive and application scenarios in the area of occupational safety. Often UX is already part of industry standards in these areas. But also in less critical application areas like e-commerce, UX is becoming more and more an economical factor.

However, at the moment the assessment of user experience is still mainly based on subjective criteria, which are the results of surveys and experience of professionals, despite guidelines such as DIN EN 62366. This project uses artificial intelligence

© Springer Nature Switzerland AG 2019
F. F.-H. Nah and K. Siau (Eds.): HCII 2019, LNCS 11588, pp. 306–322, 2019.
https://doi.org/10.1007/978-3-030-22335-9_21

techniques to develop objective measurements for determining user experience building on non-invasive methods such as eye movements, facial expressions and measurement in the change of voice. From these measurements there will be derived criteria for evaluating user interfaces, such as anger, confusion or stress.

2 Methods to Identify User Irritations for Avoiding Mistakes

Unfortunately, there is still no standardized value for user experience in case of the optimization of interactive applications or devices. The various number of methods makes it difficult to compare results because of the different approaches.

According to Sarodnick and Brau [1] two kinds of procedures can be used for measuring user experience, see Fig. 1 and its description in Table 1.

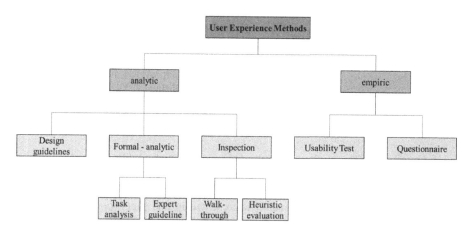

Fig. 1. User experience methods.

The major difference between the shown methods is the evaluating person. In case of analytic methods, there are experts who test and evaluate the certain user experience, whereas empirical methods are based on target-group-specific participants, who verify the system's or device's user experience during tests [1].

However, the identification and determination of user irritations is still complex and difficult to achieve. The Customer Experience Tracking Laboratory of the Offenburg University focuses on an innovative method, which is specialized on the emotion measurement, since it allows detailed and purposive conclusions by not exclusively considering usability problems [2].

Customer Experience Tracking (CXT) is a multi-level, modular and scalable process developed by Offenburg University to explore the usability of interactive systems [2]. It is based on the measurement method for user experience in which heuristics, usability tests and interviews are applied. The different methods included within the CXT process are such as analysis of facial expression, eye tracking, think aloud, electro dermal activity analysis as well as motion and gesture tracking, online-questionnaire

Table 1. User experience methods and their characteristics.

	Method	Characteristic
Analytic	Design guidelines	• Ensures usability • Easy implementation • List of principles
	Task analysis	• Evaluation of user experience by tasks to be fulfilled by the device or system
	Expert guideline	• Evaluation by rules of software ergonomics (on the basis of checklists)
	Walkthrough	• Experts evaluate proposals for the implementation of various features • Verification of an intuitive interface, also for inexperienced users
	Heuristic evaluation	• Experts evaluate by using heuristics, for example the ten heuristics according to Nielsen (1994) • Often combined with empirical methods such as usability tests
Empiric	Usability test	• Most known method • Target-group-specific participants test the device under real-life conditions by accomplishing tasks
	Questionnaire	• Enables quantitative data

and input reports. The various modules of measurement enable a development of recommendations for action and provide information on customer's emotions during the interaction which are an essential component for user experience [3].

The research project Professional UX, presented in this paper, combines the most common used modules of emotion and user experience measurement to identify signals and irritations caused during the interaction with a device. It includes the three different methods of mimic analysis, voice analysis (received data by using think aloud) and eye tracking, described below.

2.1 Emotion Psychology: Where Do Emotions Come from?

Emotions can be declared as an intermediary interface between an environmental input and a behavioral output that disconnects the stimulus itself from the resulted reaction [4].

Due to changes in state of various organismic subsystems emotions are evolved [2]. They enable the identification of user irritations by applying different methods to measure human's expression and behavior, most importantly the analysis of facial expression and voice [2].

On the basis of the so-called basic emotions it is possible to provide a selection of emotions which are intercultural universally recognized emotions. In accordance with the theory of Ekman and Friesen [6], there are six different basic emotions [5] such as joy, disgust, sadness, anger, surprise and fear with respective changes in facial expressions, which allows the measurement of emotions. The mentioned theory serves as the basis for the CXT- method of Offenburg University.

2.2   Mimic Analysis: How Do Emotions Show?

The facial expression is an important indicator for the existence of an emotion. An emotion is triggered by outer stimuli which cause changes of the person's facial expression depending on the processed stimuli and triggered feelings. During stationary testings the facial expression is recorded by a webcam. This way the data is available post hoc and can be analyzed and evaluated retrospectively, independently and unnoticed by the participants. The approach of analyzing is by Emotional Facial Action Coding System (EmFACS), a classification for interpreting mimic art. EmFACS is a reduced classification [7] of Paul Ekman's FACS (Facial Action Coding System) where the mentioned six basic emotions can be related to different action units (Fig. 2) within the definition of the primal scheme of FACS [8]. Due to the 43 muscles in our face an exact interpretation of emotions is possible [9].

Action Units

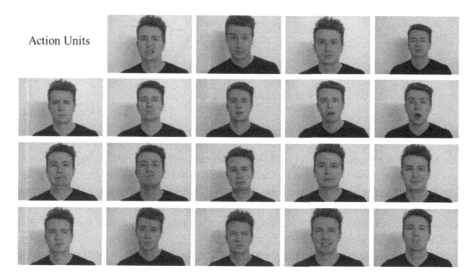

Fig. 2. Action units for the mimic analysis.

2.3   Eye Tracking: What Do Users See?

Eye tracking is one of the method's central measuring instrument for the determination of irritations and user behavior. The user's gaze is captured in real time by four cameras and infrared technology. In case of a friction the user's gaze remains longer at the certain hurdle and is shown as a fixation point. The longer the person looks at a specific spot the bigger the visualization of a fixation point gets. The results obtained are analyzed and interpreted in combination with the mimic analysis and are supplemented by the user's comments [2] (Fig. 3).

Fig. 3. Eye tracking analysis.

2.4   Voice Analysis: Can We Hear Emotions?

The human voice is not only an audible transmission of words, but rather a doorway into the human inside by providing hidden information and indications. Also, analogous to the changes of facial expression, the voice changes according to an experienced emotion. The way these changes are created and perceived enables the analysis of the acoustic speech signal and backtracking to a certain emotion and thus the origin of a positive or negative event [31].

During user experience testings by means of the customer experience tracking method, there is used the so-called think aloud method. Think aloud provides the opportunity to get information on the participant's thoughts and opinion of the tested system or product. During the tasks every participant has to manage it is requested to comment on positive or negative aspects of the system or device [10]. "Negative affects can make it harder to do even easy tasks" [11] so that especially the negative aspects give some insight into the device's frictions [12]. Think aloud can be run in two different ways. The retrospective think aloud includes a questionnaire and commenting after the testing. Whereas an interview and the participant commenting are conducted during the testing if the concurrent think aloud is used. To sum up, think aloud enables further insight into the user's mind by verbalizing their thoughts and feelings [10].

Thoughts and emotions of users, especially the negative ones, are decisive for the acceptance of devices and for the verification of user experience. For this purpose, the research project Professional UX was initiated to fathom user experience factors and emotions, and to create a device that simplifies the analysis of UX.

3 Professional UX: Soft- and Hardware Selection Criteria

3.1 Innovative Testing Technology: Cost-Effective, Easy to Use, Open Interfaces

Nowadays, since we're facing digital devices daily, it is necessary and has never been more critical to provide frictionless and intuitive experiences. Users expect devices to be optimized and without irritations, which is required as basis [13].

Therefore, it is important to understand expectations and needs of the users as soon and clear as possible and optimize user interfaces by investing in user experience. Within seconds a user is influenced by the system and forms an opinion. It is said, that "$10 would be spent on the same problem during development, and multiply to $100 or more if the problem had to be solved after the product's release" [13]. At least 50% of a programmer's time is spent on solving an avoidable problem due to frictions and bad UX [14]. Besides money good UX can save time if problems are fixed at the beginning of development, because they can cause 100 times more time waste during or after the development [15].

Due to the importance of considering user experience in the design process of devices and systems the presented research project is developing a hardware which includes the most common used methods of user experience analysis: mimic analysis, voice analysis and eye tracking. The idea of combining all three modules in a single hardware reduces the costs of purchasing hardware for each of them which would include cameras for the mimic analysis, microphones for the voice analysis and an eye tracker, the most expensive part of a purchase like this (Fig. 4).

Furthermore, the hardware not only allows agencies or UX-specialized companies to perform UX testings, which keeps down costs. Also it allows non-experts, without much expertise, to run tests on their own devices because of an intuitive use. During the development and optimization of the hard- and software within the scope of Professional UX, all usability requirements are considered which leads to a simply structured interface.

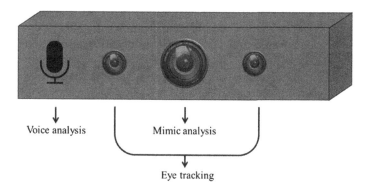

Fig. 4. Professional UX innovation.

The software, inspired by Open Interfaces for mimic analysis, is programmed accordingly so that the user has the possibility of freely selecting the desired module. In addition to this free choice, according to the test's objective, the system starts all selected modules by one single button. Thus a synchrony of all data is given, which is the most difficult and time-consuming part in the evaluation and analysis in the area of UX (Fig. 5).

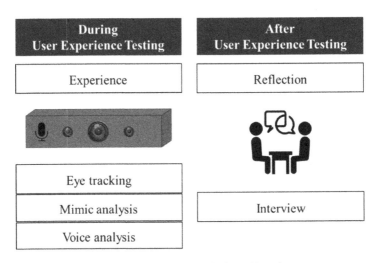

Fig. 5. Modules during and after UX-testings.

3.2   Professional UX: Learning Software

As artificial intelligence we use machine learning methods. Machine learning describes mathematical and statistical techniques that computer systems use to generate knowledge from experience. More precisely, the system automatically learns from training data including features and labels. Features are independent variables that serve as the input in our system and labels are the final output. After the learning process, the system can predict the labels of some test data using their features.

In our application we use machine learning tools to predict the emotion of a user of a graphical interface. On the one hand we analyze the facial expression of the user, on the other hand we make an analysis of its voice. So, we extract both video and audio features from a recording of this user.

We have implemented the machine learning and emotion analysis code in the programming language C++ due to performance reasons. For the facial expression analysis, we make use of OpenCV 4.0 presented in [25]. This is an open source computer vision library including many machine learning tools. For the voice analysis, the Speech Signal Processing Toolkit 3.11 (SPTK), see [26], is utilized to extract numerous audio features. Below we describe our methods in more detail.

The resulting data of our prediction analyses are visualized in a graphical user interface that we have implemented in C#, in Fig. 6.

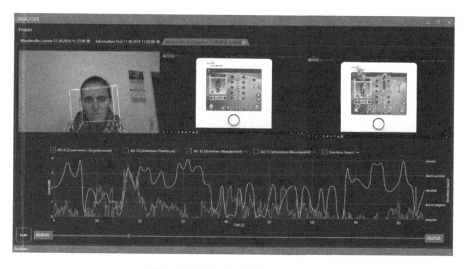

Fig. 6. Professional UX analyzer.

Mimic Analysis

The core of our emotion analysis is the automatic detection of selected action units of the Facial Action Coding System (FACS) by Ekman and Friesen [16].

In the first step, the user face is detected on each frame of the video recording. For this task, we use the very fast method proposed by Viola and Jones [17] implemented in OpenCV where we also take the pre-trained model from. This recognition is optimized respecting our special use case: For example, the face on the frame must have a specific minimum size. We get an accuracy of 99.93% on our test data which does not have challenging head poses, occlusions or lighting conditions.

In the second step, we extract 49 inner facial landmarks from the detected faces. Theses landmarks are points in the images describing eyes, eyebrows, mouth and nose, and serve later as feature set for the recognition of action units, see Fig. 7. For this landmark localization we use the method by Ren et al. [18] as implemented in (the extra modules of) OpenCV. The training features of this approach are so-called local binary patterns that describe the texture of an image. With these features we trained a model on our own data using random forests as machine learning technique. The normalized mean error of the inter-ocular distance is 6.4% on our test images. The best deep learning methods currently have an error about 4%.

In the third step, the landmarks are normalized. More precisely, we apply an affine transformation to the landmarks such that the distances between the landmarks and the points of a reference face are minimized.

In the fourth step, the goal is to detect the intensities of selected action units of the FACS in order to evaluate the emotion of the user. Seven action units have been selected to be important for emotions relating the user experience of graphical user interfaces (also see Chapter 4 "Study results for mimic analysis").

For the prediction of the intensities of these action units, we have implemented the algorithm by Werner et al. [19]. The training features of this algorithm are the

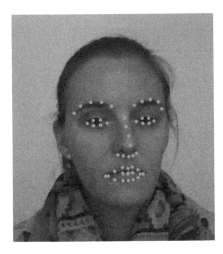

Fig. 7. Landmarks of the mimic analysis software.

normalized landmarks from the third step and the local binary patterns from the second step. The machine learning method is an ensemble of support vector machines with linear kernel. In comparison to deep learning techniques, this procedure is faster with similar detection rate.

In the fifth step, the intensities of the action units are smoothed and calibrated respecting the specific user.

In the sixth step, we predict the intensity of emotion between −1 (negative/irritated) and 1 (positive/not irritated). For this purpose, we use the computed intensities of the action units as training features and take an ensemble of support vector machines with linear kernel as machine learning method.

Voice Analysis
For emotion analysis based on voice we first split the audio recordings into intervals of two seconds. From each of these pieces we extract features by first computing certain acoustic low-level descriptors (LLDs) and then apply statistical functionals to these.

First, we split the audio pieces further into smaller segments (varying between 20 and 60 ms) and sample at 5–10 ms. From each of these samples we extract the low-level descriptors, including pitch, jitter, shimmer and formants as well as mel-frequency cepstral coefficients known to be important in emotion analysis of speech. The SPTK [26] already has methods to extract some of these features which we access in our code. We get a resulting vector containing data from the segments for each LLD and audio piece.

Having this vector, we apply functionals to it like arithmetic mean, standard deviation, arithmetic mean of the slope and some percentiles, resulting in the final feature.

Our feature selection was inspired by the Geneva Minimalistic Acoustic Parameter Set presented in [20] as well as larger known feature sets used in INTERSPEECH

Challenges, for example in the Emotion Challenge 2009 [22] or the Speaker State Challenge 2011 [23]. A nice overview of these feature sets can be found in [21]. We reduced large brute force feature sets by means of recursive feature selection and we selected features which suited our special task.

In the last step we use the features described above to predict the emotion of each interval on a scale between -1 (negative/irritated) and 1 (positive/not irritated). As machine learning method we use a support vector machine with radial kernel which was trained with the extracted features of audio files from the Berlin Database of Emotional Speech, see [24], as well as our own data. On the Berlin Database of Emotional Speech we get an accuracy of 90.2% for the classification negative/neutral/positive with a leave-one-speaker-out cross validation.

4 Professional UX-Solution: Modular System of Intelligent Hard- and Software Components

4.1 Integrated Hardware Components

In order to record synchronized video and audio as well as eye tracking, we have written a PC software to control the recordings. The user can see in advance whether all hardware components are running properly and start and stop recordings, see Fig. 8.

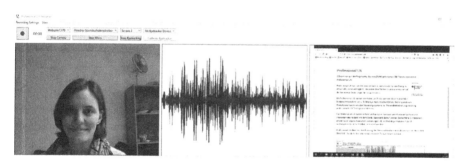

Fig. 8. Recording interface of the professional UX software.

On the hardware site we use a Raspberry Pi 3 B+ as a minicomputer to bundle the recordings. The Raspberry Pi is attached to the computer via LAN or wireless LAN for data transmission and communicates with our recording software via TCP and UDP protocols. To ensure a proper shutdown in case of a premature disconnection we use an uninterruptible power supply, namely a Raspberry USV+ by Ritter Elektronik.

On the recording site we have an Adafruit I2S MEMS Microphone Breakout attached to the GPIOs of the Raspberry Pi. The video recording is done by the Raspberry Pi V1.3 Camera from AZ-Delivery which is connected through the CSI camera port. Furthermore, we use an EyeTech Digital Systems AEye OEM Module for eye tracking via a USB connection.

We specified the recording settings according to our tasks and models from 3.2 as follows: We record video at 25 frames per second and 1280 × 720 pixel, audio at 44.1 kHz, mono and a sampling depth of 16 Bit. The speed of the eye tracker is 100 Hz and it uses dark pupil methods to calculate the gaze position.

To evaluate the functions of our prototype we conducted empirical studies on Mimic Recognition and Voice Analysis.

4.2   Mimic Recognition Method

For good UX it is indispensable to avoid negative influences caused by frictions. Therefore, a study for the consideration of emotions in user experience was carried out as part of a doctoral thesis at Offenburg University. Measuring UX as the beginning of an optimization process is quite complex, also because of numerous bias effects like social desirability or the experimenter's effect [2].

Within the doctoral thesis a pilot and a main study were performed with the objective of a mimic-based UX testing method. The method is based on the analysis of the basic emotions for the identification of frictions and aims to set parameters to a few limited trigger points. This way both time and costs can be reduced.

The purpose of the pilot study was to show the existing connection between facial expressions and emotions in the context of interactive applications by clarifying mimic as an emotion-carrier. On the other hand, the main study takes the relation between mimic, emotions and frictions in consideration and aims on finding parameters that help detect irritations. The following table presents the key data of the studies [27] (Table 2).

Table 2. Key data of mimic recognition study.

	Pilot study	Main study
Method	Videoclips which induce specific emotions are implemented in an interactive application and the facial expression is measured by Ekman's FACS	User irritations that trigger negative emotions are included in an ordering process of an onlineshop and the facial expression is measured by Ekman's FACS
Sample	33 participants, 363 videos, including 65 min. analysis material	45 participants, 45 videos, 211 min. analysis material

The study's results identify six different action units for the detection of irritations, in the study related to possible purchase abandonment at an early stage. Initial implementations focus on four following actions units, see Table 3 [27] (Fig. 9).

Concentrating only on a few action units simplifies the distinction between the action units and makes the recognition easy for non-specialists [27].

The application of a mimic-based UX method is conceivable in various areas such as the evaluation of interactive user interfaces of machines, in proactive support of online shops or interactive applications, as well as the support of e-learning applications [27].

Table 3. Relevant action units for irritation identification.

	Action unit	Percentage share	Indicator for possible purchase cancellation
AU 4	Brow Lowerer	85%	✓
AU 10	Upper Lip Raiser	100%	✓
AU 14	Dimpler	88%	✓
AU 24	Lip Pressor	94%	✓

Fig. 9. Example for action unit AU 4.

4.3 Voice Analysis Software

The objective of the presented study on voice analysis is the development of a model that enables the connection of emotions and acoustic changes of the voice. The following hypotheses built the basis of the research within a master thesis at Offenburg University (Table 4):

Table 4. Hypotheses and scientific issues of voice analysis.

No. of hypothesis	Scientific issue
Hypothesis 1	"We change the voice quality depending on the context"
Hypothesis 2	"The voice provides information about the excitement or activation"
Hypothesis 3	"On the basis of voice analysis, positive and negative emotions can be distinguished"

Phonetics describe and examine acoustic speech signals which are generated by a speech apparatus and aim to assign vocal changes to phonation types. Various areas of phonetic allow analysis of speech and voice evaluation. The part of symbol phonetic "recognizes and holds on to individual sounds and higher linguistic units" by listening carefully and by introspection, whereas phonetics "grasp physiological processes of speech and hearing" and attempts to physically add the acoustic events [28]. The presented study is based on the signal or acoustic phonetic which takes sound vibrations into consideration by the methods oscillogram and spectrogram, see Fig. 10 [29].

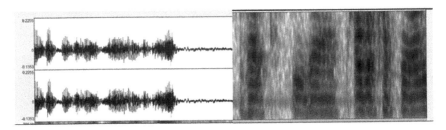

Fig. 10. Illustration of voice analysis data.

The human voice is both an interaction of various muscles and physical reactions (sound waves) for the transmission or the verbalization of information and also an insight into a person's thoughts and emotions [30].

An acoustic signal changes in response to the emotions which are triggered by certain external stimuli [31]. As an external stimulus is processed and subjectively evaluated, an emotion is triggered which is shown in the way you speak and in the acoustic or sound impression [32]. These changes also include changes in facial expression so that the combination of both methods provide information on emotions and thus possible frictions.

5   Recommendations

Professional UX provides in combination with CXT an easy handling due to a simultaneous start of all modules at the click of a button and the coded automated analysis of all gathered data during the testing.

It simplifies and improves the optimization of interfaces which leads to a reduction of risks and frictions. Using the presented method, which involves the pictured soft- and hardware, the performance of UX testings is made easier and more cost effective due to the combination of the most effective modules for analyzing user experience in a single device and its intuitive use.

In addition, the used methods and modules during Professional UX can also be transferred to other fields like tests of online shops, websites, e-learning platforms or further interactive applications, systems and devices.

Recommendation 1: Listen to your medical user's needs
Any device is supposed to be useful and lead to the desired objective. Producers of medical devices need to design products with life-saving interfaces. Therefore, it is

indispensable to listen to your customer – both the spoken and the unspoken. Thus medical device providers have to analyze their designed interfaces and go deeper into human minds and emotions to meet their expectations and to ensure a safe usage.

Recommendation 2: Concentrate on simplicity and essentials of interaction elements in medical user-interfaces
The right amount of information is one of the key factors for a successful user experience. Too many options and functions offered during the use can distract and discourage medical users from doing their vitally important tasks. It is essential to support step by step the required tasks and to concentrate on relevant interaction features from the user's angle.

Recommendation 3: Follow the usual - even in specific medical operations
When thinking about a new medical device and during the creative process a positive user experience is fundamental. A big part of it is the warranty of an intuitive use, clarity and reasonable structure. Enabling this kind of medical device interface promotes the interaction and avoids operating errors in, for example, critical surgery situations. One of the most common causes of accidents in medical technology are operating errors that could be prevented by following several UX-guidelines. Many medical devices developed by technical specialists use to be structured in a complex way what leads to unexpected interactions [33] and incorrect operations involving high risks for patients [34]. For this reason, medical devices should be designed intuitively and oriented towards their intended purposes to ensure the patients' well-being.

6 Conclusion

Measuring non-invasive parameters in combination with artificial intelligence methods provides a way to extract quantitative estimations for the user experience of graphical interfaces. Existing methods of machine learning can be extended in a way that basic parameters of the user experience such as stress or confusion during the use of the graphical interface can be determined and visualized.

In particular combining voice and facial expression analysis allows better conclusions in contrast to focusing on just one parameter.

With the combination of the different physical outputs of human interaction, emotion becomes finally measurable. That enables the automatic evaluation of perception results while human-computer interaction happens.

7 Limitations and Future Work

Using complex medical treatment devices is a hazardous challenge: only well-trained persons apply these, but physical conditions of the medical professionals is not always the same. In case of occurring problems there is an urgent need to ensure that no mistake can happen, during a surgery.

The system Professional-UX ensures to provide a user-tested interface for medical device suppliers: all possible issues can be tested and eliminated before the sale of the product starts without huge additional expenses and loss of time.

Nevertheless, there is a chance that new, with the pretesting using the Professional-UX not identifiable problems could occur and endanger the success of the operation. It is necessary to involve medical experts in the evaluation task to make sure that the interface fulfills the needs of the users.

The results of our research project still needs more investigation: The AI-system only learns from usage data and refines with every user testing procedure. A Professional-UX prototype is in use in several companies in southwest Germany. With the gained knowledge of all the different user testing scenarios there will be a huge database for medical device interface design available. This can be helpful for future research projects.

Hochschule Offenburg and Dr. Hornecker Software will enhance their research work and apply for new projects with innovative interaction devices for the medical branch. The challenge is to provide medical experts with the best-fitting interfaces for their life-saving work.

Also, other branches and industries could use the results to optimize processes that involve human machine interaction, like the usage of a display of a forming machine or the usage of an online-shop.

In future work we will also use the recorded eye tracking data for analyzing the emotion. The results of the project provide a good base for the introduction of objective UX assessment methods in the various application areas.

References

1. Sarodnick, F., Brau, H.: Methoden der Usability Evaluation, 2nd edn. sl, pp. 119–191. Verlag Hans Huber (2011)
2. Mueller, A., Gast, O.: Customer experience tracking – Online-Kunden conversionwirksame Erlebnisse bieten durch gezieltes Emotionsmanagement. In: Keuper, F., et al (eds.) Daten-Management und Daten-Services – Next Level, Berlin, pp. 313–343 (2014)
3. Thuering, M., Mahlke, S.: Usability, aesthetics and emotions in human–technology interaction. Int. J. Psychol. **42**(4), 253–264 (2007). https://doi.org/10.1080/00207590701 396674
4. Vogel, I.: Emotionen im Kommunikationskontext. In: Six, U., Gleich, U., Gimmler, R. (eds.) Kommunikationspsychologie – Medienpsychologie. Lehrbuch (Anwendung Psychologie, 1st edn.), pp. 135–157. Weinheim, Beltz (2007)
5. Schmidt-Atzert, L., et al.: Lehrbuch der Emotionspsychologie. Kohlhammer, Stuttgart (1996)
6. Ekman, P., Friesen, W.: Manual for the Facial Action Coding System, Palo Alto (1977)
7. Noldus: FaceReader: Project Analysis Module. http://www.noldus.com/facereader/project-analysis-module. Accessed 21 Oct 2017
8. Paul Ekman Group: Facial Action Coding System (FACS) FAQ - Paul Ekman Group. http://www.paulekman.com/facs-faq/. Accessed 21 Oct 2017
9. Argyle, M.: Körpersprache & Kommunikation. Nonverbaler Ausdruck und soziale Interaktion, 10th edn., p. 155. Junfermann, Paderborn (2013)

10. Jo, M.Y., Stautmeister, A.: Don't make me think aloud! – Lautes Denken mit Eye-Tracking auf dem Prüfstand. In: Brau, H., et al. (eds.) Usability Professionals 2011, Stuttgart, pp. 172–177 (2011)

11. Norman, D.: Emotion and design: attractive things work better. Interact. Mag. **ix**(4), 36–42 (2002)

12. Wong, E.: How to Prevent Negative Emotions in the User Experience of Your Product. https://www.interaction-design.org/literature/article/how-to-prevent-negative-emotions-in-the-user-experience-of-your-product. Accessed 31 Jan 2019 (2017)

13. Paunovic, G.: The Bottom Line: Why Good UX Design Means Better Business. https://www.forbes.com/sites/forbesagencycouncil/2017/03/23/the-bottom-line-why-good-ux-design-means-better-business/#358a58c32396. Accessed 31 Jan 2019 (2017)

14. Usability.gov: Benefits of User-Centered Design. https://www.usability.gov/what-and-why/benefits-of-ucd.html. Accessed 30 Jan 2019

15. Stern, T.: Why User Experience Is the Best ROI Strategy. https://www.business.com/articles/why-user-experience-is-the-best-roi-strategy/. Accessed 30 Jan 2019 (2017)

16. Ekman, P., Friesen, W.V.: Facial Action Coding System: A Technique for the Measurement of Facial Movement. Consulting Psychologists Press, Palo Alto (1978)

17. Viola, P., Jones, M.: Rapid object detection using a boosted cascade of simple features. In: Proceedings of the 2001 IEEE Computer Society Conference on Computer Vision and Pattern Recognition, CVPR 2001, Kauai, HI, USA, 2001, p. I-I (2001)

18. Ren, S., et al.: Face alignment at 3000 FPS via regressing local binary features. In: Proceedings of the IEEE Conference on Computer Vision and Pattern Recognition (2014)

19. Werner, P., Saxen, F., Al-Hamadi, A.: Handling data imbalance in automatic facial action intensity estimation. FERA, p. 26 (2015)

20. Eyben, F., et al.: The geneva minimalistic acoustic parameter set (GeMAPS) for voice research and affective computing. IEEE Trans. Affect. Comput. **7**(2), 190–202 (2016)

21. Eyben, F. et al.: Towards a standard set of acoustic features for the processing of emotion in speech. In: Proceedings of Meetings on Acoustics (2010)

22. Schuller, B., Steidl, S., Batlinger, A.: The INTERSPEECH 2009 emotion challenge. In: Proceedings of Interspeech, ISCA (2009)

23. Schuller, B., et al.: The INTERSPEECH 2011 speaker state challenge. In: Proceedings of Interspeech (2011)

24. Burkhardt, F., et al.: A database of german emotional speech. In: Proceedings of Interspeech (2005)

25. Bradski, G.: The OpenCV library. Dr. Dobb's J. Softw. Tools **25**, 120–125 (2000)

26. Imai, S., Kobayashi, T., et al.: Speech Signal Processing Toolkit. https://sourceforge.net/projects/sp-tk. Accessed 29 Jan 2019

27. Gast, O.: User Experience im E-Commerce. Messung von Emotionen bei der Nutzung interaktiver Anwendungen. Springer Gabler, Wiesbaden (2018). https://doi.org/10.1007/978-3-658-22484-4. Dissertation Pädagogische Hochschule Freiburg, ISBN 978-3-658-22484-4, pp. 18–24, 30–46, 131–134

28. Reetz, H.: Artikulatorische und akustische Phonetik, 2nd edn., pp. 1–30, 125–137f. WWT Wissenschaftlicher Verlag, Trier (2003)

29. Carstensen, K.-U.: Computerlinguistik und Sprachtechnologie. Eine Einführung, 3rd edn., pp. 176–194. Spektrum, Akad. Verlag, Heidelberg (2010)

30. Schwertfeger, B.: Personalauswahl per Sprachtest. In: Personalmagazin, no. 12, pp. 32–34. https://www.wiso-net.de/document/PEMA__111524019. Accessed 21 Oct 2017(2015)

31. Schneider-Stickler, B., Bigenzahn, W.: Stimmdiagnostik. Ein Leitfaden für die Praxis, 2nd edn., pp. 30–34. Springer, Dordrecht (2013)

32. Schwender, C.: Medien und Emotionen, p. 34. Springer Fach-medien, Wiesbaden (2007)

33. Compamed Magazin: Top-Design gegen Pannen im OP. https://www.compamed.de/cgi-bin/md_compamed/lib/pub/tt.cgi/Top-Design_gegen_Pannen_im_OP.html?oid=17100&lang=1&ticket=g_u_e_s_t. Accessed 21 Oct 2017 (2007)
34. Dain, S.: Normal accidents: human error and medical equipment design. Hear. Surg. Forum **5**(3) (2002)

Persuaded by Electronic Word of Mouth (eWOM): Network Coproduction Model on Chinese Social-Ecommerce App

Haoning Xue[✉]

City University of Hong Kong, Kowloon Tong, Hong Kong
haoninxue2-c@my.cityu.edu.hk

Abstract. In the era of Web 2.0 with prominent feature of user-generated content, the phenomenon of coproduction prevails in inter-consumer communication as well – consumers produce contents about product experience and evaluations to share and to support each other, rather than being passively influenced by marketers or key opinion leaders. The Little Red Book (LRB), a social-ecommerce unicorn in China, encourages users to share experience and opinion on cosmetic products and other aspects of life, even though it is a weak-tie community without much intimacy. This research revolves around the Network Coproduction Model of electronic Word of Mouth (Kozinets et al. 2010) and tries to test if eWOM of ordinary users can influence others' product attitude and purchase intention. Two variables of eWOM, self-disclosure and product price, are manipulated to design a 2 (self-disclosure: descriptive, evaluative) × 2 (product price: high, low) factorial experiment. The researcher conducts an electronic experiment and a follow-up survey (N = 210) with 8 LRB prototype posts. The result indicates that LRB users mostly identity LRB as a supportive and honest community, even though they are not particularly active or involved here; product attitude and purchase intention are highly correlated; descriptive self-disclosure is more effective in persuading consumers than evaluative one is, and the combination of descriptive self-disclosure and high-cost product yields the most positive product attitude.

Keywords: Computer mediated communication ·
Electronic Word of Mouth (eWOM) · Self-disclosure · Social strength

1 Introduction

Growing grass (种草), a Chinese network buzzword, means that people are persuaded to favor a product either by celebrities or fellow consumers on social media. Little Red Book (LRB) or *XiaoHongShu*, a social-ecommerce unicorn in China, has maintained over 100 million users and raised over US$300 million [1]. LRB is a user-centered instead of product-centered community, revolving around personal experience and opinion sharing on cosmetic product mainly and other aspects of life; intimacy is not a necessity here. Without credibility of celebrity or perceived intimacy shared within an interpersonal relationship, ordinary consumers on LRB can influence their peers' product attitude and purchase intention through electronic Word of Mouth (eWOM).

© Springer Nature Switzerland AG 2019
F. F.-H. Nah and K. Siau (Eds.): HCII 2019, LNCS 11588, pp. 323–332, 2019.
https://doi.org/10.1007/978-3-030-22335-9_22

Recent researches have shown that peer communication can influence customer decision making either directly or indirectly [2–4].

The causal relation of product attitude and purchase intention can be explained by the Theory of Reasoned Action and Theory of Planned Behavior [5], where behavior can be predicted by intention and attitude, and intention is shaped by an individual's attitude. Therefore, the researcher suspects that users are able to alter attitude toward a project and therefore change their purchase intention.

From social network analysis perspective, the society is composed of strong and weak ties [6]. Variables determining the difference include frequency, reciprocity, intimacy, emotional intensity, multiplexity, etc. [6–8]. In this case, the researcher believes that LRB is a weak-tie community characterized by social eWOM, different from other social media where users maintain strong-tie relationships or from shopping websites with focus on affiliated eWOM, according to eWOM categorization initiated by Xu [9].

On such a weak-tie community like LRB, users perform many-to-many communication most of the time, even though one-on-one instinct message is also enabled. Users contribute with their own stories and consume others' contents as well. This form of peer communication serves as a realistic scenario of Network Coproduction Model of eWOM – consumers are empowered by the Internet to become producers in their own network, although they are under the influence of marketer [10]. Adapted from Schramm's model of mass communication [11] to the eWOM field, three models of eWOM [10] picture how eWOM can be communicated. The organic inter-consumer influence model, corresponding to interpersonal communication, states that consumers communicate naturally without influence of marketers, which is motivated by organic desire to support; while the linear marketer influence models illustrates how key opinion leaders in consumer community directly inform and influence fellow consumers. Researches have been done to examine organic inter-consumer influence model (e.g. Pedersen, et al. 2014) [12] and linear marketer influence model (e.g. Samutachak and Li 2012) [13]. However, the network coproduction model has not been explored yet; even the definition of peer communication focuses on interpersonal communication instead of many-to-many model that prevails in virtual community [3].

The question remains, how do people form an attitude or even a decision based on an LRB post in a weak-tie community with full anonymity and little credibility? The researcher suspects that the content of the post shall be the key here, instead of the identity of the user, since in a network coproduction model, the consumers are treated identically without special focus on anyone in particular. From self-disclosure perspective, trust has been identified as an important factor mediating peer communication online, against concern of anonymity and credibility [4]. In the context of LRB, the researcher believes how users disclose personal information plays a role here. Personal information revealed is perceived as self-disclosure, which is classified into descriptive (DS) and evaluative (ES) ones [14]. Descriptive self-disclosure reveals personal facts about oneself, while evaluative ones are more about expressions of personal feelings and opinions. However, most of the researches are conducted from the perspective of the discloser, such as motivation; the effect of self-disclosure on the recipient has not been covered yet.

Apart from that users may respond to the post differently based on the level of self-disclosure, users proactively seek peer review to try to lower down the uncertainty and risk aroused by experience products. Laurent and Kapferer [15] have identified that consumers' involvement with product is determined by variables such as perceived risk, cost, and emotional appeal. Besides, familiarity with product would influence consumers' preference for sources [16]. Consumers would resort to eWOM to purchase services instead of physical goods [17]. Adopting Xu's classification [9], the researcher focuses on high-risk product with both high (HC) and low costs (LC), since LRB users mainly post and browse content related to high-risk product.

To fill the research gap and to understand how different aspects of self-disclosure in eWOM influences product attitude and purchase intention in a weak-tie community, the researcher designed a 2 (self-disclosure: descriptive, evaluative) × 2 (product price: high, low) experiment to examine the effect of self-disclosure in eWOM on product attitude (PA) and purchase intention (PI).

2   Method

2.1   Pretest

Initially, 12 eWOM in three cosmetic categories (lipstick, make-up foundation, and serum) are adapted based on real eWOM on LRB. The researcher selected eWOM with strong DS or ES characteristics and categorize them based on product price. The content is modified in order to augment its characteristics and lessen potential confusion, as most contents on the platform contain strong subjective favors that may dilute self-disclosure effects. Still, the originality of the content is mostly preserved to optimize the authenticity of this experiment. Besides, photos attached with eWOM are also modified to produce simulated brands as predominated perception of existing brands would affect the result.

By using *Mockingbot*, the researcher developed 12 simulated eWOM about 12 different virtual brands. After pretest (N = 35), eight valid eWOM (2 in each factor) are selected for formal experiment. In the process, with feedback from first 12 participants, the eWOM was modified again to better eliminate confusion caused by imprecise wording and understanding confusion. It came to the researcher's attention that many pretest participants did not realize the difference between descriptive self-disclosure and product description, though the definition and example are provided. In this way, this particular difference was specified before later participants start the survey. Therefore, the researcher took into account both overall result and result after modification (Table 1).

2.2   Electronic Experiment

The researcher collected data with wjx.com paid sample service – wjx.com filters participants with three filtering questions and pay them with fixed amount by completing this experiment. In total of 401 people are exposed with filtering questions,

Table 1. Pretest Result

	Manipulated post with virtual product							
	Tarin foundation	Fresh herb serum	American beauty lipstick	Spiritual herb mask	Athena foundation	Elec Monc serum	Les deux foundation	Glory mask
Self-disclosure	1	1	0	0	1	1	0	0
Product Cost	L	L	L	L	H	H	H	H
Result 1–19	0.79	0.84	0.32	0.32	0.74	0.47	0.32	0.47
Result 20–32	0.92	0.85	0.31	0.46	0.62	0.77	0.31	0.08
Result 1–32	0.84	0.84	0.31	0.38	0.69	0.59	0.31	0.31

Descriptive Self-disclosure: 0
Evaluative Self-disclosure: 1
High Product Cost: H
Low Product Cost: L

leaving 210 valid samples to answer this survey. There are three parts in this experiment. In the first section, participants are asked to review eight eWOM content in random order and to eight-scale questions (mark: 1 to 8) on their personal experience after reviewing. The second section consists of questions regarding user behavior on LRB and perception of this community, while the last part revolves around demographic information of the participants.

Demographic Information

The data collected (N = 210) focuses on Chinese women who age 18 to 35 and are users of *LRB*. Here is a summary of demographic and behavioral information of participants: 12% participants have received an associate degree or below, 80% have received a bachelor's degree, and 8% have earned a master's degree and above. 24% are currently full-time students, others work mostly on management (11%), administration (10%) and finance (9%). More than half of the participants live in relatively affluent areas in China, including Guangdong (20%), Beijing (12%), Shanghai (10%), Jiangsu (7%), and Zhejiang (5%), which matches the geological distribution of LRB user base as well. 84% participants earn monthly income lower than ¥10,000 ($1,484), and 89% spends less than ¥1,000 ($148) on cosmetics monthly.

Social Tie Strength

By examining 9 questions on social tie strength, LRB users maintain a relatively weak-tie relationship (M = 3.56) with each other. Even though participants mostly perceive the community as mutually supportive (M = 6.12), their engagement is overall low in terms of multiplexity (M = 4.90), frequency (M = 3.17) and intimacy (M = 2.77). Therefore, the researcher believes that it corroborates the idea that LRB is a weak-tie community.

In addition to social strength related questions, all participants have used the LRB and 95% of them have been using the LRB for more than three months. 67% participants produce less than 5 posts every month, but 86% visit the LRB more than 6 times per month. Most participants perceive their experience on LRB as positive (M = 6.19) and helpful (M = 6.43), regarding this community as necessary (M = 6.35) and relatively honest (M = 5.54).

Product Attitude and Purchase Intention
This section of results is based on six questions about eight prototyped posts, where three questions in terms of satisfaction, pleasure and overall evaluation are used to indicate the tendency of attitude, while the others are intended for intention-related actions, including adding the product to Wishlist, shopping cart and buying it over the counter.

The following table summarizes the mean of product attitude and purchase intention with regard to four categories and relevant categories. Overall, PA and PI are highly correlated, and there is a causal relationship between PA and PI, as explained by the Theory of Reasoned Action.

3   Discussion

3.1   Social Tie Strength on LRB

Overall, social tie strength on LRB is weak, as indicated in Table 2. However, the results of behavioral and cognitive indicators are extremely different. First of all, most of the time, consumers are audiences and rarely post actively, which can be explained by the power law distribution, where 20% users contribute 80% of the content. This is why most participants score higher on the frequency (M = 3.67) of following, messaging and liking than that of the reciprocity (M = 2.57). Nevertheless, relatively high following and liking frequency indicates that users are actively following what is trendy on the LRB, even though they do not gain much interaction.

Information, instead of intimacy, is perceived as more important in the eyes of LRB users. Most users do not know many users in real life (M = 2.28), which suggests that this relationship is basically maintained online and separated from the offline life of most users. However, users do perceive this community as highly supportive (M = 6.12) and helpful (M = 6.43), even though the level of interaction and involvement is quite low. Therefore, it can be concluded that interaction is not a determinant in how users evaluate how helpful a community is, instead, how informative it can be is more significant here.

Low level of interaction and high level of belongingness coexist and are not contradictory because consumers expect to gain more useful information rather than interaction from such a community, even though these are two crucial indicators of social tie strength. The weak tie strength does not necessarily mean that it is a negative thing; on the contrary, it implies that it is necessary for consumers to have a place to honestly discuss about real experience with cosmetic products.

Last but not least, it is worth noticing that users believe the LRB is not particularly honest (M = 5.54) compared with their more positive evaluation of LRB (M = 6.27) in

Table 2. Social tie strength on LRB

Topic	Mean	Description
Following frequency	3.67	*How many LRB users are you following?*
Following reciprocity	2.37	*How many LRB users are following you?*
Messaging frequency	2.79	*How many direct messages do you send every month?*
Message reciprocity	2.68	*How many direct messages do you receive every month?*
Liking frequency	4.55	*How frequently do you like others' posts on LRB?*
Liking reciprocity	2.67	*How frequently do you receive likes from others?*
Multiplexity	4.90	*I talk with LRB users about topics other than cosmetics*
Intimacy	2.28	*I know LRB users in my real life*
Emotional intensity	6.12	*I think LRB is a mutually supportive community*

terms of necessity and usefulness. At the point of this research, LRB is crowded with advertisers and key opinion leader who mask themselves as ordinary users under no influence from marketers. Hence, ordinary users usually suspect the trustworthiness before believing in the information in the post.

3.2 The Effect of Self-disclosure and Product Cost

As indicated in Table 3, the product attitude toward the eight manipulated brands are relatively positive, which is purely generated by the post in the experiment, as users are never exposed to these brands before and therefore, there is no product attitude toward them. This is necessary to eliminate the external influence on the result. Besides, purchase intention is usually lower than the product attitude; this is probably because attitude is not the only determinant of intention, which is also influenced by financial status and current need, even though these two concepts are highly correlated.

Table 3. Correlation: product attitude & purchase intention

	Product attitude	Purchase intention	Correlation
DS × HC	5.80	5.28	.68
ES × HC	5.57	5.17	.81
DS × LC	5.70	5.47	.86
ES × LC	5.39	5.03	.82
DS	5.75	5.38	.79
ES	5.48	5.10	.83
HC	5.69	5.22	.74
LC	5.54	5.25	.86

DS: Descriptive Self-Disclosure
HC: High-cost High-risk Product
ES: Evaluative Self-Disclosure
LC: Low-cost High-risk Product

First of all, descriptive self-disclosure is much more effective in persuasion than evaluative self-disclosure with regard to both product attitude ($M_{DS} = 5.75$, $M_{ES} = 5.48$) and purchase intention ($M_{DS} = 5.38$, $M_{ES} = 5.10$). However, the difference of effect on product attitude and purchase intention is minimal, as indicated by the percentage of M_{DS} on M_{ES} ($M_{PA-DS}/M_{PA-ES} = M_{PI-DS}/M_{PI-ES} = 1.07$). One reason for this phenomenon is that descriptive self-disclosure is more informative and significant than evaluative self-disclosure, as consumers usually care how similar their situation are to that of others to determine how relevant a post about cosmetic product is. As it is discussed above, information is valued more by users, while evaluative self-disclosure revolving around personal feelings is not particularly pertinent or valuable.

Secondly, the difference between high and low product price is negligible ($M_{HC-PA} = 5.69$, $M_{LC-PA} = 5.54$, $M_{HC-PI} = 5.22$, $M_{LC-PI} = 5.25$). It can be noticed that high-cost product is related to better product attitude but lower purchase intention, which can be explained by the fact that higher price usually yields lower purchase intention for price-sensitive consumers. However, the limited absolute difference can probably be random and meaningless, so the explanation above may not be solid. But in the case of product attitude, there is an observable difference between high-cost and low-cost product. The researcher suspects that people tend to perceive expensive products as better in comparison with cheaper ones, which is why the product attitude is more positive in high-cost product. In conclusion, product price may not be particularly relevant in this case by analyzing it separately.

However, the effect of product price on purchase intention is much more conspicuous when self-disclosure and product price are analyzed together, especially in the case of descriptive self-disclosure. The percentage of M_{PI} on M_{PA} ($M_{PA-DSHC}/M_{PI-DSHC} = 1.10$, $M_{PA-DSLC}/M_{PI-DSLC} = 1.04$) and the correlation of M_{PI} and M_{PA} ($r_{DSHC} = 0.68$, $r_{DSLC} = 0.86$) indicate that high price stalls consumers' intention to purchase, even though the product attitude does not vary significantly ($M_{DSHC} = 5.80$, $M_{DSLC} = 5.70$). This phenomenon is understandable since consumers may not purchase products that they love due to economic reasons. This is particularly true in the case of descriptive self-disclosure is that descriptive self-disclosure is more persuasive and leads to more prominent attitude, but this preference cannot be supported by average user's financial condition, which leads to the gap between purchase intention.

This conclusion can also be corroborated by the correlation between PA and PI in terms of product cost ($r_{HC} = 0.74$, $r_{LC} = 0.86$), where low-cost products yield more consistent product attitude and purchase intention, whereas the correlation is weaker when it comes to high-cost product. It is also worth noticing that the correlation between PA and PI in terms of self-disclosure is consistent ($r_{DS} = 0.79$, $r_{ES} = 0.83$), which indicates that self-disclosure does not contribute to the discrepancy between PA and PI.

In conclusion, self-disclosure is effective in determining the level of product attitude, while product price is effective in determining purchase intention. Specifically, descriptive self-disclosure leads to better product attitude than evaluative self-disclosure, while high-cost product tends to generate discrepancy between product attitude and purchase intention.

4 Limitation

The limitation of this experiment lies in several aspects in the following.

First of all, it is impossible to control all variables involved. 4 posts are eliminated in the pretest in order to experiment with contents with most prominent self-disclosure features. However, the product category is not fully controlled – there are two foundations and two serums involved in evaluative self-disclosure, while there are one lipstick, one foundation, and two skin masks involved in descriptive self-disclosure. This asymmetry of product category may generate new variable that affects the final experiment result, which is also vulnerable to individual difference in terms of cosmetic need and personal preference. Nevertheless, the researcher believes that it is priority to control the level of self-disclosure since it is one of the independent variables in this research.

Secondly, self-reporting of participants online may not be very reliable and may be vulnerable to varied influences. For instance, the level of social tie strength may not be particularly accurate because of self-reported intimacy and perception. Another source of noise is the online questionnaire platform, wjx.com, since the platform filters the validity of participants with mandatory vetting questions, even though the researcher has asked the website to shut down the vetting process, but it is standard procedure on the platform.

The third limitation is about the limited size of test samples and the artificial process to manipulate samples. After pretest, only eight posts remain for formal experiment. It can be inaccurate as there are millions of posts on the LRB and merely eight posts may not be representative enough. Besides, in order to eliminate the pre-existing influence of existing brands, all of the posts are manipulated with fake brands and more prominent feature of the two types of self-disclosure. This can be problematic as unfamiliar brands probably indicate untrustworthiness and low quality, and manipulated contents may not genuinely reflect the real scenario on the LRB, which may make this research less significant.

5 Conclusion

The researcher demonstrated how different dimensions of self-disclosure and product costs affect consumers' product attitudes and purchase intention, and how PA and PI correlate with each other under the context of a weak-tie community. First of all, consumers believe a community such as the LRB where they share product-related experience is necessary and supportive, even though consumers may not be actively involved in the interaction, since information and usefulness are much more crucial here. Secondly, it can be noticed that consumers may not care about personal evaluations and emotions, but more about the product itself and similarities they share with others. This can be explained by the Theory of Reasoned Action and Elaboration Likelihood Model, as consumers process information rationally to make a decision or to form a perception. Besides, there is discrepancy between attitude and intention when it comes to different product price, as the latter is constrained to the power of consumption.

With this research, we are able to understand Network Coproduction Model of eWOM from the self-disclosure perspective and how consumers grow grass because of peer review. This case study provides an example of evaluating the effect of user-generated content and how people interact or perceive each other in many-to-many communication.

Future works may explore the following two aspects. First, researchers can scrape data from LRB or equivalent communities to conduct content analysis at massive scale so as to accurately analyze the characteristics of eWOM in a coproduction circumstance. Second, since commercial endorsers can camouflage as ordinary consumers to promote a brand or product due to anonymous features online, consumers nowadays are able to detect masking or deception as well. Researchers can explore how consumers detect deceptions and what characteristics give endorsers away. From these perspectives, we are able to understand human's online behavior in a more comprehensive manner.

References

1. Deng, I.: Chinese social commerce unicorn Xiaohongshu raises US$300 million from investors led by Alibaba 1 June 2018. https://www.scmp.com/tech/china-tech/article/2148807/chinese-social-commerce-unicorn-xiaohongshu-raises-us300-million

2. Schivinski, B., Dabrowski, D.: The effect of social media communication on consumer perceptions of brands. J. Marketing Commun. **22**(2), 189–214 (2014). https://doi.org/10.1080/13527266.2013.871323

3. Wang, X., Yu, C., Wei, Y.: Social media peer communication and impacts on purchase intentions: a consumer socialization framework. J. Interact. Mark. **26**(4), 198–208 (2012). https://doi.org/10.1016/j.intmar.2011.11.004

4. Ardiansyah, Y., Harrigan, P., Soutar, G.N., Daly, T.M.: Antecedents to consumer peer communication through social advertising: a self-disclosure theory perspective. J. Interact. Adv. **18**(1), 55–71 (2018). https://doi.org/10.1080/15252019.2018.1437854

5. Fishbein, M., Ajzen, I.: Belief, Attitude, Intention, and Behavior: An Introduction to Theory and Research. Addison-Wesley, Reading (1975)

6. Granovetter, M.S.: The strength of weak ties. Am. J. Sociol. **78**(6), 1360–1380 (1973)

7. Brown, J.J., Reingen, P.H.: Social ties and word-of-mouth referral behavior. J. Consum. Res. **14**(3), 350–362 (1987)

8. Huszti, É., Dávid, B., Vajda, K.: Strong tie, weak tie and in-betweens: a continuous measure of tie strength based on contact diary datasets. Procedia Soc. Behav. Sci. **79**, 38–61 (2013). https://doi.org/10.1016/j.sbspro.2013.05.056

9. Xu, X.: Assessing source credibility on social media – an electronic word-of-mouth communication perspective. Dissertation Abstracts International **76**(11) (2015)

10. Kozinets, R.V., Valck, K.D., Wojnicki, A.C., Wilner, S.J.: Networked narratives: understanding word-of-mouth marketing in online communities. J. Market. **74**(2), 71–89 (2010). https://doi.org/10.1509/jmkg.74.2.71

11. Schram, W. (ed.): The Process And Effects of Mass Communication. University of Illinois Press, Champaign (1954)

12. Pedersen, S.T., Razmerita, L., Colleoni, E.: Electronic word-of-mouth communication and consumer behaviour - an exploratory study of danish social media communication influence. LSP J. **5**(1), 112–131 (2014)

13. Samutachak, B., Li, D.: The effects of centrality and prominence of nodes in the online social network on word of mouth behaviors. J. Acad. Bus. Econ. **12**(2), 125–148 (2012)
14. Derlega, V.J., Metts, S., Petronio, S., Margulis, S.T.: Self-Disclosure. Sage, Newbury Park (1993)
15. Laurent, G., Kapferer, J.: Measuring consumer involvement profiles. J. Mark. Res. **49**, 41–53 (1985)
16. Jain, S.P., Posavac, S.S.: Prepurchase attribute verifiability, source credibility, and persuasion. J. Consum. Psychol. **11**(3), 169–180 (2001)
17. Weinberger, M.G., Dillon, W.R.: The effects of unfavorable product rating information. In: Olson, J. (ed.) Proceedings of the Association for Consumer Research. Association for Consumer Research, Ann Arbor (1980)
18. Jungho, B., Byung-Do, K.: Is the electronic word of mouth effect always positive on the movie? Acad. Mark. Stud. J. **17**(1), 61–78 (2013)
19. Morton, T.L.: Intimacy and reciprocity in exchange: a comparison of spouses and strangers. J. Pers. Soc. Psychol. **36**, 72–81 (1978)
20. Chu, S.-C., Kim, Y.: Determinants of consumer engagement in electronic word-of-mouth (eWOM) in social networking sites. Int. J. Advertising **30**(1), 47–75 (2011). https://doi.org/10.2501/ija-30-1-047-075
21. Yi-Wen, F., Yi-Feng, M., Yu-Hsien, F., Ruei-Yun, L.: Establishing the adoption of electronic word-of-mouth through consumers' perceived credibility. Int. Bus. Res. **6**(3), 58–65 (2013)

Online Shopping Motives - An Empirical Investigation of Consumer Buying Behavior in Germany's Main Online Retail Segments

Silvia Zaharia[(✉)]

University of Applied Sciences Niederrhein, Krefeld, Germany
silvia.zaharia@hs-niederrhein.de

Abstract. In the perpetual battle for increased revenues, online retailers need to understand what actions to take in order to turn non-buyers into buyers. This study researches the online shopping motives of German online shoppers and their online buying behavior in the main online retail segments: marketplaces, generalists, fashion, consumer electronics, beauty and toys. 19 German online retailers (representing approx. 70% of German online sales) were analyzed.

The research is based on extensive qualitative (focus groups) and quantitative research. The shopping motives construct was conceptualized and operationalized as a multidimensional construct with nine motivational categories. The data from the quantitative survey were analyzed using exploratory and confirmatory factor analysis, and nine shopping motives within 16 total dimensions were established: recreational orientation (social & inspirational shopping), convenience orientation (search & possession convenience), striving for independence, risk aversion (privacy, product, delivery & retailer-related), price orientation (= smart shopping), assortment orientation (variety seeking & specialization), advice orientation (company owned & third party), sustainability orientation (= ecological) and quality orientation (= visual appeal).

The differences between the online shopping motives of buyers and non-buyers in each of the six online retailing segments were investigated as pair comparisons using the Mann-Whitney-U test. The result is that there are significant differences in the online shopping motives in all researched industries. Most differences exist in the beauty industry where 14 of the 16 dimensions of shopping motives differ significantly. The fewest differences are in the marketplaces segment. Only five of the 16 dimensions of shopping motives differ significantly here.

Keywords: Online shopping motives ·
Recreational orientation (social & inspirational shopping) ·
Convenience orientation (search & possession convenience) ·
Striving for independence ·
Risk aversion (privacy, product, delivery & retailer related) ·
Price orientation (smart shopping) ·
Assortment orientation (variety seeking & specialization) ·
Advice orientation (company owned & third party) ·
Sustainability orientation (ecologically) ·
Quality orientation (visual appeal)

© Springer Nature Switzerland AG 2019
F. F.-H. Nah and K. Siau (Eds.): HCII 2019, LNCS 11588, pp. 333–349, 2019.
https://doi.org/10.1007/978-3-030-22335-9_23

1 General Overview and Purpose

In 2018, German online sales reached 65.10 billion euros representing 12.5% of total retail sales (Bevh 2019). In some verticals, such as consumer electronics (31%) and fashion & lifestyle (16%), the online share of sales was significantly higher than the average (Statista 2018). The 10 highest-revenue online shops in Germany are the U.S. marketplaces Amazon and eBay, followed by generalists like Otto and vertical players from the fashion sector and the consumer electronics sector (EHI 2018).

The objective of this paper is to analyze the consumer behavior in German online retailing, with particular reference to shopping motives. The shopping motives construct originates from brick-and-mortar retail and was transferred to online and multi-channel retailing. The present research aims to conceptualize and operationalize the construct of shopping motives in a pure online commerce context.

The key questions addressed are the following:

- What are the shopping motives of German consumers who shop online?
- How can the online shopping motives construct be conceptualized and operationalized?
- Are there differences in the online shopping motives between buyers and non-buyers in the main online retail segments: marketplaces, generalists, fashion, consumer electronics, beauty and toys? And if so, what are they?

In order to answer these questions, this study researched 19 German online retailers. The present study is significant because to the author's knowledge, no research has been conducted to date on whether there are differences in the online shopping motives between buyers and non-buyers in a defined retail segment. In the perpetual battle for increased revenues, online retailers need to understand what actions to take in order to turn non-buyers into buyers.

2 Conceptual Framework

2.1 Shopping Motives in the Literature

One of the main determinants of the buying choices of a consumer (decision to buy or not to buy from a retailer, to buy online or offline, or to combine channels as part of a buying process) are the motives that trigger consumer behavior, the so-called shopping motives (Zaharia 2006; Schröder and Zaharia 2008). The online shopping motives construct originates from brick-and-mortar retail and was transferred to online shopping and multi-channel retailing. Shopping motives are defined as "fundamental, goal-oriented internal forces that can be satisfied by purchasing activities." (Kroeber-Riel and Gröppel-Klein 2013, p. 206). Therefore, the hypothesis of the study is: *"Consumers who buy products online in a retail segment differ from non-buyers with respect to their shopping motives."*

The question is which shopping motives are important in online shopping. Table 1 gives an overview of recent studies that deal with the construct of motives in the online and multi-channel context with the associated concept and research design. Many studies distinguish between utilitarian (functional shopping motives) and hedonic online motivation. Hedonic shopping motives refer to aspects of shopping that go beyond the mere supply of goods and emphasize the fun and joy they bring (Hirschman and Holbrook 1982).

Table 1. Overview of recent studies on shopping motives

Author	Focus & Research design	Motives
Martínez-López et al. 2014 and 2016	– Focus: online consumption – qualitative study: focus groups & personal interviews – quantitative study: online survey at universities in Barcelona/ Spain; n = 669	**Hedonic** • Visual appeal • Sensation seeking/entertainment • Escape • Intrinsic enjoyment/relaxation • Hang out • Socialize • Self-expression • Role shopping • Enduring involvement with a product/service **Utilitarian** • Assortment • Economy • Convenience • Availability of information • Adaptability/customization • Desire for control • Payment services • Anonymity • Absence of social interaction
Ono et al. 2012	– Focus: online shopping (mobile) – quantitative study: online survey with students in Tokyo/Japan; n = 1,406	**Hedonic** • Adventure • Social • Gratification • Idea • Role • Value
Ganesh et al. 2010	– Focus: online shopping – qualitative study: in-depth interviews – quantitative study: online survey (web panel) USA; n = 3,059	• Role enactment • Online bidding • Web shopping convenience • Avant-gardism • Affiliation • Stimulation • Personalized services

(*continued*)

Table 1. (*continued*)

Author	Focus & Research design	Motives
Falode et al. 2016	– Focus: online and offline shopping (mobile) – quantitative study: survey, shoppers from Ibadan, Nigeria; n = 400	**Hedonic** • Shopping enjoyment • Gratification shopping • Idea shopping • Shopping for aesthetic ambiance • Role shopping • Social shopping **Utilitarian** • Convenient shopping • Economic shopping • Achievement shopping
Zaharia 2006	– Focus: multi-channel shopping – qualitative data: focus groups & personal interviews – quantitative study: tel. survey, consumers of a multi-channel-retailer; Germany; n = 525	• Recreational orientation • Convenience orientation • Striving for independence • Risk aversion (dimensions: privacy, product- & delivery- related) • Price orientation • Smart shopping • Advice orientation • Quality orientation

2.2 Online Shopping Motives

After extensive literature research, the question arose whether the conceptualization and operationalization of the shopping motives construct from international studies could be transferred to the German online retailing market. To check this, a qualitative study was done as a first step. Based on the results of the focus groups and the theoretical considerations, the construct online shopping motives was conceptualized and operationalized as a multidimensional construct with 9 motivational categories. The group discussions resulted in a new motive that did not appear in any of the previous studies: sustainability, with the two characteristics ecological and corporate. This may be especially true for Germany, where environmental awareness is particularly pronounced.

1. The shopping motive *recreational orientation* represents the hedonistic aspect of shopping (Schröder and Zaharia 2008). This includes emotional and social needs for an interesting, inspiring and fun shopping experience as well as social interaction with friends and acquaintances (Zaharia 2006, Ono et al. 2012). Based on the preliminary studies, the following three-dimensional recreational orientation motive was adopted: *social shopping, gratification shopping* and *idea shopping*.

2. One of the most important shopping motives in online retailing is the *convenience orientation*. Convenience orientation can be characterized by a desire to minimize the time, physical and psychological effort to search, compare and purchase a product (Kaufman-Scarborough and Lindquist 2002, Jiang et al. 2013). We subsume under this shopping motive the *search convenience, comparison convenience, transaction convenience* and *possession convenience*.

3. The shopping motive *striving for independence* expresses the need of customers to be able to shop freely and independently, especially with regard to time and place (Schröder and Zaharia 2008). One particular aspect of location independence is related to the device used to access the retailer's online shop or app. Depending on where the customers are located, they want to have control over their purchasing process through researching and purchasing from an online retailer regardless of the device they use (smartphone, tablet or laptop). This desire corresponds to the aspects "desire for control" and "autonomy" by Martínes-López.

4. The motive *risk aversion* refers to perceived risk. This refers to the customer's uncertainty about the negative consequences of an online purchase and the significance of these consequences. In online retailing, perceived risk is seen as one of the most important barriers to buying. Privacy-related risk was mentioned by the participants of the focus groups as a sensitive aspect of risk aversion. Product-related risks can be felt by the customer because she/he has to rely on the graphical representation and product information provided by the retailer. Delivery-related risks arise when the customer has no influence on the delivery time, the correctness and the quality of the delivery (Schröder and Zaharia 2008, Iconaru 2012). The reputation of a shop also plays an important role in the perceived risk of consumers. Therefore, the following five risk dimensions will be considered by the study: *payment-related risk, privacy-related risk, product-related risk, delivery-related risk* and *retailer-related risk*.

5. *Price orientation* refers to a pronounced price interest of the consumers. The motive can be subdivided into the factors inexpensive buying and price optimization (=smart shopping). Consumer with inexpensive buying behavior seek to spend as little money as possible regardless of the product quality and the service (Zaharia 2006). In contrast, smart shopping is primarily about finding the best possible price-performance ratio. Smart-shopping consumers tend to spend considerable time and effort to achieve price savings (Atkins and Kim 2012). Above all, finding "bargains" triggers a feeling of satisfaction. Therefore, we adopted in the study the following two-dimensionality of the motive price orientation: *in-expensive buying* and *smart shopping*.

6. The shopping motive *advice orientation* refers to the consumers' need to seek advice before making a purchase (Zaharia 2006). In online retailing, consumers use different types of advice in order to make safe purchase decisions, such as online merchant's services and third-party advice (e.g. reviews from other consumers, forums or comparison websites, Hönle 2017). As a result, we propose two dimensions for the operationalization: *Company owned advice* covers all consulting services offered by the retailer. And by these we mean in particular the need for personal consulting services when choosing the product with the possibility of interacting with a service agent. The dimension *third party advice* includes the use

of consulting services offered by third parties. Above all, user-generated content directly on the website of the provider, such as product reviews and experience reports are important in this dimension (Bahtar and Muda 2016).

7. Martínes-López et al. 2014 consider *assortment orientation* an important motivational factor in online shopping. A large assortment gives customers access to a wider range of information but also to more diversified products. The aspect of variety seeking corresponds to consumers' desire for change when purchasing, and it can refer to products, brands or the choice of the online shop (Swaminathan and Rohm 2004, Zaharia and Hackstetter 2017). This contrasts with the behavior of some consumers who buy special products that are available (almost) exclusively online or in specialized online shops. For this reason, we assume a two-dimensional assortment orientation motive, namely *variety seeking* and *specialization*.

8. Another dimension of the shopping motives identified by the focus groups is the aspect of *sustainability*. When consumers pay attention to sustainability, one of their goals is to protect the natural environment and the living conditions of present and future generations (Joshi and Rahman 2015). Based on the findings of the focus group, a conceptualization with two dimensions is proposed: *ecological* and *corporate*. The *ecological* dimension describes the need to deal with the ecological consequences of the purchase. In the online context of the study, this mainly concerns the pollution from delivery (including returns) as well as the problem of packaging waste. The *corporate* dimension incorporates all concerns that have a direct relation to the company. This includes working conditions, the use of corporate profits, compliance with laws and market power.

9. *Quality orientation* refers to the importance of a product's quality or performance. In addition to product quality, the quality of the online shop's presentation also plays an important role for the focus group participants. What is meant here is that customers draw conclusions about the product quality on the basis of the shop's perceived appearance, including product photos or presentation of information. This is associated with the hedonic aspect of an online shop's visual appeal as outlined by Martínes-López et al. 2014. Based on these findings, we propose a two-dimensional conceptualization: *product quality* and *visual appeal*.

3 Research Design and Results

3.1 Research Design

As a preliminary investigation, 26 online shoppers took part in four focus groups (November 2017). The participants were between 19 and 72 years old and in equal proportions female and male. The aim was to discover which shopping motives could be relevant to the online shopping behavior in Germany. On the basis of the pertinent literature and the results of the preliminary investigation, the shopping motives were conceptualized and operationalized.

The quantitative data of the main research was obtained from a representative sample of 1,000 German online buyers, of which 993 could be used for evaluation. The online survey took place in February 2018 using an online panel. The demographic characteristics of the participants can be found in Appendix 1.

In order to investigate possible differences in the shopping motives between the different retail segments, 19 online shops were examined, which together represent approximative 70% of total German online sales in 2018 (see Table 2).

Table 2. Examined segments in online retailing with the corresponding online shops

Segments in online retailing	Online shops
Marketplace	amazon.de; ebay.de
Fashion	zalando.de; bonprix.de; hm.com; esprit.de
Generalists	otto.de; galeria-kaufhof.de; lidl.de; qvc.de; tchibo.de
Consumer electronics	notebooksbilliger.de; mediamarkt.de; apple.com; saturn.de; medion.de
Beauty	douglas.de
Toys	babymarkt.de; mytoys.de

3.2   Shopping Motives

In the quantitative phase, the study had three basic objectives:

1. To empirically evaluate a total of nine shopping motives and 23 proposed dimensions gathered from the literature review and subsequently refined by the focus groups.
2. To analyze the proposed multi-item scales considering the common scientific quality criteria.
3. To assess the hypothesis by answering the central question: "Are there differences in the online shopping motives between buyers and non-buyers in the six online retailing segments: marketplaces, generalists, fashion, consumer electronics, beauty and toys? And if so, what are they?".

In order to address the first two objectives, we adhered to the following procedure (Homburg and Dobratz 1991, p. 233):

- First, we checked whether the limit values for the quality criteria item-to-total correlation (ITC; $\geq$ 0.4) and Cronbach's alpha ($\alpha \geq$ 0.7) were met.
- Second, an exploratory factor analysis was carried out and we checked whether all indicators loaded on one factor, with the factor loadings $\geq$ 0.7 and the indicator reliability (IR) $\geq$ 0.5.
- Third, we performed confirmatory factor analysis (AMOS) and checked whether the factor loadings are significant and whether the following criteria exceeded the minimum values: factor reliability (FR) $\geq$ 0.6, average variance extracted (AVE) $\geq$ 0.5, and whether the Fornell-Larcker criterion was met. Iterative attempts were made to fulfill the quality criteria by eliminating individual indicators. If that was not possible, the respective dimension or motive was removed from the model.

- Finally, the quality of the overall model was checked (AMOS).

The final result demonstrated that the nine shopping motives could be confirmed but not the proposed dimensionality. Figure 1 gives an overview of the hypothetical and empirical dimensionality of the shopping motives construct.

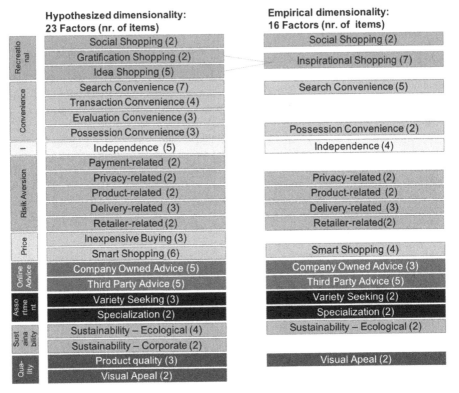

Fig. 1. Hypothetical and empirical dimensionality of the shopping motives construct

The two hypothesized dimensions of the recreational orientation, gratification and idea shopping, were incorporated into a new dimension, which we called *inspirational shopping*. Since only two dimensions of the convenience orientation exceeded the minimum value of the quality criteria, namely search and possession convenience, we focused only on these for further research. For the same reasons, we eliminated the dimension payment-related risks from the model. Also, for shopping motives price, sustainability and quality orientation, only one dimension for each was maintained. The dimensions in-expensive buying, corporate sustainability and product quality were dropped. The 16 remaining dimensions fulfill all quality criteria (see Table 3). The goodness-of-fit of this overall model is acceptable to good: $\chi2/d.f.$: 3.47; NFI: 0.859; CFI: 0.894; RMSEA: 0.05. (Note that AMOS does not report GFI, PGFI, AGFI and RMR when estimating means and intercepts.)

Looking at the strength of the purchasing motives across all respondents, the following ranking of the mean values results (5 = maximum, 1 = minimum):

1. search convenience (4.30),
2. variety seeking (4.08),
3. possession convenience (3.95),
4. smart shopping (3.62),
5. product-related risk (3.61),
6. third-party advice (3.46),
7. retailer-related risk (3.45),
8. data-related risk (3.4),
9. assortment specialization (3.25),
10. inspirational shopping (3.16),
11. visual appeal (3.05),
12. delivery-related risk (3.08),
13. independence (3.04),
14. sustainability - ecological (2.49),
15. social shopping (2.27),
16. company owned advice (2.11).

It is not surprising to see that shopping motives best met by online retail occupy the top of the list. Similarly, the last three shopping motives – company owned advice, social shopping and sustainability are those least able to be fulfilled by online shopping. Rather, these motives make up the strengths of brick-and-mortar retail.

Table 3. Factor structure of shopping motives (including quality criteria)

Shopping motives	Shopping motive dimensions	Indicator	Factor loadings (≥ 0.7)	ITC	C. Alpha	FR	AVE
			(IR $\geq$ 0.5)	(≥ 0.4)	(≥ 0.7)	(≥ 0.6)	(≥ 0.5)
Recreational orientation	Social shopping	SoS_1	0.914 (0.835)	0.670	0.802	0.803	0.671
		SoS_2	0.914 (0.835)	0.670			
	Inspirational shopping	GS_1	0.746 (0.557)	0.643	0.880	0.883	0.520
		GS_2	0.708 (0.501)	0.599			
		IS_1	0.802 (0.644)	0.713			
		IS_2	0.786 (0.617)	0.690			
		IS_3	0.760 (0.577)	0.663			
		IS_4	0.762 (0.581)	0.665			
		IS_5	0.785 (0.617)	0.694			
Convenience orientation	Search convenience	SC_1	0.718 (0.516)	0.570	0.842	0.847	0.527
		SC_2	0.822 (0.676)	0.698			
		SC_4	0.771 (0.595)	0.627			
		SC_5	0.775 (0.600)	0.635			
		SC_6	0.840 (0.705)	0.720			
	Possession convenience	PC_1	0.880 (0.775)	0.550	0.710	0.712	0.553
		PC_2	0.880 (0.775)	0.550			

(*continued*)

Table 3. (*continued*)

Shopping motives	Shopping motive dimensions	Indicator	Factor loadings (≥0.7)	ITC	C. Alpha	FR	AVE
			(IR ≥ 0.5)	(≥0.4)	(≥0.7)	(≥0.6)	(≥0.5)
Risk aversion	Privacy-related	PvR_1	0.948 (0.899)	0.797	0.887	0.887	0.797
		PvR_2	0.948 (0.899)	0.797			
	Product-related	PR_1	0.950 (0.903)	0.806	0.892	0.893	0.807
		PR_2	0.950 (0.903)	0.806			
	Delivery-related	DR_1	0.847 (0.718)	0.638	0.779	0.778	0.545
		DR_2	0.815 (0.665)	0.590			
		DR_3	0.835 (0.698)	0.619			
	Retailer-related	RR_1	0.872 (0.760)	0.520	0.684	0.693	0.533
		RR_2	0.872 (0.760)	0.520			
Independence orientation	Independence	I_1	0.921 (0.849)	0.853	0.919	0.919	0.741
		I_2	0.897 (0.805)	0.813			
		I_4	0.886 (0.786)	0.797			
Price orientation	Smart-Shopping	SmS_1	0.784 (0.614)	0.598	0.804	0.804	0.508
		SmS_2	0.826 (0.681)	0.663			
		SmS_3	0.811 (0.657)	0.642			
		SmS_4	0.759 (0.576)	0.579			
Online advice	Company owned advice	CO_A_2	0.809 (0.655)	0.568	0.771	0.787	0.564
		CO_A_3	0.785 (0.616)	0.540			
		CO_A_4	0.894 (0.800)	0.718			
	Third party advice	TP_A_1	0.855 (0.731)	0.723	0.832	0.839	0.519
		TP_A_2	0.667 (0.445)	0.521			
		TP_A_3	0.714 (0.509)	0.57			
		TP_A_4	0.867 (0.751)	0.745			
		TP_A_5	0.780 (0.609)	0.623			
Assortment orientation	Variety seeking	A_3	0.913 (0.834)	0.669	0.801	0.824	0.707
		A_4	0.913 (0.834)	0.669			
	Specialization	A_1	0.874 (0.764)	0.527	0.687	0.723	0.576
		A_5	0.874 (0.764)	0.527			
Sustainability orientation	Ecological	S_E_3	0.880 (0.775)	0.550	0.709	0.720	0.567
		S_E_4	0.880 (0.775)	0.550			
Quality orientation	Visual appeal	Q_VA_1	0.774 (0.599)	0.532	0.763	0.779	0.547
		Q_VA_2	0.881 (0.775)	0.682			
		Q_VA_3	0.826 (0.683)	0.587			

Note: Factor loadings from explorative factor analysis. All indicators load only on one factor after the exploratory factor analysis.
All factor loadings (of the confirmative factor analysis) are significant at p < .01 level. All factors met the Fornell-Larcker criterion.

3.3   Comparison of the Buying Behavior in the Researched Online Retailing Segments

To test the hypothesis, the buyers and non-buyers of a segment were compared using the Mann-Whitney-U test. This test shows that there are significant differences in the online shopping motives between buyers and non-buyers in the six online retailing segments: marketplaces (MP), generalists, fashion, consumer electronics (CE), beauty and toys (see Table 4). Therefore, the hypothesis H1 cannot be rejected.

Buyers and non-buyers of all six online retailing segments differ with respect to both recreational motives (social shopping and inspirational shopping) and their price orientation (smart shopping). Both motives are more pronounced with buyers. Only the shopping motive privacy-related risk aversion does not differentiate between buyers and non-buyers of any online retailing segment.

1. *Recreational Orientation*: Compared to non-buyers, buyers from all segments are looking for more *social* and *inspirational shopping*. These shopping motives are the strongest in the beauty and fashion industries.
2. *Search convenience* is the strongest online shopping motive. There are significant differences with regard to this shopping motive in the generalists, consumer electronics and beauty segments. With regard to *possession convenience*, there is a significant difference in all segments besides marketplaces. The possession convenience is most pronounced in the beauty industry.
3. With the exception of the generalists, buyers and non-buyers of all industries differed on *independence orientation*.
4. *Risk aversion*: with regard to *privacy-related risks*, there are no significant differences between buyers and non-buyers in any industry. The issue of privacy seems to be relatively important to all consumers (rank 8). *Product-related risks* only differ between buyers and non-buyers in the case of generalists and in the beauty industry. Furthermore, for *delivery-related risks* there are only weakly significant differences for marketplaces and in the beauty industry. In terms of *retailer-related risks*, there are significant differences in all industries except marketplaces and toys. In general, risk aversion is more pronounced among buyers than among non-buyers. This is probably also the reason why customers bought from the large, well-known online retailers surveyed here.
5. Buyers and non-buyers of all six online retailing segments demonstrate a highly significant difference with respect to their *price orientation (smart shopping)*.
6. *Advice orientation*: while *third party advice* ranks 6th among the shopping motives, the need for *company owned advice* is the least pronounced shopping motive (ranked 16th). The need for company owned advice is most pronounced in the consumer electronics and beauty industry, where it also distinguishes highly significantly between buyers and non-buyers. With the exception of the fashion industry, the need for third party advice is more pronounced among buyers than among non-buyers in all segments.
7. As far as the shopping motive *assortment orientation* is concerned, buyers in the beauty industry are those most concerned with *variety seeking* and the desire for *specialization*. The two assortment shopping motives differ significantly between buyers and non-buyers in all sectors with the exception of marketplaces (specialization) and marketplaces and toys (variety seeking).

8. *Sustainability orientation - ecological* does not seem to be particularly important for online buyers (ranked 14). Only in the fashion industry does it rank significantly higher among buyers than among non-buyers. One reason for this may be that this industry also has the highest return rates: on average, up to 50% (Wirtschaftswoche 2018).

9. *Quality orientation - visual appeal*: The need for visual appeal is significantly more pronounced among buyers than among non-buyers in all sectors with the exception of marketplace as well as toys.

Table 4. Comparison of buyer and not-buyer of online retailing segments with respect to their shopping motives (Mean) and the significance results of the Mann-Whitney-U test

Shopping Motives	Shopping Motive Dimensions	Mean	Market-Places	Generalist	Fashion	Consumer Electronics	Beauty	Toys
Recreational Orientation	Social Sh.	2.27	***	***	***	***	***	**
	Buyer (n)		2.30 (947)	2.43 (425)	2.42 (645)	2.48 (381)	2.90 (185)	2.55 (159)
	Non-Buyer (n)		1.56 (39)	2.14 (561)	1.98 (341)	2.13 (605)	2.12 (801)	2.21 (827)
	Inspirational Sh.	3.16	**	***	***	***	***	***
	Buyer (n)		3.17 (928)	3.35 (417)	3.35 (627)	3.33 (375)	3.74 (182)	3.42 (153)
	Non-Buyer (n)		2.70 (37)	3.01 (548)	2.80 (338)	3.05 (590)	3.02 (783)	3.11 (812)
Convenience Orientation	Search Conv.	4.13	n.s.	**	n.s.	**	**	n.s.
	Buyer (n)		4.30 (951)	4.36 (423)	4.31 (647)	4.36 (383)	4.39 (184)	4.30 (158)
	Non-Buyer (n)		3.70 (38)	4.25 (566)	4.28 (342)	4.26 (606)	4.28 (805)	4.30 (831)
	Possession Conv.	3.95	n.s.	***	**	***	***	*
	Buyer (n)		3.96 (954)	4.05 (524)	3.99 (648)	4.08 (383)	4.18 (184)	4.09 (159)
	Non-Buyer (n)		3.69 (39)	3.88 (568)	3.88 (345)	3.88 (610)	3.90 (809)	3.93 (834)
Independence Orientation	Independence	3.04	**	n.s.	***	***	***	***
	Buyer (n)		3.07 (933)	3.12 (415)	3.19 (635)	3.25 (380)	3.51 (180)	3.44 (155)
	Non-Buyer (n)		2.43 (37)	2.98 (555)	2.77 (335)	2.90 (590)	2.94 (790)	2.97 (815)
Price Orientation	Smart Shopping	3.62	***	***	**	***	***	***
	Buyer (n)		3.65(942)	3.85 (422)	3.68 (643)	3.79 (378)	3.84 (184)	3.93 (158)
	Non-Buyer (n)		2.99(37)	3.44 (557)	3.52 (336)	3.51 (601)	3.57 (795)	3.56 (821)
Assortment Orientation	Variety Seeking	4.08	n.s.	**	**	**	***	n.s.
	Buyer (n)		4.10 (946)	4.15 (421)	4.14 (643)	4.15 (382)	4.31 (183)	4.13 (159)
	Non-Buyer (n)		3.64 (39)	4.03 (564)	3.96 (342)	4.04 (603)	4.03 (802)	4.07 (826)
	Specialization	3.25	n.s.	***	***	***	***	*
	Buyer (n)		3.26 (933)	3.45 (423)	3.37 (633)	3.41 (378)	3.68 (181)	3.41 (158)
	Non-Buyer (n)		3.15 (38)	3.11 (548)	3.04 (338)	3.16 (593)	3.16 (790)	3.22 (813)
Risk Aversion	Privacy-related	3.41	n.s.	n.s.	n.s.	n.s.	n.s.	n.s.
	Buyer (n)		3.40 (945)	3.43 (421)	3.39 (645)	3.43 (382)	3.47 (184)	3.38 (157)
	Non-Buyer (n)		3.54 (40)	3.39 (564)	3.44 (340)	3.40 (603)	3.39 (801)	3.41 (828)
	Product-related	3.61	n.s.	*	n.s.	n.s.	*	n.s.
	Buyer (n)		3.60 (949)	3.68 (424)	3.63 (647)	3.58 (383)	3.73 (184)	3.60 (158)
	Non-Buyer (n)		3.78 (40)	3.55 (565)	3.56 (342)	3.62 (606)	3.58 (805)	3.61 (831)
	Delivery-related	3.08	*	n.s.	n.s.	n.s.	*	n.s.
	Buyer (n)		3.09 (944)	3.11 (423)	3.07 (645)	3.12 (382)	3.24 (183)	3.13 (158)
	Non-Buyer (n)		2.81 (40)	3.06 (561)	3.11 (339)	3.05 (602)	3.05 (801)	3.07 (826)
	Retailer-related	3.45	n.s.	**	*	**	**	n.s.
	Buyer (n)		3.44 (918)	3.53 (411)	3.50 (627)	3.55 (375)	3.64 (178)	3.46 (154)
	Non-Buyer (n)		3.70 (37)	3.39 (544)	3.35 (328)	3.38 (580)	3.41 (777)	3.45 (801)
Advice Orientation	Company Owned	2.11	n.s.	*	n.s.	**	**	n.s.
	Buyer (n)		2.12 (934)	2.21 (419)	2.16 (637)	2.24 (374)	2.38 (182)	2.27 (156)
	Non-Buyer (n)		1.92 (39)	2.03 (554)	2.01 (336)	2.02 (599)	2.05 (791)	2.08 (817)
	Third Party	3.46	***	**	n.s.	***	***	***
	Buyer (n)		3.49 (937)	3.55 (420)	3.50 (636)	3.60 (376)	3.68 (180)	3.64 (156)
	Non-Buyer (n)		2.81 (36)	3.39 (553)	3.38 (337)	3.37 (597)	3.41 (793)	3.43 (817)
Sustainability Orientation	Ecological	2.49	n.s.	n.s.	*	n.s.	n.s.	n.s.
	Buyer (n)		2.50 (916)	2.50 (415)	2.56 (623)	2.54 (373)	2.53 (183)	2.59 (158)
	Non-Buyer (n)		2.26 (37)	2.50 (538)	2.37 (330)	2.46 (580)	2.48 (770)	2.48 (795)
Quality Orientation	Visual Appeal	3.05	n.s.	**	***	***	***	n.s.
	Buyer (n)		3.06 (932)	3.15 (420)	3.16 (634)	3.17 (379)	3.40 (181)	3.11 (159)
	Non-Buyer (n)		2.93 (38)	2.99 (550)	2.85 (336)	2.98 (591)	2.98 (789)	3.04 (811)

*** significant at p < .01 level, ** significant at p < .05 level; * significant at p < .10 level; n.s. not significant; n=993

In summary, it can be said that the most pronounced differences between buyers and non-buyers are in the beauty industry. In comparing the strength of motives across all industries, then most appear strongest in the beauty industry. In the marketplace segment, there are the fewest differences between buyers and non-buyers.

4 Discussion and Limitations

The first conclusion of our research is that nine shopping motives with 16 dimensions in total could be defined and confirmed:

- recreational orientation (dimensions: social & inspirational shopping),
- convenience orientation (dimensions: search & possession convenience),
- striving for independence,
- risk aversion (dimensions: privacy, product, delivery & retailer related),
- price orientation (smart shopping),
- advice orientation (dimensions: company owned & third party),
- assortment orientation (dimensions: variety seeking & specialization),
- sustainability orientation (ecological)
- quality orientation (visual appeal).

Search convenience, variety seeking and possession convenience are the top three shopping motives among German online shoppers.

Secondly, the study has shown that there are differences in shopping motives between buyers vs. non-buyers in the researched segments. Most differences exist between online buyers and non-buyers in the beauty segment, where 14 of the 16 shopping motive dimensions differ significantly. The fewest differences are in the marketplaces segment, where only five of the 16 dimensions differ significantly.

Our examination also has limitations. In connection with the results of the group comparisons, it should be noted that these are significantly influenced by the selection of online shops we examined. In order to enable an objective analysis, we studied the top-selling German online retailers for every segment. Nevertheless, variation in customer shopping motives arising out of company differences between retailers *within* an industry should also be considered. Further research should benchmark individual retailers against peers in their segment with respect to shopping motives.

Another limitation has its origin in the representativeness of the investigation. In Germany, over 90% of online buyers have already bought from Amazon (IFH 2018). As a result, there are overlaps between buyers at marketplaces and buyers in other segments.

Notwithstanding these limitations, the present work provides an important contribution to the empirical investigation of shopping motives in online commerce. Against the backdrop of a growing e-commerce industry in Germany, as well as intensifying competition among retailers, the subject matter studied here will only gain in importance for science and practice in coming years.

Appendix 1: Demographic Characteristics of the Survey Participants

Gender	Male (48.2%); Female (51.8%)					
Age	18–29	30–39	40–49	50–59	60–69	70+
	23.30%	21.70%	23.70%	23.60%	6.40%	1.30%
Monthly household income (net in €)	<1.500€	1.500–1.999	2.000–2.499	2.500–2.999	3.000–3.499	3.500+
	14.30%	12.30%	12.20%	13.80%	15.70%	29.30%

Appendix 2: Operationalization of the Shopping Motives Construct

Shopping motives	Shopping motive dimensions	Indicator	Items
Recreational orientation	Social shopping	SoS_1	While I'm shopping online, I interact with my friends and/or acquaintances
		SoS_2	I like to shop online with my friends and/or family members
	~~Gratification Shopping~~	GS_1	Online shopping is a pastime for me.
		GS_2	I like to browse through various online shops
	~~Idea Shopping~~	IS_1	I find online shopping inspiring
		IS_2	While shopping online, I become aware of new trends
	Inspirational shopping[a]	IS_3	I like to look at a compilation of preselected products through the online shop
		IS_4	I like to receive suitable product suggestions on products already selected by me
		IS_5	I like to receive personalized product suggestions that match my buying behavior with the retailer
Convenience orientation	Search convenience	SC_1	It is important to me that an online store offers several filtering options
		SC_2	In an online store, a good search function is important to me
		SC_4	It's important to me that I can quickly find the product I'm looking for online
		SC_5	It's important to me that the online store has a good structure
		SC_6	It's important to me to find my way around an online store quickly
		SC_7	It's important to me that placing online orders takes as little time as possible
	Possession convenience	PC_1	It is important to me that the online shop offers the fastest possible delivery of the goods
		PC_2	It is important to me to know the exact delivery date when sending the order
		PC_3	For me it is important that I can return products ordered online as simply as possible

(continued)

(continued)

Shopping motives	Shopping motive dimensions	Indicator	Items
Striving for independence	Independence	*For me it is important...*	
		I_1	to have access to the online store from anywhere (for example via mobile devices such as mobile phones or tablets)
		I_2	that the presentation of the online shop is also suitable for mobile devices (mobile phone or tablet)
		I_4	I like to find out about products via the mobile device (e.g. mobile phone or tablet)
		I_5	I find it convenient to make purchases via a mobile device (such as a mobile phone or tablet)
Risk aversion	Privacy-related	*When placing an order on the Internet, the risk is high, ...*	
		PvR_1	that my personal information could be misused
		PvR_2	that my payment information is not secure
	Product-related	*When placing an order on the Internet, the risk is high, ...*	
		PR_1	that a product does not meet my expectations
		PR_2	that the product does not match the illustration and/or item description
	Delivery-related	*When placing an order on the Internet, the risk is high, ...*	
		DR_1	that the ordered product is not delivered
		DR_2	that the ordered product does not arrive at the scheduled time
		DR_3	that it will be difficult to send ordered products back
	Retailer-related	RR_1	Certificates and seals (for example from Trusted Shops) are important to me
		RR_2	I'm afraid to order from unknown online stores that do not showcase certificates or seals
Price orientation	Smart-Shopping	SmS_1	I like to use price search engines and/ or comparison sites to find the best price for an item
		SmS_2	I like to compare the price of an article in several online shops
		SmS_3	Before I buy a product in an online store, I like to search for discount codes and coupons
		SmS_4	I use promotions to get products at bargain prices

(continued)

(continued)

Shopping motives	Shopping motive dimensions	Indicator	Items
Online advice	Company owned advice	CO_A_2	When buying online, I miss having the opportunity to ask a sales representative for advice
		CO_A_3	I like to use the chat function or other consulting tools offered by an online shop
		CO_A_4	When buying online, personal product advice on the phone is important to me
	Third party advice	TP_A_1	For me it is important when buying online that I can use product reviews by other customers to inform my purchase
		TP_A_2	In order to better make my decision, I like to use comparison pages
		TP_A_3	For the online purchase decision, I like to access information from forums
		TP_A_4	Detailed reviews (for example, detailed comfort description of a mattress) by other customers are important to me
		TP_A_5	Customer reviews are more important to me than talking to the sales staff
Assortment orientation	Variety seeking	VS_1	I like to use online shops that have a large and varied assortment (large selection of articles)
		VS_2	I like to use online shops that offer a variety of brands
	Specialization	A_S_1	I like to use online shops that specialize in certain items
		A_S_2	I like to order from online shops for certain brands
Sustainability orientation	Ecological	S_E_3	I feel guilty about placing multiple orders that contain only a single item
		S_E_4	I feel guilty when I return packages
Quality orientation	Visual appeal	Q_VA_1	I'm willing to pay more for online shops that are beautifully designed
		Q_VA_2	When buying a product online, it is important to me that the design of the online store fits the products
		Q_VA_3	When shopping online, I attach great importance to a visually appealing website

Note: The scores for the shopping motives were given on a 5-point Likert Scale from 1 "Strongly Agree" to 5 "Strongly Disagree".
[a]Gratification Shopping & Idea Shopping were merged into Inspirational Shopping after the empirical check.

References

Atkins, K., Kim, Y.: Smart shopping: conceptualization and measurement. Int. J. Retail. Distrib. Manag. **40**(5), 360–375 (2012)

Bahtar, A., Muda, M.: The impact of user – generated content (UGC) on product reviews towards online purchasing – a conceptual framework. Proc. Econ. Financ. **37**, 337–342 (2016)

Bevh: bevh (2019). https://www.bevh.org/presse/pressemitteilungen.html. Accessed 28 Jan 2019

EHI   (2018).   https://www.ehi.org/de/top-100-umsatzstaerkste-onlineshops-in-deutschland/.
Accessed 10 Sep 2018

Falode, B.O., et al.: Online and offline shopping motivation of apparel consumers in Ibadan Metropolis. Nigeria. Int. J. Mark. Stud. **8**(1), 150 (2016)

Ganesh, J., Reynolds, K., Luckett, M., Pomirleanu, N.: Online shopper motivations, and e-store attributes: an examination of online patronage behavior and shopper typologies. J. Retail. **86**, 106–115 (2010)

Hirschman, E.C., Holbrook, M.B.: Hedonic consumption: emerging concepts, methods and propositions. J. Mark. **46**(Summer), 92–101 (1982)

Homburg, C., Dobratz, A.: Iterative Modellselektion in der Kausalanalyse. Zeitschrift für betriebswirtschaftliche Forschung **43**(3), 213–237 (1991). S. 233

Hönle, J.: Online beraten und verkaufen, pp. 1–8. Springer Gabler, Wiesbaden (2017)

Iconaru, C.: Perceived risk when buying online: evidence from a semi- structured interview. Econ. Ser. **22**(2), 63–73 (2012)

IFH: Branchenreport Onlinehandel, Jahrgang 2018, Köln (2018)

Jiang, L.A., Yang, Z., Jun, M.: Measuring consumer perceptions of online shopping convenience. J. Serv. Manag. **24**(2), 191–214 (2013)

Joshi, Y., Rahman, Z.: Factors affecting green purchase behavior and future research directions. Int. Strat. Manag. Rev. **3**, 128–143 (2015)

Kaufman-Scarborough, C., Lindquist, J.D.: E-shopping in a multiple channel environment. J. Consum. Mark. **19**(4), 333–350 (2002)

Kroeber-Riel, W., Gröppel-Klein, A.: Konsumentenverhalten, 10th edn. Vahlen, München (2013)

Martínez-López, F., Pla-Gracía, C., Gázquez-Abad, J., Rodríguez-Ardura, I.: Utilitarian motivations in online consumption: dimensional structure and scales. Electron. Commer. Res. Appl. **13**, 188–204 (2014)

Martínez-López, F., Pla-Gracía, C., Gázquez-Abad, J., Rodríguez-Ardura, I.: Hedonic motivations in online consumption Behaviour. Int. J. Bus. Environ. **8**(2), 2016 (2016)

Ono, A., et al.: Consumer motivations in browsing online stores with mobile devices. Int. J. Electron. Commer. **16**(4), 153–178 (2012)

Schröder, H., Zaharia, S.: Linking multi-channel customer Behaviour with shopping motives: an empirical investigation of a German retailer. J. Retail. Consum. Serv. **15**, 452–468 (2008)

Statista: Anteil der Online-Käufer an der Bevölkerung nach Ländern weltweit im Jahr 2017 (2018)

Swaminathan, V., Rohm, A.J.: A typology of online shoppers based on shopping motivations. J. Bus. Res. **57**(7), 748–757 (2004)

Wirtschaftswoche 2018. https://www.wiwo.de/unternehmen/handel/neuware-auf-den-muell-die-folgen-des-retouren-wahnsinns-im-online-handel/22696156.html. Accessed 15 Dec 2018

Zaharia, S.: Multi-Channel-Retailing und Kundenverhalten. Wie sich Kunden informieren und wie sie einkaufen, 1st edn., Köln (2006)

Zaharia, S., Hackstetter, T.: Segmentierung von Onlinekäufern auf Basis ihrer Einkaufsmotive. In: Dialogmarketing Perspektiven 2016/2017, pp. 45–72, Wiesbaden (2017)

User Experience Study: The Service Expectation of Hotel Guests to the Utilization of AI-Based Service Robot in Full-Service Hotels

Yaozhi Zhang[✉] and Shanshan Qi

Institute for Tourism Studies, Macao SAR, People's Republic of China
a810708027@vip.qq.com

Abstract. With the dramatic development of AI technology, the concept of robotic hotel is entering the public's awareness. Although AI application brings in high efficiency, low labor cost and novelty, practical operation of robotic hotels still faces with challenges. This quantitative research aims at understanding the current user expectation level of AI robotic hotel and robot appliance. Based on that, it tries to make the user classification by demographic, behavioral and attitude factors. By using the refined SERVQUAL model, it gathers the expectation from five dimensions involving tangibles, reliability, responsiveness, assurance and empathy.

These research objectives were realized by using survey-designed questionnaires and distributed by a snowball sampling method conducted in Beijing. After validity and reliability test, data collected from the field were analyzed by a variety of inspections. It is found that education, attitude and income level have a significant effect on the expectation to stay in the robotic hotel, which provided the basis of market position for robotic hotel operators. Through regression analysis, the model was established to identify what factors played an important part and how they worked. It is found that tangibles and responsiveness expectation significantly and positively contributed to increases in general user expectation to robotic hotels.

This thesis drew up several conclusions, which would help industry players including hoteliers, AI robot suppliers better understand details of the user group in their decision-making process, as well as academic side to formulate a tailored model to evaluate the interaction between AI robots and hotel guests.

Keywords: User experience · AI robotic hotel · Service quality management · Hospitality

1 Introduction

1.1 Background of Study

With the development of computer hardware and big data, the AI technology has matured much faster than expectation and already entered into numerous fields such as engineering, medical treatment, machine control and so forth to cooperate or fully

© Springer Nature Switzerland AG 2019
F. F.-H. Nah and K. Siau (Eds.): HCII 2019, LNCS 11588, pp. 350–366, 2019.
https://doi.org/10.1007/978-3-030-22335-9_24

replace human beings (Li and Jiang 2017). Some scientists even have predicted that AI would lead to the next technological revolution, and Workplace Automation caused by AI robots would take place 47% jobs in the US in next two decades (Smith 2016).

With the dramatic development of AI robot technology, increasing applications has appeared and developed in the service sector as well. Since the 1980s, the AI technology has been used to help hotels to choose the most preferable room for the guests (Agnew 1987). Delivery robot, designed in a hominoid appearance, also has been successfully adopted by a number of hotels in Japan to assist staff to deliver amenities and room services (Kratochwill 2015). In 2015, the first fully robot-based hotel "Henn-na" launched in Japan, and it provides robot servers replacing all human labors and performing the job of bell service, checking in/out service and even as an in-room butler and so forth ("Welcome to the Robot Hotel: robots do most of the work at a new hotel in Japan," 2015).

The reasons for hotel sector to bring in smart robots are mainly due to its high efficiency, low cost and novelty (Labs 2017). According to Weaver (2016), the founder of an AI operation system company, claims that AI technologies not only has the ability to learn from big data and derive the pattern to make prediction, but also are capable to provide more efficient as well as novel services that creates enormous added-value. Moreover, hospitality, as a labor intensive industry, robots powered by AI technology can greatly reduce the labor cost for the long run of the hotel operation, which has been considered as another one of the significant benefits for adopting service robots in hotels (Kuo et al. 2016). Hence, the great potential of industrial AI robots application have been recognized by numerous enterprises including service industry (Labs 2017).

1.2 Problem Statement and Research Objectives

Despite the advantages and perceived potential, for hospitality industry, the practice of attaching AI robots with hotel operation is still not so prevalent in the real practice compared with other industries (Weaver 2016). In this case, together with opportunities, both hoteliers and scholars are facing challenges and uncertainties in the meantime.

Therefore, this research aims to understand comprehensive user expectation to AI applications for full service hotels by gathering the detailed information from various dimensions. More specifically, it is based on service quality appraisal tool, and focuses on finding the pattern of interaction and expectation regarding different demographic factors and the interrelation between all survey variables.

2   Literature Review

2.1 Service Quality Management

In the hospitality industry, service quality is a significant factor for the success of a hotel, and the perceived high service quality directly increases guest satisfaction, which helps create profitable business, brand loyalty, positive word-of-mouth as well as customer relationship (Knutson et al. 2010). As one of the most widely used instrument to evaluate service quality in various industries, Parasuraman et al. (1985) devised SERVQUAL Model and Service Gap Model, defining that the service quality is the consequence between customer expectation and customer perception. After that, Zeithaml et al. (1990) refined the dimension of service quality respectively into Five Dimensions: tangibles, reliability, responsiveness, assurance and empathy respectively (Fig. 1).

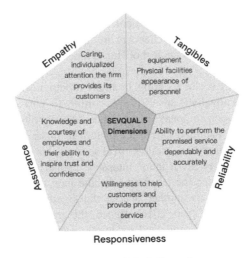

Fig. 1. SEVQUAL 5 dimensions

Tangibles. For current application, Sacarino, a service robot, providing luggage delivery service to the room as a bell and offering the enquiry service for the guests about the hotel information (Zalama et al. 2014). For contact centres, AI system has been deployed in many service sectors (Kirkpatrick 2017), which highly increase the efficiency of solving routine questions and intellectually analysis the emotion of the speakers that is beneficial for improving the customer service. Bilgihan et al. (2010) stated that in-room entertainment technologies has the same weight as hotel operation to the guest satisfaction, and they are developing and changing in a very fast speed though many up-to-date High-Tec appliances are not in a high priority among guest choices as expected. In the robot-staffed hotel in Japan, all receptionists are played by three separate intelligent robot ("Welcome to the Robot Hotel: robots do most of the work at a new hotel in Japan," 2015).

Reliability. For robot service, as same as human service, it has the concern regarding reliability, especially for those task-specific robots such as delivery robot and lifting robots (Stoller et al. 2016).

Responsiveness. Instead of measure the communication between human staff and guest, here the survey tends to measure the expected involvement between the machine and human beings.

Assurance. Concerning service assurance dimension, the first point is the language. Although the IT industry has made a huge progress on language understanding, according to the research by MIT, the great obstacle affecting task accomplishment is the transformation of language into instruct (Knight 2016). Another concern for customer to use technological service is about the data security (Park et al. 2016). Besides, based on Technology Acceptance Model (TAM), the ease to use is an essential consideration of service assurance as well (Davis 1989).

Empathy. Except for the existing question regarding customized service aspect, AI service has a special problem between SCIENCE and HUMANITY (Kakoudaki 2007). According to Kakoudaki, robot is a combined figure challenging not only technology but also traditional culture, value and justice, which are highly related to the ethical issues.

Despite the use of SERVQUAL in a wide range of industries, a number of refined models based on SERVQUAL have been developed to solely target on hospitality industries such as LODGSERV, HOLSERV, LODGQUAL and DINESERV. LODGSERV (Patton et al. 1994) and HOLSERV (Mei et al. 1999) are both for the measurement of accommodation industry. Knutson et al. redevised SERVQUAL five dimensions and then developed LODGSERV instrument, which is to focus on service quality in the lodging industry only (Getty and Thompson 1994). Although there are various schools of thought used to specially measure service quality in the hospitality industry, SERVQUAL is deemed as the most fundamental and reliable instrument having the most primary and comprehensive criteria (Stevens et al. 1995). For measurement of AI application in hotel industry, SERVQUAL is more appropriate to be selected as the basis template.

2.2 AI Robot Development

Even though AI application is still at the very beginning stage, a large number of application has been launched in the hospitality industry. In the near future, there will be increasingly advanced robot being introduced and tested as well (Fig. 2).

Countries	Focus of development	Government policies and projects	Robot products
America	1.National defense 2.Space-based development 3.Innovation application	1.Robotic cooperation association (Human-robot interaction) 2.Robotic industrial association	1. Roomba vacuum cleaner robot 2. Spencer entertainment robot 3. entertainment robot
Japan	1.Humanoid robots 2.Service application	1.Next generation of robot practical plan 2.New industry innovation strategy 3.Research institutes of robotic policy 4.New economic growth strategy	1.ASIMO entertainment robot 2.Tour guide robot 3.PAPERO healthcare robot
Europe	1.Critical technology 2.Healthcare robots 3.National defense robots 4.Household robots	1.International advanced robot plan 2.Mobile assistant robot plan 3.European robotic technology network plan	1. Medicare robot 2.Cyberhand disability aids robot 3. Da Vinci robotic surgical robot
South Korea	1.Broadband network connection 2.Household robots 3.Entertainment robots 4.Medical robots	1. Program of IT839 strategy 2.Ten new growth engine industries 3.Robot museum 4. Ubiquitous Robotic Companion	1.Genibo entertainment electronic pet 2.SR9630 cleaner robot

Fig. 2. AI development status in different countries

3 Methodology

3.1 Research Design

A descriptive quantitative research based on a survey design was conducted, because it best served to answer the research questions and the purposes of the study, which is to collect market voice based on SERVQUAL dimensions toward staying expectation in robotic hotels. The design of the questionnaire was mainly a closed questionnaire firstly gathering the general willingness of staying in AI-robotic hotel, and then followed by modified survey questions based on SERVQUAL model to investigate the intrinsic motivation and how can they relate to the general willingness (Fig. 3). The questionnaire was structured into modified Likert fashion. To the expectations respondents should provide points from 1–5. 1 meant a very low level for expectations and 5 indicated the highest level of expectations. The specific content of questions was modified in accordance with the robotic hotel service blue print as well as the realizable application of AI technology context. There was one open question gathering the expectation of potential service robot. In the end, three parts of information were gathered for segmenting the market. Demographic information including age, gender, educational level and income level was the first part; traveling behavior and attitude toward AI robotic hotel were gathered in the following to also help formulate the market segmentation for AI-robotic hotels. Due to the high validity of SERVQUAL model, no pilot study was conducted. All data were primary data that would be used in data analysis process.

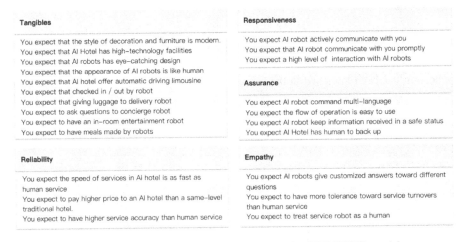

Fig. 3. The questions in the survey based on the SERVQUAL model

3.2 Sampling Design

The target population defined for this study was the adult residents living in Beijing city and those who had lived in Beijing for more than one year. As Beijing is the capital city of China, as well as the center of culture, education and technology, the residents were expected to understand IT and High-Tec notion better than other tier 2 and 3 cities, and to have more chances to travel and stay in a hotel. As a result, the technological knowledge combing hotel experience can lead to a more effective conclusion that are more representative for the whole developed cities in China where there are more potential customers who have higher purchasing power. This is also more appropriate to be used to deduce future market potential for China.

Regarding the sample size and sampling method, since this research was limited by the time, budget and geographical convenience, it was impractical to use random sampling method to cover all population in Beijing. For this reason, the research was set a margin of error of 0.05. Thereafter, the survey was made into an online-based e-questionnaire, distributed by using a snowball sampling method to facilitate the dissemination, and finally reached a sample size of 108 in total. Eventually, to enhance the validity, those surveys that costs less than 3 min were excluded. Finally, 102 of them were chosen as valid samples, based on the time limit of answering the questionnaire.

3.3 Data Analysis Design

The data collected from the field were analyzed by four dimensions. First of all, a descriptive data analysis was conducted to understand the demography of respondents, travelling behavior and attitude, and then the average willingness and expectation level toward staying in the robotic hotels were calculated. Besides, the average expectation toward the service hardware was calculated as well to understand the specific needs from the market. For the second dimension, mean tests (t-test and one-way Anova) were used to detect the specific difference between various groups in terms of socio-demography, travelling behavior and attitude toward AI-robotic hotel, aiming at formulating the proper market segments for AI robotic hotel. For the third level, a correlation analysis was made to detect whether there is internal relation between SSERVQUAL five dimensions and living expectation. Lastly, a regression analysis based on the data from SERVQUAL and general willingness was made to understand the essential interrelationship among them.

To ensure the validity of questions, they were strictly based on standard questions used in original SERVQUAL model. Since SERVQUAL has been proved to be a valid tool and model to measure service expectation, the validity of questions should be very high. To ensure the validity of the results, all respondents are strictly selected by the requirement measured by time of answering questions; only the process lasting for more than three minutes could be chosen as valid sample.

4   Results

4.1   Descriptive Data Analysis

In terms of socio demography, the proportion of the gender distribution was relatively balanced, with 51.9% (male) and 48.0% (female). More than 70% of respondents are people below 40 years old. The majority of sample (77.4%) had bachelor degree background. For income level, the majority is below 12000 yuan per month (Table 1).

Table 1. Socio-demographic profile of respondents

VARIABLE	FREQUENCY (N=102)	PERCENT (N=100%)
GENDER		
MALE	53	51.96%
FEMALE	49	48.04%
AGE		
18-29	46	45.1%
30-39	25	24.51%
40-49	17	16.67%
50-59	11	10.78%
60 OR OLDER	3	2.9%
EDUCATION LEVEL		
HIGH SCHOOL OR BELOW	7	6.86%
COLLEGE	10	9.8%
BACHELOR	79	77.45%
MASTER OR ABOVE	6	5.88%
INCOME LEVEL		
BELOW 4000	26	25.49%
4000-8000	33	32.35%
8000-12000	37	36.27%
ABOVE 12000	6	5.88%

Based on Tables 2 and 3 (Fig. 4), around 59% of travelling activities were leisure ones and 41% were business and others. For the attitude toward robotic hotel, 63% of respondents had heard the notion of AI robotic hotel. Among them, 72% showed the interest in staying in the such hotels. Other than those who fell neutral toward this idea, only one respondent felt negative toward the idea of robotic hotel. Table 4 (Fig. 4) shows the overall willingness level toward staying in such hotels, and the final result was 3.73. Table 5 (Fig. 4) shows expectation level toward specific service hardware in future AI robotic hotel. In room butler and entertainment robots was the only one that had an expectation value over 4. Table 6 shows the average value of SERVQUAL five dimensions.

Table 2. Traveling Behaviors and attitude of Respondents

TRAVELLING TYPE	PROPORTION
Leisure	59%
Business and others	41%

Table 3. Respondents Attitude toward AI robotic hotel

PEOPLE WHO HAVE HEARD ABOUT THE NOTION OF AI ROBOTIC HOTEL	FREQUENCY(N=102)	PERCENT
People who have heard	65	63.73%
People who have never heard	37	36.27%
FOR THOSE WHO HAVE HEARD THE NOTION	FREQUENCY (N=65)	PERCENT
Interested	47	72.31%
Neutral	17	26.15%
Not interested	1	1.54%

Table 5. Respondents expectation toward specific AI robot's application (n=102)

	Strongly unexpected	Unexpected	Neutral	Expected	Strongly expected	Average
Arriving at hotel by autonomous vehicles	6(5.88%)	17(16.67%)	21(20.59%)	33(32.35%)	25(24.51%)	3.53
Giving and storing luggage to the delivery robot	4(3.92%)	7(6.86%)	19(18.63%)	36(35.29%)	36(35.29%)	3.91
C/I & O by receptionist robots	6(5.88%)	12(11.76%)	22(21.57%)	40(39.22%)	22(21.57%)	3.59
Making inquiries to concierge robots	7(6.86%)	8(7.84%)	24(23.53%)	37(36.27%)	26(25.49%)	3.66
Communicating with in-room butler robots	2(1.96%)	5(4.9%)	15(14.71%)	37(36.27%)	43(42.16%)	4.12
Enjoying meals made by cooking robots	8(7.84%)	11(10.78%)	30(29.41%)	32(31.37%)	21(20.59%)	3.46

Table 4. General expectation toward staying in AI robotic hotel

	Strongly expected	Unexpected	Neutral	Expected	Strongly expected	Average
Expect	2(1.96%)	8(7.84%)	23(22.55%)	52(50.98%)	17(16.67%)	3.73

Fig. 4. Table 2. Traveling behaviors and attitude of respondents; **Table 3.** Respondents attitude toward AI robotic hotel; **Table 4.** General expectation toward staying in AI robotic hotel; **Table 5.** Respondents expectation toward specific AI robot's application (n = 102)

Table 6. Average value of SEVQUAL five dimension

	N	Mean	Std. Deviation	Variance
Tangible_Average	102	40074	0.7799	0.608
Reliability_Average	102	40613	0.81252	0.660
Responsiveness_Average	102	38,260	0.81355	0.662
Assurance_Average	102	42206	0.75558	0.571
Empathy_Average	102	38,554	0.7703	0.593
Valid N (listwise)	102			

4.2 Reliability Test

The research questions had an acceptable reliability after the modification based on SERVQUAL five dimensions. As can be seen from Table 7, all of the Cronbach's Alpha were over 0,7, which means the data were highly reliable and able to be used in further data analysis process.

Table 7. Cronbach's Alpha value of the research questions

Dimension	Cronbach's Alpha
Tangibles	0.844
Reliability	0.855
Responsiveness	0.807
Assurance	0.823
Empathy	0.723

4.3 Mean Test

Independent Sample T-test

Mean test was conducted to find the difference between various groups to set the market segmentation. By conducting independent samples t-test, Table 8 shows that there was no significant difference in staying expectation between genders, and whether they have heard about the notion of robotic hotel made no difference either (Significance values were both over 0.05). Meanwhile, there was no significant difference between leisure and business groups as well, with p value of 0.673. The results of T-test show that in-group average expectation was not affected, to the extent of statistical significance, by factors of gender, awareness or travelling type.

Table 8. Independent samples T-test results: sex v.s. staying expectation; heard v.s. not heard; leisure group v.s. business and other groups

	Group	n	Mean	T-value	df	Sig.
Expectation	Male	53	3.81	0.999	100	0.32
	Female	49	3.63			

	Group	n	Mean	T-value	df	Sig.
Expectation	Heard	65	3.83	1.572	100	0.119
	Not Heard	37	3.54			

	Group	n	Mean	Group	n	Mean
Expectation	Leisure	58	3.76	Leisure	58	3.76
	Business	44	3.68	Business	44	3.68

One-Way ANOVA

Table 9 (Fig. 5) shows that there is no statistically significant difference between means (p-0.097) in different age groups. However, there was statistically difference between group's means by the criteria of educational level (p-0.006). Then, post-hoc test was conducted by using Scheffe method for these two groups. It could be seen in Table 10 (Fig. 5) that there was a significant difference between people having high school and below diploma and bachelor degree people toward the willingness to stay in an AI robotic hotel.

In terms of attitude, it was found that among different types of attitude groups there was significant difference (p-0.01). By conducting post-hoc analysis, it could be clearly seen that people who are interested in the concept of IT and robotic related things have significantly different expectation to stay in robotic hotel to the group who hold neutral position toward the same topics and who have never heard this concept (Tables 11 and 12 in Fig. 5).

As determined by Table 13 (Fig. 5), the Income level had significant effect which was at .003 with an F statistic of 4.998. It could be interpreted that the income level had a significant influence on the overall expectation to stay in robotic hotel. Seeing from the post–hoc test, for the income groups, there was statistically significantly different expectation for low-income people (4000 and below) to people who have 8000–12000 monthly income. In conclusion, education, attitude and income level of consumers take significant effect on the expectation to stay in robotic hotel. Thus, in promotion process the hotel management should focus on these three dimensions to carry out market segmentation and market positioning.

Table 9. ANOVA: Age Group and Educational level

Overall Expectation Age Group	Sum of Squares	df	Mean Square	F	Sig.
Between Groups	6.338	4	1.585	2.023	0.097
Within Groups	75.975	97	0.783		
Total	82.314	101			

Overall Expectation Educational level	Sum of Squares	df	Mean Square	F	Sig.
Between Groups	9.679	3	3.226	4.353	0.006
Within Groups	72.634	98	0.741		
Total	82.314	101			

Table 10. Multiple Comparisons (Educational level)

Dependent Variable: Overall Expectation

Scheffe

Educational Level	(J) Educational Level	Mean Difference (I-J)	Std. Error	Sig.	95% Confidence Interval	
					Lower Bound	Upper Bound
High School and Below	College	-0.343	0.424	0.884	-1.55	0.86
	Bachelor	-.991*	0.34	0.042	-1.96	-0.03
	Master and Above	-1.143	0.479	0.135	-2.51	0.22
College	High School and Below	0.343	0.424	0.884	-0.86	1.55
	Bachelor	-0.648	0.289	0.177	-1.47	0.17
	Master and Above	-0.8	0.445	0.362	-2.06	0.46
Bachelor	High School and Below	.991*	0.34	0.042	0.03	1.96
	College	0.648	0.289	0.177	-0.17	1.47
	Master and Above	-0.152	0.365	0.982	-1.19	0.89
Master and Above	High School and Below	1.143	0.479	0.135	-0.22	2.51
	College	0.8	0.445	0.362	-0.46	2.06
	Bachelor	0.152	0.365	0.982	-0.89	1.19

*. The mean difference is significant at the 0.05 level.

Table 11. ANOVA (Attitude)

Overall Expectation	Sum of Squares	df	Mean Square	F	Sig.
Between Groups	16142	3	3381	7969	0.001
Within Groups	66171	98	,675		
Total	82314	101			

Table 12. Multiple Comparisons (Attitude)

Dependent Variable: Overall Expectation

Scheffe

	(J) Interest	Mean Difference (I-J)	Std. Error	Sig.	95% Confidence Interval	
					Lower Bound	Upper Bound
Not Heard	Interested	-,590*	,181	,018	-1,11	-,07
	Neutral	,423	,241	,384	-,26	1,11
	Not Interested	,541	,597	,844	-1,16	2,24
Interested	Not Heard	,590*	,181	,018	,07	1,11
	Neutral	1,013*	,233	,001	,35	1,68
	Not Interested	1130	,594	,311	-,56	2,82
Neutral	Not Heard	-,423	,241	,384	-1,11	,26
	Interested	-1,013*	,233	,001	-1,68	-,35
	Not Interested	,118	,614	,998	-1,63	1,87
Not Interested	Not Heard	-,541	,597	,844	-2,24	1,16
	Interested	-1130	,594	,311	-2,82	,56
	Neutral	-,118	,614	,998	-1,87	1,63

*. The mean difference is significant at the 0.05 level.

Table 13. ANOVA(Income level)

Overall Expectation	Sum of Squares	df	Mean Square	F	Sig.
Between Groups	10.922	3	3.641	4.998	0.003
Within Groups	71.391	98	0.728	71.391	98
Total	82314	101			

Table 14. Multiple Comparisons (Income level)

Dependent Variable: Overall Expectation

Scheffe

(I) Income Level	(J) Income Level	Mean Difference (I-J)	Std. Error	Sig.	95% Confidence Interval	
					Lower Bound	Upper Bound
Below 4000	4000-7999	-0.469	0.228	0.234	-1.1	0.17
	8000-11999	-.796*	0.218	0.006	-1.42	-0.17
	12000 and Above	-0.938	0.367	0.118	-2.04	0.18
4000-7999	Below 4000	0.469	0.224	0.234	-0.17	1.1
	8000-11999	-0.33	0.204	0.46	-0.9	0.23
	12000 and Above	-0.47	0.376	0.675	-1.55	0.61
8000-11999	Below 4000	.796*	0.218	0.006	0.17	1.42
	4000-7999	0.33	0.204	0.46	-0.23	0.9
	12000 and Above	-0.14	0.376	0.987	-1.21	0.93
12000 and Above	Below 4000	0.954	0.367	0.126	-0.18	2.04
	4000-7999	0.47	0.379	0.675	-0.61	1.55
	8000-11999	0.14	0.376	0.987	-0.93	1.21

*. The mean difference is significant at the 0.05 level.

Fig. 5. **Table 9.** ANOVA: age group and educational level; **Table 10.** Multiple comparisons (educational level); **Table 11.** ANOVA (Attitude); **Table 12.** Multiple comparisons (attitude); **Table 13.** ANOVA (Income level); **Table 14.** Multiple comparisons (income level)

4.4 Correlation and Regression Analysis

One main hypothesis of this study was SEVQUAL five dimensions affect the overall expectation level in staying robotic hotels. Pearson's correlation analysis was employed to test the hypothesis and the results were presented in Table 15. It was hypothesised there is a positive correlation between the SERVQUAL 5 dimensions and the overall expectation level. The final result supported for this hypothesis (r = .657, 442, 602, 438, 501, and all p are less than .001). Based on these results, it supported the need to conduct further regression analysis as well. What' s more, Pearson Correlation corf-ficients between SERVQUAL five dimensions significantly reach over 0.5, which shows that these 5 factors may affect each other.

As all five dimensions are positively related with the general expectation level, a multiple regression analysis was conducted to find out whether SERVQUAL five dimensions can effectively predict the expectation level. Using the enter method it was found that SERVQUAL model did significantly predicted the expectation level ($p < .05$, R2 = .499, R2Adjusted = .472). From the Table 16, the simulation model of SERVQUAL passed F-test, showing that the equation established was efficacious.

It can be found in the Coefficient table that only Tangibles ($p < .05$, beta = 0.566) and Responsiveness ($p < .05$, beta = 0.359) explained a significant amount of the variance in the value of expectation level. Each unit increase in Tangibles and Responsiveness expectation would lead to 0.138 and 0.353unit increase in the overall expectation level. In comparison, the responsiveness expectation played a more important role. However, other three factors did not significantly predict the value of staying expectation (Table 17).

Combined with VIF values in Table 18, results in the collinearity diagnostics show that there was multicollinearity relation between factors of the formula. It can be found that Eigenvalues of dimension 2 to 6 approximate to zero and condition Index values are more than 10. As far as multicollinearity problem, on the one hand, insufficient

Table 15. Pearson correlation coefficients results for overall expectation and SERVQUAL five dimension (n = 102)

Correlations

		Expect.	T_Aver	R_Aver	R_Aver	A_Aver	E_Aver
Expect.	Pearson Correlation	1	.657**	.442**	.602**	.438**	.501**
	Sig.(2tailed)		0.001	0.001	0.001	0.001	0.001
	N	102	102	102	102	102	102
T_Aver	Pearson Correlation	.657**	1	.711**	.695**	.706**	.623**
	Sig.(2tailed)	0		0	0	0	0
	N	102	102	102	102	102	102
R_Avetr	Pearson Correlation	.442**	.711**	1	.698**	.727**	.670**
	Sig.(2tailed)	0	0		0	0	0
	N	102	102	102	102	102	102
R_Aver	Pearson Correlation	.602**	.695**	.698**	1	.616**	.674**
	Sig. (2-tailed)	0	0	0		0	0
	N	102	102	102	102	102	102
A_Aver	Pearson Correlation	.438**	.706**	.727**	.616**	1	.684**
	Sig.(2tailed)	0	0	0	0		0
	N	102	102	102	102	102	102
E_Aver	Pearson Correlation	.501**	.623**	.670**	.674**	.684**	1
	Sig.(2tailed)	0	0	0	0	0	
	N	102	102	102	102	102	102

**. Correlation is significant at the 0.01 level (2-tailed).

Table 16. Model summary

Model	R	R Square	Adjusted R Square	Std. Error of the Estimate	Durbin-Watson
1	.706ª	0.499	0.472	0.656	1.485

a. Predictors: (Constant), Empathy_Average, Tangible_Average, Responsiveness_Average, Assurance_Average, Reliability_Average

b. Dependent Variable: Overall Expectation

samples may lead to weakening of statistical characteristics. On the other hand, the factors depict 5 dimensions of consumer expectation, which are closed related in the real sense (Table 19).

Table 20 was conducted to examine residuals of the model. The absolute value of Standard residuals remained below 3, showing no unusual value. In the normal P-P plot, the observed residuals distribute around standard normal distribution curve. It can also be proved by the Histogram for the residuals that they are normally distributed in

Table 17. ANOVA (regression test)

ANOVA[a]

Model		Sum of Squares	df	Mean Square	F	Sig.
1	Regression	41.037	5	8.207	19.088	.001[b]
	Residual	41.277	96	0.43		
	Total	82.314	101			

a. Dependent Variable: Overall Expectation

b. Predictors: (Constant), Empathy_Average, Tangible_Average, Responsiveness_Average, Assurance_Average, Reliability_Average

Table 18. Coefficients

Coefficients[a]

Model	Unstandardized Coefficients		StandardizedCoefficients	t	Sig.	Collinearity Statistics	
	B	Std. Error	Beta			Tolerance	VIF
1(Constant)	0.558	0.396		1.409	0.162		
Tangible_Average	0.655	0.138	0.566	4.747	0.001	0.368	2.717
Reliability_Average	-0.219	0.138	-0.197	-1.59	0.115	0.34	2.944
Responsiv ness_Average	0.353	0.129	0.319	2.751	0.007	0.39	2.567
Assurance_Average	-0.133	0.144	-0.111	-0.925	0.357	0.36	2.776
Empathy_Average	0.167	0.131	0.142	1.269	0.207	0.415	2.41

a. Dependent Variable: Overall Expectation

Table 19. Collinearity diagnostics

Collinearity Diagnostics[a]

Model	Dimension	Eigenvalue	Condition Index	Variance Proportions					
				(Constant)	Tangible_Average	Reliability_Average	Responsiveness_Average	Assurance_Average	Empathy_Average
1	1	5.929	1	0	0	0	0	0	0
	2	0.024	15.627	0.84	0.01	0.03	0.1	0	0.01
	3	0.014	20.33	0.01	0.26	0.08	0.06	0.03	0.59
	4	0.014	20.397	0.11	0.01	0.04	0.62	0.17	0.16
	5	0.01	23.864	0.02	0.49	0.68	0.01	0.01	0.07
	6	0.008	27.316	0.02	0.23	0.18	0.21	0.79	0.16

a. Dependent Variable: Overall Expectation

line with the condition of regression hypothesis. Figure 6. shows that most of the model residuals remain between −2 to 2, able to effectively explain predicted value of the dependent variable in the formula. In sum, residuals of the model apply to basic regression hypothesis.

Table 20. Residuals statistics

Residuals Statistics[a]

	Minimum	Maximum	Mean	Std. Deviation	N
Predicted Value	1.16	4.71	3.73	0.637	2
Std. Predicted Value	-4.022	1.55	0	1	2
Standard Error of Predicted Value	0.076	0.355	0.149	0.056	102
Adjusted Predicted Value	1.21	4.86	3.73	0.633	2
Residual	-1.829	1.714	0	0.639	2
Std. Residual	-2.789	2.613	0	0.975	2
Stud. Residual	-2.941	2.702	-0.003	1.009	2
Deleted Residual	-2.034	1.833	-0.005	0.686	2
Stud. Deleted Residual	-3.067	2.797	-0.004	1.023	2
Mahal. Distance	0.362	28.614	4.951	5.092	102
Cook's Distance	0	0.162	0.012	0.026	2
Centered Leverage Value	0.004	0.283	0.049	0.05	2

a. Dependent Variable: Overall Expectation

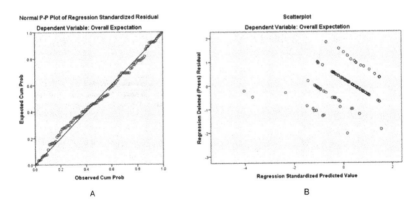

Fig. 6. (A) Normal P-Plot of regression standardized residual; (B) Regression deleted residual scatterplot

5   Discussion

5.1   Implications of the Study

First of all, based on the descriptive result analysis, it can be seen that at current stage, the general willingness toward staying at AI robotic hotel was between "neutral" and "expected" with average expectation value of 3.73. This means that for the general population as a whole, the market expectation toward living in an AI-based robotic hotel was not agreed to be very high. Thus, if currently an experimental business is established, market segmentation has to be well conducted to cater to those users who have better living wiliness.

In terms of market segmentation, based on the mean test, by socio-demographic factor, it can be seen that people who generally have higher educational level and income level are more likely to have a try in robotic hotel. Age and gender are not decisive factors affecting the willingness of staying in an AI Robotic hotel. In my opinion, the reasons include that high-income level people normally have higher educational background and are more confident on handling High-Tec and IT-related things. Therefore, education level might be the ultimate factor affecting the staying willingness. This hypothesis needs to be tested by further study.

In terms of travelling behaviors, there was no significant difference between leisure group and business group. It can be inferred that whether the aim of traveling is for enjoyment, business, and others, it did not manifestly affect the staying willingness. In other words, according to this study, the robotic hotel can be designed for people with any aim of travelling. Thus, for potential entrepreneurs, AI-based robotic hotels can be applied to business hotels, resorts and various types of hotel, because the study did not show a significant difference among people in different traveling groups.

For attitude toward AI robotic hotel, there was no significant difference between the people who had heard the idea and people who did not. Nevertheless, the people who has the interest of the AI and technology related notion had significantly higher staying expectation compared with those who has mild interest in such fields. In other words, people who are positive toward technology are more likely to be attracted by such hotels. Thereby, the promotion of the idea "AI-robotic hotel" should specially target on the group who is highly interested in and positive to IT topic (Fig. 7).

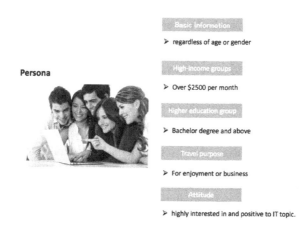

Fig. 7. General persona about target users of AI-based service hotels

Among all current AI hardware, in-room entertainment robots were liked at most with an expectation average of over four, which is followed by the delivery robot. In this case, entertainment robots should be deemed as a realizable and welcomed hardware by the general market.

Another significant aim from this study is to understand how SERVQUAL five dimensions formulate and predict the overall willingness. From the study, we can conclude that Tangibles and Responsiveness are two significant factors positively affect the general expectation. Based on the survey, it is found that normally for people who is willing to stay in robotic hotels usually because that they have a higher expectation on tangibles and responsiveness. Based on this logic, it can be concluded that the intrinsic motivation of staying in robotic hotels is due to the expectation of trying the new service hardware and experience the communicational process with them. Thus, for industrial designer, it should focus on optimizing the hardware design and produce more fancy elements. Besides, communicational functions should be primarily enhanced to strengthen the interaction between the users and robots. For hoteliers, key factors increasing the potential of success are also the same points. When designing the service process and blue print, they should definitely focus on these two points, because they are highly related with the expectation level. the foremost is the service hardware that are attractive and special.

5.2   Limitations and Future Studies

The first and foremost limitation of this study is the sample size. Limited by the time, finance and access to relevant information as well as relevant resources, only 102 valid samples were collected. This, to some extent, affects the trustworthy and quality of the findings. After that, failure to use a probability sampling technique also limits the ability to make broader generalizations from the results and to make statistical inferences from the sample. In the future, a large-scale study conducted by random sampling method is expected to be conducted to verify the study result.

Another limitation of this study is the validity of the model modification. Although the survey questions are mainly based on SERVQAUL model that has high question reliability, some modification cannot be proved that has a similar validity compared with the original model. To enhance the model to evaluating robotic hotels still has a long way to go; it could be improved by more validity test methods such as professionals and literature verification. Pilot study for relevant professionals can also be conducted for more advices.

Last but least, for this survey, about some questions, it is quite abstract to describe the robotic service. There might be a gap existing and misunderstanding between the researcher and respondents. A more comprehensive description for those applications can be written for the future study to minimize the discretion.

In the future, a fixed-interval survey can be conducted regularly, such as 2 years per time, which is to monitor the change of expectation level of staying in robotic hotel as well as the preference for guests. With the development of service hardware and more practice in this field. It is expected to see a positive trend toward AI- based robotic hotel. Meanwhile, similar study could be conducted in different cities all around the world to detect whether similar pattern exist in difference cultural and socio-demographic background. The expectation might also vary from distinct economic scale. All these questions can only be answered by obtaining the voice from the market.

6 Conclusion

This study firstly set out to determine the current market expectation toward AI appliance in hotel context. It is reached that the current expectation level is between neutral and expected. Nevertheless, this study has found that some specific groups are more willing to try AI robotic facilities. They will be called as the targeted market segments for AI robotic hotel. As a conclusion for the market segmentation and target segment, the groups of people significantly expecting staying in AI robotic hotels are those who: (1) Highly interested in the notion of AI and technology-related things (attitude dimension) (2) Have higher educational background such as bachelor and above (sociodemographic dimension (3) With more than average monthly income (sociodemographic dimension)

However, through this study, business and leisure guests did not show a significant difference toward the willingness. Therefore, at this stage, hoteliers should specially target on the focused groups stated above and conduct relevant positioning strategy to cater to these people.

In terms of specific service hardware, in-room entertainment robot is the most welcomed robot, followed by delivery robots. This result provides the reference for designing the specific service robots in AI robotic hotel for both supply chain and hotelier.

The ultimate objective of this study is to understand how expectation toward robotic hotel formed from an academic side is. The results of the findings support the hypothesis of SERVQUAL model can explain the expectation level of staying in a hotel. Based on the regression test, it also proves that tangibles and responsiveness are two significant factors positively affecting the willingness of staying in such hotels. Thus, in order to improve the market attraction and meet the expectation of customer, these two focus points should be concentrated for promotion and further improvement. In other words, service hardware and the human-machine interaction are the areas where the market should pay the most attention to. For academic sides, this result helps predict the expectation value and build the basis for refining the new service evaluation model to specifically evaluate the expectation and perception in AI robotic hotel context.

References

Agnew, J.: Artificial intelligence with a marketing use: hotel computer matches guests with their favorite rooms, p. 1 (1987)

Bilgihan, A., Cobanoglu, C., Miller, B.L.: Importance-performance analysis of guest entertainment technology amenities in the lodging industry. FIU Hospitality Rev. **28**(3), 84–108 (2010)

Kuo, C.-M., Huang, G.-S., Tseng, C.-Y., Boger, E.P.: SMART SWOT strategic planning analysis: for service robot utilization in the hospitality industry. Consort. J. Hosp. Tour. **20**(2), 60–72 (2016)

Davis, F.D.: Perceived usefulness, perceived ease of use, and user acceptance of information technology. MIS Q. **13**(3), 319–340 (1989)

Friedman, M., Sen, S.: The road to 2025. Hospitality in the digital era (2017). https://www.cognizant.com/whitepapers/hospitality-in-the-digital-era-codex2543.pdf

Kakoudaki, D.: Studying robots, between science and the humanities. Int. J. Humanit. **5**(8), 165–181 (2007)

Kirkpatrick, K.: AI in Contact Centers: Artificial intelligence technologies are being deployed to improve the customer service experience. Commun. ACM **60**(8), 18–19 (2017). https://doi.org/10.1145/3105442

Knight, W.: AI's unspoken problem: extraordinary progress has been made in artificial intelligence of late. But to achieve their full promise, machines must understand language, and that will be the most difficult step yet, p. 28 (2016)

Knutson, B.J., Beck, J.A., Seunghyun, K., Jaemin, C.: Service quality as a component of the hospitality experience: proposal of a conceptual model and framework for research. J. Foodserv. Bus. Res. **13**(1), 15–23 (2010). https://doi.org/10.1080/15378021003595889

Kratochwill, L.: The robot whisperer upgrades your hotel stay, p. 17 (2015)

Labs, W.: Robots now and in the future, pp. 77–92. BNP Media (2017)

Patton, M., Mark Patton, P.S., Knutson, B.J.: Internationalizing LODGSERV as a measurement tool: a pilot study. J. Hosp. Leis. Mark. **2**(2), 39–55 (1994)

Park, Y.-W., Herr, P.M., Kim, B.C.: The effect of disfluency on consumer perceptions of information security. Mark. Lett. **27**(3), 525 (2016). https://doi.org/10.1007/s11002-015-9359-9

Shostack, G.L.: Designing services that deliver. Harv. Bus. Rev. **62**(1), 133–139 (1984)

Stoller, O., Schindelholz, M., Hunt, K.J.: Robot-assisted end-effector-based stair climbing for cardiopulmonary exercise testing: feasibility, reliability, and repeatability. PLoS ONE (2) (2016). https://doi.org/10.1371/journal.pone.0148932

Weaver, T.O.M.: Artificial intelligence: the forthcoming hospitality renaissance. Publican's Morning Advert. (8), 57 (2016)

Welcome to the Robot Hotel: robots do most of the work at a new hotel in Japan. Scholastic News/Weekly Reader Edition 6 (2015)

Li, X., Jiang, H.: Artificial intelligence technology and engineering applications. Appl. Comput. Electromagn. Soc. J. **32**(5), 381–388 (2017)

Zalama, E., et al.: Sacarino, a service robot in a hotel environment. In: Armada, Manuel A., Sanfeliu, A., Ferre, M. (eds.) ROBOT2013: First Iberian Robotics Conference. AISC, vol. 253, pp. 3–14. Springer, Cham (2014). https://doi.org/10.1007/978-3-319-03653-3_1

Zeithaml, V.A., Parasuraman, A., Berry, L.L.: Delivering Quality Service: Balancing Customer Perceptions and Expectations. Free Press, Collier Macmillan, New York, London (1990). ©1990

Effects of Conscientiousness on Users' Eye-Movement Behaviour with Recommender Interfaces

Lin Zhang and Heshan Liu[✉]

Mechanical Engineering School,
Shandong University, Jingshi Rd. 17923, Jinan, China
zhanglin209n@163.com, liuheshan@sdu.edu.cn

Abstract. Organisation-based recommender interfaces (ORGs) have drawn attention from both the academia and the industry as they allow users to determine their preferences for product attributes. Considering that users' personality traits may deeply influence their shopping behaviour, we performed an eye-tracking lab experiment to compare two types of recommender interfaces, namely the classified evaluation ORG and the non-classified evaluation list. The results showed that highly conscientious users paid significantly more attention to ORG, evaluated slightly more products, and placed more fixations on each product in the ORG. Whereas, low conscientiousness users exhibited more fixations on the LIST interface. Hence, the empirical findings suggest that users with different personalities adapted their visual searching behaviour to the change in the recommendation presentation.

Keywords: Recommender interface · Conscientiousness of personality traits · Eye-tracking experiment · User experience

1 Introduction

Organisation-based recommender interfaces (ORGs) have become increasingly popular in various web environments [7, 10, 11]. Previous studies have indicated that ORG can increase the users' product knowledge and preference [8, 9]. Hence, users could be assisted in gaining a quicker overview and understanding of the recommended items. According to the related work, the level of users' conscientiousness may influence their subjective perception of the recommender interfaces. People with high conscientiousness are often highly disciplined, organised, cautious, dutiful, and consistent in their behaviour and styles, whereas those low in this trait tend to be more impulsive, creative, easy-going, and flexible [25]. For instance, conscientiousness has been demonstrated to be related to the preference for different levels of recommendation diversity in the music and movie domains [4]. The findings show the necessity of considering individual traits while designing diversity-aware interfaces. In [1], researchers proposed a strategy that embeds personality to adjust the diversity degree of recommendations; the results showed that it significantly increased the users' perceptions of system competence and the recommendation accuracy. A study of 1840 users

© Springer Nature Switzerland AG 2019
F. F.-H. Nah and K. Siau (Eds.): HCII 2019, LNCS 11588, pp. 367–376, 2019.
https://doi.org/10.1007/978-3-030-22335-9_25

of MovieLens showed that conscientiousness was associated with the preference for the diversity degree and that highly conscientious participants were more satisfied with diverse lists [21]. However, most of the studies conducted thus far have focused on recommendation algorithms, without considering the users' personality traits. Therefore, it is meaningful to explore the relationship between these personality traits and an organisation-based recommender.

In our work, we built two distinct interfaces, namely an ORG interface (classified evaluation ORG) and a list interface (non-classified evaluation list). Then, we used the Five Factor Model (FFM) to classify the score of uses with high and low levels of conscientiousness. In an eye-tracking experiment, we compared the noteworthy differences between the interfaces of the uses with these two levels of conscientiousness and conducted a data analysis at the category level and the product level. We recorded and analysed the eye-movement behaviour of conscientious users, summarised the experimental findings, and provided valuable proposals for future work.

2 Related Work

2.1 Recommender Interfaces

With respect to the general e-commerce site design in usability studies, it has been suggested that users are likely to adapt their decision strategies to information representations. For instance, in [16], the researchers reported that a product list interface can induce a significant effect on the users' decision strategy. From the structural viewpoint, previous studies such as the one reported in [17] claimed that a site's navigational structure directly affects shopping behaviour. In [19], the researchers discussed the effectiveness of one-column and multi-column layouts for rendering large textual documents in a web browser. They indicated that users spent less time scrolling and performed fewer scrolling actions in the case of a multi-column layout. In addition, in [18], the researchers claimed that a well-organised interface, well-designed product lists, and sufficient product information, such as product descriptions and images, can improve the accessibility of product information to online shoppers. Most of the existing systems, e.g., case-based systems, CF-based systems, and commercial sites, typically use the ranked list structure, where all items are displayed one after the other. The ranking is primarily based on scores that the system computes to predict a user's interest in the items [20]. For instance, MovieLens is a typical CF-based movie recommender system. By locating neighbours who have similar interests to the current user, the system recommends a set of movies that are preferred by these like-minded people [23]. Indeed, according to [24], in the list structure, researchers have found that people more frequently viewed and clicked the top results on the list.

To the best of our knowledge, and according to [6], keyword-style explanations are significantly more effective than recommended-item lists. For example, one study showed that the ORG interface performed substantially better at improving the quality of user-perceived recommendations [7, 10]. There has been some research on increasing the users' decision effectiveness. For instance, by using a case-based reasoning system in [15], the researchers highlighted the need to help users to effectively explore the product space by explaining the existence of the remaining products. Meanwhile, for interface design, in [11], the researchers explored all the design issues to derive effective principles, such as how to generate categories and whether to use short or long text for the category explanation. In [22], the researchers reported two experiments on recommender interfaces; the results showed that the ORG can significantly attract the users' attention and allow users to view more recommended items. However, as mentioned earlier, few studies have been conducted on the effect of layout design on users' behaviour in a recommender system. Given that the list interface is so far the most popular presentation style, it should be meaningful to compare the ORG interface with it, so as to identify the interface's genuine benefits to users. We were hence motivated to conduct user evaluations to investigate the effect of the category structure particularly in recommender systems.

2.2 Conscientiousness of FFM with Recommender Interface

The most commonly used model personality is the FFM [13], and it is traditionally captured by questionnaires such as the Big Five Inventory [5, 12]. Personal characteristics influence the form of recommendation interface [11]. As our work focuses on the effects of personality traits on the users' eye-movement behaviour with recommendation interfaces, we mainly introduce the related work on the relationship between conscientiousness and recommendation interfaces, and the empirical results. Prior work found that conscientiousness is negatively correlated with rating items and an ability to undertake difficult activities [2]. In [3], the researchers considered personality traits to be an indicator of satisfaction and attractiveness on differently diversified music recommendation lists. The results showed that conscientiousness is related to a preference for a higher degree of diversification and is increasingly more attracted to more diversified recommendation lists. In a recommendation system [1], the researchers reported that conscientiousness can affect user behaviour in a variety of ways, such as newcomer retention, intensity of engagement, activity types, and item categories. In [21], the researchers claimed that conscientiousness is associated with a greater degree of diversity in preference, and highly conscientious participants are more satisfied and attracted to diverse lists. In another work [4], the users' personality traits influenced the design of a diversity-aware recommendation interface. The results showed that higher conscientiousness led to a higher preference for more meta information. Moreover, they indicated that users scoring high on conscientiousness showed a preference for browsing by activity. In [14], the researchers simulated an online music streaming service to identify the relationship between personality traits and the way users browse for music (Table 1).

Table 1. Personality traits of conscientiousness on recommender interface identified in literatures.

Related work	Conscientious attributes	Recommender interface	Baseline	Evaluation metric
[1]	Influence user behaviour	Film recommendation list	Personality-based recommender systems	User evaluation
[21]	Degree of diversity	Recommendation list	CF-based movie recommender system	User preferences
[4]	Diversity-aware	Recommendation interface	Music recommender systems	User satisfaction
[3]	Degree of diversity; satisfaction; attractiveness	Music recommendation list	Diversifying recommendations	Subjective evaluations; user modelling; user-centric evaluations
[2]	Rating items; ability to perform activities			User model; online survey

3 Eye-Tracking Experiment

3.1 Materials

An experiment was conducted to measure users' performances in ORG and list interfaces, which chose smartphone as the product domain. For the ORG interface, the top candidate was displayed on the top of the interface. 24 recommended products were divided into four groups, with a title at the top of every group explaining the pros and cons of the products. For the list interface, we only displayed one line of 24 products. The experiment allowed us to further identify and judge the effects of users' conscientiousness level on their eye-movement behaviours in two different interfaces.

3.2 Materials Experimental Procedure and Participants

The user's task was to identify a product that he/she would buy if he/she had an opportunity to do so. An administrator was present to help the participants complete the experiment. The experiment consisted of four parts:

- The subjects were initially tested on the Big Five Inventory. The participants were asked to answer 44 questions.
- According to their daily habits, the users assumed a shopping scenario and selected their preferred products.

- The participants entered their choices to select a product in the ORG and the list interface.
- In the experiment, we used the Tobii Pro TX300 eye tracker to record the fixation duration.

We launched an online user study through various channels. Finally, we recruited 136 participants to join the study. Each participant was rewarded with an incentive. Most of the participants had bachelor's degrees or above and had some shopping experience. Meanwhile, the participants were averaged over each group. Through a median split, we classified the users into two types in each dimension, that is, high or low level of conscientiousness. Finally, we filtered out the data where the fixation time was less than 30 s and screened out 108 valid data items (Table 2).

Table 2. Demographic profiles of participants.

	Contrast experiment by eye tracker (108)
Gender	Male (54), female (65)
Age (years)	18–25 (98), 26–30 (9), 41–50 (1)
Education (degree)	Bachelor's (59), master's (43), PhD (6)
Profession	Student (106), teacher (2)

3.3 AOI Definitions and Metrics

In our work, the AOI was determined at two levels: category level and product level. At the category level, there were five areas in each interface. In the ORG interface, each recommendation module as a group was an AOI area. In the list interface, the top of the interface was an AOI area, and six products as a group were an AOI area. At the product level, each recommended product was defined as an AOI, and each recommended title was regarded as another AOI. According to the experiments, we selected the following metrics:

- Time to first fixation: time from the start of the stimulus display until the test participants fixate on the AOI for the first time
- Fixation duration: duration of each individual fixation within an AOI

3.4 Hypotheses

Combined with the relevant literature, in total, we had three hypotheses:

- Hypothesis 1: Highly conscientious users spend more time browsing the ORG interface than the list. Users with a low level of conscientiousness are the opposite.
- Hypothesis 2: A high level of conscientiousness correlates with the ORG interface, and conscientious users prefer to browse ORG.
- Hypothesis 3: Highly conscientious users are more significant in terms of the numbers of products and the degree of attention.

4 Eye-Tracking Experiment

According to the valid data, we quantified the effects of individual traits on the user experience with the recommender interfaces. In the following paragraphs, we present the results in two forms, namely the heat map, and the AOI analysis result.

4.1 Result 1: Heat Map

We will first present the heat map because it is a powerful way of visualising the users' fixation distribution. We summed all of the participants' fixations on an interface to produce the heat map (see Fig. 1). The red/orange colour indicates that almost all of the users halted their gaze at a specific part of the interface, and the green colour shows that few users halted in the area. High C stands for a high level of conscientiousness, and Low C stands for a low level of conscientiousness.

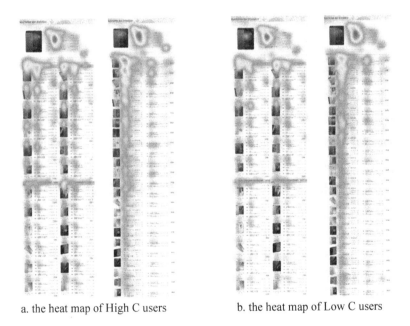

a. the heat map of High C users   b. the heat map of Low C users

Fig. 1. Heat map for the two interfaces. (Color figure online)

The heat map shows that High C users paid greater attention to category titles and read more product details in the ORG interface. This indicated that users with a high level of conscientiousness preferred to browse product information and compare products comprehensively and preferred a more comprehensive and organised product recommendation interface.

4.2   Result 3: AOI Analyses

In the following text, we present an in-depth AOI analysis for identifying whether the differences between ORG and LIST were significant.

Category Level. According to the time to first fixation in AOI, both the High C and the Low C users scanned products by basically following the same path on the two interfaces: Top Candidate → Category-1 → Category-2 → Category-3 → Category-4. The difference between the two user groups was that the High C users took longer to fixate on Category-3 and Category-4 in ORG. In contrast, the Low C users took longer to notice the two bottom categories in LIST (see Fig. 2)

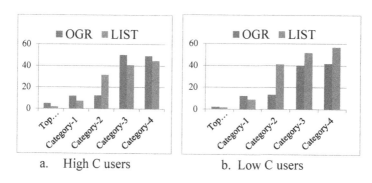

a.   High C users   b.   Low C users

Fig. 2. Time to first fixation at category level of AOI analysis.

With respect to the fixation duration, users with high C paid significantly more attention to ORG (54.09 s vs. 43.79 s in LIST, p = .035). Concretely, the comparison of fixations at each category level of AOI between the two interfaces showed that all the five category-level AOIs received more fixations in ORG. In particular, the differences for Category-2 and Category-4 were significant (Category-2: 13.37 s vs. 10.08 s in LIST, p < .01; Category-4: 7.69 s vs. 3.86 s in LIST, p < .01, see Table 3).

In contrast, for users with low C, significantly more fixations were placed on LIST (53.84 s vs. 39.20 s in ORG, p = .028). To be specific, all the five category-level AOIs received more fixations in LIST, with a significant difference for Category-1 (18.51 s vs. 10.88 s in ORG, p < .01, see Table 3).

Table 3. AOI results for fixation duration at high and low levels of conscientiousness of users at the category level (in seconds).

	Top Candidate		Category-1		Category-2		Category-3		Category-4	
	High C	Low C	High C	Low C	High C	Low C	High C	Low C	High C	Low C
	$F_{(1,106)} = 4.234$, $p = .042$		$F_{(1,106)} = 8.195$, $p = .005$		$F_{(1,106)} = 2.456$, $p = .120$		$F_{(1,106)} = 2.332$, $p = .130$		$F_{(1,106)} = 10.488$, $p = .002$	
ORG	7.74	7.10	15.89	10.88	13.37	10.46	7.19	4.92	7.69	4.05
LIST	6.66	9.14	15.30	18.51	10.08	11.83	6.26	7.17	3.86	5.58
p	.235	.136	.943	.002	.016	.437	.462	.083	.000	.538

Therefore, the interaction effect between the interface and the conscientiousness level was significant with respect to Top Candidate (F (1,106) = 12.181, p = .001), Category-1 (F (1,106) = 8.195, p = .005), and Category-4 (F (1,106) = 10.488, p = .002, see Table 3).

Product Level. We further conducted a product-level AOI analysis for both units of individual product and category explanation (in ORG). The results showed that users with High C evaluated slightly more products in ORG (19.46 vs. 19.26 in LIST) and placed more fixations on each product (2.34 s vs. 2.12 s in LIST). Among the Low C users, both the number of evaluated products and the fixation duration for each product in the case of ORG were significantly lower than those in LIST (6.63 vs. 18.71, p = .076; 1.98 s vs. 2.60 s, p = .031, see Table 4).

Table 4. AOI analysis results for fixation duration at high and low levels of conscientiousness of users at the product level (in seconds).

	The Number of evaluated products		Fixation duration per product (s)	
	High C	Low C	High C	Low C
	F (1,106) = 3.020, p = .085		F (1,106) = 6.818, **p = .010**	
LIST	19.26	18.71	2.12	2.60
ORG	19.46	16.63	2.34	1.98
p	.807	.076	.292	**.031**

With respect to the fixations on the category explanations in ORG, both the High C and the Low C users did not show a significant difference (the number of viewed explanations: 2.84 vs. 2.61; fixation duration per explanation: 1.44 s vs. 1.12 s, see Table 5).

Table 5. Fixation duration in explanations at high and level conscientiousness of users at product level of AOI analysis (seconds).

	The Number of evaluated explanations			Fixation duration per explanation (s)		
	High C	Low C	p	High C	Low C	p
ORG	2.84	2.61	.349	1.44	1.12	.319

5   Conclusions

Traditional product recommender interfaces normally present multiple recommended items in a ranked list, which we call the LIST interface. Recently, ORG has been developed to well combine the ideas of presenting diversity, and trade-off reasoning. According to the related work, there is a relationship between personality traits and shopping behaviour. Hence, in the work reported in this article, we studied the eye movements of users with different personalities through an eye-tracking experiment. We reported the results from a high or low level of conscientious user study performed by comparing an ORG interface to LIST. Specifically, we observed the user's objective behaviour, including the fixation count, fixation duration, and the user's final decision. The study revealed that users with different personalities adapted their visual searching behaviour to the change in the recommendation presentation. The results interestingly showed that highly conscientious users were significantly attracted by the ORG interface, while low conscientiousness users exhibited more fixations on the LIST interface. Therefore, for the highly conscientious users, we suggested that the ORG would more likely encourage a rigorous choice-making process and enable more users to reach an informed decision at the end. In the future, we intend to analyse other personality traits so as to further enhance our ORG.

Acknowledgement. This research work was supported by the Fundamental Research Funds of Shandong University, China. We thank all participants who took part in our experiments and teachers and friends who support us.

References

1. Wu, W., Chen, L., He, L.: Proceedings of the 24th ACM Conference on Hypertext and Social Media - HT. Using Personality to Adjust Diversity in Recommender Systems, pp. 225–229 (2013)
2. Hu, R., Pu, P.: Exploring relations between personality and user rating behaviors. In: UMAP Workshops, Rome, Italy (2013)
3. Ferwerda, B., Graus, M., Vall, A., Tkalčič, M., Schedl, M.: The influence of users' personality traits on satisfaction and attractiveness of diversified recommendation lists. In: Proceedings of the 4th Workshop on Emotions and Personality in Personalized Systems (2016)
4. Jin, Y., Tintarev, N., Verbert, K.: Effects of individual traits on diversity-aware music recommender user interfaces. In: Proceedings of the 26th Conference on User Modeling, Adaptation and Personalization, pp. 291–299 (2018)
5. Costa Jr., P.T., McCrae, R.R.: Revised NEO Personality Inventory (NEO PI-R) and NEO Five-Factor Inventory (NEO-FFI). Psychological Assessment Resources, Odessa (1992)
6. Herlocker, J.L., Konstan, J.A., Riedl, J.: Explaining collaborative filtering recommendations. In: ACM Conference on Computer Supported Cooperative Work, vol. 22, pp. 241–250 (2000)
7. Chen, L., Pu, P.: Interaction design guidelines on critiquing-based recommender systems. User Model. User-Adap. Inter. **19**(3), 167 (2009)
8. Xie, H., Wang, D.D., Rao, Y., Wong, T.L., Raymond, L.Y.K., Chen, L., et al.: Incorporating user experience into critiquing-based recommender systems: a collaborative approach based on compound critiquing. Int. J. Mach. Learn. Cybern. **9**(6), 1–16 (2016)
9. Chen, G., Chen, L.: Augmenting Service Recommender Systems by Incorporating Contextual Opinions from User Reviews. Kluwer Academic Publishers, Hingham (2015)
10. Chen, L., Chen, G., Wang, F.: Recommender systems based on user reviews: the state of the art. User Model. User-Adap. Inter. **25**(2), 99–154 (2015)

11. Bollen, D., Knijnenburg, B.P., Willemsen, M.C., Graus, M.: Understanding choice overload in recommender systems. In: Proceedings of the fourth ACM conference on RecSys, pp. 63–70. ACM (2010)
12. Tkalčič, M., Chen, L.: Personality and recommender systems. In: Ricci, F., Rokach, L., Shapira, B. (eds.), Recommender Systems Handbook, pp. 715–739 (2015)
13. Goldberg, L.R.: An alternative description of personality: the big-five factor structure. J. Pers. Soc. Psychol. **59**(6), 1216–1229 (1990)
14. Ferwerda, B., Schedl, M.: Personality-based user modeling for music recommender systems. In: Berendt, B., Bringmann, B., Fromont, É., Garriga, G., Miettinen, P., Tatti, N., Tresp, V. (eds.) ECML PKDD 2016. LNCS (LNAI), vol. 9853, pp. 254–257. Springer, Cham (2016). https://doi.org/10.1007/978-3-319-46131-1_29
15. Yan, H., Wang, Z., Lin, T.H., Li, Y., Jin, D.: Profiling users by online shopping behaviors. Multimedia Tools Appl. **5**, 1–11 (2017)
16. Jedetski, J., Adelman, L., Yeo, C.: How web site decision technology affects consumers. IEEE Internet Comput. **6**(2), 72–79 (2002)
17. Markus, M., Soh, C.: Structural influences on global e-commerce activity. J. Global Inf. Manag. **10**(1), 5–12 (2002)
18. Callahan, E., Koenemann, J.: A comparative usability evaluation of user interfaces for online product catalog. In: Proceedings of the 2nd ACM Conference on Electronic Commerce, pp. 197–206. ACM, NY (2000)
19. Braganza, C., et al.: Scrolling behaviour with single- and multi-column layout. In: Proceedings of the 18th International Conference on World Wide Web (WWW), pp. 831–840. ACM, NY (2009)
20. Adomavicius, G., Tuzhilin, A.: Toward the next generation of recommender systems: a survey of the state-of-the-art and possible extensions. IEEE Trans. Knowl. Data Eng. **17**(6), 734–749 (2005)
21. Karumur, R.P., Nguyen, T.T., Konstan, J.A.: Personality, user preferences and behavior in recommender systems. Inf. Syst. Front. **6**, 1–25 (2017)
22. Chen, L., Pu, P.: Experiments on user experiences with recommender interfaces. Behav. Inf. Technol. **33**(4), 372–394 (2014)
23. Konstan, J.A., et al.: GroupLens: applying collaborative filtering to usenet news. Commun. ACM **40**(3), 77–87 (1997)
24. Dumais, S., Cutrell, E., Chen, H.: Optimizing search by showing results in context. In: Proceedings of the SIGCHI Conference on Human Factors in Computing Systems, pp. 277–284. ACM, NY (2001)
25. Hogan, J., Ones, D.S.: Conscientiousness and integrity at work. In: Hogan, R., Johnson, J. A., Briggs, S.R. (eds.) Handbook of Personality Psychology, pp. 849–870 (1997)

Correction to: HCI in Business, Government and Organizations

Fiona Fui-Hoon Nah and Keng Siau

Correction to:
F. F.-H. Nah and K. Siau (Eds.):
HCI in Business, Government and Organizations, **LNCS 11588,**
https://doi.org/10.1007/978-3-030-22335-9

The chapters 2, 4, 6 and 12 were mistakenly published as regular chapters instead of open access. This has now been corrected.

The updated version of these chapters can be found at
https://doi.org/10.1007/978-3-030-22335-9_2
https://doi.org/10.1007/978-3-030-22335-9_4
https://doi.org/10.1007/978-3-030-22335-9_6
https://doi.org/10.1007/978-3-030-22335-9_12
https://doi.org/10.1007/978-3-030-22335-9

Author Index

Printed in the United States
by Baker & Taylor Publisher Services